Novel Constitutions and the Making of Race

LAW AND LITERATURE

The *Law and Literature* series publishes work that connects legal ideas to literary and cultural history, texts, and artefacts. The series encompasses a wide range of historical periods, literary genres, legal fields and theories, and transnational subjects, focusing on interdisciplinary books that engage with legal and literary forms, methods, concepts, dispositions, and media. It seeks innovative studies of every kind, including but not limited to work that examines race, ethnicity, gender, national identity, criminal and civil law, legal institutions and actors, digital media, intellectual property, economic markets, and corporate power, while also foregrounding current interpretive methods in the humanities, using these methods as dynamic tools that are themselves subject to scrutiny.

Series Editors

Robert Spoo, Princeton University
Simon Stern, University of Toronto

Novel Constitutions and the Making of Race

A Literary and Legal History of Slavery in the Anglophone Atlantic, 1688–1818

SARAH MARSH

OXFORD
UNIVERSITY PRESS

OXFORD
UNIVERSITY PRESS

Great Clarendon Street, Oxford, OX2 6DP,
United Kingdom

Oxford University Press is a department of the University of Oxford.
It furthers the University's objective of excellence in research, scholarship,
and education by publishing worldwide. Oxford is a registered trade mark of
Oxford University Press in the UK and in certain other countries.

Published in the United States of America by Oxford University Press
546 Fifth Avenue, New York, NY 10036, United States of America

British Library Cataloguing in Publication Data
Data available

Library of Congress Control Number: 2026941478

ISBN 9780197917862

DOI: 10.1093/9780197917855.001.0001

The manufacturer's authorized representative in the EU for product safety is
Oxford University Press España S.A. of Parque Empresarial San Fernando de Henares,
Avenida de Castilla, 2 – 28830 Madrid (www.oup.es/en or product.safety@oup.com).
OUP España S.A. also acts as importer into Spain of products made by the manufacturer.

Novel Constitutions is dedicated to
Mom, Dad, Matt, and Emma, with love.

Acknowledgements

This book has been more than a decade in the writing, accumulating many debts along the way.

My literary education began in earnest at Washington & Jefferson College, where Carolyn Kyler, Lauryn Mayer, V. Penelope Pelizzon, Dana Shiller, and Dwayne Thorpe first opened to me the wonders of language. Fr. Augustine Flood was an early academic mentor, who taught me to treasure a life of the mind.

At the University of Pittsburgh, Phil Smith helped me to see my first academic article into print, teaching me how to weather the rejection that often comes with writing literary criticism. Tomaž Šalamun, who directed my MFA manuscript in poetry, nurtured my writing with enthusiasm and his abiding sense of wonder.

During my doctoral studies at the University of North Carolina at Chapel Hill, this project took its earliest form as a study in the medical humanities. I thank my dissertation committee—Mary Floyd-Wilson, Beverly Taylor, James Thompson, and Jane Thrailkill—for their thoughtful guidance, excellent teaching, and formative critique. Inger Brodey's friendship and collaboration have extended beyond Chapel Hill to our work together on the Jane Austen Summer Program. Neil Vickers welcomed me to King's College London as an exchange student in literature and medicine, where I began asking questions about the literary history of the body. John McGowan mentored me during the years after I earned my doctorate, offering wisdom and encouragement at a time when I considered setting this project aside. Jeanne Moskal has been, since my first semester at UNC, a gifted adviser, a sensitive reader, and a compassionate mentor. The book's final chapter, on *Frankenstein*, is dedicated to her with love.

As a lecturer at American University, I was fortunate in wonderful colleagues who read drafts, recommended more reading, convened lively conversation, and generally made this study better: Mandy Berry, Fiona Brideoake, Ed Comstock, Mary Ellen Curtin, Eileen Findlay, Borden Flanagan, Keith Leonard, Mary Mintz, David Pike, Richard Sha, Anita Sherman, and Sarah Trembath. Arielle Bernstein and David Keplinger both read this manuscript as it was taking shape; their affirmations assured me that the work was worth finishing. Heather McDonald read every page with a careful and inquisitive editorial eye. Martyn Oliver was, and is, an enduring source of understanding and generosity.

I am grateful to the Smithsonian Institution for my appointment as a Margaret Henry Dabney Penick Resident Scholar at the Dibner Library of the History of Science and Technology. This fellowship, which allowed me to undertake archival research on Benjamin Banneker (and work next door to the Batmobile!), shaped the book in important ways. When the pandemic cut my residency short, Lilla Vekerdy of the Smithsonian Libraries went above and beyond to keep me in touch with sources critical to my work. My thanks go as well to the American Society for Eighteenth-Century Studies, whose annual meetings have given me a forum for workshopping the ideas in this book.

My colleagues and mentors at Seton Hill University have given me an intellectual home and an experience of university life at its best: Mike Arnzen, Casey Bowser, Mark Boyle, Christine Cusick, Debra Faszer-McMahon, Dennis Jerz, Camille Kaszubowski, Tony Krzmarzick, Fran Leap, Jim Paharik, Laura Patterson, Nicole Peeler, Adam Pellman, Robin Rohrer, Msgr. Roger Statnick, Kathy Tobolewski, David von Schlichten, Emily Wierszewski, and Sr. Susan Yochum.

At American University and Seton Hill alike, my students have provided valuable research support: Summer Griffin, Talia Marshall, and Emma Zuder, whose collective diligence and resourcefulness deserve special recognition; Talia's extended research assistance improved this book at every possible turn.

The librarians of Seton Hill's Reeves Memorial Library performed wonders with our small collection, tracking down everything I needed to bring this book to fruition.

Three friends deserve distinctive thanks. Susan Allen Ford read the *Mansfield Park* chapter and saved me from a critical error. Tom Merrill, through many conversations, encouraged me to consider the relationship of racism to sin; this book is the outcome of his good questions, and his friendship. April Shelford has given me what is perhaps most rare in the middle of one's academic life: a kind of ongoing moral guidance in the work of historical scholarship. Her wisdom and good humor have sustained me.

My greatest scholarly debt is to Simon Stern, who plucked this book's idea out of obscurity four years ago and gave me the opportunity to see it into print. Without his confidence and unstinting support, *Novel Constitutions* would not exist. I am grateful to him and to Robert Spoo, the book's editors, for their attentive readings of the manuscript and their stewardship of it through to publication. Two anonymous readers improved the book considerably, and I thank them for their time and intellectual generosity. The first chapter of this book originally appeared as an essay in *ELH*; an earlier version of Chapter 5 was published in *Eighteenth-Century Studies*. Both are reprinted here in revised form by permission of Johns Hopkins University Press. At Oxford University Press, Jo Spillane and Jack McNichol smoothed the book's path to completion. Jane Robson provided copyediting support, and Dolarine Sonia Fonceca saw the manuscript through production. Jolanta Komornicka prepared the index with exemplary care. While I have done my best to tell the truth about my subject, I expect that there are errors in these pages yet unknown to me; they are mine alone.

My beloved friends have made these years of writing happy ones: Erin Allingham, Jesse and Jennie Berney, Arielle Bernstein, Jon Bisesi and Meg Brennan, Eric Bontempo, Erin Branch, Patrick Horn, Matt Kelly and Liz Rich, Martyn Oliver and Jenn Rogers, Cacie Phelps, David and Helen Stone, Usha Vishnuvajjala, and Breckyn Wood. Lindy and Hazel, who will never read this book, gave me furry companionship, long walks in the woods, and much-needed distractions—mostly right when I needed them.

My family has lived with this book for as long as I have. Thank you from the bottom of my heart to Chris and Krista; Tom and Lunda; Bekah and Jeff; Megan and Michael; and Uncle Ed and Aunt Joanne. Special thanks are due to Chris for explaining some finer points of Euclidean geometry to me while I was writing the chapter on Benjamin Banneker.

My parents, Lou and Jane, are models of constancy and love: long before the day I told them I was leaving pre-med for literature, and every day since, they have nurtured my life in every way that matters. Mom and Dad, I love you.

My deepest gratitude is reserved for Matt and Emma. Emma has never had a mother who was not writing this book, and for the whole of it she has been the greatest joy of all. Matt—beloved husband, editor, and friend—has read every word of this study, many times over, and wrangled with me over questions of law with characteristic integrity and thoroughness. His intelligence, steadiness, and patience are everywhere evident in these pages.

Contents

Introduction

Constitutions Ancient and Novel

Racial slavery is the original sin of the American republic. It is the serpent, in the idiom of John Jay Chapman, coiled around the legs of the table on which the Declaration of Independence was signed.[1] The image conjures a world where some are born into Edenic freedom and others into hellish bondage. *Novel Constitutions* contends that original sin—while an eloquent metaphor for the birth of a freedom-loving, slaveholding nation—also describes a fundamental, yet little understood, historical reality of how Englishmen developed racial slavery in their western Atlantic colonies. My reading of early modern texts, literary and legal, reveals that Englishmen's enslavement of Africans was an overseas adaptation of seventeenth-century struggles over the nature of government in England. Of central importance in these struggles was the political theology of divine right absolutism through which the Stuart kings, like Adam and Eve in the Garden and English slaveholders in the colonies, sought to be like God.

The racial character of the American founding cannot be fully understood, *Novel Constitutions* argues, without reference to this earlier struggle over the rights of Englishmen against their monarch during England's Civil Wars (1642–51). The story of race in America is, in fact, shot through with citation of Parliament's bloody conflict with King Charles I. A striking case in point is Victor Fleming's 1939 blockbuster, *Gone with the Wind*, an adaptation to film of Margaret Mitchell's 1936 novel. Mitchell's story of a doomed romance between Scarlett O'Hara and Rhett Butler is set against the violent end of the American Confederacy and its institution of chattel slavery. As one critic writes, "The movie is, in many ways, a repository of the originals that have shaped American culture's tortured descriptions of race since."[2] But woven through *Gone with the Wind*'s familiar American racial fabric are threads of an older English history. Consider this example from the film's exposition (Figure 0.1): "There was a land of Cavaliers and Cotton Fields called the Old South," the crawling scroll reads. "Here in this pretty world, Gallantry took its last bow. Here was the last ever to be seen of Knights and their Ladies Fair, of Master and of Slave."[3]

Here, twentieth-century Hollywood filmmakers invoke the Cavaliers, King Charles I's supporters during the English Civil War, to contextualize the American Civil War (1861–65) and the institution of slavery over which it was

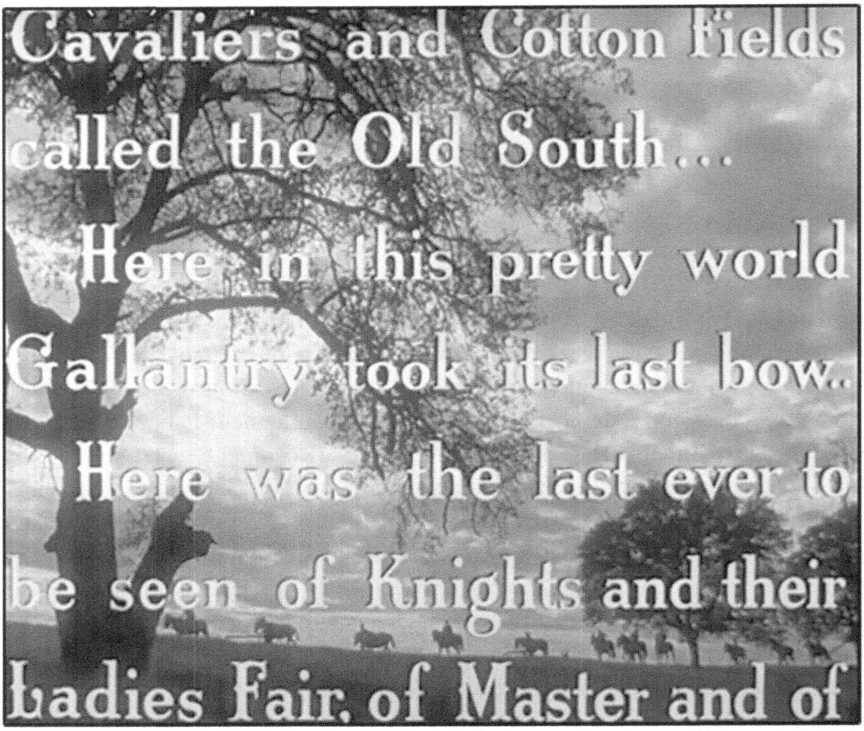

Figure 0.1 Still from *Gone with the Wind* (dir. Victor Fleming; Metro-Goldwyn-Mayer, 1939), opening title sequence.

fought. But how did seventeenth-century English royalists end up slaveholders in the American South?

Novel Constitutions answers this question with a new theory of Atlantic-world racial formations, which integrates the racial enslavement of African-descended people into a broader transatlantic history from England's Civil Wars of the seventeenth century to the American Revolution of 1776. In this way, *Novel Constitutions* fundamentally enlarges our understanding of race in America as a political, moral, and spiritual struggle between divine right absolutism and popular democracy. This struggle, first undertaken in England,[4] acquired transatlantic character through that nation's imperial ambitions, including entry into the African slave trade in 1562.[5] Paroxysms over how to govern this empire at home and abroad under the English common law culminated, in part, in the great paradox of 1776: the founding of the United States as a freedom-loving, slaveholding republic.[6] If we understand English slavocracy as a colonial expression of political disagreements in England, we can highlight the constitutional role of slavery and anti-slavery in the development of American Revolutionary ideals.

The Englishmen who took up arms against Stuart absolutism during the seventeenth century understood their political rights as embodied, heritable, and expressed by the common law of England. They called these rights their "ancient constitution." This was not a written document, as American readers might think, but a deeply and widely held belief that Englishmen could not be deprived by the Crown or its agents of life, liberty, or property without due process of law. Their immemorial protections against tyranny, Englishmen held, were fundamental to their nature and character as a people. The ancient constitution, they believed, had been passed from generation to generation with the common law, which was its perfect expression. An Englishman's claims to immemorial liberty, furthermore, bound his sovereign to the common law: when the Stuart monarchs advanced theories of their absolute power over English subjects during the seventeenth century, the ancient constitution became a vital political rhetoric for fencing in the monarch's prerogative.[7]

The Stuart kings, like their subjects, framed their right to rule as embodied and heritable. However, in pursuit of absolute power by divine right, they placed their prerogative above the common law that bound their people: English kings, the Stuarts held, made answer to God alone. Royalists therefore attacked ancient constitutionalism to justify absolutism.[8] The most influential was Sir Robert Filmer, whose Civil War-era *Patriarcha, or The Natural Power of Kings* (first published posthumously in 1680), grounded English sovereignty in Adam's paternal authority. Monarchs, he argued, ruled as fathers over their political households and thus were not bound by Englishmen's supposed ancient rights. Adam's lordship "over the whole world," conferred by God's command in Genesis, granted Adam's successors "the absolutest dominion of any monarch which hath been since the creation."[9] Absolutism, Filmer maintained, was divinely ordained in Adam's heirs, and thus the only true source of the people's freedom: the "greatest liberty in the world," Filmer concluded, "is for people to live under a monarch."[10] By tracing absolutism all the way to Genesis, Filmer made an end run around the ancient constitutionalists: if Adam's paternal authority persisted by natural, hereditary right, it was necessarily anterior to any ancient rights the people could claim.

This profound ideological conflict between absolute monarchy and ancient constitutionalism crystallized in a passionate contest to interpret the Norman Conquest of 1066. To imagine its pitch, Americans might recall the tension ensuing when 1619—the year a number of stolen Africans were exchanged for supplies in colonial Virginia—was proposed to replace 1776 as the year expressing the founding spirit of the United States.[11] Was the country founded in freedom, or in slavery? Stuart-era ancient constitutionalists insisted on freedom: England's fundamental laws and liberties had survived the 1066 moment because, when William I assumed the throne, he bound himself to the customary rights of Englishmen and accepted limits on his power: he could not deprive free English subjects of life, liberty, or property without due process of law.[12] In this way, English jurists and common lawyers maintained that the nation had never been conquered by a foreign king, preserving an ideology of immemorial, indigenous rights.

Royalists like Filmer and Sir Henry Spelman challenged this version of history. Spelman drew upon his antiquarian studies of feudal tenure to emphasize that William I's victory at Hastings imposed a new feudal order, replacing earlier Anglo-Saxon customs and making English law dependent on royal grant rather than immemorial right.[13] In *Patriarcha*, Filmer argued that pre-Conquest England had never been a single, continuous kingdom with one settled body of law or a national parliament; instead, it had been fragmented among Britons, Romans, Saxons, and Danes.[14] This evidence denied the possibility of a unified ancient constitution, undermining any claim that English kings were bound by timeless popular rights predating 1066.[15] By casting 1066 as the introduction of a new kingly order under William I, a fresh expression of Adam's originary right and not a moment of constitutional stability, both Filmer and Spelman bolstered Stuart claims to absolute power ordained by heaven.

A principal contention of *Novel Constitutions* is that all of these rights, the people's and the sovereign's, were "racial" in the modern sense of that term. Put historically: the hereditary, embodied, and legally embedded qualities of these rights were important—perhaps necessary—conditions of the emergence of modern American conceptions of race. This system of meaning rested on the old legal sense of "heredity": before the nineteenth century gave this term its modern biological meaning of transmitting genetic traits, it referred to the passing of property and status from one generation to the next.[16] Neither sovereign absolutism nor ancient constitutionalism began in England as a system particularly interested in human skin color; yet each relied entirely on ideas about embodiment and inheritance to define rights, organize property, and negotiate political authority. The contest in seventeenth-century England between the rights of the people and the rights of the king made these racial ideas available for legal application when skin color variance entered the frame of English colonial administration in the seventeenth-century Atlantic world. In this study, the phrase "novel constitutions"—a counterpoint to the ancient constitution—will describe legal practices through which chattel slavery emerged from conflict between the English people and their sovereign, each claiming the legal supremacy of embodied rights. Race in America, in its complexionary, rights-related form, was created by this constitutional process.

Writers hailing from Africa, America, Britain, and the Caribbean[17] took notice of this transoceanic struggle between the rights of the people and the rights of the monarch. They responded to it with great imaginative energy and, to a significant degree, they set and challenged its terms with their fiction and their poetry, their autobiographies, and even their mathematics. We are not wrong to understand colonial history as a period characterized by the dehumanizing effects of colonial power on both oppressors and oppressed. The enormity of this tragedy, however, and its overwhelming erasure of human beings and their stories, can also distract us from important texts in this history that have survived, and the complex perspectives they grant on our past. The writers in this study made recourse to the humanizing discourses of literature, science, and religion in an effort to describe the world that they perceived with nuance, discernment, and creativity—even as other accounts of that world were lost forever because of the silencing effects of colonial power.[18] That these authors' accounts survive at all is testament, however, that power is never absolute and that, in some measure, it does depend on what people decide to think, say, write, and do. By engaging with ideas about race in their lifetimes, these authors inscribed a revelatory literary history of slavery and anti-slavery in the early modern Atlantic world, which is the subject of this book.

This history, of slavery and anti-slavery, has been obscured in postcolonial scholarship by the powerful racial symbolism of body color that took root when England established racial slavery in its colonies by positive law. *Novel Constitutions* reframes the field with a different literary-historical model. Early modern anglophone texts, which describe bodily surface while granting access to the human interior, are not only repositories of racist tropes but also vital records of the political conflicts, legal decisions, moral drama, and spiritual struggles through which those ideas arose, met critique, and were exposed as legal fictions. In this way, *Novel Constitutions* takes seriously about literature what Vincent Brown says about Atlantic slavery's wider archive: "as surely as wind and water change the contours of stone," Brown writes, "slavery's archival sources have been shaped by the black people they rarely describe."[19] This insight, that oppressed people can and do exert influence on texts, extends Henry Louis Gates, Jr.'s critique of white supremacist mythographies that cast Africans as without writing and Europeans as sole bearers of authorship.[20] By these lights, *Novel Constitutions* proceeds on the premise that the literary record of slavery and anti-slavery in the Atlantic world reveals the human content of race, disclosing what racism sought to collapse under its dehumanizing logic of color.

The American color line, *Novel Constitutions* concludes, is a profoundly significant but in the end contingent artifact of the struggle between hereditary divine right monarchy on one hand and a fitfully emerging, frequently receding, and not yet fully realized democratic republic on the other. The color line has proven a durable legacy of America's original sin of chattel slavery in which colonial slaveholders—like English divine right kings—fell from grace when they sought absolute power over other human beings. This legacy stretches at least from the Stuart monarchy of seventeenth-century England to twentieth-century film, where Charles I's "Cavaliers" occupy a lost and longed for antebellum world in the American Confederacy.

Absolute Monarchy and the Ancient Constitution in a New Atlantic World

To understand how Stuart absolutism and English ancient constitutionalism bore the bitter fruit of American slavery, a summary of their dense political history is next in order. Formalized by Magna Carta in 1215, but popularly believed and legally asserted to have existed since time immemorial, the English ancient constitution was "a precious right not to have one's body or one's land taken by the king without due process" of law.[21] Edward the Confessor, the penultimate Anglo-Saxon king of England, was the central figure in the political mythography of the ancient constitution. His 1066 death without an heir precipitated a succession crisis, culminating when his brother-in-law Harold Godwinson briefly assumed the throne. Harold's storied death at the Battle of Hastings became a pivotal moment in the contested historiography of uninterrupted English liberty.[22] For nearly six centuries thereafter, Edward—king, saint, and lawgiver—served as a versatile political symbol closely linked to the ancient constitution because he came to represent a pre-Norman body of law that bound the king to stand as the guarantor of peace. The symbol of the Confessor, Janelle Greenberg concludes, "stood at the center of a credible and compelling historical narrative" that afforded resistance to absolutism.[23]

After the Conquest, English jurists elaborated ancient constitutionalism into a theory of significant political importance: in *De Legibus et Consuetudinibus Angliae* (c.1235, *On the Laws and Customs of England*), the thirteenth-century cleric Henry de Bracton emphasized the subordination of the sovereign to both God and law.[24] In the fifteenth century, Sir John Fortescue, chief justice of the Court of King's Bench during the reign of Henry VI, articulated in *De Laudibus Legum Angliae* (c.1470, *In Praise of the Laws of England*), a political theory of the English common law emphasizing that its immemorial quality made it superior to continental law: because English laws were "rooted in antiquity," Fortescue reasoned, "there is no gainsaying nor legitimate doubt but that the customs of the English are not only good but the best."[25] Under the Tudors in the sixteenth century, ancient constitutionalism was recruited to legitimize the English Reformation, Laura Doyle writes, "by establishing evidence of a pre-Roman, Saxon church, native to England, and Christian, but without ties to Rome."[26] This mere handful of examples discloses the political versatility of ancient constitutionalism as the late medieval period gave way to early modernity.

In the 1600s, as the Stuart kings sought to expand the royal prerogative, jurists mounted opposition by drawing on the history of early English governing assemblies and Magna Carta.[27] These scholars traced English liberty to the unconquered Germanic Anglo-Saxons, overwriting the island's tribal Britons, who had been conquered by imperial Rome.[28] In response to scholarly challenges to the primacy of his rule, King James I disbanded the Society of Antiquaries, "lest it should be the source of plots."[29] Ancient constitutionalist scholars nevertheless pursued a theory of history in which "parliament stood at the center of government" and the people enjoyed a "right to resist, depose, and even kill a king who broke the terms of his agreement with the people."[30] This theory of popular sovereignty through parliamentary representation became a reality in the 1649 execution of James I's son and heir, Charles I, for crimes against the English people. We will revisit this episode of great political trauma throughout *Novel Constitutions*.

During King James I's reign, Edward Coke became England's leading expositor of ancient constitutionalism. In 1613, James appointed Coke as Chief Justice to the Court of King's Bench in an effort to recruit the jurist's formidable legal mind to Crown interests.[31] Coke seems never to have swayed, however, from his dual convictions of the antiquity of the English common law as well as the subordination of the monarch to both law and God, a position at odds with James I's burgeoning theory of his divine right to rule his kingdoms.[32] Coke's *Institutes of the Laws of England*, published in four volumes from 1628 to 1644, emphasizes the principles of the ancient constitution as a form of individual obligation to human-made laws: "I say to thee (Gentle Reader)," he began in the second volume of the *Institutes*, "next to thy Duty and Piety to God, and his Anointed, thy Gracious Sovereign, and thy Honour to thy Parents, yield due Reverence and Obedience to the Common Laws of England: For of all Laws (I speak of human) these are most equal and most certain, of greatest Antiquity."[33] Coke's horizontal positioning of the common law "next to" sovereign power, instead of below it, became a point of great contention.

As ancient constitutionalists and absolutists scoured history for authoritative theories of power, each side amplified its hereditary claims in ways that we would recognize today as distinctively racial. For example, to counter royalist claims of hereditary rights derived from Genesis, ancient constitutionalists appealed to custom and ontology, arguing that fundamental English liberties had been conserved locally in the people themselves. Writing in 1612, the Attorney-General for Ireland, Sir John Davies, personified the ancient constitution by praising England's common law as the "*Common Custome* of the Realm," which could be "recorded and registered no-where but in the memory of the people."[34] He continued, echoing Fortescue:

> this Customary Law is the most perfect and most excellent, and without comparison the best, to make and preserve a Commonwealth. For the *written Laws* which are made either by the Edicts of Princes, or by Councils of Estates, are imposed upon the Subject before any Triall or Probation made, whether the same be fit and agreeable to the nature and disposition of the people, or whether they will breed any inconvenience or no. But a *Custome* doth never become a Law to bind the people, until it hath been tried and approved time out of mind.[35]

Davies concluded that the English common law was "connatural to the Nation," because it was embodied in "the People of this Land, which have made their own Laws out of their wisedome and experience, (like a silk-worm that formeth all her web out of her self onely)."[36] Davies's comparison of English people's jurisprudential self-reliance to the silkworm—making a web from "her self onely"—situates the English people as the source of the law. This understanding of the ancient constitution, as always having been so yet always evolving with the people, had clear racial, but not yet colorist, meanings. The ancient constitution, having been "tried and approved" by the English themselves since time immemorial, was a self-authorized birthright.

As English constitutional tensions rose in the middle of the seventeenth century and sparked civil war, antiquarian scholars like Nathaniel Bacon advanced an Anglo-Saxonist rhetoric of ancient English rights by emphasizing the ancient constitution as the political inheritance of an unconquered Germanic race. The "original Saxons," he claimed, "were a free people, governed by Laws, and those made not... by the great men, but by the people; and therefore called a free people, because *they are a law unto themselves*."[37] Bacon underscored that the "Saxons [*sic*] fealty to their King, was subservient to the publick safety; and the publick safety is necessarily depending upon the liberty of the Laws."[38] In this sense, the inheritance of the English from their Anglo-Saxon forebears was the safety of their persons from public threats. This ontological liberty of English people, Anglo-Saxonist racial ideology claimed, superseded English subjects' fidelity to the monarch by leveraging all of history—remembered and unrememberable—as its precedent.

These developments of ancient constitutionalism in England cohere with broader European patterns. As Jacob Levy observes, ancient constitutionalists contended that the "rights, liberties, and privileges" of intermediate governing bodies—such as the French Estates or the English Parliament—functioned as a bulwark against the emerging power of centralized absolutism.[39] As the Anglo-Irish peer and Stuart opponent Robert Molesworth put it in 1694, "slavery has within these last 200 years crept upon Europe," his use of "slavery" indicating the deep degree to which, in his view, the European subject had been subordinated to absolute monarchy.[40] The ancient constitutionalists further maintained, Levy writes, that Europe's traditional constitutional orders were Germanic in both origin and structure, deriving more from the "primordial liberty" of the Goths and other so-called barbarian tribes than from the legacy of imperial Roman rule.[41] Ancient constitutionalism was a useful political technique for resisting absolutist incursions inside and outside of England.

In response to the creep of slavery, some seventeenth-century Englishmen—most famously John Locke—began asserting that they possessed rights to their own labor. This marked a significant departure from feudal economies where labor was owned in common and could be compelled. Orlando Patterson,

Christopher Leslie Brown, and Robert J. Steinfeld have suggested that free labor—not the widespread form of slavery—is the real "peculiar institution" of the early modern period.[42] The protections of the ancient constitution were, John Brewer and Susan Staves explain, "exfoliated" during this period "into a more general right to be secure in one's property," including an interest in one's own capacity to create value through work.[43] Notably, in his philosophy of self-owned labor, Locke appealed to human sources even more universal than the ancient constitution: natural rights, consent, and reason.[44]

This domestic struggle, between the rights of the people and the rights of the monarch, became a central dynamic in England's imperial jurisprudence and policy. As Holly Brewer demonstrates, absolutist policies were developed in Tudor and Stuart England as jurists and colonial governors began pursuing neo-feudal theories of labor to enlarge the royal prerogative and build an empire overseas. Brewer has shown that English labor law permitted children—as young as 8 years old—to be bound without parental consent, a domestic precedent for severing children from parents in order to alienate their labor.[45] This practice would become a procedure by which the English enslaved people of African descent, as we will see in Chapter 1's reading of Aphra Behn's *Oroonoko*. It was also possible, under the 1547 Vagrancy Act, to bind a vagrant person in slavery; while there is no evidence that this law was ever enforced, its presence suggests burgeoning legal interest in the alienability of the subject's labor.[46]

Another important pro-slavery maneuver in early seventeenth-century Stuart courts was the redefinition of feudal villeinage to justify absolutist and imperial forms of bondage.[47] In medieval England, a villein was an unfree tenant: *villeins regardant* were bound to the land while *villeins in gross* were bound only to the will of a lord. Despite this degraded status, the villein still retained customary rights: to husband land for subsistence, to seek protection against arbitrary mistreatment, and to petition the courts if those rights were violated.[48] In a neo-feudal argument consonant with his theory of the Conquest, which had subordinated the English people to Norman rule, Sir Henry Spelman stripped the category of these medieval safeguards, emphasizing instead its hereditary, perpetual, and transferable character.[49] This reinterpretation allowed jurists to present villeinage as a legal precedent for creating absolute, heritable bondage, a technique that bolstered royalist claims of absolutism at home and created legal conditions under which racial slavery would emerge in England's colonies.[50]

Under the 1629 royal charter that Sir Henry Spelman drafted for Carolina, for example, colonial labor became inheritable and transferable by eliminating customary protections feudal villeins enjoyed from sale and bodily violence.[51] Spelman modeled the charter on the Palatinate of Durham, a medieval jurisdiction notable for its lack of parliamentary representation and for granting its lord sweeping powers.[52] Carolina's 1629 charter gave Robert Heath and his heirs the status of "absolute lords and proprietors" over Carolina's land and people; it explicitly authorized them to condemn or pardon anyone in the territory—the power of life and death—and assume the King's right as a Christian prince to expropriate the lands of non-Christians.[53] These provisions tied colonial governance to hereditary lordship and patriarchal power, detached from parliamentary oversight, and projected a model in which colonial subjects could be dispossessed or killed under royal authority.[54] These neo-feudal elements of Stuart charters prevented the establishment of customary ancient constitutional protections in colonial jurisdictions.

English colonial governors also pressed domestic legal developments into service to arrogate absolute power over labor to themselves. In 1636, Governor Henry Hawley of Barbados, drawing upon revised legal definitions of the villein, declared that Africans and Indians arriving in the colony without contracts must serve for life.[55] The 1639 case of *Bell v. Providence Island Company* treated human beings as alienable incidents of political office.[56] At the same time, merchants were testing procedures for buying and selling people in English colonial markets without contracts.[57] Between 1635 and 1675, for example, privateers who arrived in Barbados with stolen Africans typically sold them "on the spot" for whatever goods buyers had at hand; those purchasers then began treating the people they bought as feudal villeins bound to the land.[58]

These trends created a legal atmosphere in early English America wherein the freedom of the colonial subject was bound by the authority of the Crown and its administrative representatives. As an inducement to the colonial settlement of Jamaica, for example, King Charles II issued a 1661 proclamation that "All children of any of our Naturall born Subjects of England to be born in Jamaica shall from their respective Births, be reputed to be, and shall be free Denizens of England and shall have the same privilege to all intents and purposes as our free born Subjects of England."[59] Here is the monarch's claim that to be a "free born Subject" under his transatlantic sovereignty is the best security for English liberties, both at home and abroad—a perhaps dubious proposition, given the degree to which he and his relatives were using the courts to erode labor protections for the subject. What is more, Charles II offered transatlantic security for English liberties even as his own courts continued to insist that the English common law did not necessarily extend "beyond the seas," a problem we will consider in our reading of *Calvin's Case* (1608) and Daniel Defoe's *Robinson Crusoe* (1719).

One hundred years later, American revolutionaries would dispute King George III's claim that their best bid for liberty was subjection to an overseas monarch. To do so, they drew on their forebears' ancient constitutionalist arguments from earlier centuries. As Bernard Bailyn writes, these Anglo-Americans interpreted the ancient constitution, and specifically the immemorial common law, as "a unique inheritance of liberty."[60] Because they were possessed of legal and cultural institutions that had conserved this liberty since "time out of mind," Bailyn writes, they wielded a temporal frame that allowed them to arrogate to themselves powers that otherwise would belong to the sovereign.[61] As we will see in the final chapter of this study, Thomas Jefferson made this claim in his 1774 *Summary View of the Rights of British America*. Like Nathaniel Bacon before him, Jefferson asserted that British America's timeless and unique liberty was racially Anglo-Saxon; two years later, he would transpose that claim into supra-British terms in the Declaration of Independence.

Reading Racecraft in Literature of the Long Eighteenth Century

These transatlantic legal developments, driven by the Stuarts' pursuit of absolute power, are the conditions under which the American regime of chattel, racial slavery developed. Already we have seen how claims to political power in England, made through appeals to history in general and heredity in particular, were seeding the legal landscape with ideas about how a person's lineal descent (from Adam, the Anglo-Saxons, or otherwise) indicated his position in the present social hierarchy. *Novel Constitutions* is interested in how some writers of the long eighteenth century[62] responded to this legal environment, where they questioned, amplified, critiqued, and defied arguments for chattel slavery. To access that human detail, this study considers some literature of the long eighteenth century as an Atlantic story, a good deal older than the United States itself, of what Barbara J. Fields and Karen E. Fields call "racecraft."

Racecraft, Fields and Fields argue, is the sociohistorical process by which race is brought into being. Importantly, Fields and Fields write, the concept of racecraft does not deny "the rationality of those who have accepted" racist ideas as true; rather, racecraft seeks to account for "the processes of reasoning" that make racism seem "plausible" to the people who accept it.[63] For example, the Stuarts' racial claims to absolute power over their subjects were plausible to a thinker like Sir Robert Filmer because he believed sincerely, it seems, in Adam's historically transcendent dominion over his household. As Brewer has written of Filmer's logic in *Patriarcha*: "One was born a slave, just as one was born a prince."[64] Both were forms of racecraft.

The writers who occupy *Novel Constitutions* are of great interest to us precisely because they, like Fields and Fields, sought to narrativize "the processes" by which seventeenth-century Englishmen developed the racial, chattel enslavement of African-descended people out of the constitutional thought of their time—as well as those countervailing processes through which slavocratic governments were challenged on constitutional grounds by novelists, theologians, autobiographers, and mathematicians. Under this logic, *Novel Constitutions* gathers early modern authors' stories of racecraft, and opposition to it, to understand what was happening with human beings and their institutions as people from England racecrafted themselves into slaveholders and racecrafted people from Africa into slaves.

As Fields and Fields note, the process of racecraft operates rhetorically as a kind of "shorthand" that transfigures "something an aggressor *does*," like asserting property rights in other human beings or stripping away their legal protections from violence, "into *race*, something the target *is*."[65] The Fieldses provide an instructive example of how racecraft operates, even at the level of grammar: "Consider," they write, "the statement 'black Southerners were segregated because of their skin color'—a perfectly natural sentence to the ears of most Americans, who tend to overlook its weird causality."[66] "But in that sentence," Fields and Fields continue, "segregation disappears as the doing of segregationists, and then, in a puff of smoke—*paff*—reappears as a trait of only one part of the segregated whole."[67] We will see this in *Novel Constitutions*' extended engagement with the Barbadian slave code of 1661, the oldest known anglophone law to attach human skin color to labor condition.[68]

English slavocrats vanish in this legislation of their own enactment, disguised as their perception of Africans. As the writers of the 1661 code claimed, "Negroes" were a "heathenish, brutish and uncertain dangerous pride of people."[69] In the rest of the 1661 code, Barbadian slavocrats use the term "Negro" instead of the term "slave." As historian Edward Rugemer writes, this transposition of terms "asserted equivalence between slave status and the complexion of sub-Saharan Africans. 'Negro,' meaning 'African,' derived…from Portuguese and Spanish usage and was rooted in the word for black."[70] Thus, the 1661 Barbadian code links seventeenth-century English perceptions of body color ("Negro"), religious difference ("heathenish"), social unpredictability ("uncertain"), and animal status ("brutish," "pride") to African descent and the condition of slavery. Rugemer concludes that "race served" in the 1661 code "as an intellectual technology to justify the brutally distinct treatment of a people defined as inferior."[71] As we will see, this treatment included the deprivation of constitutional protections extended at law in the colony to other laborers. Racecraft—in 1661 as in the Jim Crow South as in 2020—is a historically transcendent practice in which politics masquerades as ontology.

The 1661 Barbadian code thus covered under the term "Negro" a repertoire of neo-feudal labor practices that English jurists friendly to absolutism had been pursuing for nearly a century. Those practices included: separating children from parents, tying persons to estates in perpetuity, and alienating labor through sale.[72] English concerns about the potential for their labor to become unfree in colonial jurisdictions arose in the context of colonial institutionalization of unfree labor for Africans.[73] Peter Charles Hoffer has shown that one key right that English people enjoyed in the colonies was that of litigating infractions against their labor contracts: "Court dockets were filled with servant-related cases," Hoffer explains, and early English servants in the colonies actively used the courts to enforce their legal rights: suing masters for proper treatment, payment, and end-of-service benefits—and often winning.[74] Servants' persistent litigation frustrated masters, who sought to avoid these challenges by investing in the unfree labor of Africans, people who, especially in the early years of English slavery, did not enjoy access to colonial courts or the English Parliament.[75] Consonant with neo-feudal alterations to the common law, enslaved Africans were systematically denied the very constitutional rights—such as the ability to sue, own land, and maintain families—that English servants began successfully to vindicate at law.[76]

In these colonial legal developments, the imperial absolutism of the Stuarts invaded the property protections of the ancient constitution in a tragic and decisive act of racecraft. We have seen that, before Africans were enslaved in England's colonies, Tudor and Stuart jurists had begun turning life and liberty into alienable property by revising villeinage law. Colonial lawmakers adapted these precedents into slavocratic property statutes, transforming an ancient constitutional safeguard—once meant to protect freeborn English subjects from royal seizures of land and chattels—into a rationale for denying those same rights to Africans, who under the 1661 Barbadian code were themselves defined as property. People of African descent had no easy recourse to the King's courts in early English America; nor could they easily lay claim to inherited English rights, although some tried and succeeded, as the well-known case of Elizabeth Key attests.[77] But without widespread opposition in the colonies, absolutist definitions of life and liberty as transferable forms of property created two new legal identities: the colonial slaveholder, subject to royal power yet empowered to hold others' lives and liberties as chattels; and the slave, whose life and liberty, and that of her children, belonged to her enslaver. As we will see in our reading of Olaudah Equiano, enslaved people of African descent eventually would appeal to Westminster for relief from bondage, emphasizing a Christian form of transatlantic constitutionalism that was deracializing in orientation.

By considering the absolutist techniques by which English imperialism freighted body color with legal significance, we can lift what W. E. B. Du Bois called the "veil"[78] of the color line, allowing us to see the human dynamics of race and racism with less interference from the evidently hypnotizing fact that human beings have, among other variances, different colors of skin. *Novel Constitutions*' attention to racecraft—as a process that remade heritable rights-deprivations as body color in English colonial law—does not in any sense overwrite scholarship on the color vocabularies of "darkness and light," described by Kim F. Hall, or humoral-climatologic theories of racial difference elaborated by Mary Floyd-Wilson in the earlier literatures of the English Renaissance.[79] These scholars and others have opened to us a dynamic world of English color signification that, Hall explains, through an "insistent association of 'black' as a negative signifier of different cultural and religious practices with physiognomy and skin color is precisely what pushes this language into the realm of racial discourse."[80] When Englishmen crafted race at law in the seventeenth century, they could not avoid this web of older ideas about the moral meanings, religious significance, and humoral explanations of human body color. Roxann Wheeler notes that, despite Enlightenment claims to study nature, Europeans still relied on classical "truisms" about climate: "Climate and humoral theory...provided the most important rubric for thinking about human differences in the eighteenth century, in regard to both complexion and civil society."[81] Whatever we conclude in *Novel Constitutions* about racecraft at law in the seventeenth century, we must understand it as one of many junctures in the broader historical processes of racial signification.

Novel Constitutions seeks to close a particular gap in the scholarship between body color's early modern meanings in English and the rise of color-based slavery in England's western Atlantic colonies. We still lack an account of how English "truisms" (about climate and humors) and "association[s]" (of body color with moral meaning) were transmuted into a broadly consistent and astonishingly durable transatlantic chattel economy in human beings, backed by the power of state violence. To bridge this gap, scholars of the last half century have relied on the explanatory power of skin color differences that Englishmen perceived between themselves and others, describing in great detail the destructive and transformational character of color-based racism in our past.[82] Given the powerful role that white supremacy has played in American history, we might posit that even *thinking* about race in America as something other than body color has been its own epistemological struggle.[83]

Novel Constitutions holds that body color alone was never sufficient to explain the enormity of racial slavery as it developed in England's western Atlantic colonies. To understand how Englishmen could claim absolute property rights in rightless Africans—and act with world-shifting conviction upon such laws for centuries—we must first grasp what they believed about themselves as bearers of racial rights against monarchs who also claimed legitimacy by racial means. *Novel Constitutions* argues that a key taproot of English racecraft, if not *the* taproot, was the ancient constitution in existential conflict with absolute monarchy during the seventeenth century. Anglo-American racial ideology has had extraordinary staying power because it was deeply rooted in how the English understood themselves—as a freeborn people since time out of mind—when they first made Africans into slaves. In the next section, we will examine how the constitutional conflicts of early modern England lent themselves to reinscription as human body color in imperial labor regimes.

"As the Constitution of this Place Shall Requyre": Color, Climate, and Constitution

Englishmen's claim in themselves against their sovereign—flowing from the "nature and disposition" of the "People of this Land"—was consonant with the humoral framework through which they conceptualized their personalities, manners, health, and skin color. The English called this set of individual traits a "constitution."[84] As Mary Floyd-Wilson has shown, the early modern English understood their bodily appearances and national manners to result from a fundamental relation between native geography, local climate, and their bodies' four humors: blood, bile, phlegm, and choler.[85] The English gleaned these ideas primarily from Hippocrates's influential medical and ethnographic treatise, *Airs, Waters, Places* (c.400 BCE), which posits that a people's political disposition grows from its climatologic circumstances. For example, Hippocrates reckoned that "the Asiatic race" was "feeble" because of "the nature of the seasons, which do not undergo any great changes either to heat or cold."[86] Unchanging local weather, Hippocrates claimed, caused "Asiatic" persons to experience "neither excitement of the understanding nor any strong change of the body" over the course of their climatologic year.[87] Hippocrates concluded that the "feeble" nature of "Asiatic persons" also was "owing to [Asiatic] laws; for monarchy prevails in the greater part of Asia, and where men are not their own masters nor independent, but are the slaves of others."[88] How these "others" in Asia had escaped the political effects of the seasons is unclear. The early modern English adapted this Hippocratic logic, contending that their laws and political customs, namely the ancient constitution, were rooted in their bodily constitutions, seasoned in the bracing northern weather of an island where no king ever had usurped the people's fundamental rights to life, liberty, and legal due process.[89]

The word "constitution" was used in English to connote the condition of the individual human frame for more than 300 years before it was recruited during the 1689 Protestant Settlement to describe the fundamental principles according to which a nation is governed. This new meaning of "constitution" adopted ancient constitutionalism's opposition to absolutism as justification for William and Mary's deposition of King James II. In this way, ancient constitutionalism naturalized the Glorious Revolution by invoking the personified rights of the English people, long associated with their habits of mind and composition of body. For example, in his 1553 *Art of Rhetorique*, an elocution manual, the humanist and diplomat Thomas Wilson drew on humoral medicine to claim that "The temperature of the mynde folowes the constitucion [*sic*] of the bodie." In common parlance, medical historians Roy and Dorothy Porter note, the constitution was a person's "inner stock of vitality and strength," a humoral body in which bile, blood, phlegm, and choler were well-balanced and in harmony with the environment.[90]

A healthy constitution was solidified alongside political character in childhood, the early modern English believed, by exposure to native geography and climate. As one sixteenth-century commentator put it: northern climates like England's brought forth "a dull inflexible people obstinately affectinge barbarous liberty & Jelous of all aucthority [*sic*]."[91] John Locke wrote in *Some Thoughts Concerning Education* (1693) that the inhabitants of Malta seasoned their children to promising effect by forcing them to go naked in the heat until their tenth year; the English might expect the same good results if they took care to "accustom [themselves] from [their] Infancy,"[92] to England's geo-aerial environment. He recommended that children wear leaky shoes in the rain and not be kept too warm in the wintertime. Coddling children during infancy, Locke warned, risked creating a race of weaklings, with bodies maladapted to their natural surroundings. "Our Bodies will endure any Thing," Locke noted, "that from the Beginning they are accustom'd to."[93] Locke's understanding of everyday living as an exercise in physical and moral co-formation links the vicissitudes of quotidian life in particular climates to more generalizable characteristics of racial types, physical and affective.[94]

This dense network of ideas, all signified by the term "constitution" and bound by the metaphor of balanced vital forces within the body and the body politic, connected embodied political liberty to English physiological identity. This was a modern racial ideology if ever there was one. In 1694, the ancient constitutionalist Robert Molesworth put it this way: "Want of *Liberty* is a Disease in any Society or Body Politick, like want of *Health* in a particular Person."[95] As legal historian Mary Sarah Bilder has written, the constitution signified "an almost anthropomorphic, organic body politic, with its history, geography, social and cultural composition, and wellbeing."[96] That *most* English people (women, children, the unpropertied, and the poor) did not enjoy the full protections of the ancient constitution in any meaningful sense did not prevent this idea from organizing how the English understood their ontological condition both at home and abroad.

Imperialism tested both the ancient and bodily constitutions of English subjects abroad. As Karen Kupperman has observed in a classic essay, the English perceived the heat of lower latitudes as a threat to their constitutional health. Writing in 1598, the English merchant George Wateson observed that these "intemperate Climats" were the source of "tropical diseases," signaling at once the importance of climate to English ideas of wellness, and the role of latitude in maintaining bodily health.[97] Lower latitudes, like those of England's Caribbean colonies and major slave-trading outposts in west Africa, were associated in the early-modern English imagination with the humor choler, and the element fire. This heat prompted Richard Ligon, an early colonist in Barbados, to fear that he and his shipmates were being "fricased," as they experienced "great failing in the vigour" of their constitutions.[98] When Ligon contracted yellow fever in Barbados in 1647, he described his illness as the "power of Tyranny" in his body, leaving him "without any appearance of life."[99] Englishmen Edward Hayes and Christopher Carleill reckoned similarly that the heat of all localities below 40° latitude "is unto our boddies offensyve, Which cannot prosper in dry and scalding heates more naturall to the Spaniard than us."[100] They offered these recommendations in a 1592 discourse on "Places Most Apt for the Constitution of our

Boddies, and the Spedy Advauncement [*sic*] of a State," a title linking the health of the body to the durability of an imperial polity.[101]

Under this epistemological regime, outward appearance signified inward well-being: "as it is for the outward complexion, so it is for the inward constitution," explained the Swiss physician Samuel Tissot.[102] For early modern English people, however, "complexion" did not mean skin color alone. It could denote health, motive, political disposition, or affect—outward signs of inner being, whether of a body or a body politic. Thus Matthew Hale described the common law in 1713 as "the Complection [*sic*] and Constitution of the *English* commonwealth."[103] Benjamin Franklin used the term for political outlooks, writing of the "Complexion of the next Assembly" and the "Complexion of Ministers and Measures"; and in 1775, Moses Mather denounced the "blackest complexion" of Parliament's tax policy, language that expressed political menace rather than racial identity.[104] So, while body color and freedom status began to travel together in the language of English colonial law starting in the seventeenth century, the two concepts were neither uniquely nor universally correlated. Nell Irvin Painter, for instance, cites Domesday Book (1086) statistics estimating that up to one-fifth of the English population was enslaved in the eleventh century—proof that English bondage was not always grounded in color, nor were the ancient rights of the English people consistently upheld.[105]

Rather, English slavocrats developed body color difference as a shorthand for their complex adaptations and suspensions of the English common law to shape chattel slavery in colonial jurisdictions. As Jonathan A. Bush explains, even when colonists invoked Attorney-General Richard West's 1720 declaration that the "Common Law of England, is the Common Law of the Plantations," they were not seeking to replicate English common law in full. What the colonists wanted instead, Bush observes, was the latitude to select and adapt particular common-law principles in order to legitimize a form of labor—racial slavery—that the common law itself had never recognized.[106] Holly Brewer's more recent work shows that this selective adaptation of the common law began not in the colonies but in the Stuart courts. Long before West's pronouncement, we have seen, Crown jurists were reinterpreting feudal precedents, especially the category of villeinage, to make labor inheritable and transferable, violating protections guaranteed by the ancient constitution.[107] By transforming villeinage into an alienable property right, Stuart jurists created an imperial precedent for hereditary servitude that colonial governors codified later.[108] English slavocrats, then, did not merely pick and choose common law doctrines; they extended their monarchy's legal innovations in absolutism into still newer legal claims of personal power over other human beings.

Securing this new asset of the chattel slave, economic historian Robert William Fogel writes, required an "enormous, almost unconstrained degree of force available to masters who wanted and needed to transform ancient modes of labor into a new industrial discipline."[109] "Centuries of tradition," Fogel adds, "shielded European laborers from the degree of force that was permitted against African or Afro-American slaves."[110] This "tradition," broadly speaking, was ancient constitutionalism's defense against sovereign absolutism's threats to "publick safety." To racecraft African-descended people into chattels and themselves into slavocrats, then, English colonists followed sovereign absolutism to novel constitutions in their overseas colonies.

These Englishmen said as much in the early slave codes they composed. When the English slavocracy of Jamaica codified racial bondage in 1664—by adopting the barely revised text[111] of the 1661 Barbados code—they emphasized two critical points. First was that "all the liberties and previledges [*sic*], immunities and freedoms conteyned [*sic*]" in the English common law "have allwayes bin [*sic*] of force and are belonging unto all" King Charles II's subjects in Jamaica "as theyre Byrthright [*sic*]."[112] The clause uses ancient constitutional rhetoric (English "freedoms" that always were) to co-authorize royal prerogative and slavocratic power on the island. Though the 1664 Act invoked certain "liberties" as the "Byrthright" of Charles II's overseas subjects, Jamaica had not been founded by sovereign charter at all. Rather, it had been acquired by conquest of the Spanish in 1655, during the Interregnum, and governed after the Restoration through the King's prerogative administered by his colonial governor, the "Right Trusty and Welbeloved *Thomas* Lord *Windsor*."[113] The Jamaican code's appeals to timeless English "immunities and freedoms" masked a regime grounded first in martial and then in hereditary rule. The "allwayes" in the code is likewise ideological, not historical: the English had seized Jamaica from Spain less than a decade earlier.[114] Importantly, these Anglo-Jamaican slavocrats stipulated that English laws might have to be "mittigated altered lessened or enlarged" in colonial Jamaica "as the constitution of this place shall requyre."[115] Thus, English slaveholders racecrafted Africans into chattels, and themselves into slaveholders, by displacing ancient constitutional protections with what the "constitution of [Jamaica] . . . requyre[d]": a new form of power, derived from absolute monarchy, "for the better ordering and Governing of Negro Slaves."[116] This was a novel constitution.

The Literary History of Novel Constitutions: Theory, Method, and Chapters

Novel Constitutions contends that we can see in vivid human detail these complex transatlantic processes of racecraft, and resistance to them, unfolding in Atlantic-world literature of the long eighteenth century. This story is important for its own sake—and also because it recontextualizes the American founding with attention to pro- and anti-slavery forms of transatlantic constitutionalism during the colonial period. To illuminate this detail, I pair selected literary works with contemporary legal texts that created race as a matter of positive law. When we understand that English colonial slavocracies were projections of monarchical absolute power, we appropriately contextualize the history of slavery and antislavery in the wider politics of the anglophone Atlantic. Consequently, our interpretive capacity to see racecraft, and its limits, in literary history swells with possibility.

Novel Constitutions is not an exhaustive reading of eighteenth-century stories of racecraft. Rather, it is a series of demonstrative examples. The first two chapters treat works of fiction by English authors who narrate how race is brought into being: Aphra Behn's *Oroonoko; Or, the Royal Slave* (1688) dramatizes the making of slaves and Daniel Defoe's *Robinson Crusoe* (1719) explores the corollary process for the creation of slaveholders. The next two chapters turn to nonfiction work by authors of African descent who challenge the legal fiction of race: in his autobiographical *Interesting Narrative* (1789) Olaudah Equiano makes a theological case for abolition in constitutional terms; Benjamin Banneker turns to spherical trigonometry in his 1792 *Almanack and Ephemeris* to demonstrate that racial slavery is wrong because human beings are one another's equals according to the universal laws of mathematics. The final two chapters return to fiction to examine the outcomes of English racecraft: Jane Austen's *Mansfield Park* (1813) is the story of a slaveholding family's destruction when colonial absolute power corrupts a father's relationships with his children, and Mary Shelley's *Frankenstein* (1818) shows how racecraft meets its limit in the truth of human kinship.

Here, readers will notice an important structural tension in *Novel Constitutions* between fiction written by English authors and nonfiction written by authors of African descent. This is by design. Enslaved or enslavable people writing in the eighteenth-century anglophone tradition generally turned to narrative to insist on the truth of their experiences. Nonfictional forms—autobiography, petition, and sermon—flourished among enslaved or enslavable writers because these genres could shoulder evidentiary weight to counter the fictions of race.[117] Autobiography, in particular, grounded the writer's authority in sworn testimony rather than invention, translating the first-person "I" into a witness. In slavocratic societies, where novel constitutions ratified the fiction that a person could be property, the autobiographical act became an assertion of standing. To write one's life, then, was to enter the record, to present oneself as a testifying subject capable of oath, contract, and covenant.[118] In this sense, autobiography functioned as a constitutional act through which the chattelized person claimed membership in the polity by a distinctive birthright: personal claims to narrative truth. We will see Equiano performing precisely this constituting act when he approaches Queen Charlotte's "royal presence" to "plead" on behalf of enslaved people in the Caribbean for "the rights . . . of freemen" to be extended to "themselves, and . . . their posterity."[119] Banneker will make a similar argument to Thomas Jefferson. These appeals confirm both men's status as founders in the Atlantic constitutional history of the people's rights against absolute power.

By contrast, the English writers in this study wrote novels that explore the moral contradictions and political tensions of racecraft by counterfactual means. These authors could do so, at least in part, because they were not faced with the immediate problem of their own enslavement. The novel itself, moreover, offered distinctive political affordances to these writers: its speculative and genealogical form was ideally suited to a constitutional imagination grappling with who might inherit property, exercise liberty, and belong to the polity. At the same time, fiction offered meaningful cover to writers like Aphra Behn and Daniel Defoe, whose imaginative experiments in sovereignty and subjection would have been dangerous to articulate directly under the exacting censorship of the Stuart regime.[120]

Novel Constitutions will show how the novel's unique affordances—its counterfactualism, perspectival shifts, and characterological depth all orchestrated within a distinctive genealogical structure—enabled English authors to examine the constitutional (dis)ordering of life, liberty, and property by colonial slavocracy during the early modern period.[121] Anglophone novels of this era consistently, if not universally, narrate how persons are embedded in kinship lines that transmit property and sociopolitical legitimacy, even as those same lines are fractured, subordinated, or transferred by the formal mechanism we call the plot. Characters' motivations and interior worlds are intelligible in these literary works only with reference to this constitutional system of inheritance.

Indeed, the eighteenth-century novel—composed of dynamic relations among life, liberty, and property—looks a lot like a genre that a culture would produce if it faced constitutional questions raised by racial fictions. In this book's title, the term "novel" thus signals not only a contrast with the "ancient" constitution but also the genre's early modern "rise"[122] as a narrative technology for exploring how constitutional questions figure the polity. What is this if not racecraft? By testing how kinship, property, and political legitimacy are (and are not) constituted, the novel became a cultural jurisdiction for adjudicating the human stakes of absolute monarchy's transatlantic conflict with ancient constitutionalism. Together in this study, novels and non-fiction expose how racecraft's constitutional contours shape, and are shaped by, the literary tradition of the eighteenth-century Atlantic.[123]

In this way, *Novel Constitutions* adds literary-historical texture to Mary Nyquist's pathbreaking study, *Arbitrary Rule* (2013), which emphasizes the categorical distinction early modern thought drew between political slavery (under tyrant kings) and chattel slavery (under slavocrats).[124] *Novel Constitutions* adds to this insight that monarchy and slavocracy turned on the same genealogical mechanism—but turned in opposite ways. Both political regimes mobilized paternal metaphors to naturalize absolute power: the key difference is that paternalism was asserted in the context of monarchy, as in Filmer's *Patriarcha*, but disavowed in the context of slavery. Under the colonial principle of *partus sequitur ventrem*, for example, a child's labor status followed the condition of her mother; under *filius nullius*, the bound young person was considered the child of no one.[125] With these doctrines, the colonial slavocrat assumed absolute power to separate the child from her common law inheritance and create her as a heritable chattel, reenacting the primal transgression of Genesis.

Novel Constitutions responds to this grave denial of human dignity with an impassioned defense of reading eighteenth-century literature as a dynamic archive of slavery and anti-slavery, whose meanings are up to us to discern. Reasoned debate about these texts in the present—premised on the equal dignity of all human beings—amounts to the search for wisdom in our tragic history. We have much to learn from the authors in this study: whether they were writing novels, letters, autobiographies, or almanacs, they knew that the literary arts could tell human truths about the fictions of race. In this way, *Novel Constitutions* opens new avenues of inquiry to scholars in literature, history, and political theory, as well as their subfields. This study also sheds light on a disagreement in the public square about the moral status of the American founding of 1776, which has returned during the nation's sestercentennial.[126] The conflict in contemporary American political culture—which pits pro-slavery and anti-slavery interpretations of the 1776 Revolution against each other—is a distant epiphenomenon of the conflict between absolute sovereignty and ancient constitutionalism in seventeenth-century England. These are living questions: as this book went to press, *Trump v. Barbara* (2026) reaffirmed birthright citizenship on the common-law grounds this study traces.

The following chapters thus tell a new story of race in America. By reading literary and legal history into this narrative, I have sought to reimagine not the texts themselves—which are now as they ever were—but our relation to them in the present. The authors in this study teach us that, although the fictions of race are powerful, we are free to read them as fictions, and ourselves as real human beings, instead of the other way around. It is not for me to say that America's original sin can or cannot be redeemed. *Novel Constitutions* seeks only to regain knowledge of that first disobedience, by reframing the constitutions of the world we have lost.

Notes

1. Cornel West, "A Grand Tradition of Struggle," *English Journal* 89, no. 6 (2000): 40.
2. Stephen Marche, "The Racism of *Gone with the Wind* is Still with Us," *Esquire*, December 15, 2014.
3. Victor Fleming, George Cukor, and Sam Wood, dirs., *Gone with the Wind* (Metro-Goldwyn-Mayer, 1939). By invoking the Cavaliers, the filmmakers were true to Mitchell's text, which, in the voice of Grandma Fontaine, traces the roots of the Southern aristocracy from the English Civil War to the American Civil War by way of the Haitian Revolution: "We've always bet on the wrong horses," Grandma Fontaine explains to Scarlett: "Run out of France with the Huguenots, run out of England with the Cavaliers, run out of Scotland with Bonnie Prince Charlie, run out of Haiti by

the niggers and now licked by the Yankees." Margaret Mitchell, *Gone with the Wind* (London: Pocket Books, 2008), 1000–1.

4. After the 1707 Acts of Union between Scotland and England, the nation became known as Great Britain. Accordingly, *Novel Constitutions* will use "England" to reference years before 1707 and "Great Britain" or simply "Britain" to indicate the years 1707 and after. Parliament of the United Kingdom, "Act of Union 1707." Accessed November 9, 2024. <https://www.parliament.uk/about/living-heritage/evolutionofparliament/legislativescrutiny/act-of-union-1707/>
5. Parliament of the United Kingdom. "The Transatlantic Slave Trade." Accessed July 1, 2024. <https://heritagecollections.parliament.uk/stories/the-transatlantic-slave-trade/>
6. For two recent studies that elaborate the notion of the founding of the United States as a paradox, see Sean Wilentz, *No Property in Man: Slavery and Antislavery at the Nation's Founding* (Cambridge, MA: Harvard University Press, 2018); and William E. Nelson, *E Pluribus Unum: How the Common Law Helped Unify and Liberate Colonial America, 1607–1776* (New York: Oxford University Press, 2019). "Paradox" has become an important metaphor in academic understandings of the tensions of 1776 between freedom and slavery.
7. J. G. A. Pocock, *The Ancient Constitution and the Feudal Law: A Study of English Historical Thought in the Seventeenth Century*, rev. edn (Cambridge: Cambridge University Press, 1987), 1–50; see also Corinne C. Weston, "England: Ancient Constitution and Common Law," in *The Cambridge History of Political Thought, 1450–1700*, ed. J. H. Burns (Cambridge: Cambridge University Press, 1991), 374–411.
8. Holly Brewer, "Whose Fundamental Constitutions? Locke, Slavery, and Manuscript Evidence," *Locke Studies* (2024): 1–57, esp. 11–12, on Filmer and Spelman's use of feudal history to bolster the royal prerogative.
9. Brewer, "Whose Fundamental Constitutions?" 11–12; Sir Robert Filmer, "Patriarcha, or The Natural Power of Kings (1680)," in *Patriarcha and Other Writings*, ed. Johann P. Sommerville (Cambridge: Cambridge University Press, 1991), 7.
10. Filmer, "Patriarcha," 4.
11. Nikole Hannah-Jones et al., *The 1619 Project: A New Origin Story* (New York: New York Times, 2021), pp. xvii–xxxiii; David Waldstreicher, "The Hidden Stakes of the 1619 Controversy," *Boston Review*, January 24, 2020.
12. Pocock, *Ancient Constitution*, 30–35. On the fictiveness of early modern England's self-understanding as a nation free of slavery, a fiction integral to this ideology of immemorial liberty, see Urvashi Chakravarty, *Fictions of Consent: Slavery, Servitude, and Free Service in Early Modern England* (Philadelphia: University of Pennsylvania Press, 2022).
13. Sir Henry Spelman, "The Original, Growth, Propagation and Condition of Feuds and Tenures by Knight-Service, in England," in *Reliquiæ Spelmannianæ* (Oxford: Theatre, 1698), esp. ch. 2 (sections beginning "This was a fair direction for William of Normandy..." and "To conclude therefore") and ch. 1 (definition of feud and denial of Saxon usage).
14. Filmer, "Patriarcha," 53–54.
15. Filmer, "Patriarcha," 53–54; see also: Pocock, *Ancient Constitution*, 301–4.
16. Staffan Müller-Wille and Hans-Jörg Rheinberger, *A Cultural History of Heredity* (Chicago: University of Chicago Press, 2012), 47–50.
17. Paul Gilroy has theorized this assemblage of Atlantic-rim localities, and the routes people traveled among them, as the Black Atlantic, a concept that has been foundational to the ideas in *Novel Constitutions*. Paul Gilroy, *The Black Atlantic: Modernity and Double Consciousness* (Cambridge, MA: Harvard University Press, 1993).
18. For the best, now classic, study of what is possible to know about the past despite the incursions of power, see Michel-Rolph Trouillot, *Silencing the Past: Power and the Production of History* (Boston: Beacon Press, 1995).
19. Vincent Brown, *Tacky's Revolt: The Story of an Atlantic Slave War* (Cambridge, MA: Harvard University Press, 2020), 13.
20. Henry Louis Gates, Jr., *The Signifying Monkey: A Theory of Afro-American Literary Criticism* (New York: Oxford University Press, 1988), 16; see also Henry Louis Gates, Jr., *The Trials of Phillis Wheatley: America's First Black Poet and her Encounters with the Founding Fathers* (New York: Basic Civitas, 2003).
21. John Brewer and Susan Staves, "Introduction," in *Early Modern Conceptions of Property*, ed. John Brewer and Susan Staves (New York: Routledge, 1995), 1.
22. Frank Barlow, *Edward the Confessor* (New Haven: Yale University Press, 1997), 235–44; Marc Morris, *The Norman Conquest: The Battle of Hastings and the Fall of Anglo-Saxon England* (New York: Pegasus Books, 2013), 183–88; Pocock, *Ancient Constitution*, 42–43.
23. Janelle Greenberg, *The Radical Face of the Ancient Constitution: St. Edward's "Laws" in Early Modern Political Thought* (Cambridge: Cambridge University Press, 2001), 2–3.

24. Jeffrey Goldsworthy, "From Bracton to the Reformation," in *The Sovereignty of Parliament: History and Philosophy* (Oxford: Clarendon Press, 1999), 22–50; *Encyclopaedia Britannica*, s.v. "Henry de Bracton," last modified February 16, 2024. <https://www.britannica.com/biography/Henry-de-Bracton>
25. John Fortescue, "Introduction," in *Sir John Fortescue: On the Laws and Governance of England*, ed. Shelley Lockwood (Cambridge: Cambridge University Press, 1997), p. xxxi.
26. Laura Doyle, *Freedom's Empire: Race and the Rise of the Novel in Atlantic Modernity, 1640–1940* (Durham, NC: Duke University Press, 2008), 30.
27. Glenn Burgess has noted that the contest modern historians perceive between ancient constitutionalism and absolutism during the early years of the Stuart dynasty is an artifact of Whig history more than a faithful telling of the facts on the ground. Nevertheless, Burgess concludes, the struggle between ancient constitutionalism and absolutism is an accurate way to conceive of the later Stuart era. Glenn Burgess, *Absolute Monarchy and the Stuart Constitution* (New Haven: Yale University Press, 1996), 1–62.
28. Doyle, *Freedom's Empire*, 31.
29. Doyle, *Freedom's Empire*, 31.
30. Greenberg, *Radical Face*, 4.
31. Peter Charles Hoffer, *Law and People in Colonial America* (Baltimore, MD: Johns Hopkins University Press, 1992), 4–5.
32. Allen D. Boyer, *Sir Edward Coke and the Elizabethan Age* (Stanford, CA: Stanford University Press, 2003), 67–107.
33. Edward Coke, *The Second Part of the Reports of Edward Coke, Her Majesty's Attorney-General: Of Divers Matters in Law, with Great and Mature Consideration Resolved and Adjudged, Which Were Never Resolved or Adjudged Before; and the Reasons and Causes Thereof; during the Reign of the Most Illustrious and Renowned Queen Elizabeth* (London: Printed by E. and R. Nutt & R. Gosling, assigns of Edward Sayer, for D. Bowne et al., 1727), A4.
34. Sir John Davies, *Irish Reports (Les Reports des Cases & Matters en Ley, Resolves & Adjudges en les Courts del Roy en Ireland. Collect & digest per Sir John Davis Chivaler, Attorney Gerall del Roy en cest Realm)*, unpaginated London edn of 1674; quoted in Pocock, *Ancient Constitution*, 32–33.
35. Sir John Davies, *Irish Reports*, quoted in Pocock, *Ancient Constitution*, 33.
36. Sir John Davies, *Irish Reports*, quoted in Pocock, *Ancient Constitution*, 33–34.
37. Doyle, *Freedom's Empire*, 40, my emphasis.
38. Doyle, *Freedom's Empire*, 40.
39. Jacob T. Levy, *Rationalism, Pluralism, and Freedom* (Oxford: Oxford University Press, 2015), 112–13. As Levy notes, Pocock's focus on the "insularity of the common-law mindset" of the English is "an exception." As David Resnick argues, the English of this period "shared with other Europeans a mode of thought that resisted the attempts of modern monarchies to claim sovereign power at the expense of particularistic privileges" by appealing to an immemorial constitution. David Resnick, "Locke and the Rejection of the Ancient Constitution," *Political Theory* 12, no. 1 (1984): 99, quoted in Levy, *Rationalism, Pluralism, and Freedom*, 115.
40. Robert Molesworth, quoted in Levy, *Rationalism, Pluralism, and Freedom*, 116.
41. Levy, *Rationalism, Pluralism, and Freedom*, 113.
42. Orlando Patterson, *Freedom in the Making of Western Culture* (New York: Basic Books, 1991); Christopher Leslie Brown, *Moral Capital: Foundations of British Abolitionism* (Chapel Hill, NC: University of North Carolina Press, published for the Omohundro Institute of Early American History and Culture, Williamsburg, VA, 2006), 46. More generally, see Robert J. Steinfeld, *The Invention of Free Labor: The Employment Relation in English and American Law and Culture, 1350–1870* (Chapel Hill, NC: University of North Carolina Press, 1991).
43. Brewer and Staves, *Early Modern Conceptions*, 1.
44. Resnick, "Locke and Rejection," 97–114.
45. Holly Brewer, "Creating a Common Law of Slavery for England and its New World Empire," *Law and History Review* 39, no. 4 (2021): 773; see also Holly Brewer, *By Birth or Consent: Children, Law, and the Anglo-American Revolution in Authority* (Chapel Hill, NC: UNC Press, 2005), 230–87.
46. An Act for the Punishment of Vagabonds and for the Relief of the Poor, 1 Edw. VI c. 3 (1547); see also: Cliff S. L. Davies, "Slavery and Protector Somerset: The Vagrancy Act of 1547," *Economic History Review* 19 (1966): 533–49.
47. Brewer, "Common Law of Slavery," 766–68.
48. J. H. Baker, *An Introduction to English Legal History*, 5th edn (Oxford: Oxford University Press, 2019), 32, 260, 347–48.

49. Brewer, "Common Law of Slavery," 770–71.
50. Brewer, "Common Law of Slavery," 830–32.
51. Brewer, "Whose Fundamental Constitutions?" 12.
52. Andrew Thrush, "Representation and Accountability," in *The History of Parliament: The House of Commons, 1604–1629*, vol. I: *Introductory Survey and Appendices* (Cambridge: Cambridge University Press, 2010), quoted in Brewer, "Whose Fundamental Constitutions?" 10–11.
53. Brewer, "Whose Fundamental Constitutions?" 11–12.
54. Brewer, "Whose Fundamental Constitutions?" 11–12.
55. Brewer, "Common Law of Slavery," 774.
56. In *Bell v. Providence Island Company* (1639), former governor Philip Bell sought permanent ownership of servants, including Africans, from the Providence Island Company. The court ruled that people were attached to the land rather than to individual masters, but since Bell had left the colony, he was awarded compensation for the servants he would have been entitled to as governor. Brewer, "Common Law of Slavery," 775.
57. Brewer, "Common Law of Slavery," 775–76.
58. Brewer, "Common Law of Slavery," 776.
59. King Charles II, quoted in David Barry Gaspar, "'Rigid and Inclement': Origins of the Jamaica Slave Laws of the Seventeenth Century," in *The Many Legalities of Early America*, ed. Christopher L. Tomlins and Bruce H. Mann (Chapel Hill, NC: University of North Carolina Press, 2001), 89.
60. Bernard Bailyn, *The Ideological Origins of the American Revolution: Fiftieth Anniversary Edition* (Cambridge, MA: Harvard University Press, 2017), 67.
61. Bailyn, *Ideological Origins*, 67.
62. "Long eighteenth century" is a term of art that has come to indicate a range of temporal frames in literary criticism. In *Novel Constitutions*, this phrase roughly references the period from the Stuart Restoration in 1660 until the early nineteenth century.
63. Karen E. Fields and Barbara J. Fields, *Racecraft: The Soul of Inequality in American Life* (London and New York: Verso, 2012), 19.
64. Holly Brewer, "Slavery, Sovereignty, and 'Inheritable Blood': Reconsidering John Locke and the Origins of American Slavery," *American Historical Review* 122, no. 4 (October 2017): 1042.
65. Fields and Fields, *Racecraft*, 17.
66. Fields and Fields, *Racecraft*, 17.
67. Fields and Fields, *Racecraft*, 17.
68. As Edward Rugemer has written, there was at least one earlier English law of slavery in colonial Barbados that was based on human body color: the Act concerning Negroes, which was passed in 1644. To the best of our knowledge, however, the text of this code has not survived; for this reason, *Novel Constitutions* makes recourse to the 1661 code, whose available content allows us to study early modern rhetorical mechanisms of racecraft. See Richard Hall (ed.), *Acts Passed in the Island of Barbados from 1643 to 1762* (London, 1764), 450; and Edward Rugemer, *Slave Law and the Politics of Resistance in the Early Atlantic World* (Cambridge, MA: Harvard University Press, 2018), 313.
69. Rugemer, *Slave Law*, 32.
70. Rugemer, *Slave Law*, 32.
71. Rugemer, *Slave Law*, 33.
72. Brewer, "Common Law of Slavery," 772–79.
73. See generally Don Jordan and Michael Walsh, *White Cargo: The Forgotten History of Britain's White Slaves in America* (New York: New York University Press, 2008).
74. Hoffer, *Law and People*, 17.
75. Brewer, "Common Law of Slavery," 773–79; cf. A. Leon Higginbotham Jr., *In the Matter of Color: Race and the American Legal Process, The Colonial Period* (New York: Oxford University Press, 1978), 19–40. While Higginbotham documents occasional early suits by people of African descent, such as the 1641 case of John Graweere, a black servant in Virginia who successfully petitioned for his child's freedom, such access to the English colonial courts seems to have been exceptional (25).
76. Hoffer, *Law and People*, 17.
77. Warren M. Billings, "The Cases of Fernando and Elizabeth Key: A Note on the Status of Blacks in Seventeenth-Century Virginia," *William and Mary Quarterly* 30, no. 3 (1973): 467–74; and Taunya Lovell Banks, "Dangerous Woman: Elizabeth Key's Freedom Suit—Subjecthood and Racialized Identity in Seventeenth-Century Colonial Virginia," *Akron Law Review* 41, no. 4 (2008): 799–836.

78. W. E. B. Du Bois, *The Souls of Black Folk* (Oxford: Oxford University Press, 2008), 3.
79. Kim F. Hall, *Things of Darkness: Economies of Race and Gender in Early Modern England* (Ithaca, NY: Cornell University Press, 1995), 6; and Mary Floyd-Wilson, *English Ethnicity and Race in Early Modern Drama* (Cambridge: Cambridge University Press, 2003).
80. Hall, *Things of Darkness*, 6.
81. Roxann Wheeler, *The Complexion of Race: Categories of Difference in Eighteenth-Century British Culture* (Philadelphia: University of Pennsylvania Press, 2000), 21–22.
82. The most important of these studies, too numerous to list here, is Winthrop D. Jordan, *White over Black: American Attitudes toward the Negro, 1550–1812* (Chapel Hill, NC: University of North Carolina Press for the Institute of Early American History and Culture at Williamsburg, VA, 1968).
83. For a political theorist's elaboration of epistemological struggles wrought by race, see Charles W. Mills, *The Racial Contract* (Ithaca, NY: Cornell University Press, 1997), 9–31.
84. *Oxford English Dictionary*, s.v. "constitution (n.)," last modified December 2023.
85. Floyd-Wilson, *English Ethnicity*, 1–47.
86. Hippocrates, *On Airs, Waters, and Places*, ed. A. C. Burnell, tr. Émile Littré et al. (London: Wyman & Sons for the Royal College of Physicians, 1881), 71.
87. Hippocrates, *On Airs, Waters, and Places*, 71.
88. Hippocrates, *On Airs, Waters, and Places*, 71.
89. This geohumoral body, Floyd-Wilson shows, was a foundational racialist principle of the early modern period because the English imperial project was realized, in part, through a cultural recasting of the northern, phlegmatic, globally marginal English as humorally superior to bodies seasoned in other climates. On the same imaginative program, England became cartographically central to a new imperial globe (Floyd-Wilson, *English Ethnicity*, 1–20). The success of the English geohumoral project over the *longue durée* is perhaps most evident in the 1884 adoption of Greenwich longitude as the Prime Meridian of the world.
90. Roy Porter and Dorothy Porter, *In Sickness and in Health: The British Experience, 1650–1850* (London: Fourth Estate, 1988), 32.
91. Karen Ordahl Kupperman, "Fear of Hot Climates in the Anglo-American Colonial Experience," *William and Mary Quarterly* 41, no. 2 (April 1984): 216.
92. John Locke, *Some Thoughts Concerning Education*, 12th edn (Edinburgh: Printed for J. Brown, 1752), 4–5.
93. Locke, *Some Thoughts Concerning Education*, 5, 4.
94. For further discussion, see Ann Laura Stoler, *Along the Archival Grain: Epistemic Anxieties and Colonial Common Sense* (Princeton: Princeton University Press, 2010), esp. 38 and 97.
95. Robert Molesworth, Viscount Molesworth, *An Account of Denmark, as It Was in the Year 1692* (London: Printed for Timothy Goodwin, 1694), n.p., emphasis Molesworth's.
96. Mary Sarah Bilder, *The Transatlantic Constitution: Colonial Legal Culture and the Empire* (Cambridge, MA: Harvard University Press, 2004), 2.
97. Kupperman, "Fear of Hot Climates," 213.
98. Ligon, quoted in Kupperman,"Fear of Hot Climates," 214.
99. Ligon, quoted in Justin Roberts, *Fragile Empire: Slavery in the Early English Tropics, 1645–1720* (Cambridge: Cambridge University Press, 2023), 175.
100. Kupperman,"Fear of Hot Climates," 213.
101. Kupperman, "Fear of Hot Climates," 217.
102. Samuel Auguste David Tissot, *Advice to the People in General, in Regard to Their Health* (Boston: Mein and Fleeming, 1767), 108, 190.
103. Matthew Hale, *The History of the Common Law of England*, 3rd edn (London: Printed by E. and R. Nutt, & R. Gosling for T. Waller, 1739), 44.
104. Benjamin Franklin and Moses Mather, quoted in Sharon Block, *Colonial Complexions: Race and Bodies in Eighteenth-Century America* (Philadelphia: University of Pennsylvania Press, 2018), 17.
105. Nell Irvin Painter, *The History of White People* (New York: W. W. Norton & Co., 2010), 36.
106. Jonathan A. Bush, "Free to Enslave: The Foundations of Colonial American Slave Law," *Yale Journal of Law and the Humanities* 5, no. 2 (1993): 417–70; see also Brewer, "Common Law of Slavery."
107. Brewer, "Common Law of Slavery," 773–79.
108. Brewer, "Common Law of Slavery," 774–76.
109. Robert William Fogel, *Without Consent or Contract: The Rise and Fall of American Slavery* (New York: W. W. Norton & Co., 1989), 34.

110. Fogel, *Without Consent or Contract*, 34.
111. Gaspar, "Rigid and Inclement," 89.
112. Gaspar, "Rigid and Inclement," 89.
113. Charles II, King of England, *A Proclamation for the Encouraging of Planters in His Majesties Island of Jamaica in the West-Indies* (London: Printed by John Bill and Christopher Barker, 1661). See also Brewer, "Common Law of Slavery," 765–70.
114. J. A. Ferguson et al., "Jamaica," *Encyclopaedia Britannica*, last modified July 2, 2024. <https://www.britannica.com/place/Jamaica>
115. Quoted in Gaspar, "Rigid and Inclement," 89.
116. An Act for the Better Ordering and Governing of Negro Slaves, Jamaica, 1664, in *The Laws of Jamaica, 1664–1832*, edited and digitized by the Slavery and Freedom in the British Atlantic World Project (University of New Brunswick), accessed December 28, 2025. <https://slavery-andfreedomlaws.lib.unb.ca/laws/jamaica-1664-0>
117. See also Faith Barter, *Black Pro Se: Authorship and the Limits of Law in Nineteenth-Century African American Literature* (Chapel Hill, NC: University of North Carolina Press, 2025).
118. See James Olney, "'I Was Born': Slave Narratives, Their Status as Autobiography and as Literature," *Callaloo* 20 (1984): 46–73; William L. Andrews, *To Tell a Free Story: The First Century of Afro-American Autobiography, 1760–1865* (Urbana, IL: University of Illinois Press, 1986); and *The Slave's Narrative,* ed. Charles T. Davis and Henry Louis Gates, Jr. (Oxford: Oxford University Press, 1991).
119. Olaudah Equiano, *The Interesting Narrative of the Life of Olaudah Equiano, or Gustavus Vassa, the African,* ed. Vincent Carretta (New York: Penguin, 2003), 231.
120. Burgess, *Absolute Monarchy*; and Annabel M. Patterson, *Censorship and Interpretation: The Conditions of Writing and Reading in Early Modern England* (Madison, WI: University of Wisconsin Press, 1984).
121. Here, I am drawing on Caroline Levine's theory of forms. Caroline Levine, *Forms: Whole, Rhythm, Hierarchy, Network* (Princeton: Princeton University Press, 2015).
122. Foundational accounts of the "rise of the novel" include Ian Watt, *The Rise of the Novel: Studies in Defoe, Richardson and Fielding* (Berkeley, CA: University of California Press, 1957); Michael McKeon, *The Origins of the English Novel, 1600–1740* (Baltimore, MD: Johns Hopkins University Press, 1987); Lennard J. Davis, *Factual Fictions: The Origins of the English Novel* (New York: Columbia University Press, 1983); and Nancy Armstrong, *Desire and Domestic Fiction: A Political History of the Novel* (New York: Oxford University Press, 1987).
123. Several thinkers have aided my conception of this idea. Angus Fletcher identifies literature's formal inventions as adaptive technologies of human thought, underscoring how narrative structures shape political possibility: *Wonderworks: The 25 Most Powerful Inventions in the History of Literature* (New York: Simon & Schuster, 2021). Toni Morrison reveals how "Africanisms" structure the moral and epistemological boundaries of Euro-American texts: *Playing in the Dark: Whiteness and the Literary Imagination* (Cambridge, MA: Harvard University Press, 1992), 6–7. Eric Slauter interprets the US founding as an aesthetic project, where art and constitutionality are inseparable: *The State as a Work of Art: The Cultural Origins of the Constitution* (Chicago: University of Chicago Press, 2009). Jill Lepore examines how colonial narratives of rebellion are coextensive with the novel's fictive strategies: *New York Burning: Liberty, Slavery, and Conspiracy in Eighteenth-Century Manhattan* (New York: Alfred A. Knopf, 2005), 122. Linda Colley shows that constitution-making itself was a literary enterprise: *The Gun, the Ship, and the Pen: Warfare, Constitutions, and the Making of the Modern World* (New York: Liveright Publishing Corporation, 2021), 12. Edward Said cautions against directly conflating aesthetic capacity with legislative authority, even as both arise from acts of world-making: *Culture and Imperialism* (New York: Vintage Books, 1993), 75. Jack N. Rakove reminds us that historical narrative, like the novel, depends on perspectival and structural decisions that organize political meaning: *Original Meanings: Politics and Ideas in the Making of the Constitution* (New York: Alfred A. Knopf, 1996), 6.
124. Mary Nyquist, *Arbitrary Rule: Slavery, Tyranny, and the Power of Life and Death* (Chicago: University of Chicago Press, 2013), esp. 1–7.
125. Annette Gordon-Reed explains that the legal doctrine of *filius nullius*—literally "child of no one"—classified children born out of wedlock as having no legal father and thus no claim to paternal inheritance, a rule that in slave societies enabled white men to deny legal recognition of their mixed-race children. She argues that historians have too often accepted this legal fiction as historical fact, treating enslaved children's paternity as unknowable and thereby erasing black family ties. See Annette Gordon-Reed, *The Hemingses of Monticello: An American Family* (New

York: W. W. Norton, 2008), 82–83; and Gordon-Reed, "Engaging Jefferson: Blacks and the Founding Father," *William and Mary Quarterly* 57, no. 1 (2000): 171–82.

126. Some important documents in this public controversy include the following: *New York Times Magazine*, "The 1619 Project," August 14, 2019; Jake Silverstein, "The 1619 Project and the Long Battle over U.S. History," *New York Times Magazine*, November 9, 2021; Adam Serwer, "The Fight over the 1619 Project is Not about the Facts," *The Atlantic*, December 23, 2019; Sean Wilentz, "A Matter of Facts," *The Atlantic*, January 22, 2020; Waldstreicher, "Hidden Stakes"; Leslie M. Harris, "I Helped Fact-Check the 1619 Project. The Times Ignored Me," *Politico*, March 6, 2020; Jake Silverstein, "An Update to The 1619 Project," *New York Times*, March 11, 2020; and President's Advisory 1776 Commission, *The 1776 Report* (Washington, DC: The White House, 2021). <https://trumpwhitehouse.archives.gov/wp-content/uploads/2021/01/The-Presidents-Advisory-1776-Commission-Final-Report.pdf>

Novel Constitutions and the Making of Race: A Literary and Legal History of Slavery in the Anglophone Atlantic, 1688–1818. Sarah Marsh, Oxford University Press. DOI: 10.1093/9780197917855.003.0001

1

Imoinda's Rebellion

Sovereignty, Slavery, and the Ancient Constitution in Aphra Behn's *Oroonoko*

> Indeed, the attribution of divinity to the king had probably always been motivated in some measure by the desire to limit him to actions becoming a god.
>
> —Edmund S. Morgan, *Inventing the People: The Rise of Popular Sovereignty in England and America*[1]

> Oroonoko was no sooner return'd from his last Conquest, and receiv'd at Court...like a Deity, when there arriv'd in the Port an English Ship.
>
> —Aphra Behn, *Oroonoko; or, The Royal Slave*[2]

Aphra Behn's *Oroonoko; or, The Royal Slave* (1688) is a story of how Englishmen made people of African descent into chattels. They did so in the colony of Surinam, *Oroonoko* shows, by enforcing a heritable color line between free and enslaved people. This chapter contends that Behn's narrative is an important, perhaps firsthand, account of specific procedures of English racecraft: namely, converting Africans' familial relationships into English chattel interests and removing due-process protections for the enslaved. *Oroonoko* is also an account of how African people resisted these English techniques of enslavement: both in principle and by force. These features place *Oroonoko* among the first explanations of how and why a color line emerged in English colonial law. In Behn's story, transatlantic conflicts between ancient constitutionalism and divine-right sovereignty draw this line.

Behn's tale has two central characters. The African prince, Oroonoko, and his wife, Imoinda, are each trafficked into the Atlantic slave trade from their home country. Behn calls this place "Coramantien," a name used by early modern Europeans for the region of present-day Ghana where the English first established a slave-trading outpost in the early 1630s.[3] Behn's Imoinda is sold into slavery by the Coramantee king while Oroonoko is captured by an English slave trader, operating in the region as a parasite of internecine conflict. The transatlantic traffic takes both Imoinda and Oroonoko to English colonial Surinam. At the end of Behn's story, Oroonoko and Imoinda die as insurrectionists against

Surinam's slavocratic government after refusing to live under it as chattels destined to pass unfree status to their child, with whom Imoinda is pregnant. Determined to avoid the enslavement of her baby, Imoinda emerges as a key figure in the uprising. After this rebellion fails, Oroonoko is executed by the colonial government. But first, he kills Imoinda with her consent, sparing her and their unborn child the depredations of their enslavers.

Oroonoko's readers have long seen in these details Behn's transatlantic exploration of a contested, divine-right monarchy in Stuart England and the development of chattel, racial slavery in its colonies. Their attention has been focused particularly by the brutal execution of Oroonoko and its likeness to the regicide of Charles I. The critical consensus on this aspect of the text remains best summarized by Laura Brown's 1987 insight that "both Charles I and Oroonoko are victims of the same historical phenomenon—those new forces in English society loosely associated with an antiabsolutist mercantile imperialism."[4] Charles I and Oroonoko are similar, that is, because they are overthrown by anti-monarchical proponents of England's empire.

Yet this consensus, to which I have contributed,[5] misidentifies key political allegiances of the two colonial officials in Surinam who are responsible for Oroonoko's execution: Byam and Behn's "wild *Irish* Man," Banister (99, emphasis in original). In addition to appearing in *Oroonoko*, these men are identifiable historical actors who governed the royalist outpost of English Surinam as Oliver Cromwell's Protectorate gave way to the Restoration in 1660. William Byam (sometimes spelled Byham) and James Banister (sometimes spelled Bannister) were in fact running the colony during Behn's presumptive visit there in 1663–64. Importantly, these two historical persons were not Cromwellian regicides or republican ideologues of an emergent capitalism, as some readings of *Oroonoko* imply; they were devoted royalists.[6] The violence against Oroonoko in Behn's story, therefore, is difficult to read as an anti-monarchical attack on an African prince; rather, it seems to represent the consolidation of a colonial slavocracy whose absolute power, exercised along a color line, flows from restored Stuart authority in London.

A brief digression through the history of English colonial Surinam will bring *Oroonoko*'s politics into better focus. Surinam was founded in 1650 by the sometimes-parliamentarian and sometimes-monarchist Sir Francis Willoughby, the 5th Baron Willoughby of Parham. Behn's readers will remember his Surinam estate, Parham House, which is where *Oroonoko*'s narrator stays during her visit to the colony. Willoughby was a Civil War-era moderate, who opposed Charles I but also disagreed with radical elements of English republicanism. In 1647, Willoughby and other moderates seeking compromise with the Crown were imprisoned without charge in the Tower of London. Released after protests but soon threatened with treason charges, Willoughby switched sides and became a commander in the King's navy.[7] Parliament retaliated in 1649, sequestering Willoughby's estates.[8] It was time to go.

Anticipating his exile since at least 1647, Willoughby had used his wife Elizabeth Cecil's vast fortune to lease the colony of Barbados for twenty-one years from James Hay, 2nd Earl of Carlisle, whose father had received the island by letters-patent from Charles I in 1627.[9] Because the Carlisle estates were deeply indebted, the lease suited both parties. Willoughby sailed to Barbados in 1649, joining a Bridgetown enclave of royalist exiles—some later architects of the 1661 Barbadian slave code.[10] When Willoughby reached Barbados, he found another civil war: after Charles I's 1649 execution, island royalists had seized the government, disarmed Roundheads, and declared themselves for the young Charles II. William Byam, an incendiary monarchist and "known malignant," who had become the island's treasurer during these purges, called for the summary execution of those who opposed the royalist cause on the island, people he referred to as "Independent dogges."[11] Cooler heads prevailed, however, and the offending Roundheads were merely deported from the colony.[12]

Distrusted by both royalists and republicans, Willoughby tried to calm Barbados and reopen relations with London, sending republican tobacco planter George Marten (sometimes spelled Martin) to request continued free trade with the Commonwealth. Parliament refused and instead dispatched Sir George Ayscue to subdue the island. Willoughby prepared to defend it, and briefly celebrated false reports in October 1651 that Cromwell was dead and Charles II advancing on London.[13] The rumor proved false. That week, Ayscue's fleet arrived, besieged Bridgetown for the next three months, and compelled Willoughby's surrender in January 1652; soon after, the Parliament-aligned colonial assembly expelled the remaining royalists.[14]

This was an era of contingency plans. Soon after reaching Barbados in 1650, Willoughby sent Major Anthony Rous south with forty men to scout the Surinam region for settlement. After royalists were expelled from Barbados in 1652, Willoughby and roughly 300 followers relocated there. That June he sailed to London to secure his Surinam claim—now called "Willoughbyland"—and recover his Sussex estates under the terms of surrender to Ayscue.[15] He would not return to the Caribbean for more than a decade. During his absence, the colony and its entanglements in Civil War politics would evolve into the backdrop of Behn's *Oroonoko*.

While Willoughby was in England, Surinam expanded as royalist refugees—and some republicans—arrived with families, servants, and slaves. Owing to the strange circumstances of its founding, and especially after its London-appointed governor Anthony Rous returned to Barbados, Surinam lacked a clear governmental structure.[16] Cromwell's government was, evidently, too busy elsewhere in the Caribbean to pay much attention.[17] By 1657, colonists took matters in their own hands, creating a militia and electing William Byam as governor three years in a row. Despite his elected status, Byam exercised judicial powers similar to those wielded by colonial governors under royal patent, including power over life and death.[18]

Byam responded to the Restoration of 1660 by declaring himself permanent governor of Surinam, and he moved decisively to silence his critics. In October of that year, he had the carpenter Daniel Jones clapped in irons for "abusing the authority of the colony."[19] Jones was not alone. The Surinam planter Robert Sanford held in 1660 that Byam only "pretendeth to have his Majesty's proclamation" of a right to rule Surinam; Byam's claim, Sanford elaborated, was "a meer Chimera of Byam's own Brain, invented to serve his Ambition for a Perpetual Dominion."[20] Chimera or not, Byam suspended elections in the colony the following year as "but a needlesse and unnecessary Charge and Trouble to the inhabitants."[21] In a 1662 political pamphlet, Sanford would again accuse Byam, this time of depriving him and his men of "liberty by an infamous imprisonment" through assertions of "arbitrary tyrannical" power, which have destroyed "the *Birth right*" of English subjects in the colony in violation of Magna Carta and the "*General fundamental Constitution*." Indeed, Sanford said, Byam and his men had arrogated to "*themselves a greater latitude of Power, a Power not differing from absoluteness*."[22] Factional struggle followed, rending Surinam's social fabric and pitting neighbors against one another in a distant Atlantic aftershock of the English Civil War.[23] As Sanford's accusations of Byam attest, the conflict between absolute sovereignty and ancient constitutionalism had arrived in Willoughbyland.

Meanwhile, the return of the Stuarts to the English throne brought bitter acts of retribution and repression to London. The regicides involved in Charles I's death were arrested and executed, control over the English press was tightened through licensing, and religious uniformity was enforced.[24] But as others suffered the return of the King, Francis Willoughby was rewarded handsomely for his loyalty during the Interregnum, securing a royal patent for a vast claim in the Caribbean in May 1663, including Willoughbyland.[25] He was next sent by the Crown to Barbados to replace its colonial governor, Humphry Walrond. Walrond, it seems, had failed to enforce repayment of the large debts Barbadian planters owed to merchants for slave purchases. When slavers in the colony attempted to collect these unpaid debts, Walrond protected the Barbadian planter-elite by imprisoning the slave merchants. Evidently, Walrond and his council had issued these orders to avoid paying their own debts, creating widespread financial chaos that threatened "not only ... Barbadoes, but ... all other plantations in America."[26]

In response, the Crown's Council on Foreign Plantations advised Charles II to overturn Walrond's orders and enforce legal mechanisms to ensure the debts' repayment, stabilizing the slave economy from which the Crown was poised to profit—particularly through family connection to the Royal African Company led by Charles II's younger brother, James. Francis Willoughby was sent by the Crown to Barbados to manage the job.[27] This consolidation of the Barbadian slave economy, at the Crown's behest, prevented Willoughby from returning immediately to the colony that bore his name.

It was around this time that Aphra Behn seems to have arrived in colonial Surinam. What she found there, amid the colony's smoldering Civil War tensions, was a modern race war. As we will see, it was related intimately to Francis Willoughby's errand in Barbados, on behalf of King Charles II, to shore up its slave economy. In the sections that follow, we will examine how English Civil War tensions in *Oroonoko* between royalists and republicans—between divine right sovereignty and the ancient constitution—morphed into a colonial battlefield whose lines would now be drawn by color.

The Slave Insurrection in *Oroonoko*

As I have noted elsewhere, the slave rebellion in *Oroonoko*—which dramatizes the relation of sovereignty, slavery, and race—is typically noticed by critics only in passing.[28] This is probably owing to how Oroonoko's execution, and its perceived similarity to the 1649 regicide, has captured critical attention. Abrupt and brutal, this episode is the fulcrum on which critical treatment of sovereignty, slavery, and race in *Oroonoko* has usually turned.[29] Yet it occupies just three paragraphs of Behn's story.

By contrast, the slave rebellion in *Oroonoko* consumes the attention of Behn's narrator and directs the entirety of the plot. Imoinda's justification for the rebellion, a moral claim in herself against sovereign *and* slaveholding tyranny, coordinates the novel's dual episodes in Coramantien and Surinam. Behn frames both the rebellion and its suppression in a racializing vocabulary through which Africans, regardless of social rank, are animalized into chattels along the color line. Imoinda, consort to the Coramantee heir apparent Oroonoko, rebels to stop her family's chattelization by the English; in turn, the English retrench in the colony by animalizing Oroonoko. The rebellion's nuances disclose the power dynamics of sovereignty, slavery, and race in greater detail than can be understood through Oroonoko's execution alone.

Imoinda's rebellion is a carefully measured response to the hereditary chattel slavery of the colony's developing racial regime, which deprives Africans of legal protections and creates Africans as heritable English property, based on their status as "*Negro,*" or "*Blacks* so called" by the English (41). Designed to stop this process and no more, Behn frames Imoinda's rebellion as an equivalent, and thus politically legitimate, response to racialization. To suppress this rebellion, Behn's English slavocrats redouble their claims to racial superiority in the colony, which is the absolute power to trade people of African descent as if they are livestock.[30]

Behn's account of this process in *Oroonoko* mirrors domestic legal developments. Just as Tudor and Stuart policies like the 1563 Statute of Artificers[31] enabled the alienation of English children's labor, the Surinam regime in *Oroonoko* recasts African kinship as a proprietary form of descent: maternity alone determines condition, so that a child inherits not a family but a slavemaster upon birth. The colony's absolutist regime for racial slavery, which Behn observes emerging under the governorship of the royalist William Byam, is an extension of the Stuarts' legal experiments in seventeenth-century England, which were exploring legal mechanisms for holding human beings as alienable property.

In *Oroonoko*, Behn observes English royalists in Surinam asserting the animal status of all African-descended people in the colony, including hereditary royalty like Oroonoko, Imoinda, and their unborn child.[32] When Africans enslaved in Surinam rebel against this racialized order, the African prince, Oroonoko, is executed by leaders of the English slavocracy, Byam and Banister, despite their ostensible monarchist sympathies with the Stuarts. In principle, their royalism should have inclined them to honor Oroonoko's hereditary claims as a legitimate sovereign, in the way that John Trefry, Colonel Martin, and Behn's narrator sometimes do. Yet Byam and Banister resolve this ideological tension by subordinating princely lineage to racial status: because Oroonoko is classified as "Negro" by the English, his royal blood becomes legally meaningless, and his execution becomes thinkable (and doable) by royalists in Surinam.

This narrative suggests a historical process in which English slaveholders invoke the developing concept of "race," reduced to body color, to justify a kind of absolute power that reduces people to the legal status of livestock, making them available in perpetuity to Englishmen's property rights. In this way, a form of absolute power over other human beings began overtaking the property protections of the ancient constitution. It did so by withholding from "Negroes" due process protections that define English liberty against monarchical prerogative. The effect was twofold. First, slaveholders' personal dominion was enlarged in the same way that the Stuarts sought dominion over their subjects by placing themselves above the common law. As Robert Sanford noted in *Surinam Justice*, this was an "Ambition for a Perpetual Dominion." Second, color emerged as a way for Englishmen to defend themselves against absolutist labor policies promulgated by the Crown, a dynamic in evidence when Barbados passed parallel codes for the governance of servants and slaves at the Crown's behest in 1661. The servant code defined specific protections, of families and court access, which were withheld from "Negroes" in the Barbadian slave code.[33]

In the failure of *Oroonoko*'s rebellion, Behn dramatizes how English slavocrats adapted royalist claims to absolute power during the opening years of the Restoration to make their own claims of dominion based on a racial hierarchy defined by skin color. The relation Behn perceives between royal sovereignty and racial slavery is crucial to note because Oroonoko—by turns sovereign, slave trader, and slave—sometimes seems to collapse the difference among the three, as recent readings rightly have underscored.[34] Yet, by exposing a slippage between the sovereign's customary power over life and death—and the absolutist's expanded imperial power to kill, let live, and trade[35]—*Oroonoko* plots a key English technique of colonial racialization.

Oroonoko is thus an important story of what Barbara J. Fields and Karen E. Fields call "racecraft." Racecraft, to review, is the sociohistorical process by which "something an aggressor *does*"—like selling people—is naturalized as race or as "something a target *is*"—an ontological category that Behn's narrator calls "Negroes, Black-Slaves altogether" (12).[36] Whether we read it as reportage, an early novel, or something in between, *Oroonoko*'s discursive capacity to dramatize external political conditions in tension with human interiority allows Behn to describe race as the fiction by which the colonial politics of absolutist retrenchment are asserted as human ontology.[37] *Oroonoko* is a foundational text in the literary history of slavery and anti-slavery because it may be the first English story to attach (un)freedom to body color in England's western Atlantic colonies, and to dramatize how this element of English racecraft was forestalled by its African targets.

The Ancient Constitution in Aphra Behn's Coramantien

The story of racecraft in *Oroonoko* comes into focus through the slave rebellion's complex psychic dynamics and transatlantic sources in English and African political society. The insurrection Behn describes is continuous with the preslavery history of Imoinda and Oroonoko, making *Oroonoko*'s plot an exception to the imperial formulation in which non-European societies existed, as Francis Bacon framed it, "in the privative," or as Mary Nyquist describes, "a condition without publicly ordered social or political relations."[38] Instead, *Oroonoko*'s main African characters hail from the highly ordered polity of Coramantien in West Africa, whose civic culture mixes military valor, conquest, and court intrigue.[39] Because Behn understands Coramantien as a complex political society, she can also see Imoinda as something other than an imperial subject without legal personality. Imoinda's consciousness of her rights against the king, and their continuity with her justification for slave insurrection, distinguishes *Oroonoko* from some early-modern English travel literatures, and later texts like Olaudah Equiano's *Interesting Narrative*, in which the English characterize Africans as bereft of political rights because they lack an uninterrupted history of native liberty.[40]

Behn's English contemporaries would have recognized Imoinda's rights against royal prerogative as consonant with their ancient constitution.[41] This constitution was not a written document, we have seen, but a customary claim in the self against the sovereign that forbade deprivation of life, liberty, or property without due process of law. In *Oroonoko*'s West African episode, the Coramantee king asserts over Imoinda the right of the royal veil, which he uses to bring wives and concubines into his harem. Because of her love for Oroonoko, and their yet unconsummated marriage, Imoinda is determined not to lose her virginity to the king. But she understands that the penalty for refusing the veil is death. Suspended between the sovereign's dual threats to her personhood, sexual and existential, Imoinda invokes the ancient constitution to limit the king's power.

As Edmund S. Morgan has written, one strategy of popular sovereignty during the Stuart era was to limit the sovereign's power by insisting that his human person live up to the godliness implied by divine right. For example, when the House of Commons resisted King Charles I's delegation of powers to the Duke of Buckingham in 1626 and 1628, the Commons claimed that Buckingham had become "too great for a subject," thus diminishing Charles's power. Morgan explains, "the Commons were isolating the king in his majesty, reducing his mightiest subjects to a level where they could be controlled by Parliament, fencing in divine right by keeping all subjects in their proper place...of subjects."[42] The liberty of the people is thus compatible with, indeed requisite of, the divinity of the king. The king's prerogative, in turn, is regulated by the protections of the ancient constitution, which the Commons learned to leverage.

Imoinda deploys the Commons' strategy when she resists the Coramantee king's veil. Disclosing her secret marriage to Oroonoko, but not his identity, Imoinda tells the king "how proud of the Divine Glory" she would be if she could "oblige" his desires. But, she emphasizes, Coramantee custom prevents "his Royal Goodness" from depriving "any man [of] his wedded wife," so the king would "commit a great Sin if [Imoinda] did not reveal her State and Condition, and tell him she was another's" (47). Writing in the previous century, Thomas Beard put the matter similarly: "all subjects perform that duty of honor and obedience to their Lords, Princes, and Kings, which is not derogatory to the glory of God."[43]

By reminding her king of the "great Sin" he would commit by despoiling his subjects' marriage, Imoinda delimits the sovereign's power by recalling him to divine status. A crime against Imoinda's bodily integrity becomes a crime against Oroonoko and Imoinda's marital privilege, a foundational relation in which hereditary right is constituted. To violate that bond is to offend not only the couple but also the institution the king is meant to safeguard as vicegerent to the divine in a polity where "the Obedience the People pay their King, was not at all inferior to what they pay'd their Gods" (47). Imoinda's claim in herself against the king is transacted through an appeal to his divinity, effectively dividing the king's natural (here, desirous) body against his transcendent body politic, of which she is a duly constituted member. The king's divine right to rule exists only insofar as he behaves like a deity in Imoinda's estimation. All supererogatory demands on Imoinda's personhood are, Behn's narrator reports, a "Breach of the Law" (49).

Charles I's execution had been justified by Parliament on similar terms, a fact that would not have been lost on Behn, who was an impressionable 8 year old at the time of the regicide. As the clerk of court, John Phelps, recorded during the trial in Parliament, the King had subjected "the Ancient and fundamental laws and liberties of his Nation," and raised "in their place...an Arbitrary and Tyrannical Government."[44] Accordingly, Charles I could be executed lawfully because he had denied his people their legitimate ancient constitutionalist limitations of his prerogative. As Geoffrey Robertson writes, key to the case against Charles were his "treasons, murders, rapines, burnings, spoils, desolations, damages and mischiefs to the nation," committed during the war he had provoked in 1642—and in his suspension of habeas corpus for five MPs who refused to pay tonnage and poundage taxes ordered by the Privy Council in 1626.[45] It was Charles's refusal to honor English life, liberty, and the due process protections of Clause 29 of Magna Carta that proved the people's claims of his high treason.

A seemingly lifelong supporter of the Stuart monarchy, Behn is perhaps unlikely to have held this republican view of King Charles I. At the same time, the draconian censorship regime introduced by Charles II after the Restoration makes it difficult to discern what her genuine political beliefs might have been at the time of her putative visit to Surinam, as well as twenty years later, when she published *Oroonoko*. A further complication in the book's history, of course, is that *Oroonoko* is regarded as one of the first novels written in English, a work of fiction, despite Behn's insistence in the text's dedication to the Scottish royalist, Lord Richard Maitland, that it is "the Truth" about her titular African prince, offered "without the Addition of Invention" (37).[46] A brief critical history of *Oroonoko*'s truth claims will help us to contextualize the role of ancient constitutionalism in the story's account of racecraft.

Scholars think it likely that Behn was resident in Surinam in 1663–64. The most important evidence for this claim is the text of *Oroonoko*, which contains Behn's assertion that it is largely an "Eye-Witness" account (37). There are local references and Caribbean words that, Janet Todd argues, would have been difficult for Behn to learn in the absence of a visit.[47] There is also the fact that many characters in *Oroonoko* are real members of Surinam's colonial society: documents independent of Behn's text place William Byam, James Banister, George Marten, and John Trefry in Surinam during the 1660s.[48] Several contemporaneous letters also reference a woman visiting the colony in 1663 with an entourage, which may have been Aphra Behn and the group of travelers she describes in *Oroonoko*.[49]

Even if Aphra Behn spent time in Surinam, however, she remained free to fictionalize *Oroonoko* in whole or in part. The available record suggests that she may have done so particularly in the narrative's African episode. No evidence indicates that this portion of the story is written from Behn's firsthand experience; indeed, several details point the other way. Behn's narrator never claims to have visited West Africa, noting instead that the account of Coramantien comes "from the Mouth of the chief Actor in this History, the *Hero* himself, who gave us the whole Transactions of his Youth" (37–38). Still, there seems to be literary embellishment. Janet Todd writes that "the Africa [Behn] portrayed has little in common with the West Africa described by French and English travelers and traders. Depictions of the old customs of the Fantis and Ashantis in the Gold Coast are not especially connected to the oriental activities of the harem intrigues of Behn's fantastic kingdom."[50] *Oroonoko*'s critics also note that Behn might have borrowed portions of *Oroonoko*'s Surinam episode from Michel de Montaigne's essay "Of Cannibals" (1580) or George Warren's *An Impartial Description of Surinam Upon the Continent of Guiana in America* (1667).[51] Or, *Oroonoko* may be some combination of these texts with Behn's imagination and firsthand experience. Why would Behn have fictionalized portions of a story she asserted to be true?

As Annabel Patterson has argued, authoritarian censorship programs, such as those of the Stuarts, create a set of "conventions" among "writers and the holders of power,"[52] which determine how directly writers can address contentious political questions. Byam's crackdown on his detractors in Surinam, like Jones and Sanford, suggests that these men had violated speech conventions that Byam was seeking to enforce. Within such constraints, Patterson notes, authors use techniques of coding and indirection designed so that no one in authority is "*required* to make an example of him,"[53] as in the case of Byam throwing Jones into the stocks.

Regardless of Behn's domestic political sympathies, her narrator in *Oroonoko* clearly opposes the slavocratic activities of royalists in Surinam. She calls William Byam the most "Fawning fair-tongu'd Fellow in the World," and she is appalled by Oroonoko's fate at Byam's hands, lamenting her powerlessness to stop what happens to Oroonoko under Byam's government: "*I wanted power*," she confesses to Lord Maitland in her dedication, "*to preserve*" Oroonoko (88, 37, emphasis in original). If Behn also opposed the Stuarts' role in these events, namely the enslavement and execution of African royalty, displacing that critique of sovereignty to a fictionalized royal court in Coramantien would have been one option for plausible deniability to Crown censors. As Laura Rosenthal argues, "to embed a political allegory of the Stuarts in a narrative describing the transatlantic slave trade was not random, but rather drew on common knowledge that they spearheaded English participation in this global atrocity."[54] Later in this chapter, we will see *Oroonoko*'s narrator withdraw as Byam violently suppresses the slave insurrection in Surinam. The conditions of writing *Oroonoko* thus bend comparably under Stuart censorship and Surinam slavocracy, each motivated by absolutism.

It is salient, furthermore, that Behn did not publish *Oroonoko* until James II was on the brink of an historic ouster by Parliament in 1688, nearly twenty-five years after she may have witnessed the events of *Oroonoko* in 1663–64.[55] This detail alone suggests that Behn did not want *Oroonoko* subjected to the scrutiny of the Crown censors, perhaps for reasons of her personal safety. One of Behn's contemporaries, Algernon Sydney, was executed brutally in 1683 for his alleged role in the Rye House Plot—his own unpublished writing bearing witness against him at trial. Behn certainly did not share Sydney's republican politics, but she would have been cautious to avoid contemporary legal uses of texts in state prosecutions.[56]

One certainty that emerges from this array of contingencies is that, in *Oroonoko*, Behn recognizes some legitimate ends to which the ancient constitution can be asserted against the royal prerogative. Emphasizing the justice of Imoinda's claims in her virginity against the sexual advances of royal power, Behn imagines the Coramantee king's natural body in a "second Childhood" of impotency, which prevents him from violating Imoinda's sexual purity after her claims to his divinity fail (46). When the monarch will not yield to Imoinda's assertion of his divine obligation, the writer's omnipotent pen unmans the body of the king.

Behn amplifies Imoinda's ancient constitutionalism with an allusion to the Battle of Hastings. Just before the king summons Imoinda into the harem, her father, a revered Coramantee general, is struck by an "Arrow in his Eye," just like King Harold II, brother-in-law of Edward the Confessor, at the Battle of Hastings (14). The year 1066 was the most contested site in the historiography of English liberty. As we have seen, Hastings marked "the one great apparent breach in the continuity of the nation's history," which threatened the people's claims of an immemorial ancient constitution.[57] English common lawyers solved this problem by interpreting William I's military victory at Hastings not as his tyrannical subordination of the English, but as his salutary confirmation of "the laws of the last Anglo-Saxon kings."[58] This story of King William I's acceptance of the common law affirmed the continuity of the ancient constitution and the uninterrupted liberty of the English people. Behn's reference to an invading William held additional meaning for her audience when *Oroonoko* was published in 1688, as another William prepared to depose James II at the behest of Parliament.[59]

By framing Imoinda's political consciousness with this allusion to the Norman Conquest, Behn invokes English constitutional tensions of 1066 and 1688 while underscoring that Africans enslaved in England's colonies have a preslavery political history. As we will see, Behn's Imoinda supplies a political mythography of uninterrupted African political rights: just as ancient English rights withstood William I's invasion, so, too, will Imoinda's ancient constitutionalism survive the Middle Passage. At the same time, *Oroonoko*'s implication of similarity between ancient African and ancient English rights is ultimately at odds with the developing racial absolutism that Behn sees in Surinam's colonial slavocracy.

Far from being a strict royal absolutist, Richard Kroll notes, Behn saw that the Stuarts' sovereign power required proper limitations that the ancient constitution provided, and that novelists might temper absolute power with political recommendations articulated in fiction.[60] If Behn conveyed to James II the importance of the ancient constitution through would-be African sovereigns enslaved by unprincipled Englishmen, then she also seems to imply some important relation between divine-right kingship and chattel slavery. Kroll's reading of *Oroonoko* finds that colonial slavery is an allegory for the political paroxysms of the Stuart metropole: "questions of liberty and slavery in *Oroonoko*," he says, "apply specifically to politics in 1688 rather than literally to the slave trade."[61] More recent work, particularly Nyquist's *Arbitrary Rule* (2013), lends credence to Kroll's reading.

Nyquist underscores the difference between political slavery, of the kind suffered under royal tyranny, and chattel slavery, in which Englishmen converted human beings into alienable property in the imperial economy.

Nyquist also notes, however, that these forms of slavery could be discursively blurred by their presumptive rootedness in patriarchalism, from which authority over political and chattel slaves was imagined to flow.[62] English paternalism, a central metaphor of absolute monarchy exposited by Filmer, was literalized in the chattel relation of colonial slavery when English paternity coincided with absolute power over enslaved children Englishmen fathered with enslaved women. A key example is the 1662 introduction in Virginia of *partus sequitur ventrem*, the institution under which children followed the legal condition of their mothers, an alteration of the English common law designed to consolidate English paternity and property in slaves.[63] Orlando Patterson has noted that enslaved people made recourse to their enslavers' unquestionable patriarchal authority—"the Negro principle that 'massa can do no wrong'"—as a way of limiting the power of the slaveholder by recalling him to paternal responsibility.[64] Here, we see three parallels: the archetypal appeal of the slave to his master's inability to "do wrong"; Parliament's justification for executing Charles I, who had done wrong by his people; and Imoinda's effort to prevent her king's sexual advances by insisting that he do no wrong. Thus, the power of the colonial slavocrat was similar to the power of the English monarch in its paternalistic susceptibility to limitation by moral claims of those persons under its authority. Indeed, the Stuarts, beginning with James I's *Basilikon Doron* (1599), had theorized their absolute sovereignty as a "God-given authority," over the English subject, which was "like that of a father over his children."[65]

The displacement of real family ties with Crown-authorized proprietary power is a key mechanism of racecraft in *Oroonoko*.[66] The burgeoning racial regime Behn describes in colonial Surinam promises to relegate Imoinda's child to the ownership of her English enslaver, Trefry, and displace the child's royal father, Oroonoko. Trefry's chattel claim will separate that child from its royal kinship ties and alienate its mother and father from their parental duties. This double alienation will transpose dynastic African kinship ties into English chattel value, transfiguring hereditary royalism into slavocratic absolutism, an explicit literary example of what Holly Brewer calls the early modern "rope," twisted by Crown jurists, "that combined feudalism with capitalism"[67] in treating people as perpetual forms of property.

But Behn's Cornish slaveholder, John Trefry, does not understand himself to have any paternalistic relation whatsoever to Oroonoko or Imoinda. Rather, he perceives himself in horizontal, or even subordinate, relationships to each: he is Imoinda's rebuffed lover and Oroonoko's "dearest Brother" as well as one who calls Oroonoko a "Prince" (70–71, 67). Behn thus plots racialization as a generational process through which Imoinda and Oroonoko's royal, parental authority is transmuted into Trefry's slavocratic power. In this way, *Oroonoko* links the colonial racialization of slavery to the role of sovereign absolutism in an imperial frame, a connection to which we now turn.

The King's—and the Slave's—Two Bodies

Oroonoko's Coramantee episode reaches an inflection point when Oroonoko and Imoinda consummate their secret marriage. The king discovers the lovers' meeting and, to save her own life from the king's wrath, Imoinda invents a story that Oroonoko has raped her. The king then sells Imoinda into slavery because he regards her as defiled by sex with Oroonoko, his grandson. Behn envisions an incest taboo so extreme that even Imoinda's execution by the king's hand is an unacceptable pollution of his regal stature. At the same time, Behn imagines Imoinda to have located a weakness in the king's absolute power, by which the king's regal status is contingent on his distance from her sexually polluted body. The king's sale of Imoinda into slavery ultimately prompts him to acknowledge the injustice of his power over her: "He believ'd now, that his Love had been unjust," the narrator explains, "and that he cou'd not expect the Gods...shou'd suffer a better Consequence from so ill a Cause" (58). The Coramantee king thus accepts (as Charles I did not) his subjects' estimation of his failure of godlike kingship. By making a woman into a chattel, the Coramantee god-king has made himself into a man.

The king's two bodies—the mortal body natural and the immortal body politic described by Ernst Kantorowicz—are narratively linked in *Oroonoko* to what Malick W. Ghachem and John Samuel Harpham have called the slave's two bodies: the mortal body natural and the historically transcendent body of property in the hereditarily enslaved person.[68] The fundamental political drama of *Oroonoko*'s West African episode is that the Coramantee king's two bodies become disintegrated: first when the king refuses to live up to his divine status in response to Imoinda's ancient constitutionalism, and again when he sells Imoinda into slavery, prompting his awareness of the incompatibility between the sexual impulses of his body natural and the political requirements of his regal divinity. The fundamental political drama of *Oroonoko*'s episode in Surinam is that Imoinda defies English slavocracy's attempt to divide her into a natural reproductive body and a body of heritable property in the person of her child.

In *Oroonoko,* the estrangement of the king's natural body from his eternal body politic manifests as political weakness. The king, fallen from grace through his objectification of Imoinda, is "not able to defend himself in War." And, "having no Sons of all his Race remaining alive" to "maintain him on his Throne," he begins to fear the just retribution of his grandson, Oroonoko, and the army he commands (58). The king's failure to accept Imoinda's limitations to his prerogative has diminished his authority in the face of his gods and subjects, which is signaled by Oroonoko's growing military power. The absolutist tendencies of the king's natural body—in this case the possession of women in the inner world of the harem and the outer world of the slave trade—have produced a legitimation crisis.

Behn thus invokes the legal fiction of the king's two bodies to illuminate transoceanic relationships between absolute monarchy in England and chattel slavery in its colonies. In a classic study, Kantorowicz explains that the English sovereign was a *persona mixta*, whose authority was both mortal and eternal.[69] Crown lawyers held during Elizabeth I's reign, for example, that "the King has in him two Bodies, *viz.*, a Body natural, and a Body politic." The sovereign's "Body natural" was "a Body mortal, subject to all Infirmities that come by Nature or Accident"; but his body politic was immaterial: it could not "be seen or handled" and was "utterly void of Infancy, and old Age, and other natural Defects and Imbecilities." Thus, Elizabeth I's lawyers concluded, "what the King does in his Body politic, cannot be invalidated or frustrated by any Disability in his natural Body."[70] Thus, in the well-known phrase: the king is dead; long live the king.

In Coramantien, Behn illuminates absolutism's pitfalls in the sexual tyranny of the king's natural body. The accession crisis in Coramantien is amplified when his only heir, Oroonoko, and many of the kingdom's warriors are kidnapped into slavery by an Englishman, operating as a parasite of Coramantee military conquests. The transatlantic slave trade eclipses divine-right authority by kidnapping princes out of rightful lines of accession, weakening militaries that protect the royal court, and giving English slave traders absolute power aboard their floating polities. When Oroonoko is chattelized through sale "to [an] Over-seer," he underscores the malignancy of this dynamic (66). Scorning the English captain, Oroonoko says it was worth his own "*Suffering to gain so true a Knowledge both of you, and of your Gods by whom you swear*" (67, emphasis in original). Oroonoko implies that, knowing no god but itself, English imperialism seeks to exceed even the divine right of kings because it makes no pretense to godlike behavior.[71] In this way, Oroonoko delivers a stunning rebuke to Stuart policies for stabilizing the transatlantic slave trade, such as those that Francis Willoughby was pursuing in Barbados at the time of Behn's visit to Surinam.

Oroonoko's character—which Behn figures as heir apparent, slave trader, subject, slave, and insurrectionist—suggests that imperial absolutism without constitutional guardrails is a slippery political slope indeed. Behn's Imoinda, by contrast, is the consciousness that remains steady in its ancient constitutionalist claims to personal political dignity, despite changing social and racial stature across jurisdictions: she is an aristocrat turned sexual slave in Coramantien, and a presumptive sexual slave in colonial Surinam, threatened by racialization. Imoinda thus discloses several truths about the Stuart imperial regime that perhaps Behn herself, for fear of reprisal, could not articulate directly: there are legitimate constitutional limitations on monarchs' and slavocrats' absolutisms; enslaved Africans have a preslavery political history, as well as emergent political influence in English colonies; and all individuals, including enslaved Africans, can make legitimate claims against slavocratic power. Behn's Imoinda is thus what Toni Morrison calls "an imagined Africanist persona," conjured in fiction to "act out the forbidden"[72] within the transatlantic constraints of Stuart strictures on free labor and free speech.

Imoinda's Rebellion: Natal Alienation and the Chattel Relation

Oroonoko's and Imoinda's enslavement in Surinam initiates a power struggle between African royalty and English slavocracy, which ultimately involves everyone in the colony. Oroonoko becomes a formidable alternative to the colonial government because enslavement and racialization do not diminish his sense of selfhood: a combination of military heroism and personal honor. Oroonoko is thus greeted as a rightful political authority in the colony. Even if "the King himself (God bless him) had come a-shore," the narrator notes, "there cou'd not have been greater Expectations by all the whole Plantation, and those neighbouring ones," where Oroonoko "was receiv'd more like a Governor than a Slave" (69). At first, Oroonoko is not a god to the English in colonial Surinam, but he is not exactly a slave, either.

Trefry, a savvy colonial politician, recognizes Oroonoko's extreme popular appeal, and so finds himself in the discomfiting position of quasi-subject to his own chattel property. Trefry gives Oroonoko a "Portion of Land," a "House" and his "Business," according to the English "Custom" of the country for unfree persons (69). At the same time, Oroonoko does no labor and receives various visitors, "without stirring towards that part of the Plantation where the *Negroes* were" (69). The English management of Oroonoko—particularly his separation from "the *Negroes*"—discloses the undertow of racial politics in Surinam, which is coterminous with *Oroonoko*'s narration (69). Trefry's separation of Oroonoko from people he might constitute as an anti-slavery military through their shared race ("Negro") and legal condition ("slaves")—both imposed by the English—absorbs the narrator's attention and guides the story's plot. Positioning herself as an observer of how the slavocracy manages Oroonoko, Behn's narrator catalogs the anti-slavery implications of his arrival in Surinam, and carefully gauges their threats to her personal safety.

Soon however, Oroonoko meets the enslaved people at Parham House who greet him not as mere governor, as the English do, but rather as their sovereign, "crying out, in their Language," "*Live, O King! Long live, O King!*" and paying "him even Divine Homage" (70). "Several English gentlemen" are with Oroonoko during this display, observing his popular appeal to enslaved Africans, despite that Oroonoko "was that Prince who had... sold most of 'em to these Parts" (70). Oroonoko's military conquests in Africa, under war slavery doctrine, are perhaps being asserted here by the Africans as a legitimate source of his sovereign power in the colonies. Perhaps these people greet their original enslaver with joy because they see in his incompatibility with bondage a lever for their own liberation. If this is the case, Behn has imagined enslaved Africans using popular sovereignty to incite Oroonoko to govern them like a god-ordained king, and overthrow the royalist elements of England's slavocracy in Surinam, a curiously deracializing gesture that would return colonial politics to a feudalist contest between lords and their lieges.

The English slavocrats' absolute power is further challenged in *Oroonoko* when Behn reintroduces Imoinda to the plot: Trefry tells Oroonoko that he has become sexually captivated by a "she-slave." And yet, despite nearly overwhelming lust, he has not raped her. As he tells Oroonoko:

> *when I have, against her will, entertain'd her with Love so long, as to be transported with my Passion; even above Decency, I have been ready to make use of those advantages of Strength and Force Nature has given me. But oh! she disarms me, with that Modesty and Weeping so tender and so moving, that I retire, and thank my Stars she overcame me.* (71, emphasis in original)

Trefry thus indicates that Imoinda's claims in herself—the same ones she made against the Coramantee king—now "*disarm*" the sexual power of her enslaver. Her ancient constitutionalism, and its capacity to limit men's sexual tyranny, has a transatlantic range. This may be why Behn's narrator suddenly remembers that Imoinda's body is "Cut and Rac'd all over" with flowers and birds, reminding her of "our Ancient *Picts* that are figur'd in the Chronicles," likening Imoinda to figures of ancient liberty, just as her father's heroic death is identified with the mythic preservation of ancient freedoms at Hastings (48). In this digression, Behn implies that enslaved Africans, again like the English, have a political history of native liberty which Imoinda has transported in her person to the western Atlantic. It is not dependent upon jurisdiction.

In the intervening paragraphs between Trefry's forestalled rape and Imoinda's appearance as an "Ancient *Pict*," Oroonoko and Imoinda are reunited with a wedding. They also conceive a child, suggesting the possibility in the colony of an African dynasty arising jointly from Oroonoko's sovereign status and Imoinda's ancient constitutionalist limitations of sovereign and slavocratic power.[73] Aware of these changes to the colony's politics, Behn's narrator promises the couple their "Liberty, as soon as the Governor" arrives in the colony (73).[74] The unspoken drama is that an insurrection, organized along the color line drawn by the English, and led by African royalty, must be forestalled.

Tensions heighten with Trefry's delays in manumitting the couple as Imoinda's pregnancy advances. The English, including Behn's narrator, continue to ply Oroonoko with promises of freedom at "the coming of the Lord Governor, who [is] every Day expected" in the colony (75). But, recalling the lies of the slave ship captain, who promised during the Middle Passage to "set both [Oroonoko] and his Friends a-shore on the next Land they should touch at," Oroonoko begins to "suspect [the English] of falshood [sic], and that they wou'd delay him till the time of his Wives [sic] delivery, and make a Slave of that too, For all the Breed is theirs to whom the Parents belong" (64, 74). Here, English abandonment of war slavery doctrine, in the enslavement of people they have not conquered, is linked to the hereditary mechanism of chattel slavery, producing race in its modern form.[75] This is not yet the doctrine of *partus sequitur ventrem*; however, the narrator's invocation of heritable property in livestock indicates a burgeoning English colonial property ideology which consolidates racial hierarchy by asserting the heritable animal status of African people.[76]

The English threat of inherited, color-based slavery before *partus sequitur ventrem* is well documented. In 1654, Henry Whistler noted on Barbados the condition of the "miserabell Negors borne to perpetual slauery thay and thayer [*sic*] seed," indicating the English adoption of color-based ("Negors") hereditary ("thay and thayer seed") slavery in that other colony.[77] The replacement of Oroonoko and Imoinda's noble lines with hereditary chattel status will make them and their child racially identical to other enslaved Africans in the colony, who are defined only as being Negro and unfree, despite the fact that they are of "several Nations" (70). This outcome is incompatible with Imoinda's and Oroonoko's sense of political personality. Thus, it is the *specific* consequence of slavery's racialization based on heritable body color that transposes slave rebellion from a political potential of Oroonoko's popular appeal in Surinam into a narrative inevitability of the chattel relation. In this way, royalist assertions of slavocratic absolutism in the colony are met with absolute African resistance.

As Charlotte Sussman has argued, what Patterson calls "natal alienation" incites Oroonoko and Imoinda to foment the rebellion they command. The violent phase of the Surinam revolt is activated when Imoinda's pregnancy becomes evident, and the natal alienation of her child becomes imminent. Patterson writes that natal alienation instrumentalizes the chattel relation through

> loss of ties of birth in both ascending and descending generations. It also has the important nuance of a loss of native status, of deracination. It was this alienation of the slave from all formal, legally enforceable ties of "blood," and from any attachment to groups or localities other than those chosen for him by the master, that gave the relation of slavery its peculiar value to the master.[78]

For Sussman, "Oroonoko rebels against the possibility that his child will be born into a natally alienated state" because it is "[o]nly through the recognition of genealogical descent" that the early modern child can "receive its cultural inheritance" of royalty.[79] An English expression of absolute power, the Coramantee child's status as "Negro" will be asserted by slavocrats to destroy customary rights in the self, an obliteration of the ancient constitution's protections concomitant with the creation of Trefry's absolute proprietary claims in the child. By racializing the ancient constitution's protections, the colonial slavocrat becomes like the tyrannical sovereign, who refuses ancient constitutionalist limits in order to gain personal dominion.

As Patterson further notes, "proprietary claims are made" during the early-modern period "with respect to many persons who are clearly not slaves...any person, beggar or king, can be the object of a property relation." Outside of the chattel relation, Patterson continues, "the proprietor's power is limited by the fact that nonslaves always possess some claims and powers *vis-à-vis* the proprietor." For example, despite the possessory implications of the royal veil, Imoinda successfully asserts a claim in her marital personhood against the Coramantee king. By contrast, the chattel relation developing in Surinam seeks to grant slave masters "power over all aspects of the slave's life," which, in Behn's portrayal of Oroonoko and Imoinda, threatens to destroy even parents' natal claims in their own children.[80]

"Race," in which freedom status is correlated to heritable body color, has thus rendered the sexual drama of *Oroonoko*'s courtly romance inseparable from its colonial politics. Imoinda's sexual body—where hereditary monarchy's proper limitations by the ancient constitution can be transformed by English slavocrats into hereditary slavery's expanded tyranny—is the locus of Behn's political concern. As the novel's crisis escalates, the narrator is subsumed by the emergency, "oblig'd, by some Persons who fear'd a Mutiny" to "give [Oroonoko] all the Satisfaction [she] possibly could" that he, Imoinda, and their unborn child will be freed when the new governor arrives (74). Parenthetically, the narrator discloses that slave mutinies are "very Fatal sometimes in those Colonies, that abound so with Slaves, that they exceed the Whites in vast Numbers" (74). The narrator's juxtaposition of "Slaves" and "Whites" discloses the new color politics of freedom and slavery in Surinam. This racecraft, which Oroonoko and Imoinda will oppose with their lives, now directs the novel's narration (74).

When Surinam's absent governor is lost at sea,[81] her promises of freedom to Oroonoko and Imoinda are emptied of political value. Foreclosed is a future in which the English king's agent will reauthorize the primacy of sovereign authority, including Oroonoko's, over the asserted racial absolutism of the slavocrats (71). Thus, a studied discursive distance develops between the narrator and Oroonoko because her personal safety, and the survival of the story, are subsumed by the slavocracy's colorist claims to power. Behn's narrator, pressed by fearful English colonists to spy on Oroonoko and Imoinda, is made unreliable on the page by the very political processes that have made her one of the "Whites." Formerly able to leave the behaviors of English slavers "to my Reader, to judge as he pleases," the once-disinterested narrator is implicated in the novel's action by a color politics over which no firsthand observer can be omniscient (64). This totality, and the racialism towards which it drives the colony, is the result of the slavocracy's claims to absolute power, which, seemingly accountable to nothing but its own expansion, forecloses the balancing potential of the ancient constitution.

The episode in *Oroonoko* just before the slave rebellion is the narrator's effort to divert the insurrectionists until she can leave the colony. A small group of people—including Oroonoko, Imoinda, and the narrator—leave Parham House to go "surprizing" in other parts of the colony, visiting with the local tribes, admiring strange landscapes, and hunting exotic game (77). Despite the rebellion's submersion in the details of a colonial adventure story, its restless politics are evident. The narrator's company, eager to appease Imoinda, "resolv'd to make her Chains as easy as [they] cou'd," and the English travelers "Compliment the Prince," highlighting to Oroonoko his uncompromised royal status in their eyes (84). Oroonoko, on the other hand, is of "a mind to see and talk with [Surinam's native] War *Captains*," ostensibly to understand the strategic possibilities surrounding Trefry's plantations (83). The narrator observes Oroonoko's reconnoitering with the unease of a spy.[82]

Imoinda's pregnancy refocuses the story. Beginning to "shew [*sic*] she was with Child," and taking notice of Surinam's shifted political landscape, Imoinda reasons to her husband that if "it were so hard to gain the Liberty of Two," in Surinam, "'twou'd be more difficult to get that for Three" (85). The chattel relation inhibits diplomatic solutions by making Englishmen answerable to their private profits and the overseas interests of the Crown. Convinced by Imoinda, Oroonoko seeks to exploit the English color-based system: "one *Sunday*, when all the Whites were overtaken in drink" Oroonoko goes out "to Feast amongst... about Three Hundred *Negroes*," of whom about "a Hundred and Fifty were able to bear Arms" (85). Identifying Africans with combat capabilities, and taking advantage of the whites' drunkenness (as his own was exploited by slavers), Oroonoko radicalizes Surinam's slaves by underscoring the dishonor of the chattel relation, to which they are subjected not because of war slavery doctrine, but through Englishmen's abandonment of it.

As the rebellion breaks out, *Oroonoko* exposes how racecraft affects the narrator's relationship to the story she tells. Behn's narrator discloses that the "white" laborers, who like herself are "a sort of Spys [*sic*] upon" Oroonoko, are legally distinct from the "Negroes" in Surinam because whites are indentured, or "*Slaves* for Four Years" (85). The narrator is racially aligned with indentured labor, in other words, through a shared political necessity of surveilling Oroonoko. Seizing on the difference English slavocracy makes between white and black labor, Oroonoko underscores that the English have animalized the enslaved, loading them with "Burdens and Drugeries [*sic*], as were fitter for Beasts than Men." Oroonoko also notes the perpetual nature of chattel slavery in contradistinction to indenture: "He told 'em it was not for Days, Months, or Years, but for Eternity; there was no end to be of their Misfortunes." Amplifying his appeal to the enslaved people, Oroonoko emphasizes that slaves in Surinam are below even domesticated animals: "an Ass, or Dog, or Horse having done his Duty, cou'd lye [*sic*] down in Retreat, and rise to Work again, and while he did his Duty, indur'd no stripes." By marked contrast, enslaved people in Surinam "whether they Work'd or not... suffer'd the infamous Whip" (86). Oroonoko thus frames the political goals of the slave rebellion—indeed, it is race war—as a finely tailored military response to chattel-racialization in colonial Surinam.[83]

Oroonoko and the Color Line

Despite Oroonoko's eloquence in framing the insurrection as a surgical response to English racecraft, the rebellion in Surinam fails. This is partly because a group of Surinam colonists, led by the narrator, forestall Oroonoko's full identification with the political interests of enslaved people in order to secure their personal safety from the uprising. Recognizing his potential military power in the colony, slaveholders like Trefry exempt Oroonoko from "the Toil and Labour" of other slaves, promise him liberation and repatriation, and thereby postpone his political identification with other chattelized people (75). As Oroonoko's anti-slavery politics become evident, the narrator discourages his racial solidarity with other Africans: after Oroonoko addresses the narrator "with an Air impatient enough to make [her] know he wou'd not be long in Bondage," she decides not to trust him "out of [her] View," or to visit the "Plantations of the negroes," without English "Spies" masquerading as his "Attendants." Oroonoko's emphatic promises to the narrator that he "wou'd Act nothing upon the White-People" are no consolation to her (75). Thus, the political importance of the color line increases with the narrator's fear of Oroonoko's defiance of chattel status.

Oroonoko's failure of political understanding is his imperfect knowledge of the familial attachments formed among the people he seeks to lead out of bondage, revealing his incomplete apprehension of chattel slavery's new political realities, and, relatedly, the success of Behn's narrator in slowing his identification with the enslaved. After his stirring speech to the enslaved rebel force—in which Oroonoko reminds the people that they are not animals—they, in turn, remind him that they are not "*only Men*," but rather "*Husbands and Parents too*" (87, emphasis in original). The slaves' vertical family bonds with their children are, for them, a necessary defiance of slavery's natal alienation, developed in Surinam despite the chattel relation imposed by English claims to absolute power.

But, perhaps because Oroonoko's child is yet unborn, he does not fully fathom the special force of parental love that characterizes the most deeply held political commitments of his new rebel army. Oroonoko's plan to "Travel towards the Sea" and "Plant a New Colony" with the rebels until they "find a Ship" and travel back "to their own Countries" promises a deracializing expression of slaves' "Liberty" (87–88). Through this program of emancipation, the enslaved would no longer be Negroes, so-called by the English, but deracialized people repatriated to their homes with their families. This plan fails because Oroonoko misunderstands the changes chattel slavery has made to enslaved people's moral and political psychology. When the English pursue the rebels and lash them "in the Eyes" with whips, the "Women and Children, seeing their Husbands so treated" run "all amongst" them "crying out, *Yield, yield; and leave* [Oroonoko] *to their revenge*" (89, emphasis in original). Here, domestic paternalism among the enslaved outstrips Oroonoko's kinglike patriarchalism, a subtle challenge to slavocrats and Stuarts alike.

To explain the failed insurrection, Behn's narrator characterizes the enslaved women and children as having "fearful Cowardly Dispositions," emphasizing their natural suitedness to enslavement (89). Oroonoko does the same, affirming the racial categories of his enslavers. *Oroonoko* thus underscores limitations of political identification that racecraft has brought into being. After sale into slavery by Oroonoko, and experiencing the natal alienation of chattel status, the people enslaved in Surinam have reconstituted themselves as nuclear families, a social structure their enslavers harness to produce more property in slaves, but which also affords enslaved people a human community in the colony.[84] When Oroonoko arrives in Surinam, the enslaved people see a pathway out of slavery that exploits English racism, which has placed all the "Negroes" together to form a group with common political concerns defined by chattel slavery. Oroonoko's personal honor, which defies English racial hierarchies, simultaneously limits his perception of the family solidarity with which enslaved Africans have responded to English colorism. The slaves rebel with Oroonoko because they choose deracializing marronage under a Coramantee slave(-seller) instead of racial bondage under English slavocrats. But because the enslaved value their kin more than the man who sold them to the English—indeed the women "pay an intire [*sic*] Obedience to their Husbands"—their fealty to Oroonoko is transactional: it is only as strong as his ability to protect their families (63).

When the women and children see their husbands and fathers blinded by Englishmen with whips, an arresting mixture of Oedipal and slavocratic iconography, they abandon Oroonoko to his now-broken relationship with absolutists in Surinam's colonial administration. This is unsurprising because Oroonoko sold these Africans in the first place to the slaving class of Englishmen. Herein lies a great political tragedy at the heart of *Oroonoko*. The English chattel system has convinced Oroonoko to die pursuing liberty for his yet *un*racialized family. At the same time, this English chattel system has coerced racialized people to live in kinship structures defined by enslavement. These family bonds motivate Oroonoko's would-be compatriots to abandon the rebellion, doom it to failure, and thereby ensure the survival of English Surinam's slavocratic government.

Unable to accept racialization when the rebellion fails, Oroonoko and Imoinda make a family suicide pact as a last hedge against kinship structures defined by the terms of chattel slavery. In killing Imoinda and their unborn child, Oroonoko dramatizes the absolute choice, forced by slavery, between preserving native family relationships in death or accepting destroyed kinship structures in life. This acknowledgment of the English slavocracy's power is, for Oroonoko, existentially unbearable: after killing Imoinda, "his Brains turned round," "his Eyes were dizzy," and "Objects appear'd not the same to him [as] they were wont to do" (96). In this textual rupture, Oroonoko's disorientation signals the incompatibility of his political personality with chattel slavery and its human depredations, authorized by the fiction of race. Indeed, Oroonoko kills Imoinda out of the conviction that "*she may be first Ravaged by every Brute [in the colony]...and then* [suffer] *a shameful Death*" (94, emphasis in original). The tragedy of Oroonoko, like the tragedy of the Stuart regime, is to have misunderstood the limits of power.

In the falling action of the story, barbarism and lawlessness overtake the plot. Realizing their inferiority to the military skill and numbers of other groups of people on the island, the English grasp at power through deceit, revenge, and violence that Behn figures as illegitimate in its sheer disproportion.[85] Oroonoko and his lieutenant, Tuscan, surrender to the English on favorable terms of manumission and repatriation, offered by Trefry and Byam. But these English promises, ratified by contract, are immediately and brutally broken. Tuscan and Oroonoko are whipped "like Dogs" by their English betrayers, achieving—in Oroonoko's first experience of this punishment—the animal status of *all* African-descended people in the colony. Byam also enforces the separation of African people from written agreements, what Behn's narrator calls "the common way of contract between Man and Man amongst the Whites" (91).[86] These details of *Oroonoko* rehearse historical developments in the English practice of slavery, wherein people from Africa were being sold by merchants in the Caribbean without contracts and declared slaves for life by alterations to the legal category of villein, all according to absolutist policies for subduing labor.[87] African claims of equality with the English—that is, a common understanding "between Man and Man"—are rebuked in Behn's telling by royalists like Byam precisely through the abandonment of common law principles of contract.

Oroonoko's brutal execution by Byam's corrupt government, exemplified by the wild Irishman Banister, underscores the endgame of racecraft in Behn's story: the power to kill, scattered from the body of the king into every white person in the colony, is now the sum of politics. In Behn's telling, this decentralized tyranny emerges through the chattel relation, which grants slavocrats not only the monarch's power to kill, but also the imperial power to convert humans into saleable goods in perpetuity. As Pocock has written, during the financial revolution of the 1690s, there was a "sudden and traumatic discovery of capital in the form of government stock." This resulted, Pocock reckons, in the emergence of a "[s]pecialized, acquisitive, and post-civic man."[88] *Oroonoko* narrates a similarly traumatic event, in which Englishmen realize, in the racial fiction they call "Negroes," a continent of capital in the form of enslavable people and their future children.

The Company of Royal Adventurers Trading into Africa was formed in 1660 by the newly restored monarch for precisely this purpose.[89] In *Oroonoko*, "acquisitive, and post-civic man" finds his consequence, through racecraft, in the hereditary chattel slave. Behn's narrator disapproves of these political developments in England's colonies, but she is ultimately powerless even to observe their human consequences.

Just as Byam breaks his contract with Oroonoko, Behn's narrator finally breaks her promise to tell her readers "the Truth" about "this Royal Slave" (37). She does not, in fact, witness Oroonoko's execution because she is "perswaded [*sic*] to leave" the scene of her own writing when moral identification with Oroonoko, across new racial lines, threatens her with "Fits of dangerous Illness" from the "extraordinary Melancholy" of Oroonoko's downfall, in which she has played an outsized and catastrophic role (98). In this way, Behn affirms the ancient constitution as the subject's rights against royal power, exemplified by Imoinda's transatlantic resistance to tyranny; but Behn rejects the alteration of the ancient constitution by absolute property rights Englishmen had begun to assert in their colonies over all people of African descent.

Notes

1. Edmund S. Morgan, *Inventing the People: The Rise of Popular Sovereignty in England and America* (New York: W. W. Norton & Co., 1989), 21.
2. Aphra Behn, *Oroonoko; or, The Royal Slave*, ed. Catherine Gallagher with Simon Stern (Boston: Bedford/St Martin's, 2000), 62. Hereafter cited parenthetically by page number.
3. Matthew Parker, *Willoughbyland: England's Lost Colony* (London: Windmill Books, 2015), 171–72; Julie M. Svalastog, *Mastering the Worst of Trades: England's Early Africa Companies and their Traders, 1618–1672* (Leiden: Brill, 2021), 92.
4. Laura Brown, "The Romance of Empire: *Oroonoko* and the Trade in Slaves," in *The New Eighteenth Century: Theory, Politics, English Literature*, ed. Felicity Nussbaum and Laura Brown (New York: Methuen, 1987), 58–59.
5. Sarah Marsh, "Imoinda's Rebellion: Sovereignty, Slavery, and the Ancient Constitution in Aphra Behn's Oroonoko," *ELH* 90, no. 3 (2023): 639–66.
6. Janet Todd, *Aphra Behn: A Secret Life* (London: Fentum Press, 2017), 32.
7. Parker, *Willoughbyland*, 75–77.
8. Parker, *Willoughbyland*, 77.
9. Parker, *Willoughbyland*, 72; Edgar Anderson, "The Couronians and the West Indies: The First Settlements," *Caribbean Quarterly* 5, no. 4 (1959): 264–71.
10. Parker, *Willoughbyland*, 77.
11. Parker, *Willoughbyland*, 78–79.
12. Parker, *Willoughbyland*, 79.
13. Parker, *Willoughbyland*, 86–88.
14. Parker, *Willoughbyland*, 86–88.
15. Parker, *Willoughbyland*, 92–93.
16. Parker, *Willoughbyland*, 112.
17. Parker, *Willoughbyland*, 111.
18. Parker, *Willoughbyland*, 138.
19. Parker, *Willoughbyland*, 137.
20. Parker, *Willoughbyland*, 139.
21. Parker, *Willoughbyland*, 139.
22. Robert Sanford, *Surinam Justice in the Case of Several Persons Proscribed by Certain Usurpers of Power in That Colony* (London: Printed for the author, 1662), 27.

23. Parker, *Willoughbyland*, 138–46.
24. Jason Peacey, *The Regicides and the Execution of Charles I* (Basingstoke: Palgrave Macmillan, 2001), 1–13; Benjamin Woodford, "Developments and Debates in English Censorship during the Interregnum and Restoration," *Early Modern Literary Studies* 11 (2010): 6–9; Parliament of the United Kingdom, "Act of Uniformity 1662." Accessed November 1, 2025, <https://www.parliament.uk/about/living-heritage/transformingsociety/private-lives/religion/collections/common-prayer/act-of-uniformity-1662/>
25. Parker, *Willoughbyland*, 124.
26. Brewer, "Common Law of Slavery," 781.
27. Brewer, "Common Law of Slavery," 781–84.
28. The exception is Charlotte Sussman, who notes that the rebellion Behn describes in *Oroonoko* is, through the character of Imoinda, an expression of "conflict between two distinct codes of property relations: colonial slavery and a traditional tribal system, which, although it uses slaves, would never enslave the wife of its leader." From Sussman, "The Other Problem with Women" in *Rereading Aphra Behn: History, Theory, and Criticism*, ed. Heidi Hutner (Charlottesville, VA: University Press of Virginia, 1993), 217.
29. Critics disagree about how *Oroonoko*'s execution structures the relation of sovereignty and slavery. An illustrative, though not exhaustive, survey of interpretations is as follows. Catherine Gallagher enlarges Laura Brown's reading in *Nobody's Story: The Vanishing Acts of Women Writers in the Marketplace, 1670–1820* (Berkeley, CA: University of California Press, 1995), 77, 85. She suggests that Oroonoko's "intrinsic, nonnegotiable kingship" is "paradoxically figured in the same blackness that designates the principle of [chattel] exchange itself." After Oroonoko becomes an object of "marketplace exchange" through racialization, he disembowels himself to resist colonial "ownership and exchange"; colonial authorities then dismember his body. Gallagher understands Oroonoko's execution as the concomitant obliteration of sovereignty and chattel property in enslaved Africans. However, Richard Frohock, in "Violence and Awe: The Foundations of Government in Aphra Behn's New World Settings," *Eighteenth-Century Fiction* 8, no. 4 (1996): 437–52, argues that Oroonoko's execution highlights the different constituencies vying for power in colonial Surinam. For Frohock, Oroonoko's execution illustrates different justifications for colonial rule: brute force on the one hand, and sociopolitical hierarchy on the other. Srinivas Aravamudan interprets Oroonoko's execution as a consequence of his chattel-racialization, characterized as "petting," in *Tropicopolitans: Colonialism and Agency, 1688–1804* (Durham, NC: Duke University Press, 1999), 45. First, Oroonoko is made from a man into an animal, and then from an animal into a pet. The pet Oroonoko "is disfigured" by torture and execution, Aravamudan argues, "in a manner that suggests the totemism and trauma of the rending of another social pet, the king himself." Aravamudan thus situates chattel-racialization as symbolically linked to regicide, though not coextensive with it, as in Gallagher's reading. Additionally, Elliott Visconsi underscores that Oroonoko's execution racializes Banister, Oroonoko's executioner. For Behn's readers, Visconsi notes, "Banister's Irishness would have been a clear reference to the gothic barbarism which had been overcome in England and marginalized geographically." See Elliott Visconsi, "A Degenerate Race: English Barbarism in Aphra Behn's *Oroonoko* and *The Widow Ranter*," *English Literary History* 69, no. 3 (2002): 673–701, esp. 687. In a related vein, Catherine Molineux argues that *Oroonoko* dramatizes the "violent unsettling of sovereignty" through Oroonoko's racialized bondage and execution; for Molineux, the novel poses the critical question of "whether a black prince could be a prince." See Catherine Molineux, "False Gifts/Exotic Fictions: Epistemologies of Sovereignty and Assent in Aphra Behn's *Oroonoko*," *English Literary History* 80, no. 2 (2013): 455–88, esp. 457, 459. Cynthia Richards provides another argument, drawing on Elaine Scarry's *The Body in Pain*, and contends that Oroonoko's execution invokes "judicial and modern torture" both to legitimize "the truth of [Behn's] own narrative" and to expose "the fictional nature of [Behn's] own narrative power." Through this paradox, Richards notes, Behn "reminds the reader of the violence inherent in any appropriation of another's story." See Cynthia Richards, "Interrogating *Oroonoko*: Torture in a New World and a New Fiction of Power," *Eighteenth-Century Fiction* 25, no. 4 (2013): 647–76, esp. 647. Most recently, Megan Griffin has shown that Oroonoko's execution is a form of ritual punishment that invokes and inverts a form of execution reserved in England for regicides. By positioning the Surinam colonists as sovereigns with power to maim and kill the sovereign Oroonoko like a regicide, Griffin argues that Oroonoko's execution functions as a metaphor for the imperial project. See Megan Griffin, "Dismembering the Sovereign in Aphra Behn's *Oroonoko*," *English Literary History* 86, no. 1 (2019): 107–33, esp. 128–29.
30. Griffin's interpretation of *Oroonoko* stresses that slavocrats have absolute power over life and death in colonial Surinam, similar to what Foucault and Agamben call sovereign power to kill or let live. This interpretation holds if *Oroonoko*'s slave society is one in which public monies are set

aside for the reimbursement of slaveholders whose property is killed in (extra-)judicial processes designed to quell rebellion, suppress flight, and punish resistance. While Oroonoko is executed as a warning to other would-be insurrectionists, it is not clear that Trefry will be reimbursed by a public fund for Banister's destruction of his property in Oroonoko. This implies that the slavocratic power to kill, in *Oroonoko*, comes at the cost of lost property value. For further discussion, see David Barry Gaspar's *Bondmen and Rebels: A Study of Master–Slave Relations in Antigua, with Implications for Colonial British America* (Baltimore, MD: Johns Hopkins University Press, 1985), 199–200. In his work on eighteenth-century Antigua, Gaspar describes the establishment of public funds for slaveholders' compensation, suggesting that slavocrats developed common interest in indemnifying one another against the necessity of killing at least some enslaved people in the maintenance of the chattel regime.

31. An Acte Touching Dyvers Orders for Artificers, Laborers, Servantes of Husbandrye and Apprentises (5 Eliz. I c. 4, 1563), quoted in Brewer, "Common Law of Slavery," 773.
32. For discussion of animalization as a method of racialization, see Edward B. Rugemer, "The Development of Mastery and Race in the Comprehensive Slave Codes of the Greater Caribbean during the Seventeenth Century," *William and Mary Quarterly* 70, no. 3 (2013): 429–58.
33. Rugemer, *Slave Law*, 11–34.
34. See esp. Megan Griffin's discussion of Oroonoko's execution in light of Ernst Kantorowicz's *The King's Two Bodies* and Giorgio Agamben's *Homo Sacer* in Griffin, "Dismembering the Sovereign," 112–31.
35. Stephanie Smallwood argues the colonial plantation system "turned on perfecting the practices required to commodify people and determining where those practices reached their outer limits (that is, the point at which they extinguished the lives they were meant to sustain in commodified form)." In Smallwood, *Saltwater Slavery: A Middle Passage from Africa to American Diaspora* (Cambridge, MA: Harvard University Press, 2007), 43.
36. Fields and Fields, *Racecraft*, 17.
37. As Lynn Avery Hunt has argued, the novel was crucial to the imagination of universal human rights because it emphasized that human beings' equal dignity was self-evident from their similar inward feelings. Hunt notes that such identification was programmatically denied to people who were enslaved. I argue that *Oroonoko* plots heritable animal status as the political technique by which Africans were categorically excluded by the English from this presumption of shared human feeling. At the same time, Behn deploys narrative access to the human interior in order to show that enslaved people, animalized by slavocrats, nevertheless retained human feelings, which are the basis of their rebellion against slavery. See Hunt, "Torrents of Emotion: Reading Novels and Imagining Equality," in *Inventing Human Rights: A History* (New York: W. W. Norton & Co., 2007), 76, 35–69.
38. Francis Bacon, quoted in Mary Nyquist, *Arbitrary Rule: Slavery, Tyranny, and the Power of Life and Death* (Chicago: University of Chicago Press, 2013), 17.
39. Here, it is worthwhile to underscore a rift in the scholarship around Behn's figuration of Coramantien and Surinam, and clarify my own position. Critics like Richard Kroll emphasize that *Oroonoko* is not about Africa or the Americas at all, but rather a transposition of Stuart politics into an Atlantic register. Others, like Sussman, have taken Behn's transatlantic frame literally to mean that the book is about the enslavement of Africans. My interpretation hybridizes these stances: like Sussman, I think that Behn is writing about the English enslavement of Africans. But I also think, along the lines of Kroll's position, that the Coramantee episode of *Oroonoko* is Behn's imaginative rendering of West Africa. On the other hand, I read *Oroonoko*'s episode in Surinam as possibly based on Behn's presumptive visit to that colony. In summary, I understand both episodes in *Oroonoko* as English interpretations of non-European societies, leaving open the possibility that Behn had firsthand experience of an English colonial slave society in Surinam. See Richard Kroll, "Fatal Fluency: Behn's Fiction and the Restoration Letter," *Eighteenth-Century Fiction* 12, nos. 3–4 (2000): 417–34; and Sussman, "The Other Problem."
40. See Jennifer L. Morgan, "'Some Could Suckle over their Shoulder': Male Travelers, Female Bodies, and the Gendering of Racial Ideology," in *Laboring Women: Reproduction and Gender in New World Slavery* (Philadelphia: University of Pennsylvania Press, 2004), 12–49.
41. See Pocock, *Ancient Constitution.*
42. Morgan, *Inventing the People*, 32–33.
43. Thomas Beard, *The Theatre of God's Judgments*, quoted in David Underdown, *A Freeborn People: Politics and the Nation in Seventeenth-Century England* (Oxford: Clarendon Press, 1996), 13.
44. John Phelps, "The Act," in *Trial of Charles I*, The National Archives, accessed June 20, 2021. <https://www.nationalarchives.gov.uk/museum/additional_image_types.asp?item_id=22&image_id=30&extra_image_type_id=2>

45. Geoffrey Robertson, *The Tyrannicide Brief: The Story of the Man Who Sent Charles I to the Scaffold* (New York: Anchor Books, 2007), 15, 33.
46. Robert A. Erickson argues that Behn dedicates *Oroonoko* not only to the historical figure of Lord Maitland, but also uses him (and his lady) as a kind of "heroic pair" analogue to Oroonoko and Imoinda, and by extension a cautionary example for England's Catholic King James II, then in crisis. Robert A. Erickson, "Mrs. A. Behn and the Myth of Oroonoko-Imoinda," *Eighteenth-Century Fiction* 5, no. 3 (April 1993): 201–16, esp. 215.
47. Todd, *Aphra Behn*, 32.
48. Todd, *Aphra Behn*, 32.
49. Todd, *Aphra Behn*, 32; Parker, *Willoughbyland*, 150–51.
50. Janet Todd, "Introduction," in *Oroonoko; or, The Royal Slave*, by Aphra Behn (New York: Penguin Classics, 2003), p. xxiv.
51. Warren's tract describes many of the characteristics of the colony that Behn's later narrative also notes, including the "wretched miseries" of enslavement that drive "Negroes" in the colony "to desperate attempts for the Recovery of their Liberty." Like Aphra Behn, Warren indicates in the word "Recovery" that enslaved people are not naturally unfree. George Warren, *An Impartial Description of Surinam Upon the Continent of Guiana in America...* (London: Printed by William Godbid for Nathaniel Brooke, 1667), 13; see also Michel Eyquem de Montaigne, "Of Cannibals," in *The Complete Essays of Montaigne*, tr. Donald M. Frame (Stanford, CA: Stanford University Press, 1973), 150–59.
52. Annabel M. Patterson, *Censorship and Interpretation* (Madison, WI: University of Wisconsin Press, 1984), 12.
53. Patterson, *Censorship and Interpretation*, 12, emphasis in original.
54. Laura J. Rosenthal, *Ways of the World: Theater and Cosmopolitanism in the Restoration and Beyond* (Ithaca, NY: Cornell University Press, 2020), 132.
55. Richard Kroll has shown that Behn probably wrote *Oroonoko* in response to the developing political drama of 1688. Three days after *Oroonoko* was published that year, on June 27, Whigs and Tories dispatched an invitation to William and Mary to invade England in order to protect the rights of freeborn Englishmen against the tyranny of James II. See Kroll, "Fatal Fluency," 580, 604.
56. Sydney's unpublished treatise, "Discourses Concerning Government," was used against him at trial for treason, as the second witness required in capital cases. Todd, *Aphra Behn*; and Kroll, "Fatal Fluency," 417–34.
57. Pocock, *Ancient Constitution*, 42.
58. Pocock, *Ancient Constitution*, 43.
59. Kroll, "Fatal Fluency," 580.
60. Kroll, "Fatal Fluency," 580, 604.
61. Kroll, "Fatal Fluency," 589.
62. See Nyquist, *Arbitrary Rule*, 164–69.
63. See Annette Gordon-Reed, *The Hemingses of Monticello* (New York: W. W. Norton & Co., 2008), 45.
64. Orlando Patterson, *The Sociology of Slavery: An Analysis of the Origins, Development, and Structure of Negro Slave Society in Jamaica* (Rutherford, NJ: Fairleigh Dickinson University Press, 1969), 173.
65. Robertson, *Tyrannicide Brief*, 25.
66. See Adam Rothman, *Slave Country: American Expansion and the Origins of the Deep South* (Cambridge, MA: Harvard University Press, 2002), 20. Rothman notes that it is not until the late eighteenth century that "the rudiments of a patriarchal defense of slavery" become evident in the distinction of "the vicious commercial world of the Atlantic slave trade, which was dominated by British merchants, with the more virtuous agrarian world of the American plantation."
67. Brewer, "Common Law of Slavery," 772.
68. Malick W. Ghachem, "The Slave's Two Bodies: The Life of an American Legal Fiction," *William and Mary Quarterly* 60, no. 4 (2003): 809–42; John Samuel Harpham, "Two Concepts of a Slave in the South Carolina Law of Slavery," *Slavery and Abolition* 39, no. 1 (2018): 101–22.
69. See Ernst H. Kantorowicz, *The King's Two Bodies: A Study in Medieval Political Theology*, rev. edn (1957; repr., Princeton: Princeton University Press, 2016).
70. Edmund Plowden, *Commentaries or Reports* (London, 1816), 2122. Originally published 1571; first English translation printed in 1761.
71. Kantorowicz notes the interesting problem of property and sovereignty in later examples recorded by F. W. Maitland, notably when King George III "had to go to Parliament for permission to hold some land as a man and not as a king, 'since rights not denied to any of His Majesty's subjects were denied to him.'" Quoted in Kantorowicz, *The King's Two Bodies*, 3.
72. Morrison, *Playing in the Dark* (Cambridge, MA: Harvard University Press, 1992), 66.
73. Her success in both endeavors allows her to bear, without question, Oroonoko's legitimate royal heir.

74. The identity of this "Governor" is one of the mysteries of *Oroonoko*, which suggests that Behn engaged in some fictionalization of the story. Janet Todd demonstrates that this "Governor" is, historically speaking, Lord Willoughby; but, curiously, the narrator of *Oroonoko* also says that it is her father. While there is speculation that Willoughby and Behn's father were related, there is no conclusive evidence that I have found supporting this connection. Todd, *Aphra Behn*, 31–32.
75. For a comprehensive history of war slavery doctrine in the English tradition, see John Samuel Harpham, *The Intellectual Origins of American Slavery: English Ideas in the Early Modern Atlantic World* (Cambridge, MA: Harvard University Press, 2025).
76. For discussion of how slave codes contemporary to Behn's *Oroonoko* animalized enslaved people, see Rugemer, "The Development of Mastery and Race."
77. Quoted in Rugemer, *Slave Law*, 21.
78. Orlando Patterson, *Slavery and Social Death: A Comparative Study* (Cambridge, MA: Harvard University Press, 1982), 7.
79. Sussman, "The Other Problem," 218.
80. Patterson, *Slavery and Social Death*, 26.
81. Sir Francis Willoughby died at sea, but not until 1666, another point of potential fictionalization in Behn's tale. Todd, *Aphra Behn*, 34.
82. Critics tend to agree that Aphra Behn was engaged in espionage during the Stuart era. See Alan Marshall, "'Memorialls for Mrs Affora': Aphra Behn and the Restoration Intelligence World," *Women's Writing* 22, no. 1 (2015): 13–33; and, generally: Todd, *Aphra Behn*.
83. As Herbert Aptheker has written, "the fundamental factor provoking rebellion against slavery was that social system itself, the degradation, exploitation, oppression, and brutality which it created." See Herbert Aptheker, *American Negro Slave Revolts* (New York: Columbia University Press, 1943), 139. In *Oroonoko*, written some 250 years before Aptheker's study, Behn arrives at a similar conclusion by examining the political motivations of Imoinda and Oroonoko.
84. Citing the manifold human coercions of chattel slavery, Saidiya Hartman cautions against any straightforward interpretation of enslaved people's actions: "What was demanded by the master was simulated by the enslaved; yet the capitulation of the dominated to these demands must be considered as pragmatism rather than resignation since one either complied with the rules governing socially sanctioned behavior or risked punishment. In addition, these performances constituted acts of defiance conducted under the cover of nonsense, indirection, and seeming acquiescence." See Saidiya V. Hartman, *Scenes of Subjection: Terror, Slavery, and Self-Making in Nineteenth-Century America* (New York: Oxford University Press, 1997), 8.
85. For a discussion of Behn's description of Englishmen's "barbarous national character which prefers violence and personal independence to the mercy and moral prudence of kingly government," what I interpret as the racialization of the ancient constitution, see Visconsi's "A Degenerate Race."
86. For elaboration of the connection between racialization and the contract, which is beyond the scope of this study, see Charles W. Mills's argument that the "constitutions of [early colonial] states and their exclusionary juridical mechanisms" indicate how the social contract was first and foremost a contract among people who understood themselves as racially superior to other groups. Mills, *The Racial Contract* (Ithaca, NY: Cornell University Press, 1997), 30.
87. Brewer, "Common Law of Slavery," 774.
88. Pocock, *Virtue, Commerce, and History: Essays on Political Thought and History, Chiefly in the Eighteenth Century* (Cambridge: Cambridge University Press, 1985), 108, 112. On the relation of public credit to the transatlantic slave trade and the English novel, see Ian Baucom, "'Madam Death! Madam Death!': Credit, Insurance, and the Atlantic Cycle of Capital Accumulation," in *Specters of the Atlantic: Finance Capital, Slavery, and the Philosophy of History* (Durham, NC: Duke University Press, 2005), 80–112. See esp. Baucom's discussion, vis-à-vis Gallagher and Pocock in *Virtue*, of how the speculative culture of finance capital is articulated as the "suppositional identities of novelistic characters" (80–81). I am saying here that *Oroonoko* tells the story, perhaps even the first story in English, of how those novelistic characters came into being, and—through racecraft—acquired the "suppositional identities" we call race.
89. George Frederick Zook, *The Company of Royal Adventurers Trading into Africa* (1919; repr., New York: Negro Universities Press, 1969).

Novel Constitutions and the Making of Race: A Literary and Legal History of Slavery in the Anglophone Atlantic, 1688–1818. Sarah Marsh, Oxford University Press. © Sarah Marsh 2026. DOI: 10.1093/9780197917855.003.0002

2

"My Reign, or My Captivity"

The Ancient Constitution in Daniel Defoe's *Robinson Crusoe*

If Aphra Behn's *Oroonoko* is a story of how the English racialized Africans into slaves, Daniel Defoe's *Robinson Crusoe* (1719) plots the corollary process by which Englishmen racialized themselves into slavocrats. *Robinson Crusoe*, this chapter contends, dramatizes how the English asserted absolute rights to trade persons overseas in response to the Crown's creation of an imperial legal landscape in which human labor was freely alienable. As Defoe's plot demonstrates, these rights acquired racial character as Englishmen's customary property protections under the ancient constitution were pushed toward absolute labor power in the wider Atlantic world. Ultimately, *Robinson Crusoe* draws an important transatlantic connection between the original property rights of the English people, as they were being projected overseas according to Crown policy, and the original sin of chattel slavery.

By "racial character" I mean Crusoe's "Englishness" as it has been conflated with his distinctive "inclination"—his mysterious "propension of Nature"—to "go to sea" and "rise by enterprize [*sic*]," against the express wishes of his parents.[1] This "propension" induces Crusoe to leave his family, and then leads him into the Atlantic traffic in slaves. As Crusoe recalls, "the same influence, whatever it was, presented the most unfortunate of all enterprises to my view; and I went on board a vessel bound to the coast of *Africa*; or, as our sailors vulgarly called it, a voyage to *Guinea*" (15). On his first voyage to Africa, Crusoe changes about "40*l.*" of "toys and trifles" into "5.9 *ounces* of gold-dust," which he sells in London for "almost 300*l*" (16). These transactions do not involve the sale of people; however, the more than sevenfold return on investment persuades Crusoe that the African coast is lucrative enough to outweigh its "misfortunes," including Crusoe's own temporary enslavement at Sallee (16).

After using this capital to purchase a plantation in Brazil, Crusoe becomes more deeply enmeshed in the slave trade, recruiting fellow planters with fantastic stories of economic gain: that "trifles" like "beads, toys, knives, scissors, hatchets, bits of glass, and the like" were "easy" to exchange in Africa not only for gold, but for "*Negroes*... in great numbers" (32, emphasis in original). Enticed, the men propose to Crusoe a plan to circumvent limitations and taxes imposed by Spanish and Portuguese royal authority over the slave trade to Brazil.[2] As payment for leading their conspiracy to avoid taxation and regulation, they offer Crusoe a share of their human cargo. And, despite Crusoe's feeling that the venture is financially "preposterous" (compared to the certain fortune he will accumulate by simply staying where he is), he agrees to go along (33). On September 1, 1659, eight years to the day after defying his parents, Crusoe sets out in an "evil hour" to become a slave trader in contravention of the sovereign slave-trading power of King Philip IV of Spain and King John IV of Portugal (34).[3] In this way, Crusoe's action mirrors that of royalist slavocrats in *Oroonoko*: an Englishman seeks abroad a form of absolute power over others, including the power to treat other persons as an alienable form of property.

"That evil influence," which propels Crusoe "into the wild and indigested notion of raising [his] fortune" is, I contend, Defoe's treatment in fiction of real contradictions that ancient constitutionalism harbored for many unlanded Englishmen (15). These people, like the fictive Robinson Crusoe, were putatively possessed of political rights which emanated from the English common law: rights to life, liberty, and property against sovereign overreach. But they did not possess, and could not easily acquire, real property in England, which the common law created and protected.[4] For these people, the promises of ancient constitutionalism were empty, or at least incomplete. However, imperial expansion, with its code-based legal landscape promoted by the Stuarts in the late seventeenth century, offered these unlanded subjects an opportunity to make real what the fiction of ancient constitutionalism had promised. In the face of this fundamental contradiction in the national status quo, some unpropertied Englishmen left their home country and created new legal capacities in themselves as colonists. They did so by asserting that England's ancient constitution—and its immemorial, Crown-ratified protections of property—were transatlantically applicable, racially unique, and the basis for new rights of mastery. *Robinson Crusoe* is one story of how this happened.

Crusoe's Englishness is central to the novel's critical tradition. In 1837, Sir Walter Scott declared Crusoe "no bad specimen of the True-Born Englishman."[5] In 1867, Karl Marx said that he was "a true-born Briton."[6] One year later, Leslie Stephen found Crusoe a "typical Englishman of his time."[7] In 1912, James Joyce concluded that the "whole Anglo-Saxon spirit is in Crusoe."[8] More recently, Edward Said saw in Crusoe "the founder of a new world, which he rules and reclaims for Christianity and England."[9] These readers no doubt took their cue from Defoe's text, which regularly identifies Crusoe as English. The Portuguese captain, who rescues Crusoe and Xury from slavery and subsequently re-enslaves Xury, calls Crusoe "*Seignor*, Inglese" or "*Mr.* Englishman" (28). The captain gets this idea from Crusoe, who introduces himself to a Scots sailor aboard the Portuguese vessel as "an *Englishman*" (28). Although Crusoe is of mixed parentage, and from a family "not of that country" of York, where he was born in 1632, he regularly styles himself English when he is abroad (5).

To apply Barbara J. Fields and Karen E. Fields's definition of racecraft to this important dimension of Defoe's plot is to see that what Crusoe *does* in the novel (going to sea, trading internationally, enslaving African people, settling a Caribbean island, evangelizing native people, claiming dominion over others, and saying that he is an Englishman) has been understood inside and outside the text as what Crusoe *is*: English.[10] By reengaging these older claims about Crusoe's Englishness, and with new attention to the relation between divine-right sovereignty and ancient constitutionalism in *Robinson Crusoe*, I argue that Defoe's title character embodies a kind of transatlantic racecraft that could convert unpropertied inhabitants of England into landed English slavocrats in the wider Atlantic world. Ultimately, this interpretation will underscore the relation Defoe draws between racecraft and original sin, perhaps illuminating why *Robinson Crusoe* has become a shibboleth in the literary history of American slavery.[11]

Daniel Defoe and the Ancient Constitution

For all his work as a satirist of Englishness, Daniel Defoe believed sincerely in the ancient constitution. In this section of the argument, we will consider Defoe's understanding of the ancient constitution in preparation for seeing how he personified it, in a form altered by imperialism, in Robinson Crusoe. Defoe's 1702 treatise, for example, *The Original Power of the Collective Body of the People of England*, defended the idea Coke popularized during the constitutional paroxysms of the previous century of Stuart rule.[12] "There must be some Power *Prior* to the Power of King, Lords and Commons," Defoe wrote, "from which, as the streams from the Fountain, the Power of King, Lords and Commons is derived."[13] The English people's power, anterior to the monarchy and Parliament, was timeless, Defoe said, and coterminous with rationality: the rights of the English against tyranny were, for him, "*as ancient as Nature, and born into the World with our Reason.*"[14]

The "Original Right of the People," Defoe argued further, was the "very Foundation" of the English government's "Being."[15] This English body politic was like a body natural; "as in the natural Body, if any Member . . . fails in the performance of its proper Duty," Defoe said,

> the Locomotive Faculty is either interrupted, and the Body distorted, or at least the regularity of Natural Motion is invaded: So in the Body Politick, if one Branch of the general Union err, and that Error is not Corrected, the whole Constitution suffers a shock, and there is an Infraction of the general order.[16]

Defoe's English "Body Politick"—composed of people, King, Lords, and Commons—was susceptible to "Error" just as the natural body was susceptible to injury. In drawing this parallel, Defoe attacks the political theology of absolute sovereignty, in which the King was designated by godlike incorruptibility. Defoe's analogy, in which the "Locomotive Faculty is... interrupted" by the failure of "any Member," implies that divine right kingship is prone to regression because it cannot conceive of a sovereign who ought to be "Corrected." Like Behn, Defoe is interested in the novel possibility of detaching the King's body natural from his body politic with appeals to the ancient constitution.

In this effort, Defoe draws upon the ancient constitutionalist rhetoric Parliament pursued to limit the Stuart kings' claims to sovereign absolutism. As we have seen in *Oroonoko*, parliamentarians and common lawyers erected Coke's theory of the ancient constitution as a hedge against the monarch's incursions into the liberty and property of English subjects. In the first of his *Institutes of the Laws of England* (1628), Coke affirmed the primacy of the common law, or *lex terrae*, while acknowledging England's legal pluralism, noting fourteen canonical sources of other "divers lawes within the realm."[17] *Lex terrae* was both land law, in the sense of property law, and the law of the land in its subsumption of all other English principles of adjudicature. In the fourth of his *Institutes* for example, Coke invoked a body natural to describe the proper functioning of the pluralistic English justice system, under the common law:

> as the body of man is best ordered, when every particular member exerciseth his proper duty: so the body of the commonwealth is best governed when every severall court of justice executeth his proper jurisdiction....[I]f one court should usurp, or incroach upon another, it would introduce incertainty, subvert justice, and bring all things in the end to confusion.[18]

Defoe thus followed Coke and many others in imagining English civic functioning as a well-ordered natural body, whose constitution, balanced by the people's claims under the common law, ensures justice and progress for the nation by checking the monarch's fallible exercise of the royal prerogative.[19]

Jurisdictional tensions that Coke canvassed in the *Institutes*, Daniel Hulsebosch argues, were central to constitutional strain that shot through Stuart England in the 1640s, leading to the Civil Wars and the regicide of 1649.[20] We have seen that, during this period, Aphra Behn held out the possibility that divine-right absolutism (and its claims to godlike incorruptibility) might be tempered by ancient constitutionalism. But Defoe, writing in the wake of the Glorious Revolution and the constitutional monarchy it established, balked at any pretension the sovereign might make to divinity. In *Original Power*, for example, Defoe included the monarch in his claim that any "Branch of the general Union" could fail the others by neglecting "the performance of its proper Duty." For Defoe, a balanced constitution could be achieved only on the presumption that the monarch is corruptible:

the English people's rights against a human sovereign guaranteed the body politic's "Locomotive Faculty" for progress.

Defoe also followed the tradition of ancient constitutionalism when he invoked "time out of mind," from whence these ancient liberties had arisen. In the beginning, Defoe argued, the English people had in essential character been much like others living nearby. In an "Explanatory Preface" to *The True-Born Englishman*, his wildly popular 1701 send-up of "ridiculous" English claims to ancestral purity, Defoe wrote that the English were "of the same original" as "their neighbors."[21] Defoe asserted with geohumoral logic that this once shared "original" character had been "bettered by our [English] climate." He added that "our language and manufactures," all "derived from" England's neighbors, had been "improved by us to a perfection greater than they can pretend to."[22] English superiority arose, in Defoe's thinking here, not from some inherent racial purity or the superiority of the common law, but from the refining influence of England's island climate, which promoted linguistic development and national industry.

But climatologic improvements to individuals' bodily (or physical) constitutions, Defoe quipped at length in *The True-Born Englishman*, could never homogenize the "amphibious, ill-born mob" out of which the English nation had grown.[23] As Defoe riotously emphasized, the English were "themselves all derived" from:

> the most scoundrel race that ever lived;
> A horrid crowd of rambling thieves and drones
> Who ransack'd kingdoms, and dispeopled towns;
> The Pict and painted Briton, treach'rous Scot,
> By hunger, theft, and rapine, hither brought;
> Norwegian pirates, buccaneering Danes,
> Whose red-hair'd offspring everywhere remains;
> Who, join'd with Norman French, compound the breed
> From whence your true-born Englishmen proceed.[24]

Indeed, Defoe went on,

> lest, by length of time, it be pretended,
> The climate may this modern breed have mended;
> Wise Providence, to keep us where we are,
> Mixes us daily with exceeding care.[25]

The English were thus no more than "Europe's . . . offal out-cast progeny."[26] "Strolling bands" and "banish'd fugitives" found "refuge" in England, where they could borrow "new Blood and Manners from the Clime," and "proudly" learn to scorn all others.[27] This, Defoe jested, was the *real* "race" of "true-born Englishmen."[28] The "new Blood" of Defoe's imagination signals an ontologic change rooted in climate difference, a concept that will be of importance in Crusoe's racial transformation in the novel that bears his name. In *The True-Born Englishman*, the English climate could refine inferior foreign manners; but its improving effects were continually offset by England's position as "Europe's sink, *the jakes*, where she / Voids" her "miscellaneous crowd," who arrive with "Diseases, and no money."[29] Here, the scatological joke is on Englishmen who believe in the purity of their family lines.

The truth in Defoe's wry hyperbole about the motley English—in tension with his serious claims for ancient constitutionalism in *The Original Power*—raises important questions with implications for understanding the rise of English slave-holding in *Robinson Crusoe*. How did Defoe think that the English people's inborn ancient rights against sovereign overreach had survived tumultuous mixing with new people who arrived in England without regard for common law protections of life and private property, those very ones that the king was bound by the ancient constitution to uphold? What became of the ancient constitution's protections against tyranny in the midst of "ransack[ing]" and "dispeopl[ing]" by the "horrid crowd" of diseased interlopers without money? If Defoe's "Maxims" in *The Original Power* held true, and "no Collective... Body of Men whatsoever, in Matters of Politics any more than Religion, *are or ever have been Infallible*," then how had the English people's original right survived the imbalancing onslaught of "hunger, theft, and rapine" introduced by these outsiders turned English not by legal process, but rather the imperfect action of the climate?[30] How had the body politic of the English nation, the one governed by law, maintained its likeness to a well-ordered natural body with "Locomotive" powers for progress?

The answer is in Defoe's understanding of who "the people" of England really were. In *The Original Power*, he writes in a clarifying passage that:

> I do not place this [original] Right upon the Inhabitants, but upon the *Freeholders*; the *Freeholders* are the proper Owners of the Country: It is their own, and the other Inhabitants are but Sojourners, like Lodgers in a House, and ought to be subject to such Laws as the Freeholders impose upon them, or else they must remove; because the Freeholders having a Right to the Land, the other have no right to live here but upon sufferance.[31]

As Defoe saw it, English freeholders had a "natural Right of Possession" that had been "handed down by Custom and ancient Usage"—and thus it was an "Inheritance from the still more ancient Possessors, and Prescription, as the Lawyers call it, or Usage time out of mind."[32] While the English climate anglicized the blood and manners of everyone who happened to be in England, only English land vested its owners, and its owners alone, with the original "Right of the

People," which was conserved by possession and prescription, via primogeniture, for the next generation of landed proprietors. In its heritable and embodied character, this "Right" of the English people was racial, but it did not belong to everyone in the country.[33] All others, Defoe said, were "Inhabitants" who either paid "Rent [to] live [in England] upon Conditions" or were "the Freeholders [*sic*] Servants."[34] Like other heritable characteristics, English land rights included, and conveyed, rights to the labor of those unpropertied people resident in England. Robinson Crusoe, born landless in England to German immigrants, is consigned to a lifetime of labor on freeholders' behalf. This way of imagining who "the people" are produces two strata within English society—freeholders and those who stand in a subordinate relation to freeholders, and owe those freeholders their labor. This division will matter when we examine Defoe's choice to represent Crusoe as originally unlanded and subsequently a landholder, a change Crusoe realizes, in part, through overseas assertions of his Englishness.

The possibility of conquest, however, gave the lie to England's system for conserving original rights through heritable property. After all, successful invaders could acquire and transfer land title, labor rights, and all. For Defoe, like many others before him, the Norman Conquest was an object lesson in how ancient English rights had been preserved—or not—since time out of mind. In *The True-Born Englishman*, for example, Defoe figured William I's invasion of 1066 as a widespread form of land expropriation:

> The great Invading *Norman* let us know
> What Conquerors in After-Times might do.
> To ev'ry *Musqueteer* he brought to Town,
> He gave the Lands which never were his own;
> When first the *English* Crown he did obtain,
> He did not send his *Dutchmen* home again.[35]

An invading foreign power with a superior army could thus insinuate itself into England, not as mere "Inhabitants," but as "freeholders" with unencumbered claim to the full protections of the ancient constitution, and even "lords" with seats in Parliament.[36] Climate could anglicize a person's manners, but only conquest could create and destroy English rights to land and labor. Gerrard Winstanley, the famous activist Digger of the Interregnum, had argued similarly in his 1652 "Law of Freedom in a Platform," that "When the Norman power had conquered our forefathers, he took the free use of our English ground from them, and made them his servants."[37] So much, perhaps, for ancient custom. William I, a foreigner, used military might to claim the ancient constitutional rights of English landowners for himself and "his *Dutchmen*," an important historical dynamic that we will see reverberating in Defoe's treatment, in *Robinson Crusoe*, of England's other famous invader, William III.

Read together, *The Original Power* and *The True-Born Englishman* disclose that the Englishness Defoe imagines in the character of Robinson Crusoe is not the Englishness of the rights-endowed freeholder. Rather, Crusoe is a kind of fictional Englishman outside and inside the novel: not really "of that country," as he says himself in the very first sentence of the story (1). Crusoe, then, embodies Defoe's quip in *The True Born Englishman* that "A *True-Born Englishman's* a Contradiction, / In Speech an Irony, in Fact a Fiction."[38] Merely an "inhabitant" at home, where he and his labor were subject to the rule of the Crown and freeholders, Crusoe acquires real property abroad in Brazil and the Caribbean. With this property, he gains the authority of a freeholder as well as of a sovereign. He commands absolute power over his African slaves in Brazil, and he exercises authority over at least two unnamed European servants and the Carib he names Friday. This is how Crusoe invents his Englishness as he goes: in part through the labor and property rights he claims in these people overseas, and in part through the racial claims he makes for his own Englishness in that imperial frame. Belief in these claims, or not, is one of *Robinson Crusoe*'s most resonant legacies.

Unlike William I's newly landed "*Musqueteer*[s]," however, who acquire English rights and government power through conquest, Crusoe's rights to property and labor result primarily from trade—often, Crusoe believes, the exchange of nothing for something. As Crusoe says of his first seafaring venture from Hull to London, it "cost me nothing for my passage" (8). Later, the Portuguese Captain will "take nothing of [Crusoe] for his passage" to Brazil (28). Once established in Brazil, Crusoe sets out on a slaving expedition to West Africa on his fellow planters' promise that he "should have [his] equal share of the negroes, without providing any part of the stock" (33). But Crusoe is wrong to count his cost as zero. As Defoe persistently dramatizes, Crusoe accepts extraordinary personal risk to life and limb in the project of raising his fortune through imperial acquisition, a point underscored by his elder brother's death in the Battle of the Dunes during the Franco-Spanish War of 1648–59, a militarized expression in Europe of English empire-building, mirrored by the Anglo-Spanish conflict Robinson experiences in the western Atlantic. Defoe's assessment of imperial expansion in *Crusoe* underscores that unpropertied inhabitants of England, like the Crusoe boys, can be persuaded to value their lives at naught, even less than those "trifles" that can be exchanged for people in Africa.

Robinson Crusoe's many occasions of economic acquisition, in which the protagonist believes himself to be getting something "for free," consolidate the novel's crucial tropes: Crusoe's Englishness abroad though not at home; his knowledge of an irresistible inward compulsion to improve his fortune by trade; and his rejection of the authority of parents and monarchs alike, by which he ultimately arrogates their traditionally superior powers for domestic and civil government to himself in the Caribbean. Crusoe's obsession with raising his fortune prevents him from reckoning the cost of ambition, which he laments with repeated references to Job, whose loss of property to the Chaldeans is the originating fact of his trial before God.[39]

Defoe situated the wreck of Crusoe's transatlantic ambition on the Island of Despair at "the mouth of the river *Oroonooko*" (170). This recalls, Jay Fliegelman says, the story of that real Englishman, Sir Walter Raleigh, who "having failed to plan Eden in Virginia, sought Eldorado, the City of Gold."[40] It may also prompt us to remember Behn's storied African prince, whose English enslavers, like Crusoe, sought for themselves "Perpetual Dominion," as Robert Sanford saw it exemplified in William Byam. By crafting—or, as I am arguing here, racecrafting—Crusoe into an Englishman, whose acquisitive power is elsewhere because of his family's unlanded status and his government's policies, Defoe prepares a novel thought experiment in imperial ancient constitutionalism. In *The Original Power* and *The True-Born Englishman*, Defoe considered the idea of ancient English rights exercised domestically, what Coke called "the ancient and excellent laws of England," which "are the birthright, and the most ancient and best inheritance that the subjects of this realm have" because they granted enjoyment of "inheritance and goods in peace" as well as "life and his most dear country in safety."[41] *Robinson Crusoe*, by contrast, explores the fate of those original rights when they are projected abroad by someone who may, or may not, be English. In the next section, we will examine how, in the figure of Crusoe, Defoe plots a transformation of ancient English liberties into justifications for racial domination in the empire.

The Imperial Constitution in *Robinson Crusoe*

In the preface to *Serious Reflections during the Life and Surprising Adventures of Robinson Crusoe* (1720) Defoe's protagonist defends the first two volumes of his story against popular insults that it is a fiction. "I have heard," an indignant Crusoe begins,

> that the envious and ill-disposed Part of the World have rais'd some Objections against the two first Volumes, on Pretence...that (*as they say*) the Story is feign'd, that the Names are borrow'd, and that it is all a Romance; that there never were any such Man or Place, or Circumstances in any Mans [*sic*] Life; that it is all form'd and embellish'd by Invention to impose upon the World.[42]

Crusoe continues: "I *Robinson Crusoe* being at this Time in perfect and sound Mind and Memory, Thanks be to God therefore; do hereby declare, their Objection is an Invention scandalous in Design, and false in Fact; and do affirm, that the Story, though Allegorical, is also Historical." In addition to emphasizing the legal character of the first two novels, this droll sworn testimony, by a fictional character of the truth of his story, is Defoe's provocative ruse on the nature of fiction.[43] It invites us to see *Robinson Crusoe* as, at once, a parable of the origins of government, a tale of religious conversion, the symbolic rendering of an English past, and other gradations of allegorical and historical tableaux. If we misread the subtle oscillations Defoe has orchestrated in *Robinson Crusoe*, we risk likeness to his protagonist, a tragically incapable interpreter of his own circumstances and in this way his "own destroyer" (33).

Defoe thus designed Crusoe across the eponymous trilogy as a multivalent literary technology for involving readers in the historical processes we now call early modernity.[44] At times, Crusoe strikes us as a plainclothes character in a colonial adventure story, recording a mundane diary of survival and conquest, often mistaking one for the other, an error that characterizes the racial supremacy he claims. At other times, Crusoe is most evidently an allegory for human origins, a new Adam seeking to establish the world of social relations and government out of an isolating Hobbesian state of nature. In this way, Crusoe is also C. B. MacPherson's possessive individualist, a Hobbesian natural man, "reduced to a meer state of nature," as Crusoe says, yet in fact a highly socialized English subject turning to overseas acquisition because he cannot get socioeconomic traction in England's landed political order.[45] Crusoe is furthermore a tortured Christian figure of ever-incomplete human redemption. The Calvinist doctrine of human depravity finds expression in Crusoe's persistent un-Christlike self-enrichment that he does not reliably understand as sin. At other times still, Crusoe's most pronounced referent is imperial politics. The point of having a protagonist who functions in this ambivalent way—with "Variety not to be met with in the World"—is, as Crusoe explains, for the "common good of Mankind." Defoe proposes through Crusoe that we need "Representation" not of "the World" to see what that world is. No less than law, fiction constitutes an understanding of where and who we are.[46]

Read in this light, Robinson Crusoe is Defoe's imaginary test case of an unpropertied inhabitant of England, who carries abroad and asserts over others modified property protections of the ancient constitution, namely forms of neo-feudal domination that were being explored by the Stuart courts to promote absolute power over labor. Defoe's effort to explore the transatlantic status and moral consequences of these rights in *Robinson Crusoe* is consonant with specific high court disputes about the slave trade in the years leading up to the novel's publication.[47] In these disputes, Defoe played an important and shifting role. Here, the backstory of Defoe's complicated relationship with Queen Anne's government in the years following King William III's death in March of 1702 will be instructive to our interpretation of the 1719 novel.

During William III's reign, Defoe enjoyed his sovereign's generous patronage and the political latitude this granted his career as a government operative and satirist.[48] During these years, George Boulukos notes, Defoe was critical of

English imperialism and voiced concern about the moral implications of English slavery.[49] In *Reformation of Manners* (1702), for example, Defoe wrote that slave-trading Englishmen were predators along the African coast: "The harmless Natives basely they trepan, / And barter Baubles for the Souls of Men,"[50] the very pattern of exchange that would become the rising action of *Robinson Crusoe*.

But later, Boulukos writes, notably by 1709 and certainly in *An Essay Upon the Trade to Africa* (1711), Defoe made an about-face on the question of the slave trade.[51] Defoe's political tract focuses on the "Separate Traders"—independent merchants legally permitted after 1698 to trade to Africa outside the Royal African Company so long as they paid a 10 percent duty for use of its forts. Defoe expressed concern that these traders were destabilizing the Company's operations by bribing its factors in Africa and agitating in Parliament to strip the Company of its property without compensation. These bribes, Defoe explained, depressed prices on the coast while inflating the cost of enslaved labor in the colonies.[52] Defoe argued further that, unless the trade remained entirely under the RAC's charter, authorized by Charles II in 1672, Britain risked losing both the security of its African forts and a reliable supply of enslaved people to its Caribbean plantations.[53] Surviving Royal African Company records clarify aspects of Defoe's involvement: RAC accounts show a payment of £12 10s 6d to Defoe on 12 April 1711, suggesting that his pro-slavery advocacy was, at least in part, financially supported.[54] Why had Defoe changed his position on Englishmen's practice of slavery?

The answer may be in his prosecution, conviction, and punishment by Queen Anne's government following his publication of *The Shortest Way with Dissenters* (1702), a political satire in which Defoe adopts the voice of an extreme High-Church Tory to propose the brutal suppression of Protestant Dissenters.[55] Defoe's biographer Maximillian Novak reckons that, when Defoe published *The Shortest Way*, he had not yet grasped the sea change in his political circumstances wrought by the loss of his sovereign patron, William III.[56] Anne's accession in 1702 had emboldened High-Church ministers and reignited pressure for stricter enforcement of religious conformity, and her government proved sensitive to perceived threats against ecclesiastical order. Anne's early reign created political conditions under which a text like Defoe's, parodying Tory zealotry while the Crown was supporting High-Church measures such as the Occasional Conformity Bill, could be treated as a genuine incitement.[57] At points of the proceedings against Defoe, the Queen was personally present, and she seems to have laid the groundwork for his prosecution by delivering a speech in the House of Lords in February 1703, decrying "Scandalous Pamphlets and Libels," which had been harmful to her government.[58] In the end, Defoe's irony in *The Shortest Way* was interpreted as sedition, and the Queen's ministers moved quickly: the pamphlet was condemned, burned by the common hangman, and Defoe was charged with seditious libel. Ultimately, he was convicted, fined, imprisoned at Newgate for five months, pilloried in July 1703 (a dangerous punishment that sometimes resulted in death), and mandated by the Crown to seven years of silence. It was a humiliation that left him financially and politically vulnerable.[59]

In response to this devastation of his family and career, Defoe wrote to Queen Anne, promising her "my hand, my Pen, or my head" if he could but "Obtain Her Majties [*sic*] Pardon" for his offenses in *The Shortest Way*.[60] After this episode, Defoe seems to have entered into a period of political dependence, during which he served as a spy and propagandist for Anne's government.[61] In light of this history, Defoe's subsequent work for the Royal African Company, including the 1711 *Essay Upon the Trade to Africa*, may reflect his new professional reality under the Crown's watchful eye and evident willingness to suppress political speech.

But here, too, were ideas that Defoe would revive in *Robinson Crusoe*. In *An Essay Upon the Trade to Africa*, Defoe warns that England's commercial interests in the African trade had been effectively "shipwreck'd…to all Intents and Purposes" by the policies of the Separate Traders, who, imagining they had brought their business "to an Issue," instead "run themselves upon a Rock which split their Cause," leaving both their project and the nation's trade in ruins.[62] This figurative shipwreck in the pages of the *Essay* anticipates the central catastrophe of *Robinson Crusoe*, published eight years later. In the novel, shipwreck is the narrative device that isolates Crusoe and enables the project of imperial self-fashioning that begins when he, much like the Separate Traders Defoe castigates in 1711, acts beyond (Spanish and Portuguese) Crown authority to acquire saleable property rights in human beings. In this sense, the "shipwreck'd" metaphor from *An Essay Upon the Trade to Africa* is not merely Defoe's figure for the Separate Traders' political miscalculations; it anticipates *Robinson Crusoe*'s plot, revealing how Defoe's state-sponsored advocacy for the Royal African Company, perhaps under the duress of Anne's government, shaped the political logic and imaginative terrain of the novel.

Indeed, Defoe imagines Robinson Crusoe as a new kind of Englishman who, once overseas, translates the ancient constitution's customary protections of English freehold into neo-feudal justification for owning property in persons. Defoe cultivates this dynamic carefully by identifying Crusoe with the ancient constitution itself. For example, the ancient constitution was popularly asserted to have arrived in England with the ancient Germanic liberties of the Saxons. Nathaniel Bacon's *Historical and Political Discourse of the Laws and Government of England* (1689) exemplifies how this story was told during Defoe's lifetime. As Bacon summarized, the Saxons, who according to the Venerable Bede introduced their unique German "Liberties" to Britain in the fifth century, were "a free people, governed by Laws," which were made not "by the great men, but by the people; and therefore called a free-people, because they are a law unto themselves." "This," Bacon continued, "was a privilege belonging to all Germans, as Tacitus observeth."[63] Defoe recapitulates this history by writing Robinson Crusoe as the child of a German immigrant who marries an Englishwoman, a point we will soon elaborate.

The constitutional history that Bacon perceived in *Historical and Political Discourse* was clear: "the *Saxons* came into [England] a free people, and so . . . continueth to this day: I say, that in those first times, they did take into the consideration of Parliament the regulating of the fluctuating motions of Sea-laws: nor were they then, or after, properly imposed by the King's Edict."[64] As Brewer has shown, these ideas were not merely antiquarian musings; they reflected the reasoning of the high-court jurists who reshaped the common law to define people as property in the late seventeenth century. As we have seen in our reading of *Oroonoko*, judges under Charles II and James II used the rhetoric of ancient constitutional liberties—especially the status distinctions derived from transformed feudal labor categories—to create new precedents that made enslaved people legally recoverable as goods, thereby fusing absolutist power with emerging capitalist regimes.[65]

Bacon followed these imperial legal frameworks to assert that trade was a mechanism of rights-creation in those unpropertied inhabitants of England, and he associated those rights with the ancient constitution carried into England by the Saxons. According to "many *Saxon* Laws," Bacon wrote, "Merchants shall have free and safe passage, and trade without unjust Taxes, as by ancient custome they ought." He continued:

> So as it appeareth, that not onely the *English Free-men* and Natives had their liberties asserted by the Law, but also Forreiners, if Merchants, had the like liberties for their persons and goods, concerning Trade, and maintenance of the same; and were hereby enabled to enjoy their own under the protection of the Law, as the *Free-men* had.[66]

In *Robinson Crusoe*, Defoe develops the idea that "Forreiners, if Merchants, had the like liberties for their persons and goods," including property in persons. In *Crusoe*, Defoe extends these claims to include real estate and labor power overseas.

Defoe's interest in transatlantic projections of English property rights manifests in Robinson Crusoe's personification of the ancient constitution, an idea we noted above in Crusoe's Anglo-German parentage. In the novel's opening passage, Crusoe notes that his German father's family are the Kreutznaers "of Bremen," a city known for its ancient civic liberty (1). In 1404, a statue of Charlemagne's heroic knight, Roland, was erected in Bremen's Rathausplatz as a testament to the medieval trading privileges of the city. Throughout Europe, Roland statues are erected in locations that used the ancient Saxon law. Dietlinde Munzel-Everling explains that, by the middle of the thirteenth century, the "Saxon law and, in particular, the 'Sachsenspiegel' came to be considered as imperial law ('Kaiserrecht') set by the Christian rulers Constantine and Charlemagne.... The God-given sword "Durendart" carried by Roland symbolizes the divine origin of imperial law."[67] In this way, Defoe identifies Crusoe as an Anglo-German figure of ancient liberty authorized by a tradition of European imperialism that lays claim to holy ordination.[68]

The Kreutznaers of Bremen have emigrated to England where their name has been corrupted in a linguistic process prefiguring the novel's central concerns about alterations to its protagonist's character. In German, "Kreutzen" is cross, and the "Kreuzer" was a German coin with a cross on each face, signaling the mixture of religion with money, a key element of Crusoe's moral character and its failures. The name "Kreutznaer" is anglicized as Crusoe, perhaps via the French "Crusiaux," a toponymic surname from a diminutive of "creux," which means "hollow." The English corruption, via French, of the German surname "Kreutznaer" suggests etymologically the Norman invasion of the Anglo-Saxons in 1066. Robinson, or "son of Rob," is from Middle English "robben" via the Anglo-Norman "robber," from Late Latin "raubāre," from Frankish "raubōn" and Old High German "roubōn," which is to rob, steal, or plunder.[69] Crusoe's names suggest a motley combination of conquest, professed Christianity, theft, and capitalist accumulation commingled with the ancient constitution through the history of Saxon liberty embedded metonymically in Crusoe's family history. In this way, Robinson Crusoe is precisely the kind of true-born Englishman Defoe imagined in 1701, "Who, join'd with Norman French, compound the breed."

Defoe pens yet a further connection to the ideology of immemorial English rights when Crusoe's "very ancient" German father intends him "for the law" (5). Consumed by imperial desire, Crusoe balks at the domestic patrimony his ancient German father offers him: the English common law. Crusoe's seemingly originless desire to go to sea is, in fact, Defoe's imperial development of ancient constitutionalism, which sought to universalize English rights to property and labor by reimagining the source of those rights. In Bacon's words, this was "free trade without unjust Taxes," a theme that American colonists would elaborate in the next half century as the basis of their revolt against the Crown.[70] The original power of the people of England, which arose, Defoe said in *The Original Power*, from land ownership and labor power in England, gives way in *Robinson Crusoe* to an Atlantic frame in which English power could arise from land acquisition and labor ownership anywhere in the world. Defoe's protagonist personifies a profound insight that, in fiction and in fact—allegorically and historically—a new kind of Englishman was required by the Crown's vision for its expanding empire.

Calvin's Case and the Jurisprudence of *Robinson Crusoe*

In imagining Robinson thus, Defoe entered a long, consequential, and ongoing legal debate about the jurisdiction of the English common law. The lawyer

Richard West, in his capacity as legal adviser to King George I's Privy Council, articulated a theory of the English common law's universal jurisdiction in an influential opinion letter the year after Defoe published *Robinson Crusoe*. "[L]et an Englishman go where he will," West proclaimed; "he carries as much of law and liberty, as the nature of things will bear."[71] West went on: "the Common Law of England, is the Common Law of the Plantations, and all statutes in affirmance of the Common Law passed in England, antecedent to the settlement of a colony, are in force there, unless there is some private Act to the contrary."[72] As West saw it, and as contemporary charters affirmed, the common law followed Englishmen abroad and allowed for "contrary" measures to be added to their expressions of the common law by "private Act[s]."[73] He thus envisioned a transformation of the repugnance principle: instead of being restricted abroad by the domestic common law, Englishmen saw their overseas powers enlarged by neo-feudal alterations to that legal tradition.[74] By moving Crusoe through a variety of legal identities—unpropertied second son in England; Atlantic slave trader; naturalized Portuguese slaveholder in Brazil; slave in Sallee; and castaway in the Caribbean turned colonial governor—Defoe plots the possibilities and limits of English law and liberty at and beyond the ends of the empire. The question Defoe dramatizes in *Crusoe* is whether—and how—the protections of the ancient constitution followed Englishmen overseas: not merely as an emanation of the judicial system in England, but as an embodied, which is to say a racial, right to trade and command the labor of others.

Calvin's Case first considered the jurisdictional limits of the common law in a different form more than a century earlier, and the case remains a key precedent in the Anglo-American law of citizenship.[75] Robert Colville, called "Robert Calvin" in the court pleadings of his suit, was born in 1605 to Scottish parents living in Scotland. In 1608, an assize of novel disseisin[76] was brought on Robert Calvin's behalf by his guardians, John and William Parkinson, who alleged that Richard Smith and Nicholas Smith had "unjustly, and without judgment...disseised [Calvin] of his freehold...in the parish of St. Leonard" in Shoreditch, England.[77] The Smiths argued that, because Calvin, a Scot, was an alien in England, he could not assert freehold rights in the realm under protections of the English common law. Scottish by birth, that is, Calvin did not have access to the English jurisdiction in which his freehold claim to lands in Shoreditch could be adjudicated.

Calvin's guardians argued on his behalf, however, that the Scottish-born infant had in fact become an English subject when his sovereign, James VI of Scotland, ascended the English throne in 1603. This was, in part, the reasoning of the Norman Conquest: liegance followed the person of the king, so that when a monarch acquired a new realm, his natural-born subjects became so in all dominions under his sovereign body. In this way, King Charles II affirmed the rights of his English subjects in the colony of Jamaica after the Restoration; in 1701, Defoe would note a similar principle in *The True-Born Englishman*: William I's conquering "*Dutchmen*" acquired English freehold rights under his sovereign power.

At Robert Calvin's 1605 birth, King James had reigned as James VI of Scotland for thirty-eight years and as James I of England and Ireland for two years, encompassing the child's short life under both crowns. Thus, the infant Calvin owed liegance to James of Scotland and to James of England and Ireland. James owed Calvin reciprocal protection of liberty and property, which included Calvin's land claims in England. As Hulsebosch explains, this bond between sovereign and subject was created "naturally upon birth within the king's territory from parents who were under the king's obedience"; the subject's liegance to the sovereign was "spatial, temporal, and genetic" in character, binding James and Robert in an all-encompassing legal relationship that transcended national boundaries.[78]

Asserting the legal supremacy of Calvin's natural liegance to James's natural body, itself a racial idea, Calvin won his suit as well as English citizenship for all *postnati*, or Scots born after James's accession to the English throne. Scottish *antenati*, those born before James's accession in England, remained subjects of the Scottish king's political body only and thus could not access the protections of the English common law in the south. *Calvin's Case* had the watershed implication of making *postnati* Scots and Englishmen equal under the English common law and underscoring the national supremacy of the same.[79] As Defoe put it in *The History of the Union between England and Scotland*, "We could get a King anywhere, but England is the only country where we could get a Constitution."[80]

However, and as Coke emphasized in *Reports*, while the Scottish *postnati* were "subject to all services and public charges within this realm, as any Englishman," and enjoyed reciprocal access to the English monarch's common law courts, those courts did not have jurisdiction beyond England.[81] Further, the common law protections that the *postnati* enjoyed in England did not follow anyone—English, Scottish, or otherwise—abroad. As Hulsebosch writes, the king's "mandatory and remedial writs," which included all common law writs, did not in any sense extend beyond the realm. By contrast, the king's "mandatory and non-remedial writs," which required the subject to return to answer the king in person, were not tied "to any place" but rather followed the subject wheresoever he went.[82] The monarch thus had jurisdiction via subjection and liegance over all subjects in other dominions and at home, but the sovereign's common law courts did not. What changed, then, between *Calvin's Case* of 1608 and West's 1720 declaration that Englishmen carried "law and liberty" everywhere they went?

As Robert Calvin's case made its way through the courts, the Virginia Company, newly chartered by James I in 1606, prepared to found a new colony in North America, two decades after the disaster at Roanoke. James's capacious recharter granted the Virginia Company lands stretching 400 miles north-to-south on the eastern seaboard of North America and spanning westward. The kingdoms of Scotland and England, united at the head by James as of 1603, would now project their union abroad in a tract of land that colonial advertisers called "New Britain." Coke, who had drafted the Virginia Company's original charter under Elizabeth

I, would be influential in framing how lawyers and colonists understood the new imperial relationship between James's kingdoms of Scotland and England and his dominions in the western Atlantic.[83]

Borrowing from Roman law, Coke divided the sovereign's transatlantic land claims into those acquired through inheritance on one hand and conquest on the other. (There was, as yet, no legal category for a settlement in the king's name, although one would soon appear in the English legal imagination.) Coke further divided conquered lands into Christian and infidel territory, a contrast important for the limits on the monarch's lawmaking powers as well as the consequences for the legal rights of native inhabitants. In a conquered Christian country, the victorious sovereign was bound, Coke said, by pre-existing laws until they could be changed by the consent of the people expressed in representative assembly.[84] But in conquests of lands belonging to non-Christian people, the sovereign immediately, and without consent, could abrogate the laws because they were "against Christianity," "against the law of God and nature," and thus ostensibly an affront to the personage of the monarch.[85] While these categorizations had monumental implications for imperial rule, they were designed primarily as ballast for Coke's mythology of the ancient constitution: the Anglo-Saxons had *not* been conquered by the Normans in 1066, thus preserving the antiquity of the English people's rights.

Key to understanding the ancient constitution in *Robinson Crusoe* is a third category of land acquisition, neither by inheritance nor conquest, but by settlement. Although Coke never elaborated a theory of settlement in his writings, late seventeenth-century jurists and political theorists, most influentially John Locke in his *Second Treatise of Government* (1689), framed colonization as the settlement of empty land under the doctrine of *res nullius*, or the "property of no one." This is why finding a footprint on the Island of Despair is of prime real estate importance for Crusoe. As James Tyrrell argued in *Patriarcha non Monarcha* (1681),

> no man in the state of nature, had a right to more land or territory than he can well manure for the necessities of himself and Family; that is, can reduce into actual possession, otherwise a man that first sets his foot on an uninhabited island, would have an absolute right to the whole, even though it were a Thousand miles long, or to all the Territory he could discover with his Eyes, so that no man could make use of one foot of land, in that Island but by his permission.[86]

Tyrell's remarks are important for their definition of possession as an epiphenomenon of small-scale land husbandry, as well as their differentiation of "man in the state of nature" from those who had entered into the social contract. Defoe dramatizes the inherent instability of these categories in *Robinson Crusoe* by shipwrecking a highly socialized person on an island that is visited, but not evidently inhabited, by cannibals whom Crusoe sometimes regards as "national" (137). Locke's *Second Treatise* developed these ideas about the techniques of imperial possession, arguing that the labor required to settle overseas colonies created the laborers' property interest in the improved land: "this Labour being the unquestionable Property of the Labourer," Locke wrote, "no Man but he can have a right to what that is once joyned to, at least where there is enough, and as good left in common for others."[87] As Hulsebosch concludes, it "took little more to argue that English liberties were conveyed along with title."[88]

But which liberties were these? The subject's extranational liegance to the king, established by *Calvin's Case*, and reciprocal access to English common law courts, expanded in the intervening century to include at least some universal constitutional rights for Englishmen, most saliently jury trials and the protection of property contracts. The definitive event in this historical process may be best understood by looking backward from May 19, 1649. On that day, an Act of Parliament established the Commonwealth and thereby replaced the king's natural and political bodies. This feat was made possible by the execution of the king's natural body several months earlier, the incarnation of a racial link between subjects and sovereign established four decades earlier by the principle of liegance in *Calvin's Case*. This Act, and the new legal fiction of transatlantic English popular sovereignty it ushered in, declared that:

> The People of England, and of all the Dominions and Territories thereunto belonging, are and shall be, and are hereby Constituted, Made, Established and Confirmed to be a Commonwealth and Free State: And shall from henceforth be Governed as a Commonwealth and Free State, by the Supreme Authority of this Nation, The Representatives of the People in Parliament, and by such as they shall appoint and constitute as Officers and Ministers under them for the good of the People, and without any King or House of Lords.[89]

As Robert Schuyler has argued, this "tremendous innovation, for which no precedent can be found before 1649" made it "necessary that the [overseas] dominions be claimed as possessions of the English people unless the empire was to be dissolved."[90] Three years later, in 1652, the Anglo-German Robinson Crusoe, Defoe's avatar of the ancient constitution, sets out to make his own claim of dominion as an English person in the Atlantic economy underpinned by the English people's new overseas possessions.

After the Restoration in 1660—which returned overseas dominions to the monarch—suits including *Craw v. Ramsey* (1681), *Blankard v. Galdy* (1691), and *Dutton v. Howell* (1694) adjudicated an ongoing ebb and flow of Englishmen's rights, which had been extended into overseas dominions, and into the persons of Englishmen, during the Interregnum.[91] Said another way, these actions relocated the situs of common law protections from the realm of England to the natural bodies of English subjects, who could go anywhere in the world. In *Craw v. Ramsey*, the court ruled that a "subject born in any dominion belonging to the Crown of England is inheritable in England as well as native Englishmen. So the natural born subjects of Ireland, Guernsey, Jersey, Berwick, and all the English plantations inherit... they are born liege-men to the same king."[92] *Craw* also confirmed the supremacy of English law in the context of naturalization: "*Naturalizing* in *Ireland*," Sir John Vaughan ruled, "gives the same effect in *Ireland* as being born there, so in *Scotland* as being born there, but not in *England*, which consents not to the *fiction of Ireland* or *Scotland*, nor to any but her own."[93] Thus, the customary protections of the ancient constitution were attached by birth to the natural bodies of English-born children in any of the monarch's dominions; but the parliamentary process of naturalization had this effect only if it was conducted in England, creating slight but significant legal differences among the English, Irish, and Scottish.

Blankard v. Galdy adjudicated the extension of parliamentary statutes to overseas plantations. Because the English seized Jamaica from the Spanish, the plaintiff argued, English laws should rule "till the King shall think convenient to make any alteration."[94] Justice Holt disagreed, implicitly affirming the ancient constitution's survival of the Norman Conquest and extending the principle of ancient constitutionalism to Jamaica. Holt found that "[t]he laws by which the people were governed before the conquest of the island do bind them till new laws are given, and Acts of Parliament made here since the conquest do not bind them."[95] What in Coke's hands was a device for preserving a doctrine of uninterrupted English liberty became, in *Blankard v. Galdy*, a tool for smoothing the contradictions of imperial rule.

In *Dutton v. Howell*, Sir Richard Dutton sued for false imprisonment in Barbados. However, the Lords found that Howell, the colonial official who had conducted the imprisonment, was "not conusable [subject to legal jurisdiction] here in *Westminster-hall*" and rather was only "censurable by the King." Dutton argued by contrast that Barbados was a "new Settlement of *Englishmen* by the King's Consent in an uninhabited Country," thus opening Anglo-Barbadians' access to the King's common law courts in England, as Calvin had opened those same courts to the *postnati* Scots. Dutton asserted by extension that there is "no Reason why the *English* Laws should not follow the Person of *Englishmen*."[96] The Lords roundly rejected both of Dutton's arguments and held fast to the doctrine of the ancient constitution: because Barbados was known to have been inhabited upon the arrival of the English by the Tainos, Caribs, and—salient here—the Christian Spanish, English common law could not be established there without the consent of the Christian people assembled, as Coke had outlined. Howsoever the English claimed domestic supremacy of their common law, they could not indiscriminately assert that supremacy beyond the seas without calling into question their own tradition's survival of the Norman Conquest. Colonial pressures on the ancient constitution thus created a momentous paradox. On one hand, English law knew no territorial or geographical limits: each individual Englishman and his children were possessed of portable legal supremacy because their English bodies were invested via subjection with protections against tyranny promised by the ancient constitution. On the other, the English common law, as expressed in the court system of England, did not extend beyond the seas.[97]

The imperial creation of chattel property in slaves, another significant area of seventeenth-century rights expansion for Englishmen, proceeded in part by analogy to the racial principle of liegance through which Robert Colville had laid claim to his lands in Shoreditch. That is, the hereditarily enslaved person, like the king's natural subject, came to owe a personal duty of lifelong labor, as well as a genetic duty of progeny, to the slaveholder, who in this way held a neo-feudal sovereign power. Scholars often note the royal names that English planters gave to the African people they enslaved: Caesar, Primus, Hagar, Prince, Augustus, Nero, and so on. One interpretation of this convention is that slaveholders mocked the degraded condition of the people they owned.[98] But these names signaled in other ways. For the English, such conventions referenced a royal class of people an ocean away who created their absolute property rights in the persons they named accordingly.

Instead of enjoying reciprocal common law protections in exchange for their subjection, the enslaved person—who had no evident legal relationship to the English sovereign, and certainly did not owe him liegance—enjoyed few if any constitutional protections in the king's overseas dominions. Rather, the English slaveholder, who acquired abroad chattel rights in the enslaved, might seek to establish legal protections of those chattel rights through the trade mechanism Nathaniel Bacon described: "Merchants, had the like liberties [of freeborn Englishmen] for their persons and goods, concerning Trade." This would change if the enslaved person was brought under the jurisdiction of the English common law. As we will see in a later chapter, this is a question on which Lord Mansfield and Jane Austen would opine.

The legal condition of an enslaved person was thus degraded in transmutations of sovereignty that transfigured the natural relationship of subject–sovereign, via liegance, into the chattel relationship of slave–slaveholder, based on the legal principle of property ownership. This people-to-chattels conversion was enabled by racializing English common law protections overseas, a process set in motion by the legal history we have canvassed. After these developments, the slave owed his enslaver his life and the lives of his children. But, as Behn dramatized in *Oroonoko*, the enslaver's reciprocal duties were not protective of the enslaved person's rights. They were rerouted—through the animalization of Africans into livestock and emerging imperial labor markets—to the slaveholders' bottom line. English colonial slaveholders, despite being unpropertied in England could, under Bacon's logic, have "their liberties asserted by the Law" not because they were "*English Free-men* and Natives" but because they were, like Defoe's Crusoe, "Merchants"—that is, merchants of people.

Slavocratic Constitutionalism and Defoe's Western Atlantic

"West Indian constitutionalism," a term coined by legal historian Liam O'Melinn, illuminates how these legal developments altered the imperial constitution in practice.[99] A key example of this phenomenon occurred after the Restoration in the colony of Barbados, when King Charles bade Barbadian slaveholders to codify their regime of human bondage. As Edward Rugemer has shown, the Barbadian slave code of 1661 is, to the best of our knowledge, the earliest surviving example of Englishmen making, under the Crown's order, distinct legal systems for free and enslaved labor based on human skin color. In doing so, they created new racial rights of mastery for themselves.[100]

In the autumn of that year, Rugemer writes, "the newly elected Barbados Assembly formulated two distinct comprehensive labor codes: an Act for the Good Governing of Servants, and Ordaining the Rights between Masters and Servants, and an Act for the Better Ordering and Governing of Negroes." These titles clarify that "only servants deserved the codification of their 'Rights.' And while servants were named by the contracts they had signed, slaves were named as a peculiar people, Negroes."[101] In turn, this colonial legislation affirmed that planters owed reciprocal protections to their servants, similar to the way that King James I owed Robert Colville property protections in exchange for his liegance. But the Barbadians did not extend such equity to their African slaves.

Rather, they concluded in the 1661 code that "we are not to leave [our slaves] to the arbitrary, cruel, and outrageous wills of every evil disposed person, but soe farr to protect them as we doe many other goods and Chattels, and alsoe somewhat further as being created Men, though without the knowledge of God in the world."[102] By asserting that enslaved Africans were legally similar to "many other goods and Chattels," Barbadian slavocrats followed Crown jurists to create neo-feudal rights for absolute labor power. At the same time, the Barbadians recognized that enslaved people required more legal "protect[ion]" than goods because they were "Men, though without the knowledge of God." Here, there may be an important ideological link between the Barbadians' essentially rights-less Africans, "without the knowledge of God," and Coke's conquered non-Christians, who were immediately subject to the laws of their conquerors without consent. Indeed, the Barbadians' withholding from enslaved Africans of jury trials, freedom of assembly, habeas corpus, and other fundamental protections of the ancient constitution suggests their racializing impulse to emphasize that Africans were unchristian "goods and Chattels" while deemphasizing their acknowledged status as "created Men."

This legal process, by which Englishmen racialized colonial labor, was correlated to skin color according to a humoral-constitutional logic: English servants engaged in overseas indentures, exchanging self-owned labor through an act of will protected by ancient constitutionalist claims to liberty and property; these same servants, had they stayed in England, would not have been understood, at least by thinkers like Defoe, as "the people" because, like Robinson Crusoe, they had no freehold claims in the country. Enslaved Africans, by contrast, were legally consigned in Barbados to ontologic unfreedom by the English word "Negro," which no one in Africa understood herself to be prior to colonial contact. Although writers like Aphra Behn imagined African freedom from chattel status in the terms of repatriation, it is not clear that any significant number of African-descended people were able to return to their ancestral homes during the seventeenth and eighteenth centuries.[103] At the very least, this possibility does not seem to exist for the "Negroes" whom Crusoe enslaves in Brazil. In these ways and others, African-descended slaves in the western Atlantic were in a fundamentally different legal and geopolitical situation from that of their indentured counterparts.

The preambles of both Barbadian laws indicate that servants and slaves in Barbados were disposed to behavior their masters regarded as unlawful. But only "Negroes," Rugemer notes, were marked out for "inherent barbarism," their enslavability imagined by the English as ontological: "Negroes[,] ... *being* brutish Slaves," the Barbadian legislation proclaimed, was the basis of legal differentiation in the first place.[104] Underscoring the inborn nature of their own lawmaking powers, carried across the Atlantic, the Barbadians said that their 1661 code was meant to clarify the "Constitution of this Government in relation" to enslaved Africans, "to whom ... we may extend the legislative power given us of provisionary Lawes," so long as the new code was not "contradictory to the Lawes of England."[105] This is an extraordinary passage.[106] It shows the Barbadians invoking the ancient constitution to, in one absolutist stroke, racialize Africans and arrogate to themselves a legislative power distinct from Parliament's—so long as their new laws are not repugnant to the laws of England.

At the same time that Africans were reduced to the legal status of "goods and Chattels," the natural bodies of servants in Barbados were protected against the "Violence and great Oppression" of their masters; their marriages were acknowledged, so that husbands and wives who made the Atlantic passage together would be "sold and disposed of together, and not severed;" young servants, under 18 years of age, "having made no Contract in England or elsewhere" were protected from lifetime servitude by a legislative limit on service to "Seven Years and no longer."[107] Together, these enactments planted, along a burgeoning color line, some protections of the ancient constitution. At the same time, the slave code revoked from African-descended people due process protections that were the hallmark of the ancient constitution's celebrated protections of life and liberty.

The effect was to render slavocrats kinglike among their servants and godlike among their "Negro" slaves. By law, servants retained recourse against breach of labor contracts and physical abuse, mistreatment and abuse. Slaves did not.

Servants in Barbados would not be called "white" in the island's colonial legislation until 1699; nevertheless, the 1661 slave and servant codes were coeval, manifesting a binary between free servants and unfree slaves, as well as implying a corresponding color binary between white skin and black skin in the Acts' dependence upon the word "Negroes" to discriminate those people who did not enjoy labor protections against absolute power from those who did. When Crusoe sets out from Brazil on his slaving venture for "Negroes" in 1659, these legal developments in Barbados were yet on the horizon. Whether or not Defoe knew of them when publishing the *Crusoe* trilogy is less important than the constitutional potentials that Barbados, and other Caribbean claims—what Crusoe calls "our *English* islands"—represent in *Robinson Crusoe*'s constitutional experiment. Here, a brief history of the settlement of Barbados is important (35).

Prior to European colonization in the sixteenth century, the Tainos began arriving by canoe in Barbados from the Orinoco Valley around 350 CE, and they established settlements by 800 CE. Kalinago migrants, or Caribs—the people Crusoe believes himself to encounter on the Island of Despair—arrived in Barbados in the thirteenth century. The island was briefly claimed by the Spanish, and then by Portugal from 1532 to 1620. Blown off course in a voyage from Brazil to England, not unlike Crusoe's disastrous 1659 slaving venture, the first English ship touched the island by accident on May 14, 1625. Captain John Powell, who seems to have been unaware that his sovereign had died in March, claimed the island for James I.[108]

Two years later, King Charles I granted the colony to the Scottish Earl of Carlisle as a palatinate named Carliola, a fresh expression of Anglo-Scottish imperial unification demonstrated a half century earlier by *Calvin's Case*. As we have seen in our reading of *Oroonoko*, Carlisle's powers were extensive. Similar to the palatinate of County Durham—governed by bishops wielding kinglike powers and tracing its ancient liberty back to (no surprise) the Anglo-Saxons[109]—Carliola was subjected to expansive powers. As O'Melinn writes, English settlers under the overseas palatinate arrangement may have worried legitimately that they had emigrated to the Caribbean only to lose their freehold claims in Barbados, these claims' protection by the English monarch, and other customary rights that conveyed with English freehold.[110] Indeed, when Carlisle's first appointed governor, Charles Wolverstone, pledged to make a "Collony of the people" of the island by telling the Anglo-Barbadian settlers that they owed Carlisle liegance, the settlers responded that they had already elected their own Governor and claimed freehold lands for themselves. Taking up arms, they declared that they were entitled to "Inioy [i.e., enjoy] the freedome of Englishmen."[111] In response, Wolverstone granted them freehold rights in Barbados; the colonists in turn confirmed Wolverstone in the governorship and began paying rents to Carlisle.

Carliola's royal charter supported the Barbadians' claims against Carlisle in this struggle. "Whatsoever Lawes whither for the publique state of the province, or the private Utility of every man are appointed," it declared, "must be with consent of Councell, and approbacon of the free Inhabitants."[112] The 1627 charter also affirmed *Calvin*'s extension of common law protections to the king's overseas dominions. Barbadian freeholders were "to have and possesse [*sic*] all the Liberties Franchises & Privileges of this our Kingdome," which included rights to command the labor of others.[113] Three decades and a half later, as we have seen, these imperial rights would be enlarged in 1661 Barbadian legislation to include the slaveholder's hereditary power to command the bound labor of Africans in perpetuity. In turn, this expanded the possibilities for English property rights abroad to include the holding of lands in fee simple, the ancient constitutional protections afforded by subjection to the monarch, the power to assemble in advocacy for English "Liberties Franchises & Privileges," and a new racial power both to demand the natural liegance of slaves and their progeny, and to own and trade them as "Merchandise" under the protection of the laws.

Thus, when Crusoe was born in York city in 1632—without domestic landed interest, but nevertheless full of imperial ambition—precedents for his overseas attainment of something *like* English freeborn status through trade, freehold, and slaveholding were already set down in royal charter, imperial jurisprudence, and colonial practice. Crusoe's Atlantic story comprises the dizzying political, legal, and moral complexities of this historical process, as it was unfolding from Scotland to England, from Barbados to Jamaica, and the ocean's vast expanse between. By moving his title character through these jurisdictions, Defoe's plotline plumbs the strange new possibilities and limits of imperial constitutionalism, affording a novel forum for its arbitration. Even if such constitutionalism was not always, as in *Dutton v. Howell*, admissible in the courts at Westminster, Defoe had admitted it nevertheless into the jurisdiction of fiction.[114]

Crusoe's Glorious Revolution and the Mastery of Friday

By landing Crusoe alone, on an evidently uninhabited island, with supplies enough to settle there, Defoe invokes the many debates we have above summarized about the imperial doctrines of *res nullius*, inheritance, conquest, and settlement, as well as the evolving overseas power of the ancient constitution into a racial right to possess others as property in perpetuity. As Patricia Seed has argued, European powers had a variety of rituals for proclaiming overseas power of this kind, and Crusoe stakes his claim to the Island of Despair with English methods: erecting structures, building fences, and planting gardens.[115] It is notable that, in *Robinson Crusoe*, a novel centrally concerned with racial identity and its alterations, the "white" people in the novel are persistently identified, by both Friday and Crusoe, as European. This happens, for example, when Crusoe explains Friday's account of the Spanish Black Legend:

> [Friday] told me that up a great way beyond the moon, that was beyond the setting of the moon, which must be west from their country, there dwelt white bearded men, like me, and pointed to my great whiskers, which I mentioned before; and that they had killed much mans, that was his word: by all which I understood he meant the Spaniards, whose cruelties in America had been spread over the whole country, and were remembered by all the nations from father to son. (170)

Thus the Spanish, differentiated from the English in both nation and religion, are at times subsumed in the novel under the modern racial term "white." This appellation appears and recedes in *Robinson Crusoe* according to the political dynamics of the plot: in Crusoe's theological disagreements with the Spanish, national and religious identities prevail as indices of human difference; but in contact zones populated by non-European people, human complexion sometimes (although not always) overthrows nation and religion as the category of importance. A similar racializing phenomenon is at work in both Behn's *Oroonoko* and the Barbadian code of 1661, when people from Africa are called "Negroes," based on their complexion, despite their different places of origin. The disappearance of skin color in *Robinson Crusoe*, behind European national identity, is coherent with Seed's observation that rituals of imperial possession were motivated primarily by competition among Europeans.[116]

In 1519, the Coventry dramatist and barrister John Rastell noted these signs of English possession, with his regret that the English had not outpaced the Spanish and Portuguese in possession of overseas colonies:

> O what a thynge had be than
> yf that they that be englyshe men
> Myght haue ben the furst of all
> That there shulde haue take possessyon
> And made first buyldynge & habytacion.[117]

Crusoe repeats these acts of settlement on the Island of Despair, erecting several "buyldynge[s] & habytacion[s]," constructing a fence "so strong, that neither man nor beast could get into it or over it," and planting barley and rice (49). But at his 1659 landing on the Island of Despair, Crusoe is uninterested in claiming lands on behalf of the Commonwealth of England, its colonial administration guided by Cromwell's Western Design, or any other nation.[118] Rather, Crusoe styles himself "king and lord of all this country indefeasibly" with "a right of possession" (80). Crusoe goes on to imagine this dominion as precisely the kind of real property that preserved the original rights of freeborn Englishmen through primogeniture: "if I could convey it," he muses, "I might have it in inheritance, as compleatly [*sic*] as any lord of a manor in *England*" (80). In this way, Crusoe has become like one of Defoe's "Conquerors in After-Times" from the *True-Born Englishman*, following in the footsteps of William I.

Unlike the real Barbadian freeholders, however, who had subjected themselves to Carlisle in exchange for freehold claims on that other Caribbean island, the fictive Crusoe is subject only to himself. In time, when he acquires his own subjects in Friday, Friday's father, and an unnamed Spaniard saved from the cannibals, Crusoe styles himself with an "undoubted right of dominion," as "absolute lord and law-giver," and his people "perfectly subjected" (190). But, in the absence of contact with the wider Atlantic economy, Crusoe characterizes his time on the island as "my reign—or my captivity" (109). Here, Defoe suggests the necessity of trade to the development of Crusoe's overseas political rights on the program outlined by the king's courts. There is also an insight here that absolute sovereigns, like Charles I, could—indeed, had—become political prisoners of their own ambitions in combination with their people's ancient constitutionalist claims.[119] It is suggestive that Defoe stages in Crusoe's island government not the divine right of kings, but rather its alteration as a limited constitutional monarchy that allows for "liberty of conscience throughout [his] dominions" (190).

Crusoe's limited sovereign power on the island is accompanied by his compulsion to command the labor of others. But, while Crusoe exhibits a desire for labor power in Brazil to make his land valuable, his wish for a servant on the Island of Despair is motivated by a more powerful yearning to return to the wider Atlantic economy, where that island possession can be transmuted into monetary and social value, alongside his plantation and slaves in Brazil. In this way, Crusoe's mastery of his African slaves and his ambiguous labor relationship with Friday in the Caribbean dramatize important developments in imperial constitutionalism.

Even before we meet the man who will be named Friday, there is a place of subjection reserved for him in Crusoe's imagination: "I dream'd," Crusoe says,

> that as I was going out in the morning as usual from my castle, I saw upon the shore, two *canoes*, and eleven savages coming to land, and that they brought with them another savage, who they were going to kill, in order to eat him; when on a sudden, the savage, the savage that they were going to kill, jumpt away, and ran for his life; and I thought in my sleep, that he came running into my little thick grove, before my fortification, to hide himself; and that I seeing him alone, and not perceiving that the other sought him that way, show'd my self to him, and, smiling upon him, encourage'd him; that he kneel'd down to me, seeming to pray me to assist him; upon which I shew'd my ladder, made him go up, and carry'd him into my cave, and he became my servant. (157)

The dream is notable for its recapitulation of Crusoe's desire to leave the island he inhabits (first England, now this); its breathless conversion of cannibalistic consumption into voluntary servitude; as well as for its curious double vision. The narrator Crusoe can see the cannibals and "the savage that they were going to kill," but the Crusoe of the dream sees the fleeing savage "alone, and not perceiving that the other [savages] sought him." Without knowledge that the person at his castle door is a runaway from those who would consume him, the half-perceiving Crusoe of the dream—that is, the Crusoe who is unaware of the cannibals' lethal force—creates a servant, not a slave: "I shew'd my ladder, made him go up, and carry'd him into my cave, and he became my servant" (157).

Daniel Carey has argued that the presence or absence of mortal consequence in the novel is a significant index of historical difference between servitude and chattel slavery, over and above the racial distinctions that exist fictionally in Defoe's Brazil and factually, as we have seen, in Barbados. Friday "is not a slave but a subject," says Carey, "under the authority of a master whose political power is absolute. As a subject, he may owe his service but he is not held as property."[120] Carey supports this reading by showing that Crusoe cannot rightfully enslave Friday under the early modern theory of just war: because Friday is "innocent" with reference to Crusoe, with no evident designs on Crusoe's life, Crusoe cannot justly kill or enslave Friday in an act of self-preservation. Carey's interpretation is supported by other elements of the text, not least of all Defoe's plot which, for twenty-eight years, divides Crusoe from even the possibility of converting Friday into a chattel in the imperial economy.

In fact, Crusoe's earliest expressions of loneliness and anguish in the Caribbean are in the terms of specie rendered valueless by his solitary condition. Upon finding coins and precious metals in the wreck of his would-be slave ship, Crusoe cries out in despair, "O drug!... what art thou good for?... I have no manner of use for thee—e'en remain where thou art, and go to the bottom as a creature whose life is not worth saving" (47). As McKeon notes, "Robinson is not slow to realize that there is no marketplace to be found on the island."[121] With this detail—inverting Cortez's rumored claim before Montezuma's court that he and his men were sick at heart, and the only cure was gold[122]—Defoe prompts us to wonder if conventional colonial labor categories of servant and slave pertain in Defoe's legal fiction that removes Crusoe not only beyond the seas, but beyond the imperial economy. In this legal *terra incognita*, Defoe makes new claims for ancient constitutionalism abroad by drawing upon the revolution of 1688.

When Crusoe wakes, he experiences "a very great dejection of spirit" in finding that this new situation of mastery over a savage is no more than a dream (157). Anguished, he resolves to "get a savage into his possession," preferably "one of [the cannibals'] prisoners, who they had condem'd to be eaten," suggesting, along the lines of Carey's reading, that Crusoe seeks as a precondition of "his possession" a person he regards as uncivilized ("a savage") who also faces a particular kind of death and dishonor: the appalling transfiguration of a human being into food (157).[123] Crusoe's idea of colonial mastery emerges not through Giorgio Agamben's figure of *homo sacer*, the holy man whose only social purpose is to be sacrificed, but rather *homo vore*, the animalized man whose only social purpose is to be eaten.[124]

Similar to the real property claims Crusoe makes in the Island of Despair through English rituals of proprietorship, his dream of "getting a savage into [his] possession" is, as he says, "realized" through another distinctively English process, although perhaps not the one that Stephen, Marx, Joyce, Said, and others have perceived. Crusoe determines to rescue his "savage" from the cannibals who frequent the Island of Despair to ritually kill and consume their prisoners of war. At length, Crusoe wakes one morning to find "no less than five *canoes*" carrying two prisoners (158). The cannibals' first victim is "knock'd down," and the cannibals "were at work immediately cutting him open for their cookery" (159). While the hideous scene unfolds, the cannibals' other prisoner, "seeing himself a little at liberty," makes a break for it and runs, unbeknownst to him, toward Crusoe's "habitation" on the coast (159). Crusoe is overcome with fear at this turn of events, noting his expectation that "part of [his] dream was coming to pass" (159). Three of the cannibals pursue their runaway victim, coming to a deep creek at the edge of the island, swollen with the tide. One cannibal stops at the edge of the water; the other two continue their pursuit. "It came now very warmly upon my thoughts, and indeed irresistibly," Crusoe discloses, "that now was my time to get me a servant, and perhaps a companion or assistant; and that I was call'd plainly by Providence to save this poor creature's life" (160). Woven together here are Crusoe's imperial desire for overseas labor mastery, the irresistible nature of this feeling that compelled him to leave England in the first place, and the divine ordination Crusoe reads in these events. Prepared to die for his acquisitions, Crusoe takes up arms and runs down the hill from his hiding place, inserting himself "between the pursuers, and the pursu'd" (160). As Crusoe charges down the hill, Defoe orchestrates a striking set of resonances with the Glorious Revolution. These resonances are important because they show Crusoe embracing the constitutional principles of the Glorious Revolution, treating Friday as "the people" in one location while enslaving Africans elsewhere in the empire. As we will see, Defoe will ultimately figure such enslavement as Crusoe's original sin, despite his redemption of Friday from the cannibals' devouring tyranny.

Not wishing to alert the other cannibals with the report of a gun, Crusoe knocks down the first chaser with the buttstock of his musket; the second cannibal he shoots, however, to defend his life when the man takes aim at him with a bow and arrow. Seeing his pursuers thus struck down by Crusoe, the cannibals' would-be victim, whom Crusoe soon names Friday, begins to tremble with fear "as if he was taken prisoner" and about to be killed (160). Crusoe "gave him all the signs of encouragement," and the man comes nearer, kneels down, kisses the ground, lays his "head upon the ground, and taking [Crusoe] by the foot, set Crusoe's foot upon his head." Friday's enthusiastic ritual of subjection looks, at least from some angles, like his effort to enlist Crusoe as protection against the cannibals. Crusoe interprets

Friday's gesture as a "token of swearing to be my slave forever" (161). As Carey notes, Friday repeats this ritual later, in the absence of the cannibals' lethal force, and the episode is characterized by language of "subjection, servitude, and submission," but not slavery.[125] In this distinction, Defoe perhaps invokes just war theory as a legitimate basis for human slavery in the novel. Also absent from this scene is the stranded Crusoe's status as Atlantic "Merchant," which has created his slaveholding power in Brazil. These dual lacunae—the missing lethal force and the missing imperial labor power—indicate a difference between Crusoe's chattel enslavement of Africans in Brazil and his domination of Friday on the Island of Despair.

After submitting himself to Crusoe, Friday sees that one of his pursuers has awakened from the stupor Crusoe induced with a blow from his musket's buttstock. Friday swiftly takes the sword Crusoe lends him and beheads the disoriented cannibal with a stroke so efficient that, as Crusoe says, "no executioner in *Germany*, could have done it sooner or better" (161). This bizarrely specific remark, distinguished by italics and prickling with allusion, invokes the English people's execution of their sovereign in 1649, when the ax also fell once and cleanly. Rumors still circulate that an executioner for Charles was sought outside the country, Germany perhaps, because no Englishman could bring himself to behead his king. Richard Brandon, London's headsman, refused to carry out the sentence and was compelled from his home by a troop of horse to do the awful job. Even then, the question of who beheaded Charles I remained so contested that at least five men were accused of the deed, and William Hulett was condemned for it in 1660, eleven years later, before being pardoned.[126]

This peculiar detail of *Crusoe* is important because it signals Robinson's subjection of Friday in relation to a revolution in English constitutional history. The fates of the three cannibals who chase Friday—one stranded by the influx of the ocean, one beheaded, and one shot dead—reveal a Caribbean beach strewn with the bodies of the last Stuart kings. Charles I, we have noted, is figured as the cannibal whom Friday beheads. His son, Charles II, is insinuated into the scene by the first cannibal, who is stranded on the far side of the flood. In 1670, Charles II struck two treaties with his Catholic cousin, King Louis XIV of France. The first was a public treaty that aligned the English military with the French against the Dutch Netherlands in exchange for French monetary support for Charles II, which would make him financially independent of a close-fisted Parliament. The second treaty was a secret agreement, covered publicly by the first, promising French military support to Charles if he carried out his plan to convert openly to Roman Catholicism. In 1672, the English-allied French forces advanced on the Dutch Netherlands, and the Catholic invasion of William's Protestant republic was forestalled when the Dutch opened their Waterline's sluices, allowing the ocean to intervene, as it does on Defoe's imaginary island.[127] Finally, James II is implied by the cannibal whom Crusoe has shot and killed. Crusoe shows a curious Friday "the wound the bullet had made" in the cannibal's breast, "where it had made a hole, but no great quantity of blood had follow'd, but he had bled inwardly" (161). Crusoe's evidently bloodless dispatch of this cannibal references the Glorious, or Bloodless, Revolution, in which William and Mary overthrew James II at Parliament's behest with "no great quantity of blood" spilled, yet great inward bleeding in Scotland and Ireland.[128]

It would not be strange for Defoe to liken the Stuarts to *Robinson Crusoe*'s cannibals, signaling Charles I's crypto-Catholicism, his sons' actual Catholicism, and the wider English suspicion of transubstantiation as a form of person-eating. Embedded here is also Defoe's stringent critique of absolute monarchy, a system of government that, he believed, required the protections of ancient constitutionalism to prevent the enslavement of the English people. In *The Original Power*, Defoe held that "when the Governours devour the People they should protect...the People themselves, who are the Original of all Delegated Power, have an undoubted Right to defend their Lives, Liberties, Properties, Religion and Laws, against all manner of Invasion or Treachery."[129] As Defoe styles it in *Robinson Crusoe*, the Catholic Stuarts had been devouring the people of England since the English Civil Wars of Charles I's reign. Friday's righteous defense of his own life, and Crusoe's interventions in the cannibals' grisly depredations, examine in fiction the complex dynamics of absolute rule in tension with the people's ancient constitutionalist protections. What is more, *Robinson Crusoe* suggests that Caribs, like Aphra Behn's Africans in *Oroonoko*, can assert ancient constitutionalist protections in the same ways that Englishmen can.

When Crusoe sets out to take a "savage into his possession," he notably makes his way to the "*west* end" and to the "*south west*" corner of the Island of Despair. Here, again with italics, and in a register of historical allusion whose bizarre specificity distinguishes it from the surrounding text, Defoe reminds his English readers that they, too, recently had been saved from devouring Catholic absolutism when William III landed at Torbay. In this episode, Defoe invokes not just the "*south west*" corner of the Island of Despair, but also the southwest coast of England where William landed after the English people's invitation, through their representatives in Parliament, of William and Mary's revolution of limited constitutional monarchy. Similarly, Friday welcomes the relative safety of Crusoe's dominion by placing his "foot upon his head" (161). Then, Crusoe names Friday after "the day I saved his life" (163). Suggestively in Defoe's novel mythography of transatlantic constitutionalism, the day of William's ceremonial entry into Exeter as England's professed deliverer—November 9, 1688—was a Friday.

Original Sin and Racial Slavery in *Robinson Crusoe*

In *Culture and Imperialism* (1993), Edward Said invokes Joseph Conrad's *Heart of Darkness* (1899) to clarify the relationship he sees among salvation, redemption, and colonization. "Through Marlow," Said observes, "Conrad speaks of redemption, a step in a sense beyond salvation" because:

> if salvation saves us, saves time and money, and also saves us from the ruin of short-term conquest, then redemption extends salvation further still... in a structure that completely encircles and is revered by you, even though you set up the structure in the first place, ironically enough, and no longer study it closely because you take it for granted.[130]

In *Robinson Crusoe,* Defoe makes another distinction between salvation and redemption in the context of colonial acquisition and the ancient constitution—one that we should study closely, and no longer take for granted.

As we have seen on the beach of the Island of Despair, littered with cannibals who have died like English kings, *Robinson Crusoe* connects the twin European specters of Roman Catholicism and Stuart absolutism to Caribbean cannibalism: "I had rather be deliver'd up to the *savages,* and be devour'd alive," says Crusoe, "than fall into the merciless claws of the priests, and be carry'd into the *Inquisition*" (192). While morally and physically revolted at the anthropophagy of the Caribs, Crusoe expects that the Spanish Inquisition would be worse because of the greater claims it would make to his soul. Reasoning transatlantically, Crusoe introduces a kind of English (non-Carib and non-Spanish) and Protestant (non-pagan and non-Catholic) moral superiority into his framework for understanding the labor power he projects abroad. In this way, he transmutes the ancient constitution of the English, those ancient rights Defoe had glossed in *The Original Power,* into what Katharine Gerbner has called "Protestant Supremacy."[131] Crusoe's decision to value his English Protestantism more highly than other national-spiritual commitments is not without inward struggle: Crusoe attests that shedding others' blood is very "terrible" to him when he imagines using lethal force against the cannibals in order to acquire mastery over the local knowledge and labor power of their would-be victims. And yet, the "eager prevailing desire of deliverance" (158) from his "death of a life" (157) on the Island of Despair ultimately persuades Crusoe not only of the economic value, but of the moral righteousness, of possessing another person who can aid his return to the wider Atlantic world and its lucrative economy.

Here is the Christological metaphor of salvific deliverance from death, which Crusoe glosses to imagine himself like God in his redemptive dominion over others. The sin of Adam and Eve in the Garden was, likewise, the irresistible desire to be like God.[132] Earlier in the novel, Crusoe himself identifies this category mistake, of the human for the divine, with the Fall itself. Echoing the republican poet Milton, Crusoe acknowledges that his first disobedience was "the opposition" to "the excellent advice of my father," which grew from Crusoe's dissatisfaction with "the station wherein God and Nature hath placed" him (154). This "station," as we have seen, was as an unpropertied inhabitant of England with incomplete access to the promises of the ancient constitution. As McKeon notes, "What is crucial about Robinson Crusoe's achievement of social success is not the degree of his elevation but his capacity to justify each station to which he attains as the way of nature and the will of God."[133] Aspiring thus to more than his original position is Crusoe's "ORIGINAL SIN," and his "subsequent mistakes"—joining the African slave trade and setting out illegally to trade human beings in Brazil—were, he too-late realizes, "of the same kind" as the first (154). We have seen that they are also "of the same kind" made by the Barbadian authors of the 1661 slave code, at the behest of Charles II.

As Colin Kidd has written, "The sacred drama of Fall and redemption rests upon assumptions of mankind's common descent from Adam. Otherwise the transmission of original sin from Adam would not have polluted the whole human race" and "Christ's atonement...would not apply to the whole of mankind."[134] Defoe's complex study of Robinson Crusoe thus reveals a profound moral correlation between racial bondage in the Atlantic world and the fall of humankind. Often styled as the original sin of the American republic founded in 1776, Defoe's *Crusoe* reveals that this sin's roots are yet deeper in the imperial constitution of the English. In seeking to establish himself abroad as a holder of ancient English rights against sovereign prerogative—and of enlarged, neo-feudal rights to treat other human beings as chattels—Robinson Crusoe must overwrite "mankind's common descent from Adam" with an absolutist fiction of heritable, perpetual command of others. Adam and Eve discovered that they were naked; Robinson Crusoe discovered chattel slavery, what Paul Gilroy has called "capitalism with its clothes off."[135] Adam and Eve's sin is atoned for with Christ's universal sacrifice. The moral consequences of Crusoe's sin are visited on himself, now the imperial possessive individualist par excellence.[136]

There are significant racial consequences in the novel for Crusoe's unchecked accumulation of overseas land, wealth, and human beings. When a fleet of ships arrives in Lisbon, carrying all of the gains that Crusoe's African slaves have generated during his twenty-eight years as a castaway, he is seized by a strange fit of overwhelm: "It is impossible," he says, "to express the flutterings of my very heart, when I found all my wealth about me," and he soon "turned pale, and grew sick" (224). A cordial briefly restores Crusoe, but he succumbs again. A physician is sent for, and then—"something of the real cause of [Crusoe's] illness being known"—the physician "order'd [Crusoe] to be let blood; after which, [he] had relief, and grew well" (224). Without this intervention, Crusoe believes, he "should have dy'd." (224).

Crusoe's Anglo-German blood is spilled in this scene not for the salvation of humankind, but for the redemption of his investments in the slave trade. Bleeding preserves his natural body from a humoral glut activated by his extraordinary accumulation of capital: Crusoe is rich beyond even his wildest imaginings, and his wealth will ultimately allow him to retire to England.[137] Yet this accumulation is mostly without his own labor in Brazil, and despite the "*civil death*" he has suffered under Portuguese law according to his accountants in Lisbon (223). Crusoe's Anglo-Saxon blood,[138] the novel attests, is "the real" and "known" "cause of [the] illness" that nearly kills him. That bloodline, I have argued here, is the imperial constitution of the English, coming into being as a racial right to, among other things, buy and sell Africans as "Merchandise." Read constitutionally, *Robinson Crusoe* dramatizes a stunning correlation of original sin with the original property rights of the English people, now in force beyond the seas as a form of absolute power.

Notes

1. Daniel Defoe, *Robinson Crusoe*, 2nd edn, ed. John Richetti (New York: Penguin, 2003), 15. Hereafter cited parenthetically.
2. Crusoe says that the trade is "not only not far entered into, but as far as it was, had been carried on by the Assiento's, or permission of the Kings of *Spain* and *Portugal*, and engross'd in the publick, so that few *Negroes* were bought, and those excessive dear" (33).
3. September 1659 is also a crisis date in the late Interregnum. Parliament vacillated over constitutional reform, struggled to finance and control the army and militia, and fractured along religious and ideological lines, while army officers increasingly acted outside parliamentary authority. This breakdown would soon prompt intervention by General George Monck, commander of the English army in Scotland, who emerged in the following months as the key figure capable of restoring civil order. Ronald Hutton, *The Restoration: A Political and Religious History of England and Wales, 1658–1667* (Oxford: Clarendon Press, 1987), 59–65.
4. Stephanie DeGooyer has argued that, although Crusoe "is a natural-born subject of England, according to the law he could not have inherited real property before 1698 because his father was foreign-born. It was not until the Aliens Act of 1698 that natural-born subjects born to alien parents were permitted incorporeal rights attached to real property." Stephanie DeGooyer, *Before Borders: A Legal and Literary History of Naturalization* (Baltimore, MD: Johns Hopkins University Press, 2022), 87. Unpropertied, natural-born English subjects born of English parents obviously had no such "incorporeal rights."
5. Walter Scott, *The Miscellaneous Prose Works of Sir Walter Scott* (Paris: Baudry's European Library, 1837), 232.
6. Karl Marx, *Capital: A Critique of Political Economy* (New York: Modern Library, 1906), 88.
7. Leslie Stephen, quoted in *Defoe: The Critical Heritage*, ed. Pat Rogers (London: Routledge & Kegan Paul, 1972), 176.
8. James Joyce, "Lecture on Daniel Defoe," Università Popolare, Trieste, Italy, 1912.
9. Edward Said, *Culture and Imperialism* (London: Chatto & Windus, 1993), 70.
10. "The term *race* stands for the conception or the doctrine that nature produced humankind in distinct groups, each defined by inborn traits that its members share and that differentiate them from the members of other distinct groups of the same kind but of unequal rank." Fields and Fields, *Racecraft*, 16.
11. Roxann Wheeler, for example, has cataloged the uses of *Robinson Crusoe* in the racial colorism of the late twentieth-century United States. Wheeler, The *Complexion of Race* (Philadelphia: University of Pennsylvania Press, 2000), 49–89.
12. Daniel Defoe, *The Original Power of the Collective Body of the People of England* (London, 1702).
13. Defoe, *The Original Power*, 8.
14. Defoe, *The Original Power*, p. iii.
15. Defoe, *The Original Power*, 2.
16. Defoe, *The Original Power*, 20.
17. Edward Coke, *The First Part of the Institutes of the Laws of England*, ed. Francis Hargrave and Charles Butler, 18th edn, 2 vols. (1628; London, 1832), 11b.
18. Edward Coke, proem to *The Fourth Part of the Institutes of the Laws of England: Concerning the Jurisdiction of Courts* (1669; repr., London: W. Clarke and Sons, 1817).
19. It is worth underscoring that this is a biblical metaphor transposed into constitutional argument. See, for example, 1 Cor. 12: 12–27 and Rom. 12: 4–5 (King James Version).
20. Daniel J. Hulsebosch, "The Ancient Constitution and the Expanding Empire: Sir Edward Coke's British Jurisprudence," *Law and History Review* 21, no. 3 (Autumn 2003): 439–82, esp. 450.

21. Daniel Defoe, "An Explanatory Preface" and "The True-Born Englishman," in *The Earlier Life and the Chief Earlier Works of Daniel Defoe*, ed. Henry Morley (London, 1889), 179.
22. Defoe, "An Explanatory Preface," 179.
23. Defoe, *The True-Born Englishman*, ll. 114.
24. Defoe, *The True-Born Englishman*, ll. 181–89.
25. Defoe, *The True-Born Englishman*, ll. 190–93.
26. Defoe, *The True-Born Englishman*, l. 195.
27. Defoe, *The True-Born Englishman*, ll.196, 197, 201, 202.
28. Defoe, *The True-Born Englishman*, l. 203.
29. Defoe, *The True-Born Englishman*, ll. 194, 214, 226.
30. Defoe, *The Original Power*, 3.
31. Defoe, *The Original Power*, 18.
32. Defoe, *The Original Power*, 19.
33. As Laura Doyle has argued, "although the racialization of freedom was fed by the Atlantic slave trade and exploitative encounters with American Indians, this racialization...develops in an emergently transatlantic England in the 1620s through 1640s as what can rightly be called a post-colonial discourse...of Anglo-Saxon rights." See Laura Doyle, *Freedom's Empire* (Durham, NC: Duke University Press, 2008), 3.
34. Defoe, *The Original Power*, 19.
35. Defoe, *The True-Born Englishman*, ll. 140–45.
36. Defoe, *The True-Born Englishman*, ll. 151, 154.
37. Gerrard Winstanley, *Winstanley: "The Law of Freedom" and Other Writings*, ed. Christopher Hill (Cambridge: Cambridge University Press, 1983), 275.
38. Defoe, *The True-Born Englishman*, ll. 17–18.
39. Job 1: 13–22 (KJV).
40. Jay Fliegelman, *Prodigals and Pilgrims: The American Revolution Against Patriarchal Authority, 1750–1800* (Cambridge: Cambridge University Press, 1985), 77. Readers will note in Defoe's setting of Crusoe's story a clear echo of Behn's title character, suggesting the continuity of English interest in grappling with constitutional concerns in fiction.
41. Edward Coke, "Preface," *The Reports of Sir Edward Coke*, ed. John H. Thomas and John F. Fraser, new edn, 13 parts in 6 vols. (London: J. Butterworth & Son, 1826), 5.
42. Daniel Defoe, *Serious Reflections During the Life and Surprising Adventures of Robinson Crusoe: With His Vision of the Angelick World*, Part 3 (London: W. Taylor, 1720), sig. A2–A3.
43. For germane discussions of the tensions between fact and fiction during the early-modern period, see generally: Lennard J. Davis, *Factual Fictions: The Origins of the English Novel*; Thomas Koenigs, *Founded in Fiction: The Uses of Fiction in the Early United States* (Princeton: Princeton University Press, 2021); Barbara J. Shapiro, *A Culture of Fact: England, 1550–1720* (Ithaca, NY: Cornell University Press, 1991). Michael McKeon has noted in *Robinson Crusoe*'s journal the "ambiguous power both to confirm the historicity of those events by referring back to them, and to undermine their factuality by providing an alternative version of 'what happened.'" In this way, what McKeon calls the "peculiar existence of historicity and subjectivity in *Robinson Crusoe*" echoes Michel-Rolph Trouillot's definition of historical silence as the difference between "what happened and what is said to have happened." Part of what matters for our study of racecraft in *Robinson Crusoe* is that fact and fiction promiscuously trade places (both inside and outside the text), involving our own beliefs in the production of a novel category we still call "race." McKeon, *The Origins of the English Novel* (Baltimore, MD: Johns Hopkins University Press, 1987), 316; Michel-Rolph Trouillot, *Silencing the Past* (Boston: Beacon Press, 1995), 13.
44. Elliott Visconsi has called this the text's enactment of "equity," which is the idea that *Robinson Crusoe* is a "philosophical argument that makes affective and hermeneutic claims upon its readers." See Elliott Visconsi, *Lines of Equity: Literature and the Origins of Law in Later Stuart England* (Ithaca, NY: Cornell University Press, 2008), 191. Of further interest here are John Mullan's and Angus Fletcher's arguments about the purposes of literary texts in the real world, so-called. See generally: Mullan, *How Novels Work* (Oxford: Oxford University Press, 2006), and Fletcher, *Wonderworks* (New York: Simon & Schuster, 2021).
45. "The behavior of men in Hobbes's model of society is," MacPherson writes, "so anti-social, that when he carries this behavior into his hypothetical state of nature, it is there easily mistaken for a statement of the behavior of non-social men. But it is a statement of the behavior of social, civilized men." C. B. Macpherson, *The Political Theory of Possessive Individualism: Hobbes to Locke*, 2nd edn (Oxford: Oxford University Press, 2011), 22. Three years earlier, Toni Morrison had captured this very dynamic in her portrayal of Stuart England's barbarism, from which Jacob and Rebecca Vaark, not unlike their fictive contemporary Robinson Crusoe, seek escape. Toni Morrison, *A Mercy* (New York: Alfred A. Knopf, 2008), 76.

46. Linda Colley explains that "constitutions are often compartmentalized: treated as a category that is separate and distinct from other modes of literature and creativity"—and yet many "constitution-drafters, thinkers and advocates... were engaged as well in other literary and cultural activities." Indeed, Daniel Defoe, "a fierce Whig in politics," Colley notes, "has his hero produce—at the request of the inhabitants—'one general writing under my hand' for his no longer deserted island. Crusoe causes 'to be drawn up, and signed and sealed' a document which sets out 'the bounds and situation of every man's plantation.' 'As to the government and laws among them,' Crusoe tells them, he is 'not capable of giving them better rules than they were able to give themselves.'" Colley, *The Gun, the Ship, and the Pen* (New York: Liveright Publishing Corporation, 2021), 12, 212.
47. See generally: Brewer, "Common Law of Slavery."
48. Maximillian E. Novak, *Daniel Defoe: Master of Fictions: His Life and Ideas* (Oxford: Oxford University Press, 2001), 168–69.
49. George Boulukos, "Defoe and Slavery," in *Daniel Defoe in Context*, ed. Albert J. Rivero and George Justice (Cambridge: Cambridge University Press, 2023), 300.
50. Daniel Defoe, *Reformation of Manners, a Satyr: Væ Vobis Hypocritè* ([London?], 1702), 17.
51. Boulukos, "Defoe and Slavery," 300.
52. Daniel Defoe, *An Essay upon the Trade to Africa, in Order to Set the Merits of that Cause in a True Light and Bring the Disputes between the African Company and the Separate Traders into a Narrower Compass* (London, 1711).
53. William A. Pettigrew, *Freedom's Debt: The Royal African Company and the Politics of the Atlantic Slave Trade, 1672–1752* (Chapel Hill, NC: University of North Carolina Press, 2013), 15–17; Daniel Defoe, *An Essay upon the Trade to Africa.*
54. Tim Keirn, "Daniel Defoe and the Royal African Company," *Historical Research* 61, no. 145 (June 1988): 243–47.
55. Novak, *Master of Fictions*, 189–212.
56. Novak, *Master of Fictions*, 169.
57. Novak, *Master of Fictions*, 189–212.
58. Novak, *Master of Fictions*, 189–90.
59. Novak, *Master of Fictions*, 168–212.
60. Quoted in Novak, *Master of Fictions*, 181.
61. Novak, *Master of Fictions*, 189–212.
62. Defoe, *An Essay Upon the Trade to Africa*, 22.
63. Nathaniel Bacon, *An Historical and Political Discourse of the Laws and Government of England* (London, 1689), 9.
64. Bacon, *An Historical and Political Discourse*, 24–25.
65. Brewer, "Common Law of Slavery," 767–93. Robinson Crusoe's father, a German who "got a good estate by merchandise" in England, and not by inheritance, is perhaps suggestive of these legal developments. Doyle has argued that Crusoe is better understood as having followed his father's example rather than transgressing his command: "In turning west to seek his own estate and adventure, Crusoe simply emulates his father's entrepreneurial migrations" (*Freedom's Empire*, 187). Similarly, McKeon notes that "Robinson's father is a merchant who became successful through the sort of travel he now forbids his son" (*Origins*, 320).
66. Bacon, *An Historical and Political Discourse*, 170.
67. Dietlinde Münzel-Everling, "Imperial Law and Roland Statues," *Forum Historiae Iuris*, September 12, 1997. <https://forhistiur.net/en/1997-09-munzel-everling>
68. As recounted in *The Song of Roland*, the eleventh-century Anglo-Norman epic, Roland distinguished himself in Charlemagne's service at the Battle of Roncevaux Pass in the Pyrenees against the Saracens. According to *The Song*, Roland dies a martyr's death when, too late for his routed men, he blows the oliphant horn to summon reinforcements. Roland's last blasts on the horn are so forceful that he ruptures his temples, a scene to which Defoe perhaps alludes when, in *Robinson Crusoe*'s strange final scene in the Pyrenees, Friday shoots a bear in "his ear" (233). See *The Song of Roland*, ed. Gerard J. Brault (University Park, PA: Pennsylvania State University Press, 1978).
69. *Oxford English Dictionary*, s.v. "Robinson, n.," accessed July 2023. <https://doi.org/10.1093/OED/7491806709> "Robber, n.," accessed September 2023. <https://doi.org/10.1093/OED/1978146487>
70. Barbara Black, "Constitution of Empire: The Case for the Colonists," *University of Pennsylvania Law Review* 124, no. 5 (1976): 1157–1211; Charles Howard McIlwain, *The American Revolution: A Constitutional Interpretation* (New York: Macmillan, 1923); Robert L. Schuyler, *Parliament and the British Empire: Some Constitutional Controversies Concerning Imperial Legislative Jurisdiction* (New York: Columbia University Press, 1929).

71. Richard West, opinion on the extent to which the King's subjects who emigrated carried English law with them to the colonies (1720), quoted in George Chalmers, *Opinions of Eminent Lawyers on Various Points of English Jurisprudence* (London: Reed & Hunter, 1814), 1: 194–95.
72. West, quoted in George Chalmers, *Opinions*, 195.
73. West, quoted in George Chalmers, *Opinions*, 195.
74. On the repugnance principle, see generally: Mary Sarah Bilder, *The Transatlantic Constitution: Colonial Legal Culture and the Empire* (Cambridge, MA: Harvard University Press, 2004).
75. *Calvin's Case* (1608), 7 Co. Rep. 1a.
76. An assize of novel disseisin was a medieval and early-modern real estate action used to recover possession of land from which a freeholder had been recently and unlawfully dispossessed. Originating in the reforms of Henry II, the assize provided a jury-based remedy to restore the plaintiff to seisin (legal possession of a freehold estate in land) and determine whether the defendant had unjustly ousted the claimant. By the early seventeenth century, including in *Calvin's Case*, it remained a standard form for contesting wrongful dispossession of freehold estates. See generally: S. F. C. Milsom, *Historical Foundations of the Common Law*, 2nd edn (London: Butterworths, 1981), 137–40, 157–61.
77. Calvin quoted in Hulsebosch, "Ancient Constitution and Empire," 378. Hulsebosch explains that novel disseisin was a "medieval statute allowing a plaintiff 'recently disseised' of land to sue in the common law courts for repossession" (454–55). This means that, if a plaintiff's land is dispossessed, they can use the courts to assert title and regain practical control of their claim.
78. Hulsebosch, "Ancient Constitution and Empire," 456.
79. A similar phenomenon of English supremacy was asserted overseas; a striking example is of the copper crown given to Powhatan by the Privy Council, indicating the Indian chief's tributary relation to James I. Anthony Pagden, *Lords of All the World: Ideologies of Empire in Spain, Britain and France c. 1500–c. 1800* (New Haven: Yale University Press, 1995), 65.
80. Daniel Defoe, *The History of the Union between England and Scotland, with a Collection of Original Papers Relating Thereto*, with a life of Defoe by George Chalmers (London: John Stockdale, 1786), 73.
81. Hulsebosch, "Ancient Constitution and Empire," 456.
82. Hulsebosch, "Ancient Constitution and Empire," 457.
83. Hulsebosch, "Ancient Constitution and Empire," 460.
84. Coke did not specify whether this assembly had to be local or in London, a question that ultimately would be resolved by the American Revolution.
85. Hulsebosch, "Ancient Constitution and Empire," 461.
86. Quoted in Manuel Schonhorn, *Defoe's Politics: Parliament, Power, Kingship, and Robinson Crusoe* (Cambridge: Cambridge University Press, 1991), 156.
87. John Locke, *Two Treatises of Government*, ed. Peter Laslett (Cambridge: Cambridge University Press, 1988), 288.
88. Hulsebosch, "Ancient Constitution and Empire," 471.
89. "Act Declaring and Constituting the People of England to Be a Commonwealth," in *Acts and Ordinances of the Interregnum, 1642–1660*, ed. C. H. Firth and R. S. Rait, vol. 2 (London: His Majesty's Stationery Office, 1911), 122, accessed October 28, 2023. <http://www.british-history.ac.uk/no-series/acts-ordinances-interregnum>
90. Schuyler, *Parliament and the British Empire*, 7.
91. *Craw v. Ramsey* (1681) Vaughan 274; *Blankard v. Galdy* (1691) 4 Mod. 222, 2 Salk. 411, Holt K.B. 341; *Dutton v. Howell* (1694) 1 Show. P.C. 24.
92. Hannah Weiss Muller, *Subjects and Sovereign: Bonds of Belonging in the Eighteenth-Century British Empire* (Oxford: Oxford University Press, 2017), 29; see also Corinne Comstock Weston and Janelle Renfrow Greenberg, *Subjects and Sovereigns: The Grand Controversy of Sovereignty in Stuart England* (Cambridge: Cambridge University Press, 1981).
93. Vaughan 274, 280.
94. Hulsebosch, "Ancient Constitution and Empire," 473.
95. *Blankard v. Galdy* (1693), 2 Salk. 411, 412 (K.B.), quoted in Hulsebosch, "Ancient Constitution and Empire," 473.
96. Dutton v. Howell [1693] 1 Eng. Rep. 17.
97. Holly Brewer, *By Birth or Consent* (Chapel Hill, NC: University of North Carolina Press, 2005).
98. Sharon Block, *Colonial Complexions* (Philadelphia: University of Pennsylvania Press, 2018), 97.
99. Liam Séamus O'Melinn, "The American Revolution and Constitutionalism in the Seventeenth-Century West Indies," *Columbia Law Review* 95, no. 1 (1995): 105.
100. The Barbadian slave code of 1661 references earlier enactments for the governance of slaves. As far as I know, the text of the earlier legislation has, so far, been lost to history. Rugemer writes,

however, that as early as 1654, during the Interregnum, the clerk of court in English Barbados, John Jennings, published "a slim volume of Barbadian law... which illuminates the dialectical contest between masters, servants, and slaves." Rugemer, *Slave Law*, 23.

101. Rugemer, *Slave Law*, 28.
102. "Barbados Slave Code," 1661, CO 30/2, The National Archives (UK), Kew.
103. As Henry Louis Gates, Jr. explains, Harry Washington, a groomsman enslaved by George Washington, was the rare case of an African-descended person who settled in Africa following his enslavement at Mount Vernon. Harry Washington resettled as part of a post-Revolutionary recolonization scheme pursued in the late eighteenth century by the newly founded republic; but, in the likely event that Harry Washington was an American-born slave, his move to Africa was not a return of the kind that Aphra Behn imagines in *Oroonoko*. Gates, quoted in *The Black Atlantic: 1500–1800*, directed by Phil Bertelsen, Asako Gladsjo, Leslie Sabin, Sabin Streeter, and Jamila Wignot (Public Broadcasting Service, 2013), 42:30–45:30. <https://video.alexanderstreet.com/watch/the-black-atlantic-1500-1800>
104. Rugemer, *Slave Law*, 28–29, my emphasis.
105. Quoted in Rugemer, *Slave Law*, 29.
106. Compare to Orlando Patterson's idea that "the social construction of freedom was made possible by the relation of slavery. Slavery had to exist before people could even conceive of the idea of freedom as a value, that is to say, find it meaningful and useful, an ideal to be striven for." See Orlando Patterson, "Freedom, Slavery, and the Modern Construction of Rights," in *The Cultural Values of Europe*, ed. Hans Joas and Klaus Wiegandt, tr. Alex Skinner (Liverpool: Liverpool University Press, 2008), 117.
107. William Rawlin (ed.), *The Laws of Barbados Collected in One Volume by William Rawlin, of the Middle-Temple, London, Esquire, and Now Clerk of the Assembly of the Said Island* (London: Printed for William Rawlin, 1699), 30.
108. Vincent T. Harlow, *A History of Barbados, 1625–1685* (Oxford: Clarendon Press, 1926); Hilary Beckles, *A History of Barbados: From Amerindian Settlement to Caribbean Single Market* (Cambridge: Cambridge University Press, 2007).
109. Jean Scammell, "The Origin and Limitations of the Liberty of Durham," *English Historical Review* 81, no. 320 (1966): 449–73.
110. O'Melinn, "The American Revolution," 124.
111. Quoted in O'Melinn, "The American Revolution," 125.
112. O'Melinn, "The American Revolution," 125.
113. O'Melinn, "The American Revolution," 125.
114. This reading of Crusoe coheres broadly with Bradin Cormack's conclusion that "literary engagement with early modern jurisdiction becomes exemplary, not (according to a familiar historicist model) because literature supports or resists particular developments in Tudor and Stuart law and governance, but because it is implicated in the same process of shaping unruly practice for which jurisdiction itself stands." Bradin Cormack, *A Power to Do Justice: Jurisdiction, English Literature, and Common Law* (Chicago: University of Chicago Press, 2008), 3–4.
115. Patricia Seed, *Ceremonies of Possession in Europe's Conquest of the New World, 1492–1640* (Cambridge: Cambridge University Press, 1995).
116. See also Wheeler's *Complexion of Race*.
117. John Rastell, *A New Interlude and a Mery of the Nature of the Four Elements* (ca. 1519), reprinted in *The First Three English Books on America*, ed. Edward Arber (Birmingham, 1885), p. xxi.
118. Underscoring Robinson Crusoe's Portuguese naturalization in Brazil, Stephanie DeGooyer has argued persuasively that Defoe's title character is best understood as a figure for the porousness of national borders during the eighteenth century. Crusoe's adoption of English customs and reenactment of English history on the Island of Despair, following his naturalization as a Portuguese citizen, affirms DeGooyer's finding that the acquisitive Robinson Crusoe is no respecter of national boundaries or customs. See DeGooyer, *Before Borders*, 95–100.
119. Robertson, *Tyrannicide Brief*, 25.
120. Daniel Carey, "Reading Contrapuntally: *Robinson Crusoe*, Slavery, and Postcolonial Theory," in *The Postcolonial Enlightenment: Eighteenth-Century Colonialism and Postcolonial Theory*, ed. Daniel Carey and Lynn Festa (New York: Oxford University Press, 2009), 123.
121. McKeon, *Origins*, 324. Furthermore, McKeon notes, in Crusoe's state of solitude on the Island of Despair, "the greatest impediments to ethical behavior—other people—suddenly disappear." At the same time, in such perfect solitude, "divinity itself, the absolute moral standard" can be "internalized within one's own desires" (323). As we will see at length, a significant part of *Robinson Crusoe*'s racializing drama is when Defoe's protagonist realizes the extraordinary wealth he has accumulated in African slaves, despite his imagined separation from the global

economy. As Crusoe subsumes "the absolute moral standard" of the divine within his "own desires," he simultaneously acquires a capacious chattel property interest in other human beings.

122. Stephen Greenblatt, *Marvelous Possessions: The Wonder of the New World* (Chicago: University of Chicago Press, 2017), 170.
123. There is an important parallel here in the conversion of people into livestock under the chattel principle of racial slavery. For a discussion of the symbolic and political role of animals in the symbolic field of *Robinson Crusoe* and other novels, see Heather Keenleyside, *Animals and Other People: Literary Forms and Living Beings in the Long Eighteenth Century* (Philadelphia: University of Pennsylvania Press, 2016).
124. Giorgio Agamben, *Homo Sacer* (Stanford, CA: Stanford University Press, 1998).
125. Carey, "Reading Contrapuntally," 163.
126. "Brandon, Richard (d. 1649)," *Oxford Dictionary of National Biography* (Oxford University Press), https://doi.org/10.1093/ref:odnb/3266; Historic Royal Palaces, "Banqueting House: The Execution of Charles I,", accessed July 31, 2023. <https://www.hrp.org.uk/banqueting-house/history-and-stories/the-execution-of-charles-i/>
127. Encyclopaedia Britannica Online, s.v. "Dutch War," accessed July 24, 2014. <https://www.britannica.com/event/Dutch-War>
128. Of particular importance is the 1692 Glencoe Massacre, when thirty-seven members of the MacDonald clan were killed by the British military after the chief of the clan delayed swearing an oath of allegiance to William III. Encyclopaedia Britannica Online, s.v. "Massacre of Glencoe," accessed October 14, 2023. <https://www.britannica.com/event/Massacre-of-Glencoe>
129. Defoe, *The Original Power*, 16.
130. Said, *Culture and Imperialism*, 69.
131. Similar to my argument about the importance of the Barbadian slave code of 1661, Katharine Gerbner cites this colonial legislation as a key document in the differentiation in Barbados of "Negroes," the people Crusoe enslaves in Brazil, from "Christian servants," which Friday becomes on the Island of Despair (42–45). Katharine Gerbner, *Christian Slavery: Conversion and Race in the Protestant Atlantic World* (Philadelphia: University of Pennsylvania Press, 2018), 42–45.
132. See generally J. B. Stump and Chad Meister (eds), *Original Sin and the Fall: Five Views* (Westmont, IL: IVP Academic, 2020).
133. McKeon, *Origins*, 336.
134. Colin Kidd, *The Forging of Races: Race and Scripture in the Protestant Atlantic World, 1600–2000* (Cambridge: Cambridge University Press, 2006), 25.
135. Paul Gilroy, *The Black Atlantic* (Cambridge, MA: Harvard University Press, 1993), 40.
136. Ian Watt, *The Rise of the Novel: Studies in Defoe, Richardson and Fielding* (Berkeley, CA: University of California Press, 1967), 60–92.
137. *The Farther Adventures of Robinson Crusoe* concludes with Crusoe in England: "To conclude: having stay'd near four Months in Hamburgh, I came from thence over Land to the Hague, where I embark'd in the Pacquet, and arriv'd in London the 10th of January, 1705, having been absent from England ten Years and nine Months. And here, resolving to harass myself no more, I am preparing for a longer Journey than all these, having liv'd 72 Years a Life of infinite Variety, and learn'd sufficiently to know the Value of Retirement, and the Blessing of ending our Days in Peace." See Daniel Defoe, *The Farther Adventures of Robinson Crusoe; Being the Second and Last Part of His Life, and of the Strange Surprising Account of His Travels Round Three Parts of the Globe*, 3rd edn (London: Printed for W. Taylor, 1722), 318.
138. For discussion of blood as a metaphor for heredity see Staffan Müller-Wille and Hans-Jörg Rheinberger, *A Cultural History of Heredity* (Chicago: University of Chicago Press, 2012), esp. 48–49, 53, 103, 122, 204, 206, 208; see also Brooke N. Newman, *A Dark Inheritance: Blood, Race, and Sex in Colonial Jamaica* (New Haven: Yale University Press, 2018).

Novel Constitutions and the Making of Race: A Literary and Legal History of Slavery in the Anglophone Atlantic, 1688–1818.
Sarah Marsh, Oxford University Press. © Sarah Marsh 2026. DOI: 10.1093/9780197917855.003.0003

3

Olaudah Equiano Petitions the Queen

Christian Constitutionalism in *The Interesting Narrative*

In March of 1788, a man signing himself Gustavus Vassa submitted an anti-slavery petition to Queen Charlotte of Great Britain and Ireland. This is how it began:

> *To the* QUEEN's *most Excellent Majesty*
>
> MADAM,
>
> Your Majesty's well known benevolence and humanity emboldens me to approach your royal presence, trusting that the obscurity of my situation will not prevent your Majesty from attending to the sufferings for which I plead.
>
> Yet I do not solicit your royal pity for my own distress; my sufferings, although numerous, are in a measure forgotten. I supplicate your Majesty's compassion for millions of my African countrymen, who groan under the lash of tyranny in the West Indies.[1]

One year later, in 1789, Vassa would publish under two names *The Interesting Narrative of the Life of Olaudah Equiano, or Gustavus Vassa, the African. Written by Himself*, which he addressed "To the Lords Spiritual and Temporal, and the Commons of the Parliament of Great Britain" (7). The *Narrative* ends by reprinting the above appeal to Charlotte, who at the time was Queen Consort as well as Regent to King George III.[2]

In addressing himself to Parliament—and to a Queen who as Regent would assume the monarch's responsibilities (including leadership of the Anglican Church) should the King be incapacitated—Equiano signals the broad constitutional dimensions of his anti-slavery appeal. This chapter contends that Equiano's *Narrative* reimagines the ancient constitutionalism of the English in a deracializing Christian register, underscoring the illegitimacy of British colonial governments through which slavocrats abroad, like Robinson Crusoe, grasped at absolute power to enslave Africans under the legal fiction that a person could be traded as a thing. Accordingly, we will read the *Interesting Narrative* as a constitutional reckoning with colonial slavery, from the position of Equiano's Christian theology.[3] Read in this way, the *Narrative* appeals to Queen, Church, and Parliament for abolition by recounting its author's religious conversion. Equiano makes this appeal by affirming God's ultimate sovereignty—over and above the sovereignty of slaveholders—and, in doing so, dramatizing a fundamental moral contradiction within the imperial constitution: Britain's enslavement of baptized Christians.

Equiano's *Interesting Narrative* thus opens an important new stage in the argument of *Novel Constitutions*. The shift from Behn and Defoe to Equiano in this chapter marks not only a change in what we would call our author's racial identity, but a shift in the location and meaning of Atlantic constitutional discourse that created at law the racial identities that are with us still. In this way, we pivot here from English authors, who grapple with the legal fictions of their Atlantic empire, to a Black Atlantic writer whose autobiographical act of truth telling exposes those fictions from within, a process through which Equiano ultimately understands himself to become English. While *Oroonoko* and *Robinson Crusoe* dramatize how divine-right sovereignty and the property protections of ancient constitutionalism were adapted into chattel slavery based on race, Equiano's *Interesting Narrative* dramatizes by contrast how those remaining elements of ancient constitutionalism—the life and liberty of the subject, particularly in their spiritual dimensions—became fundamental features of the Black Atlantic literary tradition.

For this reason, Equiano's *Interesting Narrative* is a foundational Black Atlantic freedom text, echoing the 1689 Declaration of Right and unfolding alongside the revolutionary moment of 1776. In 1993, Paul Gilroy introduced the concept of a "Black Atlantic" as a transnational counterculture of modernity, formed through the forced and chosen movements of people, texts, and ideas across the Atlantic world. For Gilroy, the Black Atlantic is not a stable cultural origin with "roots" but rather a mobile, hybrid formation produced through displacement, maritime circulation, and the "routes" of diaspora.[4] Equiano's life and autobiography exemplify this set of cultural conditions with unusual clarity. His story unfolds across shifting domestic and imperial jurisdictions—Igboland, Barbados, Virginia, the Atlantic Ocean, Philadelphia, London—and cannot be contained within a single national or constitutional frame. Yet rather than dissolving his political thought into a cosmopolitan abstraction, Equiano anchors this transatlantic subjectivity in specific constitutional claims about life and liberty—and therefore legal personhood—within a transcendent theological framework of Christian fellowship.

In this sense, Equiano's Black Atlantic does not displace the constitutional discourse within which chattel slavery developed but instead reorients that discourse against the neo-feudal fictions of race promoted by Stuart imperial rule. Indeed, the central ideological target of the *Interesting Narrative* is the transformation of human beings into masters and chattel slaves, which in the previous century had been grounded in the political theology of the divine right of kings. Equiano was perhaps unaware of the specific high-court maneuvers of jurists like Sir Henry Spelman that brought about this change in English imperial policy; Equiano was, however, a firsthand witness to their long-term effects. His spiritual labor in the *Narrative*—through which he establishes his identity as a brother in Christ against imperial counterclaims of his status as property—offers further evidence for a central claim of *Novel Constitutions*: that English slavocracy emerged through selective assertions of patriarchal relationship, affirmed under divine-right monarchy and disavowed in chattel slavery. Indeed, Equiano would conceive of abolition as the legal expression of Christian siblinghood, a leveling of hierarchical relations established by law between kings and subjects or masters and slaves. These hierarchies all derived from the patriarchal principle behind claims to absolute, godlike power.

During the reign of the Stuarts, that transformation of people into masters and chattel slaves depended not only on revived doctrines of villeinage and emerging theories of liegance, but also on the juridical construction of non-Christian "aliens" or "infidels," who were legally exterior to the political body of the monarch's subjects—and therefore eligible to be held and traded as property. In *Butts v. Penny* (1677) for example, judges explicitly justified property in enslaved people on the grounds that they were "heathens," and therefore outside the protections of the English constitution and the king's courts.[5] In our reading of *Robinson Crusoe*, we saw that Coke's ancient constitutional theory held that a conqueror of Christians was bound by their laws, but the laws of non-Christian peoples could not bind a Christian, English sovereign. Seeking the reversal of these doctrines by spiritual means, Equiano elevates Christianity as a transoceanic high court, one in which an enslaved person could assert legal standing, human status, and moral membership against an imperial racial order that had stripped him of all three.

Equiano, then, does not stand in opposition to Behn and Defoe so much as he writes from within the imperial constitutional system they narrate, offering a firsthand account of racial slavery's consequences for the chattelized person. Where Behn and Defoe register the transatlantic contradictions of English constitutionalism from the vantage point of imperial and colonial authority, Equiano exposes those contradictions from the standpoint of a human chattel—where fictions of race become real-life circumstances. All three writers engage the same Atlantic order, but importantly chose different genres to express the constitutional currents they observed: Behn seems to have blended fiction with personal narrative; Defoe wrote a novel; Equiano turned to autobiography.[6] These forms' professed relationships to veracity describe precisely the literary consequences of Atlantic world racecraft: what appears in *Oroonoko* and *Robinson Crusoe* as racial fiction is, in *The Interesting Narrative*, oppositional sworn testimony. In what follows, we weigh its truth.

Equiano and the Constitution of the Black Atlantic

Equiano's *Narrative* is a story of the author's childhood kidnapping by African slave traders in Igboland, and his harrowing Middle Passage to chattel slavery under Anglo-American colonists in Barbados and Virginia. Equiano recounts his subsequent service as a bound member of the British Navy during the Seven Years' War, defending the maritime interests of the imperial power that enslaves him. Importantly, Equiano highlights his 1759 Christian baptism, at St Margaret's Church, Westminster, as well as his subsequent betrayal by his slavemaster, Henry Pascal; Pascal has Equiano removed forcibly from London in a second Middle Passage, despite the latter's consecration in baptism. The *Interesting Narrative* then builds toward the year 1766, when Equiano's parliamentary audience repealed the Stamp Act (1765) and asserted authority over the American colonies with the Declaratory Act. As the American chapter of imperial Britain's constitutional crisis unfolded, Equiano describes how he was in Montserrat purchasing his freedom from the Quaker slaveholder, Robert King. Thus manumitted through self-purchase, Equiano began a new life as a merchant, slave overseer, missionary, and ultimately a London abolitionist after finding human slavery (even in ameliorated form) incompatible with his 1775 conversion to Christianity, some sixteen years after his London baptism. Through his dramatic autobiography of spiritual transformation within Britain's transatlantic chattel system, Equiano advocates a parallel conversion for the British government to a constitutional stance against colonial slavery.

Moving across numerous Atlantic jurisdictions of the ancient constitution in an era of its crisis and reinvention, Equiano's *Narrative* is a story of how one man liberated himself from racial slavery, in spirit and in law, just as American colonists were asserting a fundamental equality that empowered them to declare their own independence from Britain while clinging to fictions of racial inequality to justify the institution of human slavery. This last American bastion of divine-right monarchy would require another Civil War to resolve.[7] Equiano mentions the American Revolution only peripherally in the *Narrative*, perhaps because of the charged political meanings it still held for his readers in Britain.[8] Yet, his coincidental endeavors realize his and others' liberty—through free trade, religious conversion, political abolitionism, parliamentary procedure, and royal redress. Moreover, those endeavors illuminate how people enslaved in the Atlantic chattel system adopted and adapted the claims of ancient constitutionalism against tyranny, in parallel with their Anglo-American contemporaries.

However, while American revolutionaries renounced their subjectship to King George III in their Declaration of 1776, Equiano asserted a rights-conferring subjectship to Queen Charlotte as her "servant to command" on behalf of enslaved "millions of [his] African countrymen." Indeed, when Equiano wrote to Charlotte in 1788, he addressed a monarchy whose power was constitutionally limited, as of 1688, in a way that American slaveholding power would not be until the following century. This complex bifurcation of interests, between slavocratic republicanism in Britain's (former) colonies and constitutional monarchy in the metropole, exposes how the racialization of the imperial constitution along the western Atlantic rim was shaping transatlantic politics during the American rebellion and the rise of transatlantic abolitionism.[9] As we have seen in *Oroonoko* and *Robinson Crusoe*, that racialization was accomplished through colonial slavocrats' adoption of neo-feudal, Stuart-era policies to establish hereditary property in persons. The contradictions produced by this imperial legal process are why, in Samuel Johnson's famous phrase, one could hear—indeed, would *expect* to hear—"the loudest yelps for liberty among the drivers of Negroes."[10]

Equiano, of course, was never subject to Stuart absolutism. But he was enslaved under its racialized adaptations in Barbados and Virginia, where slavocrats developed chattel slavery for African-descended people beyond parliamentary regulation. These colonial slavocracies expanded their chattel regimes by arrogating to slaveholders traditional forms of sovereign power over life and death, and by creating a new commercial power to buy and sell. As we saw in *Robinson Crusoe*, the possibilities of new kinds of property represented by overseas markets, including human chattels, proved irresistible to unpropertied Englishmen who sought the ancient constitution's promises of freedom as the protection of life, liberty, and property overseas. Equiano comments on this dimension of Britain's imperial constitution when, during his colonial enslavement, he says that "by selling my goods when we arrived at Montserrat, I should have enough to purchase my freedom" (133).

Even after his self-purchase and manumission, and in full knowledge of "the anguish, and the horror" of chattel slavery, Equiano joins a slave-trading and missionary expedition on the advice of friends as a way of raising his fortunes within the transatlantic British system (50).[11] Like Robinson Crusoe, Equiano seems at first to think better of his venture; yet, although he is "happy…amongst [his] friends and brethren" in London, he is persuaded nevertheless to join a slaving expedition by his friend Dr Irving, who has a plan for a "new adventure in cultivating a plantation at Jamaica and the Musquito Shore" (202). Irving convinces Equiano to join the expansion of the British plantation system he has lately escaped by appealing to Equiano's inward sense of personal credit, remarking "that he would trust [Equiano] with his estate in preference to any one" (202).

As Ian Baucom has argued, the "capricious, seductive, anxiety-producing shadow" of Defoe's Lady Credit was a staple atmospheric element of "finance capitalism's speculative culture" during the eighteenth century.[12] The racial difference that Crown policy and colonial law imputed to Equiano did not insulate him from her influence. However, Robinson Crusoe's subjectivity is formed in tandem with acquisition of economic power in overseas markets created and underwritten by credit; in contrast, Equiano's subjective position in the market is necessarily one of extraordinary ambivalence because of the constitutional difference that colorist slave codes have made. Black people's capacity for political subjectivity through property acquisition in the Anglo-American system was never assured, indeed it was never *creditable*, as long as African-descended people remained constitutionally enslavable in this system erected through racecraft.

For Equiano, the most shocking example of this is the kidnapping of Joseph Clipson, a "free young mulatto-man," who is taken forcibly by a ship captain in Bermuda, despite showing a "certificate of his being born free in St. Kitt's" (121). As Equiano learns at his own frequent peril, this inequality among people, introduced by the racialization of ancient constitutional protections, requires a moral appeal to a sovereign power distinct from Lady Credit's transatlantic sway over British law and British religion.

Equiano structures the *Interesting Narrative* to unfold his evolving understanding of this constitutional problem to his readers. At first, Equiano shows readers his original belief that the chattel system can be made humane: "I can quote many instances," he argues,

> of gentlemen who reside on their estates in the West Indies, and then the scene is quite changed; the negroes are treated with lenity and proper care, by which their lives are prolonged, and their masters are profited. To the honour of humanity, I knew several gentlemen who managed their estates in this manner; and they found that benevolence was their true interest. And, among many I could mention in several of the islands, I knew one in Montserrat whose slaves looked remarkably well, and never needed any fresh supplies of negroes. (105)

Yet this is before he fully perceives the moral content of his constitutional precarity within the transatlantic slave economy. Later in the *Narrative*, Equiano exhibits for readers the consummate failure of his own personal efforts to ameliorate the conditions of slavery on Dr Irving's plantation. This amelioration project collapses, Equiano shows, because it remains subject to imperial policies and market forces that incentivize human beings to exert godlike power over one another instead of affirming human equality under God's undiluted sovereignty. For example, when the plantation's entire crop is washed out by rainy season storms, Equiano interprets the calamity as "in some measure a judgment upon us for working on Sundays" in service to the plantation's accounting books instead of keeping the sabbath (210).

When Equiano leaves Irving's plantation in moral disgust, the Africans enslaved there revolt, as in *Oroonoko*, against the "inhumanity and ill-judged avarice" of the next overseer; ultimately, these people perish in an effort to gain their freedom by sea. "[N]ot knowing where to go, or how to manage the canoe," Equiano writes, "they were all drowned" and Dr Irving sets off again "to Jamaica to purchase more slaves" (210). Through the clarity of his Christian conversion, which happens in the chapter before his slaving venture with Irving, Equiano frames his career as an ameliorationist overseer as "heathenish," sinful, and ultimately incompatible with his sense of personhood (210). Concerned that plantation life may cause him to "lose his own soul," Equiano ultimately renounces chattel slavery to become not a fictive Englishman, like Robinson Crusoe, but a real one (210).

The *Interesting Narrative* and the Rise of Transatlantic Abolition

When Equiano was writing in the late 1780s, the British public's serious engagement with Parliament on the question of Britain's role in the transatlantic slave system was still less than a decade old. As Christopher Leslie Brown has shown, the first known petition to Parliament on the question of the slave trade was submitted in June of 1783, signed by 273 Quakers.[13] The Quakers found it their "religious duty to lay the suffering situation" of enslaved Africans before the House of Commons "as a subject loudly calling for the humane interposition of the Legislature."[14] The Quakers continued by voicing their "regret, that a nation professing the Christian faith, should so far counteract the principles of humanity and justice, as by cruel treatment of this oppressed race, to fill their minds with prejudices against the mild and beneficent doctrines of the Gospel."[15] The Commons, which in the previous century had appealed to ideals of Christian benevolence and generosity to fence in the royal prerogative of the Stuarts, were now appealed to by members of the British public to curb the absolute power of colonial slaveholders.

The exigence cited by the Quakers for their 1783 appeal was news that "a bill for the regulation of the African trade, is now before the House, containing a clause which restrains the officers of the African Company from exporting Negroes."[16] Citing their deep moral affectation by crimes against humanity perpetrated by slave traders, the Quakers implored the Commons "that this restriction [on the African Company] may be extended to all persons whatsoever," including unincorporated slave traders, like Defoe's Crusoe.[17]

The Quakers' information about the newly introduced legislation was not wrong. Earlier that year, the African Company of Merchants Act had come before the Commons.[18] In the provisional peace signed at Versailles on January 20, 1783, to end hostilities of the American Revolution, George III of England and Louis XVI of France agreed to reorganize their respective royal claims to trading privileges along the western coast of Africa. Notably, the Fort of Senegal was ceded from Britain to France in exchange for Fort James and the River Gambia, which France in turn ceded to Britain. Because the Fort of Senegal had been vested previously in the Company of Merchants trading to Africa during the reign of George II, the African Company of Merchants Act of necessity revoked the Company's corporate claims to the Fort of Senegal. Article IV of the 1783 Act further revoked the individual slaving privileges of the Company's members:

> It shall not be lawful for any of the Officers or Servants, employed by the Committee of the said Company of Merchants trading to Africa, upon the Coast of Africa, to export Negroes from, thence upon their own Account; and that if any of the said Officers or Servants shall be found to be directly, or indirectly,

> interested in such Exportation of Negroes from Africa, he shall be dismissed from the Service of the said Committee.[19]

One indirect result of the American Revolution, then, was that Parliament made it illegal for individual "Officers or Servants" of the Company to export slaves from Africa "upon their own Account." This action does not seem to have been rooted in Parliament's abolitionist motives so much as in its efforts to limit trade conflict in Africa with the French.

Nevertheless, London Quakers seized upon this significant moment of parliamentary interposition in the slave trade, exhorting legislators to prohibit individuals from engaging in the chattel economy. In effect, the Quaker petitioners sought to make it unlawful for any Briton to do in fact what Robinson Crusoe, some sixty years earlier, had done in fiction: self-enrichment, beyond the seas, and beyond the reaches of the royal prerogative, through the Atlantic slave trade. In the following year, a group of their coreligionists in Philadelphia had the London petition reprinted to renew their abolitionist "address [to] the Congress of these American states." The Quakers of the young American republic cited their hope that "the minds of those who are invested with power here, may become so effectually moved by a sense of the enormity of the evil complained of, as to exert their authority to remove it, that the cry of this oppression may not be continued in our land."[20] Thus began the transatlantic abolition movement, to which Equiano would add the story of his life.

Christian Slavery and the *Interesting Narrative*

The British Empire's expansionist agenda of the eighteenth century, which had come to rely upon the enslavement of Africans, was riven by constitutional paradoxes presented by slave conversion. As Brown has shown, pioneer abolitionists like Equiano's friend and collaborator, Granville Sharp, saw in these challenges the possibility of collective national atonement for what we identified synecdochally in the previous chapter as Robinson Crusoe's original sin. In turn, Britons could begin to imagine an empire without slavery and take the first staggering steps toward a total abolition in their remaining Caribbean colonies.[21]

As we have seen in *Oroonoko* and *Robinson Crusoe*, Anglo-American slavocrats of the late seventeenth century committed this original sin of chattel slavery when they created a new commercial form of hereditary absolute power with novel constitutions that committed ancient English rights along new racial lines. Significantly, in the *Interesting Narrative*, Equiano bears witness before Parliament to the spiritual effects of the Barbadian slave law, under which he lived briefly in May of 1754, before being taken to Virginia: "By the 329th Act, page 125, of the Assembly of Barbadoes," Equiano writes,

> it is enacted 'That if any negro, or other slave, under punishment by his master, or his order, for running away, or any other crime or misdemeanor towards his said master, unfortunately shall suffer in life or member, no person whatsoever shall be liable to a fine; but if any man shall out of *wantonness, or only of bloody-mindedness, or cruel intention, wilfully kill a negro, or other slave, of his own, he shall pay into the public treasury fifteen pounds sterling*.' (109)

The legal innovations of slavocratic constitutions in Britain's colonies, including the legal fiction of the slave's two bodies (natural and as perpetual property, as we saw in *Oroonoko*), are in evidence here. Barbadian law converts the life of "any negro, or other slave" to "*fifteen pounds sterling*" in "*the public treasury*," if that person's life is destroyed "*wilfully*" and "*only of bloody-mindedness, or cruel intention*." There is, by contrast, no public liability if the enslaved person "suffer[s] in life or member" while "under punishment by his master, or his order." Here, the slavemaster and "his order" are elevated to sovereign status with regard to the colony's public debt, although not in relation to slavocrats' private accounts of which monetary value in the enslaved person is part, suggesting a secondary legal fiction of the slavemaster's several bodies in colonial monetary policy. During the next century, in an 1850 Rochester lecture, Frederick Douglass observed the same slavocratic absolutism in the Southern United States that Equiano perceived in colonial Barbados: "The law gives the master absolute power over the slave," Douglass pronounced; "He may work him, flog him, hire him out, sell him, and, in certain contingencies, kill him, with perfect impunity."[22]

In this way, Laura Doyle has argued, Equiano "turns the emergent British tradition of fictional autobiography on its head, revealing himself," and other people enslaved under new colonial constitutions, "as the shadow behind its narrators," most pronouncedly Defoe's Crusoe.[23] This is precisely the application of a Black Atlantic literary tradition against Anglo-American fictions of race. Colonial Barbados, where property in racialized persons was created by positive law, represented to men like Defoe's fictional Englishman an opportunity for rights-conferring property accumulation that C. B. MacPherson has called "possessive individualism."[24] Yet, at the same time that Equiano, in Doyle's phrase, "establishes the pervasive undoing effects of his predicament on the Atlantic," he also realizes an inward spiritual freedom from colonial slaveholding power because slavocratic absolutism, as Behn's Oroonoko observed in the previous century, makes no pretense whatever to the Christian comportment from which it purports to derive godlike legitimacy to govern. With the genre of spiritual autobiography, in which the human sufferer finds transcendence in the sufficiency of God alone, Equiano drives his *Narrative* into the cleft he perceives in slavocratic absolutism.

For example, by establishing himself textually as a Christian man of God, Equiano emphasizes the ontological impossibility, in a Christian society, of the slave's two bodies: the body natural and the historically transcendent body of property in which the slavocrat asserts perpetual interest in a commercial bid for eternal power on earth. Slaveholding power is not as it is in heaven, but rather similar to royal power as it was in Stuart England. In this way, Equiano modifies Locke's contention that slavery is a state of war between master and slave. In his commentary on the Barbadian code, for example, Equiano invokes the gospel of Matthew to tell the story of Mr James Tobin, "zealous labourer in the vineyard of slavery," who "gives an account of a French planter of his acquaintance, in the island of Martinico" (109). This planter showed Mr Tobin, Equiano says, "many mulattoes working in the fields like beasts of burden; and he told Mr. Tobin these were all the produce of his own loins!" (109). Equiano scorns the racial double standard that would make these people "less [Tobin's] children by being begotten on a black woman," and links his grievance to the drafters of the Barbadian code of 1754, "who estimate the lives of their sons... at no more than fifteen pounds; though they should be murdered... *out of wantonness and bloody-mindedness*!" Equiano thus underscores for Parliament slavocrats' abrogation of the constitutional principle of liegance, formed by birth as in *Calvin's Case*, that is destroyed in Tobin's by the racialized chattel principle enshrined in Barbadian law as, among other things, a liberty to contravene God's sixth commandment at the mere cost of "fifteen pounds."

Transposing this scene into the register of biblical metaphor, we might even say that Tobin is a distorted Abraham who sacrifices his children not as the highest act of obedience to God but at his personal whim for monetary gain. For Equiano, by contrast, the universal siblinghood of humankind is confirmed alone by a "God, 'who hath made of one blood all nations of men for to dwell on all the face of the earth,'" and to whom all owe Abrahamic obedience as a fundamental expression of their equality (45). When Equiano pronounces the slave trade "a war with the heart of man," he reframes Locke's account of the state of war between bondsman and master as something far more theologically charged: the slaveholder's war with God. He builds this reframing through a two-step rhetorical movement. First, Equiano underscores that enslaved Africans, as children of God, stand in a relation of siblinghood with other human persons. Second, and on this ground, he suggests that the violence slavers enact upon the enslaved is not confined to the human plane; it is a direct assault on the divine order, and thus a war waged against God.[25]

Equiano's constitutional argument against British colonial slaveholding power is further distilled in the pervasive sense of equality with slaveholders that his gradual religious conversion brings about. Originally terrified by Europeans—pale men with straight hair and strange habits of violence, who seem to have no women and live by magic in their terrifying ship—Equiano draws upon his growing understanding of universal Christian fellowship under divine omnipotence to transform the spiritual content of his racialized fears. A key episode of this alteration in his consciousness is a series of similar calamities at sea, which reveal his bodily equality with other people before God: "I belonged for a few days in the year 1758 to the Jason," Equiano remembers,

> and one night, when I was on board, a woman, with a child at her breast, fell from the upper-deck down into the hold, near the keel. Every one thought that the mother and child must be both dashed to pieces; but, to our great surprise, neither of them was hurt. I myself one day fell headlong from the upper-deck of the Ætna down the after-hold, when the ballast was out; and all who saw me fall cried out I was killed: but I received not the least injury. And in the same ship a man fell from the mast-head on the deck without being hurt. (87–88)

These events persuade Equiano of "the particular interposition of Heaven" on behalf of all people. Equiano's stories of these fallen human beings are descriptive, not metaphorical, but they nevertheless incline his attention toward the divine. Thus, says Equiano, "I began to raise my fear from man"—those originally terrifying Europeans—"to [God] alone" (88). In this way, God is separated in Equiano's political theology from the earthly authority of government, making the divine a site of neither royal ordination nor slavocratic authority, but of human equality under a higher power.

Indeed, one of the unignorable features of the *Interesting Narrative* is that, Augustine-like, Equiano becomes aware, persuaded, and ultimately convicted of the truth of the Gospel, the divinity of Jesus Christ, and the cosmic sovereignty of a provident (if not always benevolent) God. Equiano is also preoccupied with the state of his own soul and the prospect of eternal damnation in tandem with his yearning for freedom. By taking seriously the specific moral content of Equiano's Christianity, therefore, we can better understand his relationship with western Atlantic slavery, including how his experience of bondage—imbricated almost entirely with his religious conversion—produced insight about the constitutional politics of the Atlantic world. Indeed, Equiano exhorts us (alongside his Queen-in-Parliament) to consider the *Narrative* as evidence of the liberty of his mind, body, and spirit over and against slaveholding power. To make our understanding equal to the *Interesting Narrative*, then, we will make our constitutional analysis of colonial slavery accountable, as Equiano's was, to "God's holy Law."[26]

Christian Baptism's Constitutional Challenge to Racial Slavery

In the *Narrative*, Equiano separates his baptism in London (1759) from his full religious conversion aboard the slave ship *Hope* (1775), suggesting an important difference between his inward spiritual state during each of these transformative events. Furthermore, when the 14-year-old Equiano is baptized, he is still legally enslaved; at the time of his conversion, he is free by law, but none of these events—baptism, manumission, or conversion—are coincident. The upshot is that Equiano exhorts Lords, Commons, and Queen to note the specific changes that colonial slavery has made to the ordinary practice and moral authority of Christianity in Great Britain. During Equiano's life, Christian conversion and baptism had for decades been closed as legal pathways to freedom for black people enslaved in Britain's colonies.[27] Nevertheless, the historical meanings of slave conversion and baptism, as well as their moral force, structured the development of Equiano's abolition politics.

As Katharine Gerbner has written, the "concept of conversion has never been stable" historically.[28] Furthermore, slave baptism and conversion held significant—and significantly unstable—political meanings in the context of Britain's colonial slave system. During the seventeenth century, the prospect that baptizing enslaved people could destroy the colonial chattel regime was a persistent concern of slaveholders. Richard Ligon's *A True and Exact History of the Island of Barbados* (1657) illustrates a revelatory case in point.

In conversation in the late 1640s with Sambo, a man enslaved in Barbados, Ligon learns of the man's desire for Christian baptism. Ligon's response to Sambo illuminates important constitutional contours of Equiano's *Narrative*, so we will consider it at length. "I promised to do my best endeavor" for Sambo, Ligon explains,

> and when I came home, spoke to the Master of the Plantation, and told him, that poor *Sambo* desired much to be a Christian. But his answer was, That the people of that Island were governed by the Lawes of *England*, and by those Lawes, we could not make a Christian a Slave. I told him, my request was far different from that, for I desired him to make a Slave a Christian. His answer was, That it was true, there was a great difference in that: But, being once a Christian, he could no more account him a Slave, and so lose the hold they had of them as Slaves, by making them Christians; and by that means should open such a gap, as all the Planters in the Island would curse him. So I was struck mute, and poor *Sambo* kept out of the Church.[29]

The planter's response to Ligon's request for Sambo's baptism discloses the dense relationship among "the Lawes of *England*," the nature of colonial slaveholding power, and the radical legal and spiritual meanings of Christian baptism for free and enslaved people. According to Ligon, the Barbadian planter vocalizes Coke's ancient constitutionalist position from *Institutes* that English law prohibits the enslavement of Christians under arbitrary rule. Recall that, according to Coke, even if England should conquer a Christian people, that people's laws would remain intact and immediately bind the triumphant English sovereign. Thus, the ancient constitution of the English governs this Barbadian planter's political logic that, should Sambo become "a Christian, he [the planter] could no more account

[Sambo] a slave." The planter's freeborn Englishness and the various property interests he asserts—conferred by the ancient constitution via transatlantic liegance to King Charles I—rest on this principle.

The Barbadian slaveholder continues, in Ligon's account, to note the "gap" that "should open" in Barbados through Sambo's baptism: "being once a Christian, [the slaveholder] could no more account [Sambo] a Slave, and so lose the hold they had of them as Slaves, by making them Christians." Here, the transformation in Ligon's syntax is perhaps historically important. Both the planter and Sambo become a plural "they" in the second half of the sentence. This suggests that, at the time of Ligon's visit to Barbados in the late 1640s, there may have been a burgeoning synecdochal process on the island—racecraft—in which one person (slaveholder or slave) could stand in for a whole group of people who belong to the new colonial social category. As we have seen in our discussion of *Robinson Crusoe*, the social relation Ligon registers syntactically would be codified by the Barbadian slavocracy in their racialized labor codes of 1661 as a distinction between "Negroes" and "Christian servants." Ligon's account of Sambo's wish to become a Christian, who according to his master would then no longer be enslavable, sheds light on the social and spiritual processes in the Barbadian colony that preceded the 1661 law.

Through Sambo's baptism, Ligon's Barbadian planter believes all enslaved people in Barbados might become Christians in the English king's overseas dominions, thereby forcing an existential choice for the English slaveholding class: lose the property interest in their human chattels or keep their status as Englishmen who, under the ancient constitution and like their own sovereign, do not enslave Christians. In essence, Sambo's christening would signal a breach in the hedge of slaveholding power through which all the slaves in Barbados might run, thus destroying English chattel property rights in non-Christians through those people's spiritual commitment of themselves to God in Christ. Subsequent English cases like *Butts v. Penny* in the Court of King's Bench (1677) and *Gelly v. Cleves* (1694) in the Court of Common Pleas affirmed a transatlantic English commitment to the enslavable status of non-Christians.[30] In the trover case of *Gelly v. Cleves*, for example, justice Sir George Treby found that "trover will lie for a Negro boy; for they are heathens, and therefore a man may have property in them, and that the court without averment made will take notice that they are heathens."[31] By implication, then, enslaved people might alienate themselves from their masters' chattel claims through a higher transfer of their souls to God. Equiano invokes this English property idiom in his own conversion, figuring salvation as "a title to heaven" (178).

Robinson Crusoe's "double hedge" on the Island of Despair, inside of which he could "lay very secure," is an important fictional counterpoint to Ligon's story of Sambo. Crusoe's mastery over Friday is signaled in the novel by bringing Friday within the literal and metaphorical hedge of Crusoe's protection from the cannibals (or, as we have seen, the tyrannical Stuart kings). Here, Friday converts to Christianity of his own volition.[32] The novel remains ambivalent about the labor relation between Crusoe and Friday, which hovers indeterminately between slave and servant, particularly while the two remain separated from the wider Atlantic economy in human chattels. Yet, even when Crusoe and Friday leave the Island of Despair, Crusoe never conceives of Friday, the Christian, as saleable, an important distinction to the non-Christian Xury whom Crusoe sells without much hesitation to the Portuguese captain for sixty pieces of eight.[33] Here, Defoe registers the same legal difference, between Christians and non-Christians, established in 1677 by the Court of King's Bench in *Butts v. Penny*.

Friday's willful Christian conversion in fiction has, in addition to Ligon's Sambo, other historical counterpoints in fact: as Rebecca Anne Goetz has demonstrated, non-Europeans in the western Atlantic, like the Afro-Virginian Payne and Driggus families of the Chesapeake tidewater region, adopted English forms of Christianity in their social obligations to one another, as well as their private devotions to God. When Francis Payne died in 1673, his last will and testament conveyed his faith in the truth of Christian salvation: "I bequeath my Soule to my loving father my creator," Payne wrote, "and to Jesus Christ whereby his blood and passion suffered for my Sinns."[34]

When African-descended people like Payne made attestations of their Christian faith, they presented implicit constitutional challenges to the colonial slavocratic governments under which, and in tension with which, they lived. Ligon's Barbadian slaveholder clearly believes that, for initiating the destruction of his fellow planters' property in persons by opening Christian sacraments to Sambo, all those "Planters in the Island would curse him." As Willie James Jennings has observed of Equiano's case, "Christianity performed as an exchange network," in the context of colonial chattel regimes like the one in Barbados, "would become a severely limited Christianity."[35] These limitations arise, Jennings notes, because the "categories of capital," like slaveholder and slave, destroy the fundamental condition of Christian fellowship: the doctrine of the *imago dei* in which all people are believed to be made in the image of God. In this way, English racecraft finds itself at cross purposes with divine creative power, a specific tension we will consider at length in this study's final chapter on *Frankenstein*.

As Jennings's analysis makes clear, this tension is not confined to the seventeenth-century Caribbean but belongs to a longer Christian struggle to articulate what it means for human beings to be made in God's image. Dietrich Bonhoeffer's Christian humanist analysis in *Creation and Fall* (1937) offers us, Jennings argues, a theological explanation of how colonial slave societies adopted "a *sicut deus* form of communion" in which human society is not organized by the equality principle intimated by the doctrine of *imago dei*. Rather, the colonial slave society is organized by the question: "Who is like God?"—posed in scorn by Michael the Archangel after his defeat of Satan, who aspired to godlike power, an echo of the serpent's false promise to Eve.[36] In our readings of *Oroonoko* and *Robinson Crusoe*, we have seen that the Stuart kings, as well as some of their English subjects, presented themselves as an answer to St Michael's query. As Jennings observes, "Bonhoeffer speaks of the Fall... as the emergence of the *sicut deus*, the formation of the creature without limits."[37] Specifically, Bonhoeffer described this creature as a human person who believes the self "similar to God in knowing-out-of-its-own-self about good and evil and acting-out-of-its-own-resources, in its aseity, in its being alone."[38] We might be reminded here of Robinson Crusoe or those would-be British slave traders whom London Quakers sought in 1783 to keep from trading Africans "upon their own Account."

There is important continuity of characterological form among Bonhoeffer's *sicut deus* human being, MacPherson's "possessive individualist," and Pocock's "post-civic man" who, after the "sudden and traumatic discovery of capital in the form of [English] government stock," emerges during the 1690s in a "specialized, acquisitive" form.[39] A hallmark of the Anglo-American slave society—and a moral pretext for racializing other people—was a human pretense to absolute power: on the throne, in the courts, and through imperial policy. We have observed this consistently across *Oroonoko*, the Barbadian slave code of 1661, and *Robinson Crusoe* (the great myth of English aseity). In these texts, we see Englishmen leveraging and adapting their divine-right monarch's claims to absolute power, actualizing this power in new overseas markets, and acting out of their own resources within these markets formed by property claims justified by imperial adaptations of the English ancient constitution.

The grave spiritual consequences of these developments in English colonial society are well in evidence: in the case that Ligon narrates, Christianity faces social negation in Barbados because of the absolute, perpetual, and alienable property interest slaveholders assert in African-descended people. Instead of creating universal fellowship under a God who, as Equiano quotes from the Book of Acts "hath made of one blood all nations," Sambo's baptism within the chattel system would fracture the colonial polity beyond all recognition. As Ligon notes, the slavemaster believes that, by opening Christian baptism to the enslaved, he would be "curse[d]" by the very absolute power to which he aspires collectively with fellow slavocrats. Thus, the Barbadian planter discloses in this passage his own spiritual knowledge (deformed spiritual knowledge, a commentator like Jennings or Bonhoeffer might say) that sanctifying slaves in baptism is to destroy the chattel system. Personal economic ruin would ensue for all those Englishmen who, Crusoe-like, derive their social status and sense of personhood from economic standing in the transatlantic chattel system. As Marcus Rediker notes, at least one group of English sailors, lying at anchor in a slave ship off the West African coast, expressed the world-historic spiritual drama of their commercial venture by naming their first two African captives Adam and Eve.[40]

The Barbadian planter's word "curse," from the Old English *curs*, signaling "damnation" or "excommunication," bears on both Jennings's claim about the specific limitations chattel slavery places on Christianity and our forthcoming elaboration of Christian constitutionalism in Equiano's *Narrative*.[41] Sambo's desired baptism, the sacramental mechanism by which Christ's sacrifice is universalized, is transformed in the imagination of Ligon's slaveholder as a removal: not from God's grace, but from the good graces of "all the Planters" in Barbados. Read in a soteriological register, the planter foresees that the "gap" opened by Sambo's christening would be, for the enslaved, a pathway to both freedom under "the Lawes of *England*" (carried to Barbados in the English bodies of colonists) and eternal salvation (through the body of Christ, executed by imperial Rome). But in the context of the chattel relation, on which the colonial government of Barbados depends, Ligon's Barbadian slaveholder can perceive this "gap" as nothing but the road to perdition.

In Old Norse, "gap" means "chasm" or "wide-mouthed outcry" while "gape," from the Old Norse "gapa," means "to open the mouth."[42] Anglo-Saxon depictions of Hellmouth, the monstrous portal through which Christ descended to the dead to liberate captives (including the original sinners Adam and Eve) are likewise rooted in Norse culture, suggesting significant cultural context for the "gap" Ligon's planter associated with the possibility of Sambo's baptism.[43] To maintain the constitution of Barbados, then, is to keep Sambo "out of the Church," in Ligon's phrase, and thus maintain him and other slaves without the reciprocal, transatlantic protections of the ancient constitution imputed thirty years earlier by *Calvin's Case*. This system is maintained, Ligon's anecdote suggests, not only by the absolute power that slaveholders assert over their slaves, but by another novel element of colonial constitutionalism in which slaveholders corporately assert greater than human power over an individual fellow planter who threatens the collective racial sovereignty of the group.

To ease the reader's just concern that I am reading too much into a few words from Ligon's *True and Exact History*, we now turn our attention to those themes in Equiano (and in the next chapter, to Thomas Jefferson and Benjamin Banneker)—all of whom draw upon ideas of divine retribution to describe the constitutional effects of chattel slavery. Indeed, Frederick Douglass and Abraham Lincoln would become exemplars of this rhetorical tradition in the nineteenth century. For example, in his Second Inaugural Address, Lincoln invoked Psalm 19: 9 to describe the magnitude of human loss wrought by the institution of slavery in the United States, and its violent settlement by the American Civil War. He famously proclaimed:

> If God wills that [the American Civil War] continue, until all the wealth piled by the bond-man's two hundred and fifty years of unrequited toil shall be sunk, and until every drop of blood drawn with the lash, shall be paid by another drawn

> with the sword, as was said three thousand years ago, so still it must be said "the judgments of the Lord, are true and righteous altogether."[44]

This and other appeals to the divine are, I am saying here, a kind of historical affirmation that English slaveholding power was originally seized in the seventeenth-century Atlantic through colonists' Promethean bid to abrogate absolute power from their divine-right sovereign. By doing so, colonists extended the logic of the absolute toward new commercial ends, beyond the reach of Parliament, through colonial racecraft. As Jared Hickman has argued persuasively and at length, this drama of the absolute is at the heart of the Atlantic story of race and revolution.[45] To understand Equiano's role in advancing that revolution through Christian constitutionalism, we next consider the theological and political meanings of his baptism and religious conversion.

"I Saw Clearly with the Eye of Faith": Spiritual Transformation in the *Interesting Narrative*

Equiano narrates his London baptism at St Margaret's in a familiar idiom that Alistair Duckworth has associated with the moral economy of Jane Austen's fiction. As Duckworth argues, Christian humanism finds salutary cultural expression in the English country house system of Austen's *oeuvre*—although, as we will note in our reading of *Mansfield Park* in Chapter 5, not without the significant moral exception created by Britain's chattel regime. In this system, Duckworth argues, the proper stewardship of the estate is tantamount to the earthly nourishment of the soul.[46] As Equiano says of his own burgeoning Christianity, he saw his London baptism as "an opportunity of improving" himself, which he "gladly embraced" (78). And yet, Equiano's understanding of himself in London, which he describes in the Austenian idiom of "improvement," is immediately invaded in the *Narrative* by the constitutional fact that he does not creditably own an estate in himself because of the racialization of the law.

In the 1759 baptism episode, we learn that this is not the first time that Equiano and his enslaver's cousins, the Guerins, have sought his christening. The *Narrative* discloses that the eldest Miss Guerin, Elizabeth Martha, had earlier "asked [Equiano's] master to let [him] be baptized, but [Pascal] had refused"—perhaps for the same reasons cited by Ligon's Barbadian slaveholder, although the *Narrative* is silent on this point (78). Nevertheless determined to promote Equiano's Christian life, the eldest Miss Guerin applies anew to her slaveholding cousin, this time insisting on Equiano's baptism (78). Equiano, we learn, has sought this support from his friend. Having heard from the Guerins' servants that christening is necessary for admittance to heaven, Equiano has been "press[ing]" the eldest Guerin sister to advocate on his behalf (78). Ultimately we then learn that, because Captain Pascal is "under some obligation to [Miss Guerin's] brother," he eventually "complied with [Elizabeth Martha's] request" (78).[47]

Unfolding a century hence, this tableau of baptism is a noteworthy metropolitan counterpoint to Sambo's desire for the sacrament in seventeenth-century Barbados. Both episodes are governed not by a widening Christian fellowship implied by the indrawing sanctification of a faithful person, but by slavocratic interests that obstruct Christian life and spiritual voluntarism. As Jennings has noted of the *Narrative*'s manumission episode, Equiano's self-purchase from Robert King "is an amazing situation not because of its rarity but because it signifies the best possible relationship between blacks and whites under the conditions of chattel slavery and mercantile capitalism: economic confraternity."[48] The same principles of market exchange, underwritten by novel constitutionalism, exclude Sambo from baptism in Barbados yet admit the enslaved Equiano to it in London. Indeed, it is only through Miss Guerin's successful appeal to "economic confraternity"—an unnamed "obligation"—between her brother and Captain Pascal that Equiano's baptism is permitted at all. The transactional structure of Equiano's access to baptism promotes the slaveholder Pascal to false clerical authority. Equiano's audience, particularly the Lords Spiritual, would have disapproved of Atlantic slaveholders' pecuniary interests bubbling up in the baptismal fonts of the Church of England.

Slaveholders like Captain Pascal may seek to capture the institutions of Christianity for their own ends; but Equiano insists that these outward signs of faith have real meaning only through rigorous self-examination beyond the reach of slavocratic government.[49] This spiritual truth is perhaps best exemplified in Equiano's profound struggle in the *Narrative* with the question of redemption's source: "whether salvation was to be had partly for our own good deeds, or solely as the sovereign gift of God" (189–90). Equiano's formulation, which distinguishes human action from God's sovereignty, is part of ongoing post-Reformation controversies around the Protestant doctrine of *sola gratia*.[50] But Equiano's understanding of this tension—between the gifts of a sovereign God of grace and deeds of a sinful and thus subordinate people—is contextualized in the *Narrative* by the profound spiritual distortions of slavocratic absolutism, which Equiano experienced firsthand in the western Atlantic colonies, and aboard Atlantic vessels. In these parts of the world, Equiano explains with knowing gravity, men "did not fear God" as he had learned to do when, as a young enslaved sailor, he fell into the gap between decks of the *Ætna* (204). Recall that Aphra Behn's Oroonoko castigates his English captors on the slave ship in similar terms, framing his suffering as a worthy price for gaining "*so true a Knowledge both of you, and of your Gods by whom you swear*," which is to say their worship of self-enrichment, covered by false professions of Christianity. Robinson Crusoe repeats this mistake, we have seen, in the novel that bears his name.

Equiano's inward struggle to comprehend the substance of Christian salvation—a struggle persisting long after his baptism and manumission—is linked with his deepening understanding of what chattel slavery does to the spiritual lives of human beings who live within its abuses, contradictions, and false consciousness. These contradictions are so hardwired into political society that Equiano's full conversion to Christianity happens not through the official event of his baptism, nor through his manumission, but only much later in the *Narrative*: when struggling inwardly with "deep consternation" about salvation's nature, Equiano says "the Lord was pleased to break in upon [his] soul with his bright beams of heavenly light" (190). In this passive moment of spiritual clarity, Equiano is met with a vision of "the crucified Saviour bleeding on the cross." Suddenly, "the Scriptures," which Equiano has been studying at Acts 4:12, become "an unsealed book," and he perceives himself "a condemned criminal under the law," not of Barbados, but of Moses (190). Equiano then perceives "the Lord Jesus Christ in his humiliation, loaded and bearing [his] reproach, sin, and shame," a vision that persuades Equiano beyond doubt that salvation is from God alone. Equiano then understands "every leading providential circumstance that happened to [him], from the day [he] was taken from [his] parents to that hour... as if it had but just then occurred" (190). These are compelling reflections, designed, it seems, to convey the truth of his faith. Why would Equiano include this series of private visions for his parliamentary audience?

Equiano's Appeal to the Spirit

Readers of the *Interesting Narrative*, including Queen Charlotte and Parliament, have in hand a text that discloses these "providential circumstance[s]" as they flash before their author's eyes in real narrative time. In this way, Equiano presents his autobiography as documentary evidence of a human life, through which he lays claim to the constitutional rights he asserts for all enslaved people in his petition to Charlotte. As Henry Louis Gates, Jr. has argued, "Equiano's text [is] a representation of becoming," and in "Equiano's mastery of self-representation,"[51] he seeks wider representation to Parliament of his fellow bondspeople. Likewise, Queen, Lords, and Commons are constitutionally united in Equiano's appeal not through a racecrafted legal identity, created by human beings, but by the universal gift of God's "sovereign free grace," available alike to English and African people (193).

Equiano's conversion episode gathers additional elements that are of great constitutional importance in the developing abolitionism of the *Narrative*: the suffering of Jesus during his execution by imperial Rome; the newly clarified message of scripture; and Equiano's revealed status as a criminal "under the law," whose punishment has been transferred to the crucified Christ. These signs lead Equiano to an "astonishing change" in his spiritual outlook: "the burden of sin, the gaping jaws of hell, and the fears of death, that weighed me down before, now lost their horror," he freely attests (191). Here, Equiano stages for Queen and Parliament a dramatic juxtaposition of his personal experience of colonial slave law with the account of Christ's crucifixion in Acts.[52] The constitutional nuances of this comparison become the blueprint of Equiano's abolitionism, a civic orientation to politics that is consistent with the truth of his inward spiritual life—in marked contradistinction to his baptism and manumission, which are each distorted by the incursions of the chattel system and the limitations it places on Christian fellowship.

In Equiano's conversion, Christ appears as a figure who is both humiliated and, with the weight of his cross, "loaded," a verb that Equiano uses frequently when referring to punishments that slaves endure in Britain's colonies. For example, as an enslaved child in colonial Virginia, Equiano has a terrifying encounter with a woman enduring severe physical punishment. As Equiano recalls, "I had seen a black woman slave as I came through the house ... and the poor creature was cruelly loaded with various kinds of iron machines; she had one particularly on her head, which locked her mouth so fast that she could scarcely speak; and could not eat nor drink" (62–63). There is a double resonance in this passage, whose constitutional importance we are now beginning to plumb: this loading has "locked" the woman's mouth, reifying her animalization under colonial law as one who can "scarcely speak." This throughline from Golgotha to the plantation, slim though the word "loaded" at first seems, is the germ of Equiano's constitutional theory of equality, a Pauline universalism that sets the image of God borne by all persons against the slave law that turns persons into property. Before his conversion, Equiano has not yet grasped that he too bears that image, and so is periodically troubled by his complexion. As a boy in Guernsey, he had noticed that washing turned his playmate Mary's face rosy but left his own unchanged, and grew "mortified at the difference in our complexions" (69). His conversion teaches him otherwise: the likeness that matters is not complexion but the shared human capacity to suffer and die, as the "loaded" Christ did for the redemption of humankind. In the *Narrative*, Equiano learns to see this truth with the more perceptive eye of faith.

As M. Shawn Copeland has argued, crucifixion, as a judicial punishment in imperial Rome, "was intended to intimidate by example and subdue by spectacle"—the spectacle, indeed, of the "Mangled King" of the Jews, to mix phrases from *Oroonoko* and the Bible.[53] Enslaved Christian people in Anglo-America, Copeland observes, often looked to the body of Jesus, dishonored by torture and crucifixion, to understand the nature of their own suffering: "It is not too much to assume that the descriptive realism of the [African American] spirituals regarding the suffering and death of Jesus draws on the very torture that enslaved people endured."[54] Equiano, although writing outside the antebellum US context in which African American spirituals are often studied, employs precisely this mode of "descriptive realism" when recounting his own crucifixion-like torture aboard a sloop owned by a man named Hughes.

In June 1776, a profoundly dejected Equiano departs by ship from Dr Irving's Mosquito Coast plantation to return to England. The captain promises Dr Irving that the sloop will carry Equiano to Jamaica; however, Hughes, the owner of the ship, attempts to force Equiano into a separate schooner that is "in want of hands" and bound for Spanish Cartagena. Ultimately, Hughes threatens Equiano that he should "go in the schooner, or else… not go out of the sloop as a free man" (211). Urgently seeking to avoid re-enslavement, Equiano begs "to be put on shore," but Hughes refuses; Equiano defies Hughes again by saying that he "had been twice amongst the Turks, yet had never seen any such usage with them," adding with disgust that he had not "expected any thing of this kind among Christians" (211). Doubly furious with Equiano's resistance and his moral indignation, Hughes utters "a volume of oaths and imprecations" and then explodes: "Christians! Damn you, you are one of St. Paul's men; but by G——, except you have St. Paul's or St. Peter's faith, and walk upon the water to the shore, you shall not go out of the vessel!" (211). Equiano, by identifying Hughes as a fellow—equal—Christian, has manifestly unfastened the gates of damnation that Sambo sought to open through his christening in Barbados. Hughes then bids

> some of his people tie ropes around each of [Equiano's] ancles, and also to each wrist, and another rope round [his] body, and hoisted [him] up without letting [his] feet touch or rest upon any thing. Thus [Equiano] hung, without any crime committed, and without judge or jury, merely because [he] was a freeman, and could not by the law get [his] redress from a white person in those parts of the world. (212)

Equiano weeps. He begs for mercy, but the "tyrant" Hughes responds to Equiano's pleas by threatening to shoot him (212).

Given the many occasions of brutalization that Equiano references in the *Narrative*, it is striking that this is one of the only personal ordeals that he describes in any extended detail. It seems plausible that Equiano expanded upon this particular episode of abuse for the Queen-in-Parliament because of its topographical similarities to the crucifixion of Jesus, and because it recruits important themes of his Christian conversion to his argument for abolition. The scene also demonstrates definitively that baptism, manumission papers, letters of endorsement, and verbal contracts between white men like Dr Irving and the sloop's captain were useless to prevent the re-enslavement of black people, when novel constitutionalism was asserted along racial lines through arbitrary violence, beyond and upon the seas.

After his vision of Calvary during his conversion but before his crucifixion-like torture, Equiano narrates the radical transposition of "the law" from human to divine parameters. This is a significant constitutional intervention. In Equiano's conversion scene, "the Scriptures [become] an unsealed book," and Equiano sees himself "a condemned criminal under the law"—that is, the Ten Commandments, with which he has been grappling while studying the Bible. While narrating his conversion to Parliament, Equiano links his account explicitly to Romans 7, Paul's meditation on the relationship between God's law and human sinfulness. He quotes the chapter's ninth verse: "For I was alive without the law once: but when the commandment came, sin revived, and I died" (Rom. 7: 9, KJV). Since the first century, scholars have debated the meaning of Paul's remarks in this chapter. The long-standing disagreement is whether the text is autobiographical—a story of Paul's awareness of his sin before and after his conversion on the road to Damascus—or synecdochal, with the "I" of the passage standing in for all humankind and their spiritual conditions before and after Moses's giving of the law.[55] Both interpretations underwrite Equiano's constitutional argument for abolition.

The autobiographical interpretation of Romans 7 understands the historical, unregenerate Paul as the "I" of the text. As Stephen Voorwinde has written, this autobiographical reading held sway among Christian commentators until the early twentieth century. It is likely to have been the interpretation with which Equiano and his audience were most familiar, having been exposited by exegeticists including Desiderius Erasmus (1466–1536), Martin Luther (1483–1546), John Calvin (1509–64), Jacobus Arminius (1560–1609), and John Wesley (1703–91), the Methodist abolitionist who was a subscriber to Equiano's *Narrative*.[56]

In his invocation of Romans, Equiano figures himself, like Paul, in a state of personal condemnation before God, a "criminal under the law" of Moses. This is a marked distinction to Equiano's situation, just a chapter later, when he is splayed out and suspended Christlike aboard Hughes's sloop, "without any crime committed, and without judge or jury, merely because [he] was a freeman, and could not by the law get... redress from a white person in those parts of the world." It is easy to read this scene merely as Equiano framing himself as a Christlike figure, suffering arbitrarily for the original sin of English slavocrats. But seeing the scene in only this light would require us to disregard his opening remarks that the *Narrative* is "the history of neither a saint, a hero, nor a tyrant" (31). Something more constitutionally complex is implied by Equiano's biblical reference.

The synecdochal reading of Romans was pioneered by Werner Kümmel in his dissertation, *Römer 7 und die Bekehrung des Paulus* (1929), although it has sometimes been attributed to commentators as ancient as Origen. Kümmel's reading is that the use of the first-person singular is "a rhetorical device used to portray general human experiences" that "cannot be taken biographically."[57] Given the spiritual nature of Equiano's struggle in the Atlantic slave system, and his observation that the chattel principle places slaveholders at war with God, it is constitutionally important for his conversion to have both personal and universal significance. It is necessarily personal because Equiano must demonstrate the truth of his *Narrative*'s autobiographical, anecdotal evidence that African-descended people, including the unbaptized, enslaved, and unconverted like himself, can and should be understood by English law and religion as non-enslavable.

At the same time, Equiano's conversion is necessarily universal in character; in order for it to be an argument to end colonial slavery writ large, all other human beings must be bound, as he is, by "God's holy Law," which has moral legitimacy that colonial slave codes cannot pretend to hold. Granville Sharp, Equiano's collaborator and friend, had articulated a similar point in the title of his 1776 treatise, *The Just Limitation of Slavery: In the Laws of God, Compared with the Unbounded Claims of the African Traders and British American Slaveholders*. The "unbounded" claims of slavocrats and their suppliers recall Robinson Crusoe's realization of ancient constitutional protections overseas and prefigure the "creature without limits" Bonhoeffer (and Mary Shelley) would describe. Sharp's American editor extended the constitutional implications of this point in his introduction to Sharp's argument:

> if our forefathers, who emigrated from England hither, brought with them all the rights, liberties, and privileges of the British constitution (which hath of late years been often asserted and repeatedly contended for by Americans) why is it that the poor sooty African meets with so different a measure of justice in England and America, as to be *adjudged free* in the one, and in the other held in the most *abject Slavery?* (8–9)[58]

Sharp's editor then wishes for an American trial, like the 1772 case of *Somerset v. Stewart* in the King's Bench, "that it might appear and be known, that *Liberty* in America, is not a partial privilege, but extends to every individual in it" (9).[59] These trials, at length, would come.

Parliament should not consider colonial slave codes legitimate or binding, Equiano further demonstrates, because their maintenance both defies "God's holy Law," as in Sharp's argument, and thereby compromises key elements of British liberty outlined in the Bill of Rights (1689), a document drawn up by the very forebears of Equiano's audience to limit the divine-right power of James II and affirm the uninterrupted ancient constitution after the Glorious Revolution: "the rights and liberties asserted and claimed," the Bill said of itself, "are the true, ancient and indubitable rights and liberties of the people of this kingdom."[60] As John Saillant has shown, Equiano draws upon structural and linguistic elements of the Declaration of Right throughout the *Interesting Narrative* to make the case for his incontrovertible freedom and the wider emancipation of enslaved Africans.[61] Rebecka Rutledge Fisher has noted similarly that the poetic interventions of Equiano's *Interesting Narrative* enact Equiano's personhood in this racially stratified society by demonstrating how his "modern subjectivity" arises in relation to the "formation of modern nation states," not as peripheral to them as a stateless person without rights.[62]

Specifically, Saillant notes, "[t]he right of subjects to petition the Crown was guaranteed in the 1689 Declaration of the Lords Spiritual and Temporal, and

Commons," which is "the language of the opening of *The Interesting Narrative*."[63] Like Equiano, Saillant says, American revolutionaries including Benjamin Franklin, Thomas Jefferson, and Thomas Paine maintained that the people's right to petition was fundamental. Jefferson's *Summary View of the Rights of British America* (1774) began as a petition; Paine criticized King George III in *Common Sense* (1776) for refusing to read colonial petitions; and in 1790, Franklin cosigned the Pennsylvania Society for Promoting the Abolition of Slavery's petition to Vice President John Adams to intervene in the transatlantic traffic in African people.[64] Like Equiano in his address to Parliament, Franklin invoked the *imago dei* when he wrote to Adams: "mankind are all formed," Franklin attested, "by the same Almighty being, alike objects of his Care & equally designed for the Enjoyment of Happiness the Christian Religion teaches us to believe, & the Political breed of America fully coincides with the Position."[65] Equiano would have rejected Franklin's last claim, no doubt, given his experience of American slavery in colonial Virginia, but Franklin and Equiano were sanguine about the constitutional nature of human equality: "All blood is alike ancient," Franklin wrote as Poor Richard in 1745, similar to Equiano's later citation of the Book of Acts that God "hath made of one blood all nations of men."[66]

The *Interesting Narrative* and the Declaration of Right

In addition to adopting the genre of petition for his autobiography, Equiano draws yet more deeply on the 1689 Declaration of Right in his treatment of slavocratic infractions against fundamental rights in Britain's colonies. Vincent Carretta has shown that, as early as 1774, Equiano and Granville Sharp were antislavery associates in London. That year, John Annis was removed forcibly from Britain in blatant violation of the *Somerset* ruling, then 2 years old. Unsuccessfully, Equiano enlisted Sharp's support on Annis's behalf. That same year, Sharp published *A Declaration of the People's Natural Right to a Share in the Legislature*, a title which drew expressly on Parliament's 1689 Declaration to argue for universal representation in the British legislature, and which Equiano perhaps knew.[67]

In his *Declaration* of 1774, Sharp made a natural rights argument for the transatlantic stake that "all British subjects" held in the legislation of the empire. Britons, Sharp argued, "whether in Great Britain, Ireland, or the Colonies" ought to be enfranchised because "'having a share in the legislation' is not merely a British Right, peculiar to this island, but it is also a Natural Right, which cannot, without the most flagrant and stimulating injustice, be withdrawn from any part of the British empire by any worldly authority whatsoever."[68] This, he continued quoting sixteenth-century English theologian Richard Hooker, was because all were bound "by the Natural Law, whereunto he [Almighty God] hath made all subject."[69] Sharp's argument has at least three important constitutional features:

the concept of a portable, embodied ancient constitution, which English slavocrats drew upon in the 1660s to draft their first racialized slave codes; an argument for universal human equality through uniform subjection to a divine Christian parent, a claim central to the earliest anti-slavery arguments in Anglo-American history; and an implied Cokeian prohibition of Christian slavery in Britain and its overseas dominions. In this way, Sharp argued for the expansion of the transatlantic protections of the ancient constitution for those living in "any part of the British empire," a claim that lent support to the American rebellion of 1776 and contravened the American practice of enslaving African-descended Christians, like Equiano. One implication of these claims is that, if all Britons should have some share in their government because of their common subjection to God, then the legislation passed by colonial slavocracies must also come under wider public review or invite colonial legislatures' supersession of Parliament as well as divine retribution by a righteous God.[70] As Sharp declared in a footnote,

> The toleration of domestic slavery in the Colonies greatly weakens the claim or natural right of our American brethren to liberty. Let them put away the accursed thing, that horrid oppression! from among them, before they presume to implore the interposition of divine justice; for whilst they retain their brethren of the world in the most shameful involuntary servitude, it is profane in them to look up to the merciful Lord of all, and call him Father![71]

In *A Declaration of the People's Natural Right*, Sharp therefore affirmed the anti-slavery claims of the ancient constitution in the context of representative government: "because the Representation of the People...is absolutely necessary to constitute an effectual Legislature, according to the fundamental principles of the English Constitution."[72] These protections, Sharp continued, echoing Coke (and citing Bracton before him), "maintain[ed] that excellent equilibrium of power, or mixt government, limited by law, which our ancestors have always most zealously asserted, and transmitted to us, as our best birthright and inheritance."[73] Sharp thus set the terms of an argument for limited constitutional monarchy as a universal birthright within Britain's dominions, expanding the provisions of Parliament's 1689 Declaration of Right into a distinctively imperial register.

As the Lords Spiritual and Temporal and Commons asserted, their 1689 Declaration was an expression of "the true, ancient and indubitable rights and liberties of the people of this kingdom" and " the dominions thereunto belonging" following the abdication of "King James the Second" who, "by the assistance of divers evil counsellors, judges and ministers employed by him, did endeavor to subvert and extirpate the Protestant religion and the laws and liberties of this kingdom."[74] Representing Stuart England as a nation that had lost its way (and, like Defoe's Friday, nearly been eaten alive by cannibals), Parliament sought to rebalance the constitution by affirming key liberties of the subject, including speech, due process (especially jury trials), and freedom from cruel or unusual punishments. To deliver "this kingdom from popery and arbitrary power" suffered under the Stuarts, Parliament continued, the "ancient rights and liberties" of the English people should be declared in print.[75]

In his petition to Queen Charlotte (which was included in the *Narrative*'s petition to Parliament), Equiano sought for his "African countrymen, who groan under the lash of tyranny in the West Indies," many of the constitutional protections described in the Declaration of Right. Equiano's reasons, as he framed them in his letter to the Queen, are similar to those that the 1689 Parliament named: the suppression of tyranny and the preservation of the constitutional monarchy (231). As Sharp had argued in his 1774 *Declaration of the People's Natural Right*, "if there was no law, there would be no King," and so Equiano proceeded in his address to Charlotte and, through her, George III.[76] Their authority to rule Britain and its dominions, Equiano suggested in his claim of subjectship, was tied implicitly, through the 1689 Declaration of Right, to their constitutional capacity to protect fundamental freedoms of all people in their dominions, including Equiano's enslaved African contemporaries. Just as Sambo's wish for baptism forced an absolute choice for the planters in Barbados between their chattel claims in Africans and their status as Englishmen, so Equiano implied an absolute choice for the Christian King and Queen of Great Britain between abolition and the pleasure of "Almighty God," who mercifully had preserved their forebears, William and Mary, the 1689 Declaration noted, during the conflict with the powerful Stuart dynasty.[77]

Viewed in the light of these constitutional politics, Equiano's 1789 *Narrative* appears as a living document, a talking book, speaking of how British colonial slavery limited overseas the protections of the 1689 Declaration of Right and the customary rights of the English, fundamentally compromising the integrity of the imperial constitution. How, wondered MP Edmund Burke in his *Letter to... [the] Sheriffs of the City of Bristol on the Affairs of America* (1777), was a "'strong presiding [British] power, that is so useful towards the conservation of a vast, disconnected, infinitely diversified empire' to be reconciled with the preservation of traditional British liberties?"[78] In his *Narrative*, Equiano focuses on the protections Parliament had styled "freedom of speech" and prohibition of "cruel and unusual punishments" to make an argument for abolition through the framework of Christian constitutionalism.

The Christian Constitution of the *Interesting Narrative*

The constitutional plotline of the *Interesting Narrative* is, simply put, its author's loss of fundamental rights in the Atlantic chattel system as a spiritually formative process leading to his redemption in Christ. Equiano presents his childhood self as a fully enfranchised subject: he has full standing as a human person in the society of Essaka, and he understands his future in this society to be structured by the customs and institutions that have structured its past: the local systems of family, agriculture, religion, warfare, and justice are all presented in the opening chapters of the autobiography as stable, ongoing, and thus fathomable by the young child. After purchasing his freedom from Robert King in Montserrat in 1766, at the approximate age of 21, Equiano remarks that he has regained this "original free African state" described at the beginning of the *Narrative* (138). This is the very same African freedom that Aphra Behn had ascribed to Imoinda. But, by demonstrating the persistent possibility of his re-enslavement in chapters after his manumission, Equiano undercuts this joyful claim made in a moment of worldly idealism and sets the stage for his religious conversion to an understanding of human freedom that is independent of the market. This is Black Atlantic constitutionalism's answer to Robinson Crusoe's racial "freedom," which, Crusoe says himself, is really a form of captivity. Furthermore, Equiano implies that, through the legislative latitude it has allowed western Atlantic slavocrats in jurisdictions like Barbados and Virginia, Britain is at least partly responsible for the destruction of that "original free" state he enjoyed among his Igbo countryfolk, similar to those "ancient rights and liberties" that Parliament sought to restore to the English people in 1689 after Stuart rule. To adjudicate this constitutional case, then, Equiano focuses on how—against God's will, but evidently not Parliament's—Anglo-American slaveholders deprive enslaved Africans of several fundamental freedoms.

A thematic feature of Equiano's enslavement in Britain's colonial system is a persistent inability to speak freely with others, know the nature of his position in the world, and thus understand how to act in his own interests: social, economic, spiritual, or otherwise. Indeed, one of Equiano's ultimate revelations in the *Narrative* is that no human being, free or enslaved, can act in their own *spiritual* interest within the Anglo-American chattel system, which is why it must be abolished. Importantly in the *Narrative*, Equiano dramatizes how the degradation of African rights alienates Englishmen from God and leads them into a state of spiritual death.

As Jennings has argued, Equiano's journey to the slave ship is a "demonic reversal of a pilgrimage. On holy pilgrimage," Jennings continues, "those who walk depend on kind, hospitable strangers to offer them food and sometimes shelter. The pilgrimage, step after step, edging exhaustion, reveals the vulnerability of the human creature and humans' longing for God as companion and destiny."[79] Of course, Jennings says, English slave traders likely did not conceive of human traffic as having a theological dimension; yet Britons trading in the Atlantic slave system were regarded by their contemporaries as, in Jennings's term, engaged in a "demonic" enterprise. The English Dissenter Richard Baxter, for example, issued in his *Directions to Masters in foraign Plantations* (1673) a rebuke to English slave traders in precisely these terms: "To go as Pirates and catch up poor *Negro's*," he writes,

> or people of another Land, that never forfeited Life or Liberty, and to make them slaves, and sell them, is one of the worst kinds of Thievery in the Word... and they that buy them and use them as Beasts, for their meer commodity, and betray, or destroy, or neglect their Souls, are fitter to be called incarnate Devils than Christians, tho they be no Christians whom they so abuse.[80]

Notably, Baxter's anti-slavery position extended to all human beings, including non-Christians, a claim in tension with Coke's theory of conquest, which distinguished between the legal standing of Christian and non-Christian peoples.

For Equiano, the "demonic" journey to the slave ship that Jennings describes is coterminous with his steady loss of free speech, a key degradation of the "original free African state" he notes during the episode of his manumission. "From the time I left my own nation," Equiano recalls, "I always found somebody that understood me till I came to the sea coast" (51). "All the nations and people I had hitherto passed through resembled our own in their manners, customs, and language," he continues, "but I came at length to a country, the inhabitants of which differed from us in all those particulars" (53). Equiano's ultimate inability to comprehend the Europeans aboard the slave ship convinces him that he "had gotten into a world of bad spirits, and that they were going to kill me" (55). In consequence of no longer having rational capacity to comprehend his circumstances, the 11-year-old Equiano is ultimately seized by the primal fear of being eaten.

Much like Robinson Crusoe, Equiano spends a significant portion of his story concerned that he is to be consumed. Here, we are reminded of Defoe's commonplace of the "devouring" divine-right Stuart kings in *The True-Born Englishman* and perhaps also of Behn's Oroonoko, who refuses to eat as a last stand aboard a slave ship when he is deprived of liberty by English slave traders.[81] As Heather Keenleyside has argued in assessing the Lockean dynamics of *Robinson Crusoe*, "Locke's account of civil society turns on the distinction between political authority (a relation between human persons that is constituted by consent) and property right (a relation between persons and things that is constituted by appropriation). In condensed form, Locke figures these modes of relation as speaking and eating." Ultimately, Keenleyside writes, Defoe undercuts Locke's paradigm, from the *Second Treatise*, of a world neatly divided into "persons and things." Rather, she continues, "*Robinson Crusoe* composes a domestic and creaturely society that does not clearly sort humans from animals, speaking from eating, consent from coercion, family from food." In this way, Crusoe's island "is a sign of the breakdown, or the impossibility, of Lockean politics."[82] The very impossibility of political authority through consent, which Keenleyside rightly perceives in *Robinson*

Crusoe, emanates from an important feature of the novel's plot: the emergence in fiction of Robinson Crusoe as an individual, a freeborn Englishman, constituted by and through the Atlantic slave economy. Through it, human beings, like Crusoe, can transform other people, like Xury, into things and can transform themselves into rights-bearing Englishmen with commercial pretension to absolute power.

Keenleyside's discussion of Lockean political philosophy in *Robinson Crusoe* illuminates our understanding of the freedom of speech in Equiano's *Narrative*. Equiano's progress toward the slave ship, we have noted, is figured as a loss of his capacity for communication. After Equiano is taken on board the slave ship that will carry him into the Anglo-American chattel system, he finds "some of [his] own nation" and he inquires "of these what was to be done with us; they gave me to understand," Equiano continues, that "we were to be carried to these white people's country to work for them" (56). Others on the ship "made motions with their hands, signifying," Equiano conjectures, that "we were to go to their country; but we did not understand them" (57–58). Much later in the autobiography, Equiano attributes his overwhelming fear of the Middle Passage to the strangeness of his European enslavers, his ignorance of their manners and customs, and his inability to learn about them because of the language barrier. "I never felt half the alarm at any of the numerous dangers I have been in," Equiano recalls, "that I was filled with at the first sight of the Europeans.... That fear, however, which was the effect of my ignorance, wore away as I began to know them" (77). For Equiano, the capacity to listen and speak in English, and to understand the motives of Britain's slaveholding class, is to erase his own fear of men (including slavocrats), which becomes a crucial element of his religious conversion and professed constitutional theology of human equality, in which all people are rightly subordinated to God instead of to one another through violence, fear, and other coercion.

Consequently for Equiano, the degradation through enslavement of fundamental rights in the *Narrative* is a kind of Babel: the loss of human community through the loss of speech. Equiano laments his arrival in Virginia in these very terms. There was, he writes, "not one soul who could talk to me." He continues: "at last all my companions were distributed different ways, and only myself was left. I... thought myself worse off than any of the rest of my companions; for they could talk to each other, but I had no person to speak to that I could understand" (62). His isolation is horribly confirmed in Virginia when, as we saw earlier, he meets an enslaved woman loaded by her captors with an iron muzzle. Equiano's childhood terror at the sight of this awfully subdued woman induces his further paranoia: he imagines that the clock and portrait on the wall are watching him to report to his slavemaster "any thing [he] might do amiss" (63). As Keenleyside observes of the Island of Despair in *Robinson Crusoe*, here in Equiano's Virginia is evidence of a political society—a real one, in this case—that "does not clearly sort humans from animals [or] consent from coercion."[83]

When acquiring his slave name, Gustavus Vassa, from Captain Henry Pascal, Equiano associates his growing fluency in English—that is, his capacity to speak freely—with principled resistance to slaveholding power. "At that time," Equiano writes, I "began to understand him a little, and refused to be called [Gustavus Vassa], and told [Pascal] as well as I could that I would be called Jacob." When Equiano "refuse[s] to answer" to the new name, Pascal beats him cruelly, and Equiano is thereby "obliged to bear the . . . name." Whereas Robinson Crusoe hears his own words echoed back to him through the creaturely expressions of the democratically named parrot, Poll, Equiano's refusals of his new name, "Jacob," are repeated by no one and refracted in the text as violence that is necessary to maintain in fact the legal fiction of race set down by colonial slave codes. By juxtaposing Crusoe's Poll, who, as Keenleyside says, "ultimately opens the possibility that 'the Society of . . . Fellow-Creatures' might be composed of animals as well as human beings"[84] with Equiano's inability to speak meaningfully to English slaveholders, we can see the kind of discursive slippage that chattel slavery has wrought through the animalization of human beings. Indeed, as Keenleyside concludes in her analysis of *Crusoe*'s epistemic crisis: it is only after selling Xury into the Atlantic chattel system that Crusoe is first met with a kind of perceptual confusion that prompts his vocabulary to slip from signatories of the human ("Men" and "Boy[s]") to a more capacious category of "creature," which includes people and animals together, human beings styled by law as brute creation, and animals who, like Poll the parrot, are personified.[85] This slippage is the very spiritual problem that Equiano perceives in the "329th Act . . . of the Assembly of Barbadoes," under which the sons of men are saleable like cattle.

Equiano's testimony to Parliament in the *Narrative*, of the disproportionate and unusual cruelty that attends his efforts to speak freely within Britain's slave system, links the deprivation of speech to unconstitutional forms of punishment. One of Equiano's most striking indictments of slavocratic violence is captured in a series of questions: "Why do you use those instruments of torture?" he writes; "Are they fit to be applied by one rational being to another? And are ye not struck with shame and mortification, to see the partakers of your nature reduced so low? But, above all, are there no dangers attending this mode of treatment? Are you not hourly in dread of an insurrection?" (112). In *Creation and Fall* Bonhoeffer elaborates the concept of *sicut deus*, of seeking to be like God, as a kind of death-in-life: "It is true," Bonhoeffer says, "that humankind becomes sicut deus through the fall; but human beings who are sicut deus human beings can no longer live—they are in a state of death. That means that the serpent in all its attempt to pretend that God's truth is a lie, can never escape this truth."[86] This passage from Bonhoeffer illuminates the theo-juridical dimension of answers to Equiano's questions: instruments of torture, Englishmen know from their 1689 Declaration of Right, are not fit to be applied by one rational being to another. Moreover, it *is* shameful to torture another human being, and there *are* dangers inherent in colonial slaveholding because insurrections are everywhere possible. Those British slaveholders, Equiano implies further, who are Bonhoeffer's "sicut deus human beings"—living out of their own knowledge of good and evil—can make many attempts to pretend that Africans are not their equals. Slave traders *can* use torture machines. Slaveholders *can* conspire to "keep Africans in a state of ignorance," while hypocritically asserting, as Equiano says, "that [Africans] are incapable of learning" (111–12). These absurdities, rhetorically similar to the assertions of Bonhoeffer's serpent who cannot escape God's truth, demonstrate a parallel truth: colonial slave codes would not be needed at all if Africans were in fact the brutes that slavocracy asserted them to be. In this way, Equiano's questions imply subtly the profound truth that by creating others in a condition of social death in life, slaveholders effect for themselves a graver death of the spirit.

Perhaps the most important constitutional example of rights deprivation in the *Interesting Narrative* is the text's second Middle Passage of 1763 in which Captain Henry Pascal sells Equiano to Captain James Doran aboard the *Charming Sally*, which is bound for the West Indies. Although Equiano has not yet purchased his freedom, he has come to realize conditions of relative liberty as a bound member of the British Navy during wartime. He has been baptized; he has learned to write and do arithmetic; he has learned to dress hair and read the Bible with his friend Daniel Queen; and he has kept some of his own prize money from the Seven Years' War. Nevertheless, Pascal trades Equiano to Doran without warning, perhaps because Equiano's growing semblance of freedom is becoming a threat to the property interest Pascal asserts in Equiano's person.

The defense that Equiano raises to this transaction invokes a variety of English legal prohibitions of slavery. Equiano asserts to Doran that "I have been baptized; and by the laws of the land no man has a right to sell me"; in an aside to Parliament, he adds that he had "heard a lawyer and others at different times tell my master so," suggesting the customary usage of the common law to prevent the enslavement or re-enslavement of African-descended people living in Britain (93–94). Nevertheless, the transaction proceeds and Doran tells Equiano, in response to Equiano's invocations of Coke and the common law, that he speaks "too much English"—that is, has too much free speech—and that "if [he] did not behave [himself] well, and be quiet" there was "a method on board to make [him]" (94). This unnamed method, no doubt a cruel punishment, raises not for Equiano a vision of the crucified Christ but rather a memory, Equiano says, of "my former sufferings in the slave-ship" (94). Crushed by this thought, Equiano responds to Doran that, although he cannot get his "right among men here, I hoped I should hereafter in Heaven" (94).

For parliamentarians reading the *Narrative*, Equiano has demonstrated that colonial slavocracy has arrived on the shores of Great Britain, staging an invasion by a new kind of arbitrary power that, like Stuart tyranny before it, is at odds, Equiano notes, with "Heaven" itself. As Quobna Ottobah Cugoano argued just two years earlier in his *Thoughts and Sentiments on the Evil and Wicked Traffic of the Slavery and Commerce of the Human Species* (1787), "'tis impossible to conceive how such an enormous evil as the slave-trade could have been established and carried on under any Christian government."[87] Indeed, Cugoano continued, slavery had placed "one of the finest constitutions in the world" at risk for "ruin and destruction; and that the most generous and tenacious people in the world for liberty, may also at last be reduced to slaves."[88] If unanswered by Parliament, Cugoano and Equiano imply, the quiet invasion of Britain by colonial slavocrats, like the one Equiano describes by Pascal and Doran on the Thames, threatened the constitution itself and the ancient liberty of the British people.

Olaudah Equiano, Christian Englishman

In his biography of Equiano, Vincent Carretta has recorded that a writer calling himself Gustavus Vassa submitted several letters to the London *Morning Post* from 1777 through 1779, a period coincident with both the end of the American Revolution as well as Equiano's London employment with Matthias Macnamara, former governor of British Senegambia. This writer, whom Carretta strongly suspects was Equiano, is also an avowed royalist, critical of the prosecution of the war against the American rebels and well aware of the seafaring power of Britain's Navy.[89] The *Morning Post* writer's royalist sympathies are commensurate with Gustavus Vassa's assertions of his subjectship to Queen Charlotte in the 1788 petition we considered at the beginning of this chapter.

In a March 10, 1778 letter, Gustavus Vassa wrote to the *Morning Post*, referencing the Caledonian chieftain Galgacus. In Tacitus's *Agricola* (98 CE), Galgacus appears as the leader who organized British resistance to Julius Agricola's military campaign into Caledonia (the Scottish Highlands) in 83 CE. Carretta posits that the author of the 1778 *Morning Post* letter probably expected his readers to recall that Galgacus urged his followers to resist Roman enslavement.[90] As A. J. Woodman explains, Tacitus frames this episode of the *Agricola* with an "assertion that the British provincials are 'already tamed to obey, but note [*sic*] yet to be slaves.'"[91] By ethnographic contrast, Tacitus notes that the Gauls have already "lost their *uirtus* [virtue] along with their freedom"; but the same fate, Woodman suggests, awaits Britons as they undergo a gradual "transition from freedom to servitude" under Roman imperial rule.[92]

In this same section of the *Agricola*, Tacitus draws attention to Rome's reliance on dependent local rulers, such as Togidumnus, the client king installed over several British provinces in the late 40s CE. This system exemplifies Rome's practice of turning compliant local elites into "the instruments of servitude."[93] By invoking Tacitus's account of these imperial strategies, and their degradation of free but vulnerable Britons, the *Morning Post* author invites his eighteenth-century readers to reflect on similar dynamics within Britain's empire, particularly the possibility that Britain will be invaded by minor kings—which is to say colonial slaveholders—returning from the outer reaches of the empire. We will study one of these minor kings, Sir Thomas Bertram, in a reading of Jane Austen's *Mansfield* Park in Chapter 5.

If Carretta is correct, and the *Morning Post* writer is Equiano, we can see across his *oeuvre* a compelling historical alignment of the first-century Romans with the British slaving class. The imperial Romans both crucify Jesus in the conversion vision from the *Narrative* and slowly bind Britons by gradual transition from freedom to slavery in the *Agricola*, referenced in the 1778 *Morning Post* letter. Just as quietly, British slaveholders like Henry Pascal and Captain Doran invade Britain through the programmatic destruction of Christian equality by becoming *sicut deus* human beings: minor kings and the human instruments of enslavement, just like Togidumnus before them. It is now up to Parliament and Queen Charlotte, Equiano argues in the *Narrative*, to avert this transatlantic constitutional crisis for the British people and preserve the integrity of the Christian religion in Britain and its remaining colonies. In making this appeal to the sovereign-in-Parliament, Equiano seeks restoration of ancient constitutional liberties for his "African countrymen" under her transatlantic sovereignty—the ones he realized in regaining his "original free African state" by manumission. To achieve reinstatement of "original" freedom for enslaved Africans, Equiano calls for the abandonment of imperial policies that violate "God's holy Law." Equiano thus underscores to Crown and Parliament his standing as an English Christian, who under their limited authority enjoys the protections of the ancient constitution.

Benjamin Banneker, Equiano's contemporary abolitionist in the newly founded United States, would also look to the heavens for a constitutional answer to the problem of absolute power in America's racial slavocracies. As we will see in the next chapter, Banneker—with mathematics and correspondence to Thomas Jefferson—appended a trigonometric argument to Equiano's Christian constitutional case for human equality. Banneker would also calculate an answer to a novel constitutional problem: how to escape racial slavery in new American jurisdictions, where it was no longer possible to appeal to the Queen.

Notes

1. Olaudah Equiano, *The Interesting Narrative of the Life of Olaudah Equiano, or Gustavus Vassa, the African*, ed. Vincent Carretta (New York: Penguin, 2003), 231. Cited hereafter parenthetically.
2. On Queen Charlotte's constitutional and political position during the Regency debates associated with George III's periods of incapacity, particularly in 1765, see Derek Jarrett, "The Regency Crisis of 1765," *English Historical Review* 85, no. 335 (1970): 282–315; "Queen Charlotte (19 May 1744–17 November 1818)," accessed December 18, 2023, <https://www.royal.uk/encyclopedia/queen-charlotte-19-may-1744-17-november-1818>

3. John Saillant has noted the constitutional structure of Equiano's *Interesting Narrative*, which begins by addressing Parliament and ends by addressing the Queen: "Indeed, one reasonable way of looking at Equiano's narrative is that the frames at the beginning and end, which he petitioned, first, Parliament and, second, the Queen, to move against the slave trade." John Saillant, "'Profitable Reading': Literacy, Christianity, and Constitutionalism in Olaudah Equiano's *Interesting Narrative*," in *Teaching Olaudah Equiano's Narrative: Pedagogical Strategies and New Perspectives*, ed. Eric D. Lamore (Knoxville, TN: University of Tennessee Press, 2012), 154.
4. Paul Gilroy, *The Black Atlantic* (Cambridge, MA: Harvard University Press, 1993), 1–40, esp. 15–19.
5. *Butts v. Penny* (1677) 2 Lev. 201, quoted in Brewer, "Common Law of Slavery," 766–72, esp. 768–71.
6. While Equiano writes in his *Narrative* that he was born in what is now Southeastern Nigeria, Vincent Carretta has found baptismal and naval records indicating that Equiano was actually born in South Carolina. In his biography of Equiano, Carretta argues that Equiano claims African birth as a political choice for the abolitionist cause. There is not a consensus among Equiano scholars that Carretta's findings are true. Catherine Acholonu's *The Igbo Roots of Olaudah Equiano* cites oral history verifying Equiano's claim to a Nigerian birth, thus refuting Carretta's argument. Paul E. Lovejoy has been a vocal opponent of Carretta's claims, citing Acholonu's work. See generally Catherine Obianuju Acholonu-Olumba, *The Igbo Roots of Olaudah Equiano: An Anthropological Research (with a Reply to Vincent Carretta)*, rev. edn (Owerri, Nigeria: AFA Publications, 2007); Paul E. Lovejoy, "Issues of Motivation—Vassa/Equiano and Carretta's Critique of the Evidence," *Slavery and Abolition* 28, no. 1 (2007): 121–25. See also Vincent Carretta, *Equiano, the African: Biography of a Self-Made Man* (Athens, GA: University of Georgia Press, 2005), p. xiv. For the purposes of this chapter, I have taken Equiano at his word, while remaining open to the possibility that Carretta's claims are correct. If they are, we might momentously situate Equiano along the same literary arc as a writer like James Baldwin, who placed the first-person "I" in histories that "I" did not in fact inhabit in order describe the effects of racecraft on the person and his society. See, e.g., "Stranger in the Village," the essay in which Baldwin casts himself in Africa to achieve his point about the historic difference race has made to his social identity in the present: "I am in Africa, watching the conquerors arrive," he writes. James Baldwin, "Stranger in the Village," *Harper's Magazine* 207, no. 1214 (October 1953): 44.
7. The political crisis of the American Revolution was consistently framed by rebel colonists as one constitutional in nature. Bernard Bailyn, *The Ideological Origins of the American Revolution* (Cambridge, MA: Belknap Press of Harvard University Press, 2017), 55–93.
8. As Vincent Carretta writes, "except for the mention of the American privateer captured by Captain Douglass as they returned to England, as far as one could tell from *The Interesting Narrative*, the American Revolution never happened." Carretta, *Equiano, the African*, 192.
9. Lord Dunmore's Proclamation of November 7, 1775 is probably the best-known case in point; in it, Dunmore declared martial law in Virginia and promised freedom to "all indentured Servants, Negroes, or others, (appertaining to Rebels,) free that are able and willing to bear Arms" who joined His Majesty's troops, thus attempting to mobilize enslaved people's royal subjecthood against rebelling slaveholders, a gesture rooted in Dunmore's military strategy, not his abolitionism. The text survives as John Murray, Earl of Dunmore, *By His Excellency the Right Honorable John Earl of Dunmore…A Proclamation*, broadside, November 7, 1775, Broadside 1775.V852 FF, Special Collections, Library of Virginia. See also Benjamin Quarles, "Lord Dunmore as Liberator," *William and Mary Quarterly* 15, no. 4 (1958): 494–507; Sylvia R. Frey, *Water from the Rock: Black Resistance in a Revolutionary Age* (Princeton: Princeton University Press, 1991), 55–67; and James Corbett David, *Dunmore's New World: The Extraordinary Life of a Royal Governor in Revolutionary America—with Jacobites, Counterfeiters, Land Schemes, Shipwrecks, Scalping, Indian Politics, Runaway Slaves, and Two Illegal Royal Weddings* (Charlottesville, VA: University of Virginia Press, 2013), 104–5.
10. Samuel Johnson, *Taxation No Tyranny: An Answer to the Resolutions and Address of the American Congress*, 4th edn (London: Printed for T. Cadell, in the Strand, 1775), 89.
11. Notably, under Coke's theory of settlement of the previous century, the Christianization of a people through collective conversion would probably have placed them beyond the reach of perpetual enslavement; yet by the mid-eighteenth century this framework no longer governed imperial practice. In this respect, Equiano's own situation during the naval expedition is striking: though baptized, he had not yet experienced the inward conversion to Christianity that Coke assumed as a marker of non-enslavable status, leaving him in a legal and spiritual limbo—neither properly enslavable under the old formulation nor shielded from the arbitrary legal improvisations of a slaveholding empire.

12. Baucom, *Specters of the Atlantic* (Durham, NC: Duke University Press, 2005), 81.
13. Christopher Leslie Brown, *Moral Capital* (Chapel Hill, NC: University of North Carolina Press, 2006).
14. Anthony Benezet, with John Ady, John Drinker, and the London Yearly Meeting (Society of Friends), *The Case of Our Fellow-Creatures, the Oppressed Africans: Respectfully Recommended to the Serious Consideration of the Legislature of Great-Britain* (Philadelphia: Reprinted by Joseph Crukshank, 1784), 17.
15. "The Petition of the People Called Quakers" (1783), reprinted in Benezet et al., *Our Fellow-Creatures*, n. 16.
16. "Petition of the People Called Quakers," in Benezet et al., *Our Fellow-Creatures*, n. 16.
17. "Petition of the People Called Quakers," in Benezet et al., *Our Fellow-Creatures*, n. 16.
18. 1783: 23 King George III, c.65: African Company of Merchants. <https://statutes.org.uk/site/the-statutes/eighteenth-century/1783-23-george-3-c-65-african-company-of-merchants-act>
19. African Company of Merchants Act, section IV.
20. Benezet et al., *Our Fellow-Creatures*, n. 4.
21. Brown, *Moral Capital*, 209.
22. Frederick Douglass, *My Bondage and My Freedom* (New York: Miller, Orton & Mulligan, 1855), 429.
23. Laura Doyle, *Freedom's Empire* (Durham, NC: Duke University Press, 2008), 193.
24. C. B. Macpherson, *The Political Theory of Possessive Individualism*, 2nd edn (Oxford: Oxford University Press, 2011).
25. John Locke, *Two Treatises of Government*, ed. Peter Laslett (Cambridge: Cambridge University Press, 1988), 284.
26. Olaudah Equiano, quoted in Michelle Faubert, *Granville Sharp's Uncovered Letter and the Zong Massacre* (New York: Palgrave Pivot, 2018), 24.
27. Rebecca Anne Goetz, *The Baptism of Early Virginia: How Christianity Created Race* (Baltimore, MD: Johns Hopkins University Press, 2012), 86–111.
28. Katharine Gerbner, *Christian Slavery* (Philadelphia: University of Pennsylvania Press, 2018), 7.
29. Richard Ligon, *A True and Exact History of the Island of Barbados* (London: Printed for Humphrey Moseley, 1657), 50.
30. Douglas A. Lorimer, "Black Slaves and English Liberty: A Re-examination of Racial Slavery in England," *Immigrants and Minorities* 3, no. 2 (July 1984): 121–50.
31. Brewer, "Common Law of Slavery," 765–834.
32. Defoe, *Robinson Crusoe* (New York: Penguin Books, 2003), 174.
33. Defoe, *Robinson Crusoe*, 28–29.
34. Payne, quoted in Goetz, *Baptism of Early Virginia*, 96.
35. Willie James Jennings, *The Christian Imagination: Theology and the Origins of Race* (New Haven: Yale University Press, 2010), 182.
36. For additional commentary see Jens Zimmermann, "In God's Image: From *Sicut Deus* to *Imago Dei*," in *Dietrich Bonhoeffer's Christian Humanism* (Oxford: Oxford University Press, 2019), 113–47.
37. Jennings, *Christian Imagination*, 324.
38. Dietrich Bonhoeffer, *Creation and Fall: A Theological Exposition of Genesis 1–3* (Minneapolis: Fortress, 1997), 113.
39. Pocock, *Virtue, Commerce, and History*, 108, 112.
40. Marcus Rediker, *The Slave Ship: A Human History* (London: Penguin Books, 2008), 3.
41. *Oxford English Dictionary*, s.v. "curse (n.)," accessed September 2023. <https://doi.org/10.1093/OED/3690264898>
42. *Oxford English Dictionary*, s.v. "gap (n.1)," accessed December 2023. <https://doi.org/10.1093/OED/1009733633>; "gape (v.)," accessed September 2023. <https://doi.org/10.1093/OED/9539328114>
43. Meyer Schapiro argues that, "The Anglo-Saxon taste for the Hell Mouth was perhaps influenced by the northern pagan myth of the Crack of Doom and the battle with [Fenrir] the wolf, who devoured Odin [in Norse Mythology]. The wolf's great jaws are broken by Odin's son, who is later identified with Christ" (211). Meyer Schapiro, "'Cain's Jaw-Bone that Did the First Murder,'" *The Art Bulletin* 24, no. 3 (1942): 205–12, at 211; Encyclopaedia Britannica Online, s.v. "Fenrir," accessed October 19, 2023. <https://www.britannica.com/topic/Fenrir>
44. Abraham Lincoln, "Second Inaugural Address," March 4, 1865, in *The Collected Works of Abraham Lincoln*, ed. Roy P. Basler, vol. 8 (New Brunswick, NJ: Rutgers University Press, 1953), 333.
45. Jared Hickman, *Black Prometheus: Race and Radicalism in the Age of Atlantic Slavery* (New York: Oxford University Press, 2020).

46. Alistair M. Duckworth, *The Improvement of the Estate: A Study of Jane Austen's Novels* (Baltimore, MD: Johns Hopkins University Press, 1994).
47. Vincent Carretta's biography of Equiano provides the first names of the Guerin family members. See Carretta, *Equiano, the African*, 80–81.
48. Jennings, *Christian Imagination*, 184.
49. For an extended discussion of how enslaved people adopted Christian principles from their enslavers, and then turned those principles toward their own spiritual emancipation, see Robert Olwell, *Masters, Slaves, and Subjects: The Culture of Power in the South Carolina Low Country, 1740–1790* (Ithaca, NY: Cornell University Press, 1998), 103–40.
50. *Sola gratia*, Latin for "grace alone," was a central doctrinal principle of the Protestant Reformation, emphasizing salvation as entirely the work of God's unmerited favor; see Alister E. McGrath, *Reformation Thought: An Introduction*, 4th edn (Oxford: Wiley-Blackwell, 2012), 121–22, 142–43.
51. Henry Louis Gates, Jr., *The Signifying Monkey* (Oxford: Oxford University Press, 2014), 167.
52. Readers will recall that the frontispiece of the *Narrative* portrays Equiano with the Bible open to this book. Cornelius Tiebout, *Olaudah Equiano or Gustavus Vassa the African* (engraving, 1791), Library Company of Philadelphia Digital Collections, accessed January 23, 2026. <https://digital.librarycompany.org/islandora/object/digitool%3A128586>
53. M. Shawn Copeland, *Knowing Christ Crucified: The Witness of African American Religious Experience* (Maryknoll, NY: Orbis Books, 2018), 118.
54. Copeland, *Knowing Christ Crucified*, 28.
55. Stephen Voorwinde, "Romans 7: A History of Interpretation," *Vox Reformata* 83 (2018): 74. <https://rtc.edu.au/wp-content/uploads/Romans-7-a-history-of-interpretation-2018.pdf>
56. Voorwinde, "Romans 7," 76.
57. Voorwinde, "Romans 7," 74, 86. Compare to James Baldwin's use of the rhetorical "I" at Chapter 3 n. 6.
58. Granville Sharp, *A Declaration of the People's Natural Right to a Share in the Legislature, Which Is the Fundamental Principle of the British Constitution of State* (Philadelphia: Reprinted and sold by John Dunlap, 1774), 8–9.
59. Sharp, *Declaration*, 9.
60. "An Act Declaring the Rights and Liberties of the Subject and Settling the Succession of the Crown," 1 Will. & Mar. sess. 2, c. 2, in *The Statutes of the Realm*, vol. 6 (London, 1819), 142–45.
61. John Saillant, "Profitable Reading," 154.
62. Rebecka Rutledge Fisher, *Habitations of the Veil: Metaphor and the Poetics of Black Being in African American Literature* (New York: State University of New York Press, 2014), 89.
63. Saillant, "Profitable Reading," 154.
64. Saillant, "Profitable Reading," 154.
65. Benjamin Franklin, "Letter Transmitting Letter from James Pemberton and a Petition from the Pennsylvania Society for Promoting the Abolition of Slavery to Vice President John Adams," February 9, 1790, Record Group 46, *Petitions and Memorials and Resolutions of State Legislatures Submitted to the 1st Congress*, National Archives and Records Administration (NARA), Washington, DC, National Archives Identifier 306388. <https://catalog.archives.gov/id/306388>
66. "Poor Richard, 1745," *Founders Online*, National Archives, accessed January 1, 2024. <https://founders.archives.gov/documents/Franklin/01-03-02-0001>
67. Because Equiano's 1789 *Narrative* and Sharp's 1776 treatise, *The Just Limitation of Slavery*, cite the same passage from laws of Barbados, specifically the 329th Act, it seems likely that Equiano had access to Sharp's work sometime after 1776. For a more substantive comparison of the writers' engagement with the colonial law in Barbados, see Olaudah Equiano, *Interesting Narrative*, 109; and Granville Sharp, *The Just Limitation of Slavery in the Laws of God, Compared with the Unbounded Claims of the African Traders and British American Slaveholders* (London: Printed for B. White, & E. and C. Dilly, 1776), 33–34.
68. Sharp, *Declaration*, 4.
69. Sharp, *Declaration*, 4.
70. For elaboration of this general point, see Brown's chapter, "The Politics of Slavery in the Years of Crisis," on the role of colonial slavery in the politics of the American Revolution. *Moral Capital*, 114–53. As Brown notes, "British and American pamphleteers competed to assign or escape blame for the existence of slavery in the British Empire, casting slavery in the process, though with little reflection, as an archetype of injustice" (114). See also Brian Harrison, "A Genealogy of Reform in Modern Britain," in *Anti-Slavery, Religion, and Reform*, ed. Christine Bolt and Seymour Drescher (Ann Arbor: University of Michigan Press, 2009).

71. Sharp, *Declaration*, 18. In *Moral Capital*, Brown has elaborated Sharp's stance in favor of the American rebellion and against the American institution of chattel slavery; see esp. chapter 3, "Granville Sharp and the Obligations of Empire," 155–206.
72. Sharp, *Declaration*, 17.
73. Sharp, *Declaration*, 10.
74. English Bill of Rights (1689), 1 Will. & Mar. Sess. 2, c. 2.
75. English Bill of Rights (1689), 1 Will. & Mar. Sess. 2, c. 2.
76. Sharp, *Declaration*, 20.
77. English Bill of Rights (1689), 1 Will. & Mar. Sess. 2, c. 2.
78. Linda Colley, *Britons: Forging the Nation 1707–1837* (New Haven: Yale University Press, 2009), 103, 105.
79. Jennings, *Christian Imagination*, 174.
80. Richard Baxter, quoted in Mary Stoughton Locke, *Anti-Slavery in America from the Introduction of African Slaves to the Prohibition of the Slave Trade (1619–1808)* (Gloucester, MA: Radcliffe College, 1901), 16.
81. For a general discussion of the relationship between slavery and metaphors of consumption see Charlotte Sussman, *Consuming Anxieties: Consumer Protest, Gender, and British Slavery, 1713–1833* (Stanford, CA: Stanford University Press, 2000). On the contemporary cultures of accumulation see Lenora Hanson, *The Romantic Rhetoric of Accumulation* (Stanford, CA: Stanford University Press, 2023).
82. Heather Keenleyside, *Animals and Other People* (Philadelphia: University of Pennsylvania Press, 2016), 60.
83. Keenleyside, *Animals and Other People*, 60.
84. Keenleyside, *Animals and Other People*, 59.
85. Keenleyside, *Animals and Other People*, 64.
86. Bonhoeffer, *Creation and Fall*, 112.
87. Quobna Ottobah Cugoano, *Thoughts and Sentiments on the Evil and Wicked Traffic of the Slavery and Commerce of the Human Species, Humbly Submitted to the Inhabitants of Great-Britain* (London, 1787), 90.
88. Cugoano, *Thoughts and Sentiments*, 90.
89. Carretta, *Equiano, the African*, 193.
90. Carretta, *Equiano, the African*, 194–95.
91. Tacitus, *Agricola*, ed. A. J. Woodman and Christina Shuttleworth Kraus (Cambridge: Cambridge University Press, 2014), 19.
92. Tacitus, *Agricola*, 19.
93. Tacitus, *Agricola*, 19.

Novel Constitutions and the Making of Race: A Literary and Legal History of Slavery in the Anglophone Atlantic, 1688–1818. Sarah Marsh, Oxford University Press. © Sarah Marsh 2026. DOI: 10.1093/9780197917855.003.0004

4

"Disguised Directions for Escape"

Benjamin Banneker's Celestial Maps and the Science of Emancipation

> Our spirituals, now so widely admired around the world, were often codes. We sang of "heaven" that awaited us, and the slave masters listened in innocence, not realizing that we were not speaking of the hereafter. Heaven was the word for Canada, and the Negro sang of the hope that his escape on the Underground Railroad would carry him there. One of our spirituals, "Follow the Drinking Gourd," in its lyrics contained disguised directions for escape. The gourd was the Big Dipper, and the North Star, to which its handle pointed gave the celestial map that directed the flight to the Canadian border.
>
> —Martin Luther King, Jr., "Impasse in Race Relations"[1]

In 1967, the Canadian Broadcasting Corporation invited Martin Luther King, Jr., to deliver its prestigious Massey Lectures on "anything he considered of importance."[2] In the first lecture, King greeted his Canadian audience by invoking the Underground Railroad's Canadian terminus. Magnifying the Black Freedom Struggle's transnational and cosmic scope, King underscored that with quotidian means, their spirituals and the night sky, African Americans journeyed to freedom. This chapter proposes that the deep history of King's "disguised directions"—those emancipatory possibilities hidden in ordinary places—includes Benjamin Banneker's 1792 *Almanack and Ephemeris*.[3] In response to slavocrats' legal claims that one human being could have absolute power over another, Banneker appealed his anti-slavery case to a higher plane: he invoked the divine, as Equiano had done, and he added the universal truths of mathematics.

In the late summer of 1791, Banneker, the free black inventor and astronomer from Maryland, enclosed his calculations for a 1792 almanac in a pointed letter to Thomas Jefferson. "How pitiable is it to reflect," Banneker wrote,

> that altho you were so fully convinced of the benevolence of the Father of mankind, and of his equal and impartial distribution of those rights and privileges which he had conferred upon them, that you should at the Same time counteract his mercies, in detaining by fraud and violence so numerous a part of my brethren under groaning captivity and cruel oppression, that you should at the

> Same time be found guilty of that most criminal act, which you professedly detested in others, with respect to yourselves.[4]

Here, Banneker underscores the moral hypocrisy that God and history may ascribe to a freedom-loving, slaveholding republic. He reminds Jefferson, who embodied that paradox, that it is not too late for him to lend "aid and assistance to" black Americans, providing "relief from those many distresses and numerous calamities to which we are reduced."[5] Fundamentally, these "distresses" and "calamities" arose from black Americans' enslaved or enslavable condition in the Atlantic world, which we have observed in Behn's *Oroonoko*, Defoe's *Robinson Crusoe*, and Equiano's *Interesting Narrative*.

Scholars have thoroughly appraised the discrete abolitionist arguments in Banneker's letter.[6] Jared Hickman has argued convincingly that Banneker's missive was a "public performance," designed to disseminate the correspondence to the broader audience of the *Almanack*, and to circulate widely Banneker's decisive critique of American racial slavery and Jefferson's response to it.[7] Indeed, Banneker's overture and Jefferson's reply were reprinted with editions of Banneker's foreword to the 1792 almanac as "a form of antislavery propaganda" produced "in large part by Banneker himself."[8] Eric Herschthal has argued, to the contrary, that Banneker "primarily meant [the epistle to Jefferson] to be a *private* letter."[9] Herschthal's claim is founded on persuasive evidence that Banneker never offered Jefferson's letter for publication until it was needed as a prefatory letter asserting Banneker's authorship. The privacy of this letter is part of Herschthal's broader argument that "Banneker knew his most powerful antislavery weapon was not his words, but his science."[10] Yet, given Banneker's complex signification on the concept of freedom, which Hickman elaborates, Herschthal's interpretation is difficult to accept in its entirety. In Banneker's political thought, I see a more capacious abolitionism that is theological, mathematical, and literary. Banneker evinces the truth of human equality with disciplines that are more complementary than hierarchical.[11]

This view emerges clearly when we read the *Almanack* as a paratext of Banneker's appeal to Jefferson. This chapter shows that the 1792 tract is itself a significant artifact of early American anti-slavery politics, hiding in plain sight as a farmers' almanac. It challenges popular climatological justifications for racial slavery and offers a compelling alternative by proposing spherical trigonometry as a mathematical rationale for human equality. The *Almanack* also contains information that could have guided fugitives from bondage by providing what King called "disguised directions for escape." In sum, Banneker's first almanac reveals that some early American thinkers saw science not only as an opportunity for black people to prove their intelligence by sharing in its practice, but also as a venue for demonstrating empirically the truth of human equality. That these scientists' contributions have been obscured from our perception by intervening discourses of white supremacy and scientific racism does not diminish the historic and moral significance of their work. In fact, the gravity of white supremacy, and the human catastrophe it has wrought between Banneker's time and our own, bespeaks the importance of reckoning with an American archive of human equality.

Climate Science and Colonial Slavery: The 1792 *Almanack* in Context

Banneker published his series of almanacs from 1792 through 1797, in at least twenty-eight editions, collaborating with various publishers in cities like Baltimore and Philadelphia. His first almanac is best known in our contemporary scholarship, surely because of its connection to Jefferson, and is the focus of the present analysis. Although the handwritten calculations that Banneker sent to Jefferson are, to my knowledge, lost to history (Jefferson evidently mailed them to the Marquis de Condorcet), we have the letter in which they were enclosed. Banneker's argument to Jefferson was at least twofold. First, his calculations proved black intelligence and, by implication, equal personhood with whites. Second, Banneker's comparison of racial slavery in the United States to English tyranny in colonial America pressed the drafter of the Declaration of Independence to support the cause of early national abolition.[12]

The 1792 almanac, *Benjamin Banneker's PENNSYLVANIA, DELAWARE, MARYLAND and VIRGINIA Almanack and Ephemeris for the Year of Our Lord 1792*, also has survived. The text begins with remarks from Banneker's Baltimore printers, William Goddard and James Angell, and the abolitionist James McHenry. All three white men testified to Banneker's authorship of the almanac's calculations.[13] Next are Banneker's tide tables for the Chesapeake Bay and monthly ephemerides, or tables of future positions of celestial bodies, including the sun and moon. Banneker's calculations are followed by a print miscellany, probably chosen by the abolitionist James Pemberton in coordination with Goddard.[14] The selections include sentimental poetry; hymns; excerpts from London periodicals; curatives for rheumatism, bloody-flux, cancer, and corns; and agricultural instructions for manuring diseased trees. The tract concludes with a catalog of United States government officials, schedules of circuit courts, a calendar of Quaker meetings, lists of roads in the eastern part of the country, and conversion tables describing the value of currencies and contemporary rates of interest.[15]

Except for the certifying front matter from white patrons, Banneker's *Almanack* is a standard example of the genre. As Thomas A. Horrocks explains, early American almanacs typically featured a preface, a calendar, information on eclipses and other astronomical phenomena, and a list of local court and fair dates.[16] But American almanacs were not just compilations of facts and predictions; they were also subjective and argumentative. First produced at Harvard, the American genre was heavily influenced by regional Puritanism, which sought to purge "heathenish" astrology from English iterations of the genre in favor of astronomy, reason, and historical dates uncoupled from purportedly Catholic or pagan origins.[17] Cotton Mather, himself an almanac compiler, noted in 1721 the "foolish *Astrology* of the *Star-gazers*," those "*Planet-Struck*" speculators, who endeavored to discover "what the Great GOD that made them has not *written* there."[18] Mather's castigation of planet-struck people testifies to their presence in his society. In this way, almanacs were a forum of debate, imagination, and projection of relationships among human beings, civil society, the climate, and the cosmos.

Banneker's 1792 *Almanack* exercises this feature of the genre to discredit climatologic explanations of human difference that were asserted during the latter half of the eighteenth century as nature's justification for chattel slavery.[19] To understand the force of this pro-slavery argument—and appreciate why Banneker would use a genre of climatological observation to challenge American slaveholding power—we should review the eighteenth-century relationship between climate, constitution, and racial character. As we observed in this study's introduction, the term "constitution" signified a dense network of ideas in early modern England: it was a near synonym for the common law, understood as the legal expression of the nature and disposition of the English people since time immemorial; it also named bodily condition and character, which climate was thought to shape by humoral means. The conceptual proximity, even overlap, of these terms made it possible for the English to imagine that their rights were embodied—a development that, this study has argued, helped to bring the modern concept of race into being.

During the eighteenth century, British slaveholders pressed this climatologic rhetoric into service as a justification for racial bondage. Slavocrats' fundamental claim, appearing in many variations, was that African-descended people were suited to unfree labor in hot western Atlantic climates because the African environment had long predisposed them to enslavement. In the 1780s, this impulse to naturalize chattel slavery as the effect of climate became popular in direct proportion to abolition's increased political traction.[20] Of course, this was not Englishmen's first use of climate to explain the dynamics of their empire. Justin Roberts shows that the English had long understood climate as a primary challenge to empire-building in the Caribbean: in the seventeenth-century English tropics, small, disease-prone European populations were outnumbered by enslaved majorities and relied on them to hold dangerous colonial outposts, amid European rivalries and powerful indigenous polities. In that dangerous setting, Roberts explains, slavery was forged as a labor regime that underwrote an otherwise fragile empire.[21] English vulnerability in the tropics, real and perceived, is the broader context in which slavocrats embraced climatic rationalizations for African bondage. But, as Katherine Johnston has shown, slaveholders also came to understand that "Africans suited labor in American plantation environments no better than Europeans did"; slavocrats' specious arguments were "designed to protect [their] economic livelihoods," despite catastrophic human consequences.[22]

Slavocrats' eighteenth-century claims drew upon a much older intellectual tradition. We have noted Mary Floyd-Wilson's and Roxann Wheeler's arguments that, for early modern anglophone people, climate was the foundation of the human categories we now call race and ethnicity. To review: Floyd-Wilson explains that the early modern English understood bodily appearances and national manners to be rooted in a fundamental relation between native environment and their bodies' four humors, a system she named geohumoralism. Two general models of geohumoralism pertained. In one, gleaned from Hippocrates's *Airs, Waters, Places* (c. 400 BCE), a people's disposition arose in kind with its climatologic circumstances. A hot climate would produce a hot-tempered people. The second model posited an inverse relationship between humors and climate. A hot climate burned away the humors, leaving the body cold and dry. In both models, the relation of the humoral body to the surrounding climate was of singular ethnographic importance.[23]

In the seventeenth- and eighteenth-century Western world, this ancient thought system continued to hold sway. Wheeler notes that it "provided the most important rubric for thinking about human differences in the eighteenth century, in regard to both complexion and civil society."[24] European colonialism, however, and its mass movements of human beings to non-native climates, illuminated consequential problems in traditional climatologic thinking: Was human racial identity formed by local climate and permanently fixed in the body? Or could an individual's change of place produce a change of racial character?[25]

In *Some Thoughts Concerning Education* (1693) John Locke, like many thinkers of his time, blended the possibilities implied by these questions. We have noted his belief that the inhabitants of Malta seasoned their children by forcing them to go naked in the heat until their tenth year; the English might expect good results if they took care to "accustom [themselves] from [their] Infancy" to England's climate. Locke recommended that English children wear leaky shoes and not be kept too warm in the wintertime. "Our Bodies will endure any Thing," Locke noted, "that from the Beginning they are accustom'd to."[26] Here, Locke describes a common human process of physiological formation through environmental exposure that created different kinds of human beings (English and Maltese, in this case) because of variations in local climate. On the other hand, Locke's assertion seems to allow that a baby born in England could be raised naked in Malta, or that a child born in Malta could be reared in leaky shoes in England, and each become acclimated to a non-native locality through direct experience of the local environment. In accordance with his empiricist habits of mind, the human experience of climate and culture—not heredity—was the significant racializing force Locke perceived.

Others would express more rigid views about the effects of climate on human beings. In a footnote to his 1748 essay "Of National Characters," David Hume indicated his infamous supposition that "negroes" were "naturally inferior to the whites."[27] Whereas Locke focused on the individual's formation in response to her environment, Hume's analysis addressed human populations as well as single persons, reckoning that there "scarcely ever was a civilized nation of [Negro] complexion, nor even any individual eminent in action or speculation; no ingenuous manufacturers amongst them, no arts, no sciences."[28] Although he vehemently opposed colonial slavery on the grounds that it corrupted the moral character of slaveholders,[29] Hume ultimately advanced a controversial, nonbiblical argument about human difference, arguing that only an "original distinction betwixt these three breeds of men [Negroes, Germans, and Tartars]," made by "nature," could account for differences he observed in the middle of the eighteenth century.[30] While Locke allowed for racial mutability to be contingent on environment, Hume's footnote is evidence that racial determinism could be derived from climatologic thought.[31]

Importantly, however, English statutory enslavement of Africans did not arise from climate theory but through imperial policy and legal action—charters, court decisions, Crown orders, and slave codes—that first rendered human beings as property in the Stuarts' pursuit of absolute power through neofeudal jurisprudence. Yet because the term "constitution" referred both to a body of laws and to a theory of bodies, England's developing regime of human slavery was always inherently available to climatological explanation, allowing legal bondage to be redescribed as a difference of physical features. We saw this to be the case when Barbadian lawmakers used the complexionary term "Negro" to justify withdrawal of ancient constitutional protections from people of African descent in a slave code they drafted at King Charles II's behest. Over the course of the eighteenth century, and in response to growing anti-slavery agitation across the Atlantic world by enslaved people and others, climatologic meanings of "constitution" were drawn upon by pro-slavery advocates to argue that racial slavery was natural. Africans, they held, had been made for bondage by their native climate and the customs and complexions to which it had given rise.

No one understood this element of slavocratic rhetoric better than people who were enslaved. In *Thoughts and Sentiments on the Evil of Slavery* (1787), Quobna Ottobah Cugoano remembers his enslavers' claim that the "long continued practice[s] of [African] nations" had "marked out" Africans for slavery in both their "nature and complexion." Cugoano responds that his compatriots "are born as free, and are brought up with as great a predilection for their own country, freedom and liberty, as the sons and daughters of fair Britain"—the word "fair" invoking Anglo-America's burgeoning ideology of white liberty and black slavery.[32]

In his 1789 abolitionist memoir, *The Interesting Narrative*, Olaudah Equiano recalls slaveholders' geohumoral assessment of his native climate. Africans were "unfinished," they claimed, and "incapable" of enjoying nature's bounty. "You stupify [your slaves] with stripes," Equiano writes,

> and think it necessary to keep them in a state of ignorance; and yet you assert that they are incapable of learning; that their minds are such a barren soil or moor, that culture would be lost on them; *and that they come from a climate, where nature... has left man alone scant and unfinished*, and incapable of enjoying the treasures she has poured out for him!—An assertion at once impious and absurd. Why do you use those instruments of torture? Are they fit to be applied by one rational being to another?... But, above all, are there no dangers attending this mode of treatment? Are you not hourly in dread of an insurrection?[33]

Equiano illuminates that the corruption Hume saw in the institution of domestic slavery had its roots in extreme forms of interpersonal and state violence required when, as Equiano said, "one rational being" sought to enslave another. By maintaining the relational nature of his personhood in this system, and the truth of his status as a rational human being, Equiano argues that political violence, not nature, makes the only meaningful social difference among people.

Benjamin Banneker espoused this same argument, not only in his correspondence with Jefferson, but in his almanacs. Equiano's interventions in racial ideology were, we have seen, undertaken primarily in the poetics of biblical metaphor.[34] Banneker's interventions added mathematic ballast to such theological claims. As we will see, the Maryland scientist challenged the slavocratic ideology of Africans' natural-historical inferiority by maintaining that *universal* relationships pertain between human beings and their surroundings. This important contribution to the discourse on human rights addressed a significant contradiction in the status quo, to which we now turn.

Early American Racial Climates

During the eighteenth century, anglophone religious orthodoxy bolstered the notion of a single human creation, or monogenism, as opposed to multiple creations of humanity, or polygenism. With geohumoral thinking, Englishmen explained to themselves how a global diversity of human beings could, in time, follow from the monogenetic beginning described in Genesis: the original human family was scattered from the Garden to settle in various global localities where their humoral constitutions were altered over time by variations in climate, roughly the process Locke had described in *Thoughts*. Anglo-American slavocrats took up this logic in the eighteenth century to argue that climate had made some descendants of Adam naturally free and others naturally suited to slavery, as Equiano and Cugoano testify. In this way, an Englishman might ultimately reconcile belief in the Bible's account of a common human creation with the colonial reality of chattel slavery, affirming God's supreme power with one hand while usurping it with the other.[35]

English thinkers posited that varying exposure to the sun at different latitudes was a fundamental source of different humoral constitutions. The anglophone globe was thus divided into polar, temperate, and equatorial (or torrid) regions, with corresponding native human types.[36] This is evident in texts like *Othello*, in which Desdemona posits that "the sun where [Othello] was born" is responsible for drying out his humors and thus forming his unjealous moral character. Elsewhere in the play, Othello is bestialized as "an old black ram" and "Barbary horse" because his color is a sign of categorical difference, at least to the treacherous Iago.[37] Prior to inventions by writers of the Renaissance, Floyd-Wilson has demonstrated, the effects of the sun on equatorial regions and their inhabitants were, contrary to Shakespeare's Iago, not regarded by the English as diminishments of personhood. Rather, the English ascribed a range of moral attributes to these people, allowing (like Desdemona) that Ethiopians, whose humoral constitutions were dried by intense local heat, exhibited "natural wisdom and spirituality."[38] By geohumoral implication, the English believed the opposite true of their own wet, phlegmatic constitutions, whose dull wits and warlike natures arose from the chilly maritime weather of their home island. A critical part of the early modern imperial project, Floyd-Wilson shows, was the transmutation of these ideas, from the Mediterranean-centered world of classical antiquity, to characterize the English as geohumorally balanced and temperate—and thus globally central—as opposed to marginal, chilly, and barbaric.[39]

Throughout the eighteenth century, the sun remained central to anglophone ideas about human variation, not least of all in the context of British colonial expansion into the western Atlantic.[40] As John Gabriel Stedman noted in his *Narrative of a Five Years Expedition Against the Revolted Negroes of Surinam* (1796), "the [native] Americans are of a copper-colour or red, and the inhabitants of Africa, called Negroes, are black, *viz.* the one being more burnt by the sun than the other, and not because they are two distinct races of people."[41] For Stedman, the sun's differential effects cohered with the traditional meanings of Genesis. No thoughtful person, Stedman underscored, could "avoid seeing that there is but one race of people on the earth, who differ from each other only according to the soil and the climate in which they live."[42]

English colonists extended geohumoral ideas into the colonial sphere and reckoned that their humoral constitutions, seasoned at higher latitudes, would falter in the sun-heated tropics; they worried that intense heat and humidity would endanger their health, customs, and power. In 1592, we have noted, Edward

Hayes and Christopher Carleill found that European localities south of 40 degrees north latitude were, in the summer, "unto [English] bodies offensyve [*sic*], Which cannot prosper in dry and scalding heat more naturall [*sic*] to the Spaniard than us."[43] The royalist Richard Ligon, who settled in Barbados during the Interregnum, reported disbelief that an Englishman could travel to the tropics and "indure [*sic*] such scorching without being suffocated." Ligon, remember, wrote of being "fricased [*sic*]" with his shipmates in the Caribbean, and the "great failing in [our] vigour, and sprightliness we have in colder Climates."[44] Alan Bewell has elaborated these ideas, showing that colonial expansion posed physical threats to British sailors, soldiers, and marines, creating the "tropical invalid" as a medical diagnosis and literary type.[45] Thus, under the rubric of climate, eighteenth-century ideas about English somatic inferiority at low latitudes lived cheek by jowl in the Anglo-American imagination with correlative ideas about the mental and political inferiority of African-descended people. As Johnston's and Bewell's work clarifies, however, all people tended to suffer in non-native climates and disease environments; but the burgeoning political climate of race in America occluded this reality.[46]

Anglo-Americans amalgamated their physical endangerment at low latitudes, real and perceived, with claims to slavocratic power over resistant black people, who often vastly outnumbered them in those regions. The brutal slave codes produced by colonial legislators are significant evidence of their disquiet.[47] Race war seems to have been a persistent specter: "Are you not hourly in dread of an insurrection?" Equiano pregnantly asks in the *Interesting Narrative*.[48] Similarly Jefferson, in *Notes on the State of Virginia* (1785), says gravely:

> Indeed I tremble for my country when I reflect that God is just: that his justice cannot sleep forever: that considering numbers [of enslaved black and free white people], nature and natural means only, a revolution of the wheel of fortune, an exchange of situation, is among possible events: that it may become probable by supernatural interference! The Almighty has no attribute which can take side with us in such a contest.[49]

The state of war that Locke perceived in the master–slave relation in *Two Treatises of Government* is evident here.[50] So, too, is Equiano's view that slaveholders were at war with God. We can see neither this political dynamic in the western Atlantic world, nor the nuances of its moral content, without attending to older English climate ideologies with which it tumultuously interacted. Jefferson's "revolution of the wheel of fortune" invokes not only Machiavelli's *fortuna*, but a geohumoral world turned upside down, where slavocratic interpretations of African descent, perhaps even his own, are upended by a righteous God's violent intervention in human history.[51]

Thus, in the early American republic, older English beliefs about climate underwrote a burgeoning national system for the government of slave and free labor, glossing the socioeconomic outcomes of this system as the work of nature. This early American labor regime had grown from the parameters of royal land charters of the early colonial period; territorial conflicts with Native Americans whose land the English expropriated and traded for; and practices for land and animal husbandry, which depended upon local soil composition, topography, crop viability, growing seasons, annual rainfall, and access to Atlantic shipping ways. The lines that ultimately divided free and slave states along the eastern seaboard were subtended by the contours of these long-standing and often violent colonial processes. In the early national republic, a "place of still vaguely defined jurisdictions, frontiers, and marchlands," the state lines that Americans now understand to demarcate the countryside were less important to a sense of place than climate, local agrarian customs, and brutal labor and legal regimes that made those customs possible.[52] In his searing Independence Day oratory of 1852, Frederick Douglass could say with justice that "New York has become as Virginia" because the Fugitive Slave Act of 1850 had "obliterated" the Mason-Dixon line and nationalized "the power to hold, hunt, and sell men, women, and children as slaves."[53]

When Banneker wrote to Jefferson in 1791, the Northwest Ordinance of 1787 both outlawed slavery north of the Ohio River and permitted the recapture of people who escaped from slavery into that region, throwing into relief the significance of racial slavery in the new national cartography.[54] Banneker perhaps knew of Jefferson's complicated history with this legislation when he sent his letter to the Virginian. As principal author of the Ordinance of 1784, Jefferson had proposed an anti-slavery proviso barring slavery in all federal territories after 1800, a measure William Cohen describes as "the single most important antislavery act in Jefferson's career," and that William Merkel reads as an early, abortive articulation of free-soil constitutionalism.[55] Congress struck the clause by a single vote, with Jefferson one of two Southern delegates to support it.[56]

The Northwest Ordinance of July 1787, drafted by others but built on the territorial framework Jefferson had sketched three years earlier, enacted a narrower prohibition on slavery north of the Ohio River and, as Paul Finkelman has shown, simultaneously instituted a fugitive-slave provision that extended federal statutory protection for slaveholders' property claims in persons.[57] A few weeks later, in late August 1787, South Carolina delegates Pierce Butler and Charles C. Pinckney successfully moved in the Constitutional Convention to add a similar fugitive-slave clause extending that logic from the Northwest Territory to the Union as a whole, which would ultimately become Article IV, Section 2, Clause 3 of the Constitution:

> No Person held to Service or Labour in one State, under the Laws thereof, escaping into another, shall, in Consequence of any Law or Regulation therein, be discharged from such Service or Labour, but shall be delivered up on Claim of the Party to whom such Service or Labour may be due.[58]

Along with the delay of the transatlantic slave trade's abolition, and the three-fifths compromise on representation, Article IV, Section 2 exemplified the Constitution's protection of racial slavery as a pillar of the new nation's stability. The constitutional meanings of the Fugitive Slave Clause were as clear to Southern slavocrats as they were to Douglass half a century later. Pinckney proclaimed during the clause's ratification debates that "We have obtained a right to recover our slaves in whatever part of America they may take refuge, which is a right we had not before."[59] The personal dominion of slaveholders, derived from monarchical theories of absolute power, now overflowed the plantation and the state, flooding the rest of the country.[60]

When Banneker published his 1792 almanac, American slavocrats had thus accomplished a stunning ideological about-face. Drawing upon domestic English ideas about climate, colonial slaveholders had reimagined the meanings of complexion, fixing skin color as a fundamental determinant of legal personhood rather than a mere effect of environmental exposure. Those new ideas about human body color—now fully American—were established in social practices, inscribed in colonial slave codes, and ratified by the US Constitution. This interchange of effect and cause institutionalized the heritable, and presumptively immutable, chattel status of African-descended people. Pivoting on the fulcrum of slavery, the different legal meanings of skin color across American states were changing the historical significance of latitude itself. Into this revolution of ideas, Banneker's *Almanack* proposed another turn.

"When I Take the Universe for my Standard": Trigonometry and Human Equality

Banneker's *Almanack* begins by roundly rejecting constitutional American racism that is based on human skin color. In affirming Banneker's authorship, Goddard and Angell not only assert an equality of intellectual aptitude; they do so using an older geohumoral monogenism where climate and place of origin determine skin color, but where skin color does not determine human worth:

> THE Editors of the . . . ALMANACK, feel themselves gratified in the Opportunity of presenting to the Public . . . a COMPLETE and ACCURATE EPHEMERIS for the Year 1792, calculated by a sable Descendant of Africa, who, by this Specimen of Ingenuity, evinces . . . that mental Powers and Endowments are not the exclusive Excellence of white People, but that the Rays of Science may alike illumine the Minds of Men of every Clime, (however they may differ in the Colour of their Skin) particularly those whom Tyrant-Custom has too long taught us to depreciate as a Race inferior in intellectual Capacity.[61]

In this metaphor, science is an egalitarian sun, whose global effects are "alike" regardless of how human beings "differ in the Colour of their Skin." The "Tyrant-Custom" exposits specious ideas about "Race" as an indicator of human "intellectual Capacity." This assertion is particularly potent considering contemporary claims about the tyranny of American slaveholders. Banneker had styled these to Jefferson as the "State of tyrannical thralldom" experienced by enslaved black people; earlier in *Notes*, Jefferson, too, underscored "the intemperance of passions" that were "daily exercised in tyranny" by slaveholders toward their human property.[62] Here, both men continued the line of thinking earlier trod by Hume and Equiano. And, by asserting that "the Rays of Science" can equally "illumine the Minds of Men of every Clime," Angell and Goddard join Equiano in framing the rational person as a bulwark against racializing climate discourse.

The abolitionist James McHenry follows Goddard and Angell in the *Almanack*'s opening pages, saying that Banneker is "a fresh proof that the powers of the mind are disconnected with the colour of the skin," and then taking a swipe at Hume's comparison of white and black intelligence.[63] Together, the certifiers' remarks disentangle the sun's imputed outward effects on skin color from the inward reality of intelligence. This point is underscored dynamically further down the page by Banneker's prediction of two solar eclipses.[64] American white supremacists ultimately would seek to obscure Banneker and other black thinkers from our view based on slavocratic assertions of the sun's degrading effects on African intelligence. But in 1792, Banneker calculated the scientific reality of a counterclaim with symbolic importance: the sun, not human beings, would be obscured on September 16 to all people living in Pennsylvania, Delaware, Maryland, and Virginia. Together, Banneker, Goddard, Angell, and McHenry set the stage not only for Banneker's public demonstration of his facility with astronomical calculations, but also for the *Almanack*'s demonstration that slavocratic ideology was as unscientific as it was corrupting to the new nation's high ideals of equality. Here, the "Rays of Science" illuminate not only the minds of men, but the moral travesty of human slavery, which Hume had exposited in the terms of political philosophy and Equiano with biblical exegesis. However, Banneker's mathematical interventions in the *Almanack* are as theoretically significant as they are pragmatic: for anyone who could perceive it as such, the almanac's information might assist any person, wrongfully enslaved, in fugitive relocation to a freer latitude.

Discerning the fault in America's moral compass, but not necessarily in its stars, Banneker offers his *Almanack*'s readers, now as then, an alternative to the racialized world of early modern geohumoral thought, which had become a justification for racial slavery established through novel constitutionalism. Banneker's alternative worldview posits a common set of relations between human beings and the cosmos described by spherical trigonometry, a universal method for wayfinding in the absence of a fixed referent. This method provided a mathematical basis for Banneker's contribution to the early American discourse on human rights in both the 1792 *Almanack* and his 1791 letter to Jefferson.

Spherical trigonometry is a branch of mathematics describing the metrical relationships between sides and angles of spherical triangles. It was used in the eighteenth century to calculate global and extraterrestrial positions when local time and time at 0° longitude were unknown.[65] To discern the position of the sun, moon, planets, and other heavenly bodies for both the capital survey in Washington, DC, and his later ephemerides, Banneker used a telescope and quadrant to measure the altitude and azimuth of an observed celestial body. With spherical trigonometry, these measurements of vertical distance and horizontal degree could be converted into coordinates on that observed body. Using trigonometric functions, the astronomer could then use these coordinates to calculate the object's future locations relative to the fixed point on Earth, from whence the original altitude and azimuth had been gauged.[66]

Thus, Banneker took the sun's measure in the *Almanack*—not by assessing its variable and relative effects on human bodies the globe over, but by showing through a reproducible mathematical method its appearance in the sky. The activity of the sun and other celestial bodies, Banneker demonstrated, was calculable by human beings, irrespective of their skin's pigmentation or their position on the globe. Moreover, Banneker showed that human position is not determined solely by the edicts of the powerful; rather, all people possess faculties to orient themselves according to cosmic reference points, which they hold in common. This public performance by "a sable Descendant of Africa" thus offered early Americans not just proof of black intelligence, but a radically egalitarian theory of the relationship among human beings, the terrestrial world, and the wider universe. This was a direct scientific challenge to slavocratic geohumoralism.

To slaveholders like Jefferson, who publicly doubted the equality of black Americans and sought evidence that "the want of talents observed in [black Americans] is merely the effect of their degraded condition" and not "from any difference in the structure of the parts on which intellect depends," Banneker's skillful application of spherical trigonometry offered a double reproof.[67] First, Banneker showed the equality of his intellectual capacity with whites, and that black people were capable of "tracing and comprehending the investigations of Euclid," which Jefferson had doubted in *Notes*.[68] Second, Banneker undermined slavocratic geohumoralism, showing that human difference is meaningfully interpreted not according to climatologic determinism, but to the ever-moving but always measurable positions of celestial bodies. This is to say that human beings are equivalent ontologically and metaphysically; they differ only in their orientation to the sun and stars, an emphatically monogenetic way of interpreting human skin color, as well as the entire cosmos.

There is compelling evidence, in the 1792 *Almanack*'s many literary excerpts, that Banneker, Goddard, Angell, and Pemberton sought to emphasize the political implications of what Banneker's application of spherical trigonometry revealed. The most thorough example, "The Planetary and Terrestrial Worlds," is an eighteenth-century meditation, attributed to the English theologian James Hervey, on the "extreme meanness" of all human beings, and the "abject littleness of all terrestrial things" in relation to the wider cosmos, and particularly the sun, that "grand dispenser of divine munificence."[69] The "dim speck" of Earth, "hardly perceivable in a map of the universe," ultimately offers occasion to consider the insignificance of political institutions—kingdoms, countries, and patrimonies—in the context of cosmic grandeur:

> If then ... this whole system, be so very diminutive, what is a kingdom or a country? What are a few lordships or the so much admired patrimonies of those who are styled wealthy? When I measure them with my own little pittance, they swell into proud bloated dimensions: But when I take the universe for my standard, how scanty is their size, how contemptible their figure! they shrink into pompous nothings.[70]

Hervey's exhortation to "take the universe for [your] standard" invites the reader to see human similarity as an effect of the cosmic scale which is the *Almanack*'s purview, and which Banneker described mathematically in his ephemerides. As Hervey says, human political institutions "shrink into ... nothings" when considered within the macrocosm whose future movements Banneker had predicted with trigonometry just a few pages earlier.

The institution that comes under special scrutiny in the literary selections of the *Almanack* is racial slavery. In the text's extracts from *The Commonplace-Book of the Kentucky Philosopher*, we learn the epigrammatic story of the "slaves of Tartary," who, when river-crossing, "catch hold of the horse's tail that passes before them" to escape drowning.[71] The extract then pivots to the story of a Muslim scholar, who had "escaped from being impaled."[72] This scholar has spent his life studying the Quran and various sciences. In older age, the scholar's learning is great, but he is impoverished. He appeals to the Sultan Mohamet, "beseeching him to save a son of science from starving. The Sultan, having considered his case, gave him no other answer than this: '*Friend, with all your learning, don't you know that the world is a tail, and happy is he that gets hold of it.*'"[73] Taking the Sultan's metaphor as advice, the scholar changes clothes with a Russian slave and asks this person to sell him into slavery. Once enslaved, the scholar works in the fields and feigns his general ignorance. However, six or eight months hence, the story goes, he begins to preach and prophesy, quoting the Quran at length. Creating a stir, the prophet-slave is ultimately presented to the Sultan, who recognizes him, and asks if they have met before. The scholar replies, "betray me not; *you know the world is a tail, and I have but just got hold of it.*" The story concludes "that the man got a good living by his wit, and the world has got a good story."[74]

What are we to make of this strange tale of water-crossing, deep learning disguised as prophecy, and the passage of a scholar in and out of slavery? It is hard not to see Banneker in these details. He was born a free man in colonial Maryland, but his grandfather, Bannaka, came to colonial Maryland from Africa in chains. Enslaved by the Senegalese during wartime, Bannaka (or Bannka) was sold into the English Atlantic trade where he became the sometimes-chattel and sometimes-husband of the Englishwoman Mary Walsh, Banneker's grandmother. Mary was a Sussex servant convicted of larceny in 1683 for allowing a cow to kick over a pail of milk. She purchased Bannaka to work the tobacco farm she rented following her penal sentence of indentured labor in Maryland, a commutation of her original death sentence, secured when she demonstrated her ability to read. After Bannaka refused enslavement to Mary on the grounds of his royal birth, the two married.[75] Their grandson, Benjamin, thus knew from family history the arbitrariness that consigned some people to bondage, like the Muslim scholar in the *Almanack* who is forced into slavery by poverty. Certainly Banneker, a black scholar who lived in a slave state by subsistence farming, was well aware of the possibility of his own enslavement.

However, the Muslim scholar from the *Commonplace-Book of the Kentucky Philosopher* dramatizes a critical difference between the "slaves of Tartary" and the slaves of the United States. While the Muslim scholar can become a slave by switching clothes with an enslaved Russian—an alteration which, by implication, could be reversed by a wardrobe change—the colorist American regime stopped African-descended people from altering their condition of enslavement or enslavability. In May 1751, when Banneker was 19 years old, the General Assembly of Maryland passed "An Act for the more effectual Punishment of Negroes and other Slaves," as well as a supplement to an earlier "Act to prevent the tumultuous Meeting and other Irregularities of Negroes and other Slaves," which further consolidated racial slavery in colonial Maryland—and whose titles alone presume that all African-descended people in the colony are held in bondage.[76] Family and public records show the Bannekers taking care during these years to ensure that their children inherited real estate at young ages because heritable property in land was a significant, if imperfect, hedge against the potential of racial enslavement in colonial Maryland. A 1737 land indenture between Benjamin's father, Robert, and a Baltimore County landowner, Richard Gist, shows Banneker becoming a landed proprietor at the age of 5.[77]

The 1792 *Almanack*'s extract from the *Columbian Magazine* condemns these American legal developments and their reliance on the slavocratic ideologies derived from geohumoralism:

> The enlightened part of humankind begins to be ashamed of this inhuman traffic, and of the base degradation of that part of our species, who, to speak in the language of an amiable and eminent philosopher of our country [David Rittenhouse],

> "have been doomed to endless slavery by us—merely because *their* bodies may be disposed to reflect or absorb the rays of light in a way different from *ours*."[78]

In this way, the *Almanack* programmatically rebukes slavocratic geohumoralism as a rationale for chattel slavery, asserting that the sun's different effects on people are, at most, skin deep. Human beings' geographical origin in relation to the sun, that is, changes nothing more than their color, which is evidence only of itself. The volitional subject can change geographical position to secure freedom from "endless slavery," the central feature of the American chattel system. In this way, the *Columbian Magazine* excerpt emphasizes a key political implication of the universal mathematical method Banneker had used to compose his predictive tables: locations on Earth are of little consequence to the astronomer's perceptive and descriptive powers. Banneker's ephemerides thus assert, contextually to the *Columbian Magazine*'s abolitionism, an egalitarian heliocentrism as the basis for universal human rights, underwritten by trigonometric proof.

Banneker's Mathematical Civil Religion

In his collaborative effort with Angell, Goddard, and Pemberton, Banneker found himself morally unbound from a country of professed Christians swearing allegiance to liberty while holding others in bondage. We have seen in his letter to Jefferson that Banneker found it "pitiable" that Americans had forgotten their founding claims of God's "equal and impartial distribution of... rights and privileges" by "detaining by fraud and violence" their African-descended "brethren." But Banneker's critique of American slaveholding was not merely a feeling of sorrow at the suffering of others. Rather, Banneker's letter frames racial slavery as America's failure of theological discipline. He reminds Jefferson of the Christian injunction that "we are all of the Same Family, and Stand in the Same relation to" the "one universal Father." This is true, Banneker says, regardless of "Society or religion," "Situation or colour."[79] Banneker chose to include for Jefferson calculations attesting mathematically that the observable universe imitated this metaphysical truth. Banneker concludes that it is the duty of all Christians to relieve "every part of the human race" from every "burthen or oppression they may unjustly labour under."[80] If Jefferson's "love" for self and law is sincere, Banneker adds, he could not help but exert himself on behalf of enslaved people, as was consistent with the will of God. Here, Banneker seems to be exerting himself mathematically and theologically to free Jefferson from the spiritual and moral burdens of a political misunderstanding.

Jefferson may have received this idea with equanimity. In *Notes*, the Virginian had wondered rhetorically if "the liberties of a nation" could "be thought secure when we have removed their only firm basis, a conviction in the minds of the people that these liberties are the gift of God?" His implication was that slaveholding, or "permitting one half the citizens...to trample on the rights of the other," not only destroyed the "morals" and "industry" of human beings, but also that this "violation" would expose slaveholders to God's "wrath."[81] Perhaps Banneker hoped that his calculations for the 1792 almanac would evince for Jefferson human beings' common position under a benevolent and parental God, the very position Banneker described in his letter. Banneker had enclosed mathematical assurance that the Creator's universe did not naturally tend toward fortune's vengeful wheel.

After all, Banneker continued to Jefferson, the "Supreme Ruler of the universe" had assured American independence from British attempts to "reduce [the American colonists] to a State of Servitude."[82] When "every human aid appeared unavailable," Banneker recalls to Jefferson, a "miraculous and providential preservation" of the Americans had granted them "freedom and tranquility"—not as the result of any human exertion, but as "the peculiar blessing of Heaven."[83] If Banneker's letter is indeed the "public performance" that Hickman discerns, the scientist was painting the statesman into a corner of great importance: appealing to the "Creator" and "Supreme Judge"[84] of the Declaration of Independence, Banneker prompted Jefferson to acknowledge in writing the just extension of liberty to all human beings living in the United States. As Jefferson had suggested in *Notes*, white and black Americans were "citizens" all; the important difference was that the former could lawfully "trample on the rights" of the latter.

In fact, Jefferson had, in *Notes*, taken Banneker's position, but in the earthly terms of property: "The man," Jefferson said, "in whose favour no laws of property exist, probably feels himself less bound to respect those made in favour of others."[85] Banneker's argument for a common human family, and Jefferson's insight about the exclusive nature of private property, were two sides of the American coin minted by chattel slavery: the children of the same divine parent were transfigured into master and slave. Banneker's analogy—between the "universal Father" of his letter, and the egalitarian sun of his *Almanack*—illuminated the macrocosmic dimensions of the microcosmic injustice Jefferson underscored. With the ideal of universal liberty as a common referent, both men set their course: Banneker to persuade by divine appeal, and Jefferson to warn of trouble on the ground.

Unlike Jefferson and Equiano, Banneker never raised the possibility of slave insurrection as righteous and inevitable. Instead, Banneker sought to orient Jefferson away from apocalyptic visions of a racial revolution on Machiavelli's wheel, and toward an understanding of interracial brotherhood nurtured by the benevolent "Father of mankind."[86] Banneker's letter thus styles the Virginian as "measurably friendly and well disposed" to black Americans and "far less inflexible in Sentiments of [a racist] nature, than many others," who, as members of the human family, might also be persuaded.[87] This appeal to Jefferson's better angels is the rhetorical point from which Banneker's argument in the letter inclines heavenward—that is, toward those enclosed calculations that describe an egalitarian cosmos. In this way, Banneker implies to Jefferson that, when slaveholding American founders are weighed in macrocosmic scales by God and history, their moral authority—and their claims for universal human freedom—will be found wanting substance. As he makes this most subtle yet important political appeal, Banneker allows for a "friendly" and "flexible" Jefferson to yet have an historic change of heart. Indeed, Banneker's letter counsels humility to anyone who would presume a fixed correspondence between a person's sociopolitical position and his capacity for future moral action. In another deft blow to the climatologic determinism of slaveholders, Banneker implied that, while the movements of the sun and stars are predictable, the moral choices of human beings are not.

Banneker's 1792 *Almanack* elaborates this theme of intellectual humility in a key literary excerpt titled "ON OMNIPOTENCE." The poem begins:

> Learn to distinguish God from Man
> Nor think the Lord resembles Thee
> Thou never canst the Godhead scan,
> Pow'r increate, from body free.[88]

These lines exhort the *Almanack*'s reader, and perhaps especially the American slaveholder, not only to mark the difference between the human and the divine, but to accept the ultimately unknowable nature of God. Humanity cannot take God's measure by its own means because, unlike human beings the poem says, God is an uncreated, omnipotent power without a body. For this reason, human beings should not "think the Lord resembles" them in outward appearance or inward being. Read in the context of Banneker's letter to Jefferson, these lines are a clear indictment of slaveholders who legally assert Godlike power over the people they enslave, justified by earthbound ideas of their own racial superiority. Rhyming "Thee" with "free," the poem underscores an error in slaveholders' presumption that their body color grants them absolute power over others. Rather, the poem contends, God—the "Supreme Ruler of the universe" is Banneker's phrase to Jefferson—was a power free from body, and thus free from color and its human-created meanings.

"Devising Ways and Means": Banneker's Celestial Maps to Freedom

Using math to strike at the heart of slavocratic justifications of racial bondage would itself be a momentous accomplishment for a late eighteenth-century farmers' almanac.[89] Yet, as I have indicated above, there is more emancipationist potential in the 1792 *Almanack*, which is that its information could have been a resource for people escaping from bondage. While this interpretation of the *Almanack* must remain speculative considering the available evidence, we should consider it nevertheless because it animates a lasting tension in American political life: that it is one thing to assert the truth of human equality and another to live in the world as though this assertion is true.

As we have noted, Banneker's 1792 *Almanack* concludes with a standard list of federal government officials as well as schedules for the early national circuit, district, and county courts from New Hampshire to Georgia. A list of northeastward and southwestward running roads showed the number of miles between various settled waypoints as far north as New Haven and as far south as Savannah. Interspersed between the circuit court schedules and the list of roads is a calendar of local Quaker meetings from Pennsylvania to North Carolina.[90] In sum then, the 1792 *Almanack* is a palimpsest of anti-slavery arguments layered among Chesapeake tide tables, schedules of sunrise and sunset times, charts of the moon's phases, weather predictions, mile markers for northerly and southerly running roads, timetables for the movements of local law enforcement, and a meeting calendar for perhaps the best-known group of abolitionists in the early United States.

Certainly a farmer, miller, merchant, or slave trader would benefit from this constellation of texts; so, too, would the fugitive from slavery and her collaborators. As Eve Tavor Bannet explains, miscellaneous texts, like eighteenth-century American almanacs, often were engaged by readers in a discontinuous way: "As the miscellarian writer [or compiler] was free to write about subjects in any order and manner he pleased... the reader was free to read... in any order and manner s/he pleased."[91] Given the coordination among Banneker and Baltimore abolitionists like Pemberton to devise the 1792 *Almanack*'s textual contents, it seems possible, if not plausible, that some patterns and manners of reading these pages may have aided the exodus of fugitives. We know from Frederick Douglass's work that Northern abolitionists, like Mr Ruggles, often were "devising ways and means for [fugitive slaves'] successful escape."[92] Douglass, too, "bent [himself] to devising ways and means" for his 1835 attempt to escape slavery.[93] Had Angell, Banneker, Goddard, and Pemberton thus devised the 1792 *Almanack*?

We cannot be certain. Still, Douglass's *Narrative* sheds light on the immensely important role that cartographic, climatologic, calendric, and astronomical knowledge played in early national fugitivity and the rhetoric of abolition. Throughout his first autobiography, Douglass invokes the latitudinal politics of American slavery, noting slaves' general dread of being sold to the "Georgia traders," who signify distance from Mason's and Dixon's line as well as the direct relationship between degrees latitude and the probability of escape from slavery.[94] The global outlook is no more promising: "We could see no spot, this side of the ocean," Douglass writes, "where we could be free. We knew nothing about Canada. Our knowledge of the north did not extend farther than New York."[95]

With the same geographic metaphor, Douglass imagines escape in his well-known apostrophe to the Chesapeake Bay. Douglass "pour[s] out [his] soul's complaint" at the edge of the water; but the Chesapeake also represents a practical political reality to an enslaved person in Maryland: "I will take to the water," Douglass says plainly. "This very bay shall yet bear me into freedom. The steamboats steered in a north-east course from North Point. I will do the same; and when I get to the head of the bay, I will turn my canoe adrift, and walk straight through Delaware into Pennsylvania."[96] Typical of Douglass's political thought, in which well-navigated moral obstacles are a source of human dignity, the Bay is both barrier and conduit to freedom. Douglass's understanding of tides at "the head of the bay," and the latitudinal relation of Delaware to Pennsylvania—mixed with his moral courage—transforms the barrier into a conduit, making a way out of no way. Banneker's 1792 *Almanack*, which seeks to excite anti-slavery sentiment while providing information about Chesapeake tides is, in this way, a miscellanist precursor to Douglass's *Narrative*. For example, Banneker's 1792 Chesapeake tide table (Figure 4.1) includes a column emphasizing the nature of

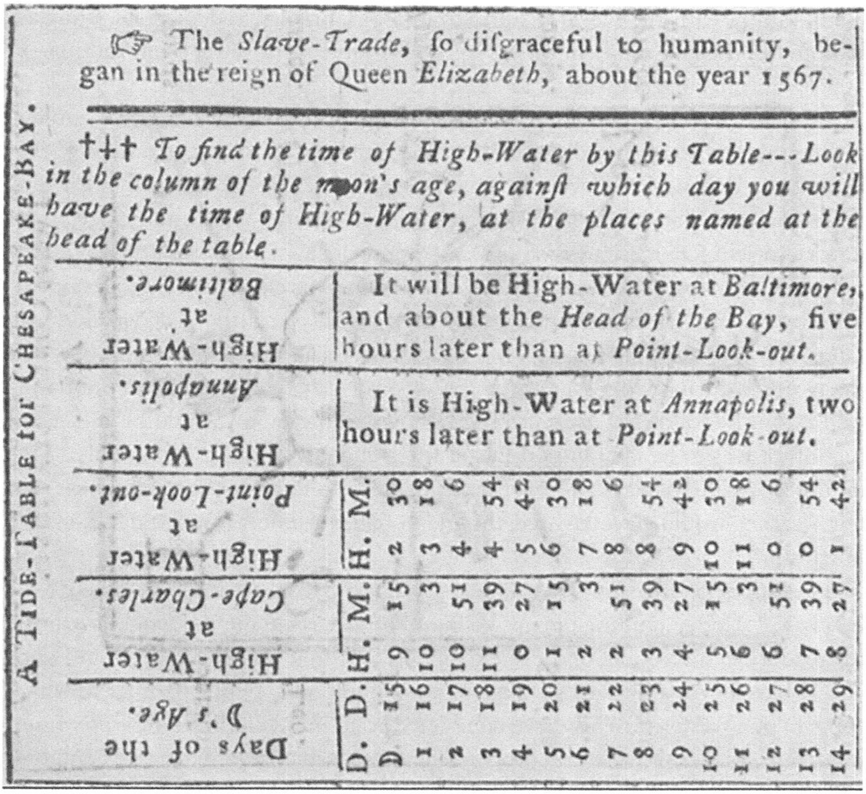

A TIDE-TABLE for CHESAPEAKE-BAY.

☞ The *Slave-Trade*, ſo diſgraceful to humanity, began in the reign of Queen *Elizabeth*, about the year 1567.

††† *To find the time of High-Water by this Table---Look in the column of the moon's age, againſt which day you will have the time of High-Water, at the places named at the head of the table.*

High-Water at *Baltimore*. — It will be High-Water at *Baltimore*, and about the *Head of the Bay*, five hours later than at *Point-Look-out*.

High-Water at *Annapolis*. — It is High-Water at *Annapolis*, two hours later than at *Point-Look-out*.

Days of the ☾'s Age. D.	D.	High-Water at *Cape-Charles*. H.	M.	High-Water at *Point-Look-out*. H.	M.
D	15	9	15	2	30
1	16	10	3	3	18
2	17	10	51	4	6
3	18	11	39	4	54
4	19	0	27	5	42
5	20	1	15	6	30
6	21	2	3	7	18
7	22	2	51	8	6
8	23	3	39	8	54
9	24	4	27	9	42
10	25	5	15	10	30
11	26	6	3	11	18
12	27	6	51	0	6
13	28	7	39	0	54
14	29	8	27	1	42

Figure 4.1 Detail from Benjamin Banneker's *Almanack and Ephemeris for the Year of Our Lord 1792* (Baltimore, MD, 1791), tide table for the Chesapeake Bay.

the slave trade, "so disgraceful to humanity" and its long-standing depredations since the "reign of Queen *Elizabeth*, about the year 1567."[97]

Calendric, cartographic, tidal, and astronomic information of the kind provided in Banneker's *Almanack* is also crucial to the escape that Douglass and his fellow fugitives formulate in chapter 10 of the *Narrative*. In the spring of 1835, the men decide

> to get a large canoe belonging to Mr. Hamilton, and upon the Saturday night previous to Easter holidays, paddle directly up the Chesapeake Bay. On our arrival at the head of the bay, a distance of seventy or eighty miles from where we lived, it was our purpose to turn our canoe adrift, and follow the guidance of the north star till we got beyond the limits of Maryland.[98]

This plan's timing, seemingly on the Saturday before Holy Week, mixes the men's need for a plausible reason to travel with the religious meanings of the holiday, suggesting a "glorious resurrection, from the tomb of slavery, to the heaven of freedom," which Douglass describes earlier in the *Narrative*.[99] Aligning the escape plan's timing with the world-historic drama of Christian redemption, Douglass illuminates the nation's twin moral-spiritual problems of slavery and racism—in other words, its original sin.

Banneker had seized upon a similar lexicon in his letter to Jefferson, underscoring his "most profound gratitude to the Supreme Ruler of the universe" that he was not "doomed" to slavery in what Douglass later would call the hellish "pit" of antebellum Maryland.[100] As we have seen, Banneker struck these scriptural notes to orient Jefferson toward his Declaration's ideal of universal human liberty. Likewise, perhaps, Banneker's 1792 *Almanack* may have oriented fugitives northward by assembling forecasted movements of the tides, courts, Quakers, and sun. One Maryland almanac for 1835, the year Douglass attempted escape, shows that the weather during Holy Week (April 12–19) was to be rainy on Palm Sunday as well as on the following Monday, the 13th, when the moon would be full. Until the 16th it was to be fair, and on Easter the cloud cover would be variable.[101] We do not know if Douglass and his friends had access to projections like these, but fair weather would have favored the men's plan to follow "the guidance of the north star."

As readers of the *Narrative* know, Douglass's 1835 escape was foiled by a betrayer.[102] Understanding the unlikelihood of successful flight, Douglass exhorts his readers to discretion, and even silence, about how slaves escape from bondage. "I have never approved," Douglass says, "of the very public manner in which some of our Western friends have conducted what they call the *underground railroad*, but which, I think, by their open declarations, has been made most emphatically the *upperground railroad*." Public declarations, he added, "do nothing towards enlightening the slave, whilst they do much towards enlightening the master."[103] If Banneker's celestial maps were indeed "disguised directions for escape," the freedom of enslaved people required this fact to be as obscure in the past as it remains to us in the present. Certainly the 1792 *Almanack* offers coordinate arguments for human equality—mathematical, theological, and literary—a conclusion that comes into focus when the almanac is read alongside Banneker's letter to Jefferson. But the almanac's role as fugitive guide is necessarily less self-evident, intimating how a humble farmers' almanac might be a declaration of independence.

Notes

1. Martin Luther King Jr., *The Trumpet of Conscience* (Boston: Beacon Press, 2011), 3.
2. Coretta Scott King, "Foreword to the 1968 Edition," in *The Trumpet of Conscience* (Boston: Beacon Press, 2011), xii.
3. The author extends heartfelt gratitude to the Smithsonian Institution's Margaret Henry Dabney Resident Scholar Program, and to Lilla Vekerdy, Head of the Special Collections Department, for the opportunity to spend three weeks with Banneker's *Almanacks* at the Dibner Library early in 2020. The author is further indebted to Christopher Marsh, for his assistance in translating between mathematical and humanistic interpretation of astronomical data.
4. Silvio A. Bedini, *The Life of Benjamin Banneker: The Definitive Biography of the First Black Man of Science* (New York: Charles Scribner's Sons, 1972), 155.
5. Bedini, *Life of Benjamin Banneker*, 156.
6. As Rusert has argued, Banneker led the way in responding to Thomas Jefferson's *Notes on the State of Virginia*, "the ur-text against which fugitive science defined itself in the early national and antebellum periods." "Fugitive science" is Rusert's term for the wide range of knowledge practices through which black thinkers resisted the sociocultural functions of state-sponsored scientific racism. Rusert catalogs a "Banneker Age," in which the philomath inspires generations of black American scientists to debunk and rebuke Jefferson's notorious claims of African inferiority in Query XIV of *Notes*. Rusert concludes that Jefferson's finding that African-descended people were "unfit for self-government and could not be trusted to bear the responsibilities of freedom," inspired these scientists to respond in ways that affirmed their intellectual capacities for civic participation. See Britt Rusert, *Fugitive Science: Empiricism and Freedom in Early African American Culture* (New York: New York University Press, 2017), 37.
7. Jared Hickman, "The Afro-Promethean 'Science of the Stars': Toward a New Metahistory of African Survivals," in *Black Prometheus: Race and Radicalism in the Age of Atlantic Slavery* (Oxford: Oxford University Press, 2017), 177.
8. Hickman, *Black Prometheus*, 177.
9. Eric Herschthal, *The Science of Abolition: How Slaveholders Became the Enemies of Progress* (New Haven: Yale University Press, 2021), 54–55.
10. Herschthal, *Science of Abolition*, 56.
11. Fraser and Herschthal have remarked on other elements of the 1792 *Almanack*, in addition to the calculations. Fraser argues that the ventriloquism of Banneker by his editors' selection of unattributed texts (in 1792 and beyond) ultimately demonstrates the limits of an early national project in racial empire-building. Fraser shows that the resulting author persona in the almanacs—sometimes a bureaucratic functionary of empire, sometimes an occultist prognosticator of American apocalypse—indicates the radical limits of the early republic's imperial ambitions. Herschthal notes that the 1792 *Almanack* includes anti-slavery arguments from the discourse of astronomy, including those by Rittenhouse. See Gordon Fraser, *Star Territory: Printing the Universe in Nineteenth-Century America* (Philadelphia: University of Pennsylvania Press, 2021); Herschthal, *Science of Abolition*, 57. See also William L. Andrews, "Benjamin Banneker's Revision of Thomas Jefferson: Conscience Versus Science in the Early American Antislavery Debate," in *Genius in Bondage: Literature of the Early Black Atlantic*, ed. Vincent Carretta and Philip Gould (Lexington, KY: University Press of Kentucky, 2001).
12. Bedini, *Life of Benjamin Banneker*, 52–58.

13. For discussion of white authorization of black literary accomplishment, see Henry Louis Gates, Jr., *The Trials of Phillis Wheatley* (New York: Basic Civitas, 2003). For a more recent treatment of Wheatley's work that emphasizes the poet's attention to legal questions of copyright and literary property, see Emma Brush, "'In My Own Handwriting': Phillis Wheatley and the Problem of the Creative Commons," *European Journal of English Studies* 29, no. 1 (2025): 50–74.
14. Fraser, *Star Territory*, 34; Herschthal, *Science of Abolition*, 54. As Fraser has shown, both the almanac's calculations and an unattributed prose selection about the cosmos, probably written by the eighteenth-century English theologian James Hervey, may have appeared to 1792 readers to have been written by Banneker. Such fictionalization, or semi-fictionalization, of the astronomer-author's persona was a distinctive generic feature of early American almanacs, Benjamin Franklin's Poor Richard being the best-known (Fraser, *Star Territory*, 34–35). In fact, Fraser underscores, only the astronomical calculations were Banneker's. I agree with Fraser about the authorship of the calculations and other ephemera, *and* hold out the possibility that Banneker's calculations and the literary selections were coordinated thematically by all collaborators on the full text of the *Almanack*.
15. Benjamin Banneker, *Benjamin Banneker's Pennsylvania, Delaware, Maryland and Virginia Almanack and Ephemeris for the Year of Our Lord 1792* (Baltimore, MD: William Goddard & James Angell, 1792), 5, 7–18, 19–36, 37–45.
16. Thomas A. Horrocks, *Popular and Print Medicine: Almanacs and Health Advice in Early America* (Amherst, MA: University of Massachusetts Press, 2008), 3. Horrocks notes that the American form of the almanac was a markedly republican departure from earlier English forms, which were organized according to the Church calendar year, with holy days noted, as well as a "*prognostication* comprising astrological predictions of political and social events" (2).
17. Horrocks, *Popular and Print Medicine*, 3.
18. Mather qtd. in Horrocks, *Popular and Print Medicine*, 3.
19. In a recent collaboration, Curran and Gates have shown that scientific explanation of racial difference in eighteenth-century France was a response to the economic significance and moral atrocity of the transatlantic slave trade. Johnston has made a similarly powerful case in the Anglo-Atlantic context, arguing that slavocrats' "defense of racial slavery in the late eighteenth century became a retroactive explanation for its establishment" in Britain's colonies. See Stuart Curran and Henry Louis Gates, Jr., *Who's Black and Why? A Hidden Chapter from the Eighteenth-Century Invention of Race* (Cambridge, MA: Belknap Press of Harvard University Press, 2021), 3.
20. Christopher Leslie Brown, *Moral Capital* (Chapel Hill, NC: University of North Carolina Press for Omohundro Institute of Early American History and Culture, 2006), 1–30.
21. Justin Roberts, *Fragile Empire* (Cambridge: Cambridge University Press, 2023), esp. 1–27, 67, 123–30, 172–74.
22. Katherine Johnston, *The Nature of Slavery: Environment and Plantation Labor in the Anglo-Atlantic World* (Oxford: Oxford University Press, 2022), 5.
23. Mary Floyd-Wilson, *English Ethnicity and Race in Early Modern Drama* (Cambridge: Cambridge University Press, 2003), 3.
24. Roxann Wheeler, *The Complexion of Race* (Philadelphia: University of Pennsylvania Press, 2000), 21–22.
25. For an extended discussion of these questions, as illuminated by early American literatures in English, see Katy Chiles, *Transformable Race: Surprising Metamorphoses in the Literature of Early America* (Oxford: Oxford University Press, 2014).
26. John Locke, *Some Thoughts Concerning Education*, 12th edn (Edinburgh: Printed for J. Brown, 1752), 5, 4.
27. David Hume, *Essays: Moral, Political, and Literary*, ed. Eugene F. Miller (Indianapolis: Liberty Fund, 1987), 208.
28. Hume, *Essays*, 208.
29. In "Of the Populousness of Ancient Nations" (1752), Hume noted the moral degradation of slaveholders in ancient times as well as in the present. He mentioned Britain's western Atlantic colonies specifically: "The remains which are found of domestic slavery, in the AMERICAN colonies, and among some EUROPEAN nations," Hume said, "would never surely create a desire of rendering it more universal. The little humanity, commonly observed in persons, accustomed, from their infancy, to exercise so great authority over their fellow-creatures, and to trample upon human nature, were sufficient alone to disgust us with that unbounded dominion." David Hume, *Political Discourses* (Edinburgh: Printed by R. Fleming for A. Kincaid and A. Donaldson, 1752), 162.
30. Hume, *Essays*, 208.

31. As Hall has shown, however, the negative meanings of blackness in English theology were persistently incorporated into anglophone understandings of African-descended people. Blackness was understood by the English as not only a property of the body but also of the soul and spirit; "death, mourning, baseness, evil, sin and danger" were all connected to the color black. Kim F. Hall, *Things of Darkness* (Ithaca, NY: Cornell University Press, 1995), 9.
32. Quobna Ottobah Cugoano, *Thoughts and Sentiments on the Evil and Wicked Traffic of the Slavery and Commerce of the Human Species* (London, 1787), 27.
33. Olaudah Equiano, *The Interesting Narrative of the Life of Olaudah Equiano, or Gustavus Vassa, the African*, ed. Vincent Carretta (New York: Penguin, 2003), 112.
34. Rebecka Rutledge Fisher, *Habitations of the Veil* (Albany, NY: SUNY Press, 2014), 89.
35. As Harpham has found in an unpublished paper, even the seventeenth-century English did not have a widespread understanding of a link between the blackness of Africans' skin and the condition of slavery. Harpham's work indicates that the intellectual sources of Anglo-American colorist slavery cannot be confined to the biblical story of Noah's male line. For earlier, influential explanations of the biblical curse, see also Robin Blackburn, "The Old World Background to European Colonial Slavery," *William and Mary Quarterly* 54, no. 1 (Jan. 1997): 65–102; and David Whitford, "A Calvinist Heritage to the 'Curse of Ham': Assessing the Accuracy of a Claim about Racial Subordination," *Church History and Religious Culture* 90, no. 1 (2010): 25–45. John Samuel Harpham, "The Causes of Complexion," presentation at Triangle Intellectual History Seminar, Oct. 25, 2020.
36. Floyd-Wilson, *English Ethnicity and Race*, 29–30.
37. William Shakespeare, *Othello: The Moor of Venice*, ed. Barbara A. Mowat and Paul Werstine, with Michael Poston and Rebecca Niles (Folger Shakespeare Library, accessed Apr. 30, 2023), <https://www.folger.edu/explore/shakespeares-works/othello/read> 3.4.31; 1.1.97, 125.
38. Floyd-Wilson, *English Ethnicity and Race*, 2.
39. Floyd-Wilson, *English Ethnicity and Race*, 1–23.
40. As Felicity Nussbaum has demonstrated, the humid atmosphere of "the torrid zone"—a name given by the British to equatorial regions—was believed to corrupt British customs and sociosexual propriety by enervating the body with heat. Felicity A. Nussbaum, *Torrid Zones: Maternity, Sexuality and Empire in Eighteenth-Century English Narratives* (Baltimore, MD: Johns Hopkins University Press, 1995).
41. John Gabriel Stedman, *Narrative of a Five Years' Expedition against the Revolted Negroes of Surinam, in Guiana, on the Wild Coast of South America, from the Year 1772 to 1777* (London: J. Johnson & T. Payne, 1813), 384.
42. Stedman, *Narrative of a Five Years' Expedition*, 384.
43. Karen Ordahl Kupperman, "Fear of Hot Climates in the Anglo-American Colonial Experience," *William and Mary Quarterly* 41, no. 2 (Apr. 1984): 216.
44. Quoted in Kupperman, "Fear of Hot Climates," 214.
45. Alan Bewell, *Romanticism and Colonial Disease* (Baltimore, MD: Johns Hopkins University Press, 1999), 277–95.
46. Johnston, *Nature of Slavery*, 3–6; Bewell, *Romanticism and Colonial Disease*, 1–26.
47. Edward B. Rugemer, *Slave Law and the Politics of Resistance in the Early Atlantic World* (Cambridge, MA: Harvard University Press, 2018), esp. the introduction and first chapter.
48. On slave rebellions see Herbert Aptheker, *American Negro Slave Revolts* (New York: Columbia University Press, 1943) and Vincent Brown, *Tacky's Revolt* (Cambridge, MA: Belknap Press of Harvard University Press, 2020).
49. Thomas Jefferson, *Notes on the State of Virginia* (New York: Penguin Books, 1999), 169.
50. John Locke, *Two Treatises of Government*, ed. Peter Laslett (Cambridge: Cambridge University Press, 1988), pp. 283–85.
51. While the francophone influence on Jefferson's racial imaginary is beyond the scope of this study, it is important to note two points in passing. First, in *Notes*, Jefferson engaged in an intellectual struggle with the French naturalist Georges-Louis Leclerc, Comte de Buffon, whose theory of American degeneracy (or the idea that American species of animals were diminished forms of European kinds) troubled Jefferson considerably. Jefferson's struggle was complicated by his regard for Buffon as "the most learned... of all others in the science of animal history" (45). In *Notes*, Jefferson refuted Buffon's claims by arguing that both sides of the Atlantic were "warmed by the same genial sun," making it unlikely that American soil, "of the same chemical composition" as that of Europe, "was less capable of elaboration into animal nutriment" (45). Second, Jefferson was likely influenced in his political and natural-historical thought by the French philosophe, the Baron de Montesquieu. Jefferson recorded significant sections of Montesquieu's

Spirit of Laws in his legal commonplace books and, as Arthur Scherr has demonstrated, Jefferson's anti-slavery stance in his early political career was likely influenced by that tract. For additional insight, see Arthur Scherr, "Intellectual Roots of Thomas Jefferson's Opinions on Slavery: Montesquieu's Impact," *Journal of Transatlantic Studies* 19 (2021): 189–214. Importantly for our purposes here, Montesquieu blended climate theory with his analysis of the nature of government, finding that "the government most conformable to nature is that which best agrees with the humour and disposition of the people in whose favor it is established" (7). See generally Winthrop D. Jordan, "Thomas Jefferson: Self and Society," in *White over Black* (Chapel Hill, NC: University of North Carolina Press for Institute of Early American History and Culture at Williamsburg, VA, 1968), 429–81; Lee Alan Dugatkin, "Buffon, Jefferson and the Theory of New World Degeneracy," *Evolution: Education and Outreach* 12, no. 1 (2019): 1–10; *The Papers of Thomas Jefferson: Retirement Series*, vol. 3, August 12, 1810 to June 17, 1811, ed. J. Jefferson Looney (Princeton: Princeton University Press, 2006), 11–15; and Charles de Secondat, baron de Montesquieu, *The Complete Works of M. de Montesquieu*, tr. from the French (London: T. Evans & W. Davis, 1777), 7.

52. Edward G. Gray, "First Partition: The Troubled Origins of the Mason-Dixon Line," in *The American Revolution Reborn*, ed. Patrick Spero and Michael Zuckerman (Philadelphia: University of Pennsylvania Press, 2016), 269.
53. Frederick Douglass, "What to the Slave is the Fourth of July?" in *Frederick Douglass: Narrative of the Life of Frederick Douglass, an American Slave, Written by Himself*, ed. and intro. Ira Dworkin (New York: Penguin Books, 2014), 135.
54. Eric Foner, *Gateway to Freedom: The Hidden History of the Underground Railroad* (New York: W. W. Norton, 2015), 9.
55. William Cohen, "Thomas Jefferson and the Problem of Slavery," *Journal of American History* 56, no. 3 (Dec. 1969): 510; William G. Merkel, "Jefferson's Failed Anti-Slavery Proviso of 1784 and the Nascence of Free Soil Constitutionalism," *Seton Hall Law Review* 38, no. 2 (2008): 555–91.
56. Cohen, "Jefferson and Slavery," 511.
57. Paul Finkelman, "Slavery and the Northwest Ordinance: A Study in Ambiguity," *Journal of the Early Republic* 6, no. 4 (1986): 343–70, esp. 345–46.
58. "Constitution of the United States," art. IV, sec. 2, cl. 3, National Archives and Records Administration, accessed Mar. 28, 2023. <https://www.archives.gov/founding-docs/constitution-transcript>
59. Pinckney, quoted in Foner, *Gateway to Freedom*, 39.
60. Still, enforcement of these constitutional provisions remained questionable. Who, if anyone, could compel a fugitive from slavery back into bondage? The answer came in the Fugitive Slave Act of 1793, which allowed a slaveholder, or his agent, to capture a fugitive and present that person in court with written or even verbal evidence of the runaway's enslaved status. The judge might then issue a certificate compelling that person back into bondage. Anyone obstructing the process could face civil action. Foner, *Gateway to Freedom*, 39.
61. Banneker, *Almanack*, 2.
62. Quoted in Bedini, *Life of Benjamin Banneker*, 154; Jefferson, *Notes on the State of Virginia*, 168.
63. Banneker, *Almanack*, 2–4.
64. Banneker, *Almanack*, 4.
65. For the related history of Harrison and "the longitude problem," or the eighteenth-century quest to calculate longitudinal position at sea, see Dava Sobel, *Longitude: The True Story of a Lone Genius Who Solved the Greatest Scientific Problem of his Time* (New York: Bloomsbury, 1995).
66. Sethanne Howard, "Benjamin Banneker and Celestial Navigation: Just How Did They Know Where They Were, Then?," *Journal of the Washington Academy of Sciences* 101, no. 1 (Spring 2015): 29–42.
67. Jefferson, quoted in Bedini, *Life of Benjamin Banneker*, 159.
68. Jefferson, *Notes on the State of Virginia*, 146. Euclidean geometry treats linear space, as on a flattened sheet of paper, while spherical trigonometry describes curved space, as on a globe.
69. Hervey, quoted in Banneker, *Almanack*, 19. Gordon Fraser writes that this extract from Banneker's 1792 *Almanack* is "an unattributed excerpt by English theologian James Hervey" that was probably "cribbed...from a version that appeared nearly four decades before in London's *Universal Magazine*." See Fraser, *Star Territory*, 35.
70. Hervey, quoted in Banneker, *Almanack*, 20.
71. Quoted in Banneker, *Almanack*, 25.
72. Quoted in Banneker, *Almanack*, 26.
73. Quoted in Banneker, *Almanack*, 26 (emphasis in original).
74. Quoted in Banneker, *Almanack*, 25–26.
75. This story of Banneker's family history is from Bedini, *Life of Benjamin Banneker*, 9–21.

76. *Acts of Assembly of the Province of Maryland, Made and Passed*: "An Act for the More Effectual Punishment of Negroes and Other Slaves" and "Act to Prevent the Tumultuous Meeting and Other Irregularities of Negroes and Other Slaves" (Baltimore, MD: Jonas Green, 1751), 15–17, accessed Apr. 3, 2023. <https://msa.maryland.gov/megafile/msa/speccol/sc4800/sc4872/003179/html/m3179-0798.html>
77. Bedini, *Life of Benjamin Banneker*, 27.
78. Quoted in Banneker, *Almanack*, 33.
79. Quoted in Bedini, *Life of Benjamin Banneker*, 153.
80. Quoted in Bedini, *Life of Benjamin Banneker*, 153.
81. Jefferson, *Notes on the State of Virginia*, 168–69.
82. Banneker, quoted in Bedini, *Life of Benjamin Banneker*, 154.
83. Banneker, quoted in Bedini, *Life of Benjamin Banneker*, 154.
84. Thomas Jefferson, "Jefferson's 'Original Rough Draught' of the Declaration of Independence," June 1776, in *Declaring Independence: Drafting the Documents*, Library of Congress, accessed Apr. 23, 2023. <https://www.americaslibrary.gov/aa/jefferson/aa_jefferson_declar_2_e.html>
85. Jefferson, *Notes on the State of Virginia*, 149.
86. Banneker, quoted in Bedini, *Life of Benjamin Banneker*, 155.
87. Banneker, quoted in Bedini, *Life of Benjamin Banneker*, 155.
88. Quoted in Banneker, *Almanack*, 35–36.
89. The words quoted in the subheading are from Douglass, *Narrative of the Life of Frederick Douglass, an American Slave* (Boston: Published at the Anti-Slavery Office, 1845), 109.
90. Banneker, *Almanack*, 36–42.
91. Eve Tavor Bannet, *Eighteenth-Century Manners of Reading: Print Culture and Popular Instruction in the Anglophone Atlantic World* (Cambridge: Cambridge University Press, 2017), 185.
92. Douglass, *Narrative*, 109.
93. Douglass, *Narrative*, 84.
94. Douglass, *Narrative*, 18, 46.
95. Douglass, *Narrative*, 84.
96. Douglass, *Narrative*, 65.
97. Banneker, *Almanack*, 5.
98. Douglass, *Narrative*, 86.
99. Douglass, *Narrative*, 73.
100. Banneker, quoted in Bedini, *Life of Benjamin Banneker*, 154; Douglass, *Narrative*, 40.
101. *Almanac for Maryland, Pennsylvania, and Virginia* (Baltimore, MD: R. J. Matchett, 1835), 10, author's personal collection. This artifact lacks a cover/title page; publication details are inferred from surviving pages.
102. Douglass, *Narrative*, 91.
103. Douglass, *Narrative*, 101.

Novel Constitutions and the Making of Race: A Literary and Legal History of Slavery in the Anglophone Atlantic, 1688–1818.
Sarah Marsh, Oxford University Press. © Sarah Marsh 2026. DOI: 10.1093/9780197917855.003.0005

5

"One Wish for Air and Liberty"

The Returns of Novel Constitutionalism and the Anti-Slavery Argument in *Mansfield Park*

> "Why, you know, Sir Thomas's means will be rather straitened if the Antigua estate is to make such poor returns."
>
> —Mrs Norris to Lady Bertram, *Mansfield Park*[1]

> "I don't think anybody here would deny that when you send chickens out in the morning from your barnyard, those chickens will return that evening to your barnyard, not your neighbor's barnyard."
>
> —Malcolm X, "God's Judgment of White America"[2]

As Benjamin Banneker's letter of August 19, 1791 made its way to Thomas Jefferson in Virginia, the Haitian Revolution broke out in Saint-Domingue. Black people in the French colony, enslaved and free, rose in armed revolt on the night of August 21 against the island's slavocratic government. By morning, French slave owners and their families lay dead amidst smoldering plantations.[3] Thomas Jefferson, author of the equal rights doctrine of the United States Declaration of Independence, thus found himself the recipient of two different claims of human equality, strikingly coincident. The first, written in ink drawn by the quill, was Banneker's trigonometric proof that human beings of all complexions are one another's equals under God. The second, written in blood drawn by the sword, was news that the race war he forecast in *Notes on the State of Virginia* had broken out in the Caribbean.

Banneker's letter and the Haitian Revolution were each, in their way, effective. The first evidently persuaded Jefferson, as he wrote to the Marquis de Condorcet that "the want of talents" the Virginian perceived in people of African descent was "merely the effect of their degraded condition [as slaves], and not proceeding from any difference in the structure of the parts on which intellect depends."[4] Led by the formidable generals Toussaint L'Ouverture and Jean-Jacques Dessalines, the enslaved and free rebels in Saint-Domingue threw off French slavocracy and founded the first republic in the western hemisphere led by people of African descent. Haitians, many of whose ancestors had arrived in the western Atlantic in chains aboard British slave ships, framed their first constitution in 1801 and formally declared independence from France in 1804.[5]

Jane Austen's brother-in-law-to-be, the Reverend Thomas Fowle, died in the Haitian Revolution. Engaged to Austen's beloved sister Cassandra, Tom was buried at sea after succumbing to yellow fever off the coast of Saint-Domingue in 1797[6] while serving as private chaplain to his distant cousin, Lord Craven of the 43rd (Monmouthshire) Regiment of Foot, aboard a British vessel deployed to the conflict.[7] As Ruth Perry has written, Fowle's deployment to the Caribbean was part of Britain's wider Atlantic campaign against Revolutionary France, and that conflict's dense entanglements with colonial slavery. Fowle sailed to the Caribbean as part of Britain's bid to capture Saint-Domingue and re-enslave L'Ouverture's forces at the behest of French slavocrats who had fled the colony and appealed to London for support. These Frenchmen had lost significant political capital in Paris following the 1793 execution of Louis XVI by the French First Republic, so they redirected their appeals for assistance across the Channel.[8]

Reverend Fowle's deployment to the Caribbean was also a domestic necessity. He could not marry Cassandra without a professional situation that the deployment might supply in the form of patronage from his commander, prize money, or both.[9] Deirdre Le Faye reckons that Tom accepted his cousin's offer because he did not wish to "offend his patron by citing his engagement to Cassandra"; the young military chaplain "made his will in October 1795 before joining the Craven entourage," leaving his entire savings of £1,000 to Cassandra at his death.[10] Lord Craven, who survived the Caribbean deployment to Haiti, is said to have deeply regretted his request of his young relative. Had he known of Tom's engagement, Le Faye writes, Craven "would never have allowed him to go to so dangerous a climate."[11]

Jane Austen was 15 years old when reports of the anti-slavery rebellion in Saint-Domingue began arriving in London, and she was 21 when news that Tom had died of yellow fever reached her family at Steventon.[12] What followed was a period of general "Affliction" in the Austen household. Jane and Cassandra's oldest brother, James, remembered his friend in a poem that envisioned Tom's body amidst "restless waves 'gainst Western India's shores."[13] Perry has argued that Fowle's death led both Austen sisters to eschew ideas of marriage for the rest of their lives.[14] In this way, the young novelist, with her closest sibling and friend, faced a painful connection among four dimensions of life in early nineteenth-century Britain: their country's colonial institution of chattel slavery; the race wars it bred across the Atlantic; the financial necessity of military service in Britain's pro-slavery wars for unlanded men seeking to establish households; and the domestic tragedy awaiting young women and their families when these men died abroad.

Written between 1811 and 1813 and published in 1814,[15] Austen's novel, *Mansfield Park,* studied these interwoven elements of British life during an important interval of pro-slavery and anti-slavery politics. Lord Chief Justice Mansfield's 1772 ruling in *Somerset v. Stewart* made it unlawful to treat human beings as saleable chattels in Britain.[16] In 1807, Britain ended its transatlantic traffic in human beings with the Slave Trade Abolition Act; but this legislation left untouched the institution of human bondage that would exist in the country's Caribbean colonies until the Slavery Abolition Act of 1833.[17] This era of abolition in Britain, Christopher Leslie Brown has shown, was marked by its density of political debate, elevating anti-slavery as an important moral idiom in public life.[18]

Thus, when Austen took up her pen to write *Mansfield Park*, she was living in a society whose government had taken steps to end its involvement in human slavery, at home and in trade, while allowing the institution to continue abroad otherwise unchecked. Austen scholars disagree[19] considerably about how to place the abolition of the slave trade in *Mansfield Park*'s internal timeline; but when the novel came out, full abolition was still years on the horizon and by no means certain. Austen, who died in 1817, would not live to see it. We proceed, then, on undisputed evidence that Austen began writing *Mansfield Park* about forty years after *Somerset v. Stewart*, about fifteen years after her would-be brother-in-law died during a deployment to a slave insurrection in the Caribbean, and about four years after Britain abolished its slave trade. These historical facts, with the manifest content of the novel to be canvassed below, allow us to read *Mansfield Park* as an anti-slavery text.

This chapter contends that *Mansfield Park*, a story of how colonial slaveholding compromises a British family and everyone they know, is an abolitionist argument in the form of a domestic novel, describing how the institution of colonial slavery corrupts British parents' relationships with their children and thus the novel's marriage plot, by which one generation of Britons gives way to the next. The literary stakes of this claim are significant because British colonial racecraft at law is intimately related to how British domestic fiction is being written in the early nineteenth century. I argue further that *Mansfield Park*'s attention to the law has been lost to literary criticism until now because of the nuanced anti-slavery position Austen stakes out in the text: the necessity of constitutional change but the futility of outright rebellion against slavery. This argument proceeds in four stages.

To open I demonstrate that Austen's first anti-slavery project in *Mansfield Park* is to create the racial consciousness of her fictional slaveholder, Sir Thomas Bertram. Next, I show that Sir Thomas's coordinate absences from his estates in Northamptonshire and Antigua are Austen's crucible of awareness that colonial racecraft destroys Britons' relationships with their children. Third, I speculate that both of Sir Thomas's estates, domestic and colonial, are in a narratively coordinated rebellion against his tyrannical dominion. Finally, the chapter demonstrates how the creation of Sir Thomas's racial consciousness, through rebellions against his tyranny on both sides of the Atlantic, is Austen's negative critique of Britain's limited anti-slavery jurisprudence in the year 1814, represented by Lord Chief Justice Mansfield's 1772 ruling in *Somerset v. Stewart*, after which she titled the novel.

While Lord Mansfield sought to insulate Britain from the treatment of human beings as saleable chattels in *Somerset*, Austen intimates that only a full abolition can begin to restore moral authority to her country's government, corroded by its overseas accommodation of human slavery through absolutist manipulations of patriarchalism, of which Sir Thomas is representative. *Mansfield Park* animates this position in two ways: the destruction of the Bertram family; and the manifest failures of several different rebellions against Sir Thomas's slavocratic authority. For these important reasons, *Mansfield Park*'s position in the literary history of the British Empire must be revised to admit the following evidence of the novel's nuanced anti-slavery position.

"Everywhere Awake": The Creation of Sir Thomas's Racial Consciousness

The present argument marks a pivot from previous chapters, which have surveyed stories of English racecraft at law by Aphra Behn and Daniel Defoe, as well as theological and mathematical responses written by Olaudah Equiano and Benjamin Banneker.[20] Importantly, Equiano and Banneker addressed their anti-slavery claims to people in government: Queen Charlotte-in-Parliament and Thomas Jefferson, respectively. We have thus established the *constitutional* terms on which pro-slavery and anti-slavery arguments proceeded in the anglophone Atlantic tradition from the seventeenth century into the eighteenth. *Mansfield Park* turns our attention to the longer term effects of racecraft—what Christina Sharpe has called the "wake" of Anglo-American colonial slavery—in early nineteenth-century Britain.

Sharpe's lyric analysis, *In the Wake: On Blackness and Being* (2016) conceptualizes the long and ongoing effects of chattel slavery as interlocking and plangent definitions of the term "wake": the path left by a slave ship, an act of collective grief for a loved one, and a state of heightened moral attention.[21] "Living in/the wake of slavery," Sharpe elaborates, citing Saidiya Hartman, "is living 'the afterlife of property' and living the afterlife of *partus sequitur ventrem*...in which the Black child inherits the non/status, the non/being of the mother."[22] As we have seen in our readings of *Oroonoko* and *Robinson Crusoe*, what Sharpe calls "the wake of slavery" and "the afterlife of *partus sequitur ventrem*" is the wake of what this study calls "novel constitutionalism." To recapitulate my argument: novel constitutionalism is the capacious transatlantic legal process, including but not limited to Virginia's 1662 introduction of *partus sequitur ventrem*, by which imperial policy, Crown lawyers, and colonial legislators accommodated the English common law's protections of life, liberty, and property to the institution of chattel slavery. In legal actions that created chattel property at cross purposes with the lives and liberties of African-descended people, Englishmen interested in absolute power—for their monarch and for themselves—divided the ancient constitution against itself in the original sin of chattel slavery.[23] The extraordinary state violence authorized by English colonial governments in order to enslave Africans and their children in perpetuity, and to make English people and their children into slaveholders in perpetuity, describes how life and liberty were subordinated at law to the singular slavocratic interest of property in persons.

For Sharpe, living in the twenty-first-century wake of novel constitutionalism means "living and dying through the policies of the first US Black president; it means the gratuitous violence of stop-and-frisk and Operation Clean Halls; rates of Black incarceration that boggle the mind," and, in the words of scholars Joy James and João H. Costa Vargas, "the immanence of death as 'a predictable and constitutive aspect of *this* democracy [in the United States].'"[24] In this sense, chattel slavery is "constitutive" of the American republic declared in 1776 in ways that, we have seen in earlier chapters, are as old as England's reckoning with absolute power during its Civil Wars of the seventeenth century.

Sharpe's insights about living "in the wake" of slavery during the current century prompt us in this chapter to consider a more local region of disturbance caused by British slave ships on the Atlantic. In *Mansfield Park*, Jane Austen examines currents of the wake in her own time, and at considerable psychological depth, establishing her as an important if heretofore misrecognized commentator on colonial racecraft. Sharpe's conception of "the wake," as an epistemic condition of African-descended people racialized into property by the Atlantic slave trade, does not apply in a categorical sense to an Englishwoman like Austen. At the same time, any conviction of the fundamental equality of human beings requires us to consider that racecrafting Africans into chattels—and dividing the ancient constitution's protections of life and liberty against its protections of property—held significant consequences for the English people who did this racecrafting at law, passed its results to their children, or bought their way into the slave system as it grew. These consequences included enslaved people's retaliatory political violence against slaveholding societies, like the French one in Saint-Domingue, a phenomenon of violent return that Malcolm X later described as chickens coming home to roost. But racecrafters also inflicted moral injury on themselves and others.

In his 1962 essay, "Down at the Cross: Letter from a Region in my Mind," James Baldwin wrote one of the best assessments we have of the moral injuries inflicted by racecrafters. Baldwin also describes ways of responding to this catastrophe, including an interpersonal method for uncrafting race in America:

> If we—and now I mean the relatively conscious whites and the relatively conscious blacks who must, like lovers, insist on, or create, the consciousness of others—do not falter in our duty now, we may be able, handful that we are, to end the racial nightmare, and achieve our country, and change the history of the world.[25]

Baldwin says that "whites" and "blacks" who are "conscious" of what racecraft has done—to human beings, to politics, and to society—can create this kind of "consciousness" in others. The endeavor is not without risk: Baldwin's *oeuvre* is a catalog of the violence facing human beings who seek to create in others a consciousness of racecraft's effects. At the same time, Baldwin argues, consciousness creation is the moral and intellectual "duty" of people racecrafted into different groups: "whites" and "blacks," Baldwin believes, can create awareness in others of both their shared humanity and the historical differences that racecraft has made.

In *Mansfield Park*, this chapter contends, Jane Austen used the British domestic novel to create "the consciousness of others" in the nearer wake of Atlantic racecraft. It has been difficult to read *Mansfield Park* in this way because postcolonial criticism first engaged the text as a harbinger of the second British Empire, not as an intervention in the first. In *Culture and Imperialism*, Edward Said argued influentially that the novel's "usable colony" in Antigua, where Austen's fictive Bertram family owns an estate, "can be read as pointing forward to" later examples of imperial exploitation in the works of Joseph Conrad, E. M. Forster, and Jean Rhys.[26] But this is Said's historical vantage point, not Jane Austen's.

In fact, the "usable colony" in *Mansfield Park* is just one detail of a plot comprehensively engaged with British colonial slavery: its violent history, its evolving legal dynamics, and its destructive results in the families of Britons who perpetuated the institution. Austen populates *Mansfield Park* with, to adapt Baldwin's phrasing, relatively unconscious Britons who, in the course of her plot, become more conscious of what it means to inherit "the racial nightmare" initiated by their forebears. The Baldwinian "nightmare" takes two forms in *Mansfield Park*: (1) the legal difference colonial racecraft has made between traditional English estates and the modern, highly capitalized, slave-powered plantation complex[27] in the Caribbean; and (2) plantation slavery's corruption of domestic estates and their denizens through transatlantic pressures exerted on the institution of marriage by British slaveholders. These domestic outcomes of colonial slavery in *Mansfield Park* are in no sense imaginary or abstract; they are grounded in Austen's manifest knowledge of the law and her family's complicity in, and opposition to, their country's transatlantic system of human bondage.

Like racialized human beings elsewhere in history, Austen's characters in *Mansfield Park* exist in varying positions of political power, social consequence, and moral authority as a result of colonial racecraft in their time. This part of *Mansfield Park*'s political allegory is extremely subtle and highly complex; it dodges back and forth as only a novel can between the factual and fictive, the present and the past, resulting in a narrative that does not correlate directly to any historical chronology I have been able to perceive. Nevertheless, the novel is an unflinching exercise in consciousness creation, similar to the kind Baldwin envisioned in 1962. Sir Thomas Bertram, Austen's absentee patriarch and slaveholder, is the focal point of her efforts.

Sir Thomas Bertram and the Wake of Colonial Racecraft in *Mansfield Park*

As I have argued elsewhere, *Mansfield Park*'s backstory describes how British colonial slaveholding, personified by Sir Thomas, shapes class inequality in Britain.[28] In this way, Austen's plot dramatizes domestic epiphenomena of novel constitutionalism in Britain's colonies, but not first-order exercises in racecraft at law. This feature of the novel is important to emphasize because some postcolonial critics have found in *Mansfield Park* that Austen's British characters, namely Fanny Price, are either actually or metaphorically enslaved[29] or representations of people who are enslaved.[30] I show in this section that Austen is doing something more legally accurate than implying that Fanny Price is held in bondage by her uncle. What Deirdre Coleman calls "Austen's acute sense of just proportion," alongside the novelist's nuanced attention to class dynamics noted by J. A. Downie,[31] would have been significant barriers to her direct substitution of a free Englishwoman for an enslaved person of African descent in her fiction.[32]

In the opening paragraphs of *Mansfield Park*, Austen intimates how Britain's slave economy, protected by the British Navy, has reconfigured domestic hierarchies in the Ward family of Huntingdon through the marriage of baronet and colonial planter Sir Thomas Bertram. As Richard S. Dunn has concluded from Barbadian census data of the 1680s, the ascendency of English colonial planters began early in the seventeenth century.[33] Writing before Dunn, in the 1920s and 1940s respectively, economic historians Lowell J. Ragatz and Eric Williams catalogued the decline of the British Caribbean planter class during the second half of the eighteenth century.[34] Ever since, Nicholas Crawford explains, scholars "have debated the various degrees to which planters' downfall stemmed from 'decline' in the sugar industry, mounting abolitionist pressure, or slave resistance and other contingent factors."[35] Sir Thomas is Austen's representative member of this group. She gives him "dut[ies] in Parliament," establishing his knowledge of abolition politics in that body, dating from the 1780s (20).[36] She also gives Sir Thomas four children, and a dependent niece, whose actions are, in Nicholas Crawford's words, "contingent factors" in the slaveholder's increasingly precarious historical position.

Mansfield Park's rising action is Sir Thomas's decision to leave Britain for his plantation in Antigua because of an unspecified but urgent threat to that estate. Through Sir Thomas's absence from Britain to attend to these colonial concerns, Austen explores the transatlantic disunification of his personality as a specific moral injury resulting from racecraft. In *Oroonoko* and *Robinson Crusoe*, we observed disunifying plots of racecraft through which Englishmen made Africans into slaves, and themselves into slavocrats, by destroying at law the bonds of kinship between parents and children of African descent. These familial bonds were occluded legally (but could not be dissolved in fact) by slavocrats' claim to the absolute power to kill, let live, or sell. In *Mansfield Park*, we glimpse the outcome of this disunification as Sir Thomas simultaneously loses his grip on slavocratic authority in British colonial Antigua and his paternal authority in Northamptonshire, England. Similar to *Oroonoko* and *Robinson Crusoe*, the colonial legal fictions of *Mansfield Park* destroy familial kinship; but in Austen's narrative action, the bonds we see destroyed belong to free Britons. Eve Sedgwick's insight of the early 1990s—that so much Austen criticism of the late twentieth century was preoccupied with the "spectacle of a Girl Being Taught a Lesson"—can be adapted to *Mansfield Park* by observing that, in ruining a British family through their overseas slaveholding, Austen is teaching a lesson to that family's patriarch and, by extension, to her readers.[37]

Austen sets this destruction in motion when "a large part of [Sir Thomas's colonial] income [is] unsettled" to a degree that requires the planter's personal attention overseas (36). This portion of the income, however, has not always been unstable. Rather, the Antiguan plantation has played a significant role in Sir Thomas's favorable expectations for his family's future. In the novel's preamble, Maria Ward, her family's middle child, marries the West Indian slaveholder Sir Thomas before the attachment of her elder sister to Sir Thomas's friend, Reverend Norris. Their youngest sister, Frances, makes the "untoward choice" of marrying Lieutenant Price of the British Royal Marines, a position "no interest could reach," not even Sir Thomas's, whose other concerns extend to Antigua (4). After the weddings, there is a breach among the Ward sisters leading to their years-long estrangement. Austen's narrator offers us a few details from the fray, namely that Frances, the youngest, has shared some "very disrespectful reflections on the pride of Sir Thomas," which her oldest sister, Mrs Norris, "could not possibly keep to herself" (4). Frances Price's unfavorable opinions of her brother-in-law are contextualized by the narrator's disclosure that Frances's husband has been "disabled for active service" in the very military force which protects the slave trade and makes Sir Thomas's wealth possible (4).[38] Thus the oldest and youngest Ward sisters, who have anticipated being married with "almost equal advantage" to their middle sister Bertram, instead find themselves in positions of disadvantage because of the colonial institution embodied by their brother-in-law (3). The Ward sisters renew contact with one another only when Lieutenant Price's disability pension from the British Royal Marines, meager by comparison to the Bertrams' colonial wealth, proves unequal to the maintenance of his nine children. Under this duress, Mrs Price writes to Northamptonshire to request her sisters' assistance. Their reply is an invitation for Frances's daughter and namesake to leave home in Portsmouth to be raised among Sir Thomas's four children at Mansfield Park. Fanny, a timid and disconsolate child, soon comes to live with the Bertrams.

While making these arrangements for his niece in a genuine spirit of concern, Sir Thomas also insists that the social inequalities introduced among the Ward sisters by their marriages will be fixed in the next generation: Fanny Price's "rank, fortune, rights, and expectations will always be different," Sir Thomas emphasizes, from those of her Bertram cousins, despite the fact that they are to be raised in the same house (11). Here, Sir Thomas means the *superiority* of his children's claims; but Austen is plotting something different. From the first paragraph of the story, Austen foreshadows that Sir Thomas's plan to elevate himself and his children, through holding slaves abroad, is an exercise in futility. The Ward sisters' uncle, an unnamed Huntingdon lawyer, "allowed [his niece, Maria] to be at least three thousand pounds short of any equitable claim" to her advantageous marriage to Sir Thomas (1). One implication of this detail is that Sir Thomas, some thirty years before the events of *Mansfield Park*, is not able to court his financial equal in marriage.[39]

Austen further plots the decline of the British planter class in *Mansfield Park* as a series of unprofitable marriages. Sir Thomas Bertram's somewhat disadvantageous union with Maria Ward initiates a pattern that intensifies in the next generation with the disastrous marriage of the couple's oldest daughter, Maria, to James Rushworth. Orchestrated during his Caribbean absence by Mrs Norris, the match is one Sir Thomas initially views with optimism. He is at first "truly happy in the prospect of an alliance" between Maria and Rushworth because it is "so unquestionably advantageous" (40). The Caribbean planter gives his "most hearty concurrence" to the engagement, approving it as "exactly of the right sort—in the same county, and the same interest" (40). His only stipulation is "that the marriage should not take place before his return" from Antigua (40). But what is this shared "interest" of the Rushworths and the Bertrams—and why must its consummation in marriage await Sir Thomas's voyage home?

Herein lies Austen's next diminishment of her fictional slaveholder. Sir Thomas Bertram and James Rushworth, Austen shows, indeed share "the same" project of improving their estates: the former is in the colonies seeking to settle his plantation; the latter appears in *Mansfield Park* primarily as a discourse on landscape improvements to his estate at Sotherton. But these improvements, colonial and domestic, cannot have a common "interest," Austen shows, because of the difference racecraft has made to the laws that govern each estate. She achieves her point by taking the slaveholding Bertrams of Mansfield Park on a tour of Sotherton.

During the visit, James Rushworth boasts to his visitors of cutting down "two or three fine old trees" to improve the view (55).[40] Improvement efforts like Rushworth's were common in Britain during the period, often mandated by legislation designed to adapt the British countryside to industrialization.[41] A different kind of improvement scheme arose in the West Indies after the 1807 abolition of the slave trade, when planters attempted to offset resulting labor shortages with "breeding schemes."[42] Slaveholders moved quickly to improve living conditions, medical care, and nutrition on their plantations with the addition of "provisional grounds," where slaves could grow their own food.[43] Writing to one of his Grenada managers, the Herefordshire slaveholder Sir George Cornewall urged "particular attention to [the slaves]; so that...such regulations will be enforced, in respect to the work, the food, the medical assistance to the negroes, & the encouragement to the women to rear their Children, as will tend to obviate this great defalcation of numbers"[44] resulting from the newly abolished trade, in combination with the long-standing Caribbean practice of working enslaved people to death.[45] Proposed chronologies for *Mansfield Park*, some of which place the novel just after the slave trade's abolition in 1807, suggest that the "great defalcation of numbers" Cornewall reported is the crisis Austen indicates with the "recent losses" on Sir Thomas's plantation (24).[46]

Reflective, perhaps, of her family's experience of Tom Fowle's death in the Haitian Revolution, Austen refracts these historical dynamics of the British slave system through her marriage plot. Every romantic tension in *Mansfield Park* is underwritten by class distinctions that colonial slavery has created domestically among the Prices, the Rushworths, the Crawfords, and the Bertrams. In Austen's fiction, these tensions are always a contest for the future of Britain, and *Mansfield Park* is no exception: wealth, social influence, and moral authority are all at stake, including the status of wealth derived from colonial slavery. Austen emphasizes this tension at Sotherton when her characters tour the grounds sharing "one wish for air and liberty" while Sir Thomas is abroad settling his slave-worked estate (90). *Mansfield Park*'s contemporary readers would have recognized in this phrase the "free air" metaphor of anti-slavery jurisprudence, in which the British legal atmosphere was imagined to set captives at liberty.[47] Let us consider Austen's insights at Sotherton more closely.

James Rushworth's boisterous exclamations—about felling Sotherton's ancient trees—are not only textual counterpoints to Sir Thomas's errand in Antigua. They are also the young man's boasts in his contest with Henry Crawford for Maria Bertram's romantic attention. While he is in the Caribbean, Sir Thomas is happy to connect his family to the Sotherton estate through Maria's ascendant engagement. The alliance, as Sir Thomas sees it from Antigua, offers stability during a period of financial strain. But, upon Sir Thomas's return to England, he discovers James Rushworth to be "an inferior young man...as ignorant in business as in books, with opinions in general unfixed, and without seeming much aware of it himself" (200)—and he admits that Maria's engagement is a mistake. "Advantageous as would be the alliance," we learn from the narrator's report of Sir Thomas's consciousness, Maria's "happiness must not be sacrificed to it" (200). Sir Thomas goes on. He tells Maria "his fears, inquire[s] into her wishes, entreat[s] her to be open and sincere, and assure[s] her that every inconvenience should be braved, and the connection [to the Rushworths] entirely given up, if she felt herself unhappy" (200). Sir Thomas goes yet further: "He would act for her and release her," taking the matter of the broken engagement upon himself (200). With these details, Austen discloses that Sir Thomas would not have encouraged the match had he been home; only from across the Atlantic does the union appear supportable. In this way, Austen shows how colonial slavery shapes the institution of marriage in Britain, particularly the relationship between father and daughter.

Maria is aware that her marriage plays a role in her family's overseas interests. This understanding is evident in the way she experiences attachment: "She had Rushworth feelings, and Crawford feelings," the narrator tells us, "and in the vicinity of Sotherton the former had considerable effect" because Maria has internalized the importance of this landed estate to her family's financial stability (81). But what Maria wants, above all, is an escape: from her father's oppressive manners and from the limited marriage prospects available to her as the daughter of a slaveholding family. That social position seems to have curtailed her ability to court landed wealth coupled with wit and intelligence, despite her beauty and engaging manners. In result, she faces a false choice: James Rushworth's landed wealth offers her release from her father's tyrannical authority, but only at the cost of her felicity in marriage. In this way, Maria's diminished prospects are an effect of her family's slaveholding status: here is a young woman who cannot have both freedom and happiness.

In the Sotherton episode, Maria's vexed effort to escape her father's household highlights some legal details of the instability radiating from the Bertrams' colonial plantation. Austen unfolds these subtleties in a narrative constellation of intertextual allusion and legal history, which we will examine in the next several pages. Observing Rushworth's bungling courtship ritual disguised as a plan to chop down old trees, Fanny whispers to her cousin Edmund that she wishes to see Sotherton "in its old state," with its tree-lined avenue preserved (56). Here, Fanny references book 1 of *The Task* (1785), an anti-imperialist poem by progressive abolitionist William Cowper. *The Task* remained popular from its publication through the period of Austen's life and beyond, especially among abolitionists. Frederick Douglass, among others, quoted *The Task* and Cowper's other works at length in their anti-slavery arguments.[48] In the twentieth century, Martin Luther King, Jr. invoked Cowper in his arguments for civil rights.[49]

Fanny's invocation of the abolitionist poet, in defense of Sotherton's "old state," extends Austen's comparison of the Rushworth and Bertram properties. Fanny cites a scene early in the poem where Cowper's speaker tours a lord's "enclosed demense," like Sotherton, and laments the "fallen avenues" destroyed by improvement schemes.[50] Fanny's critique of Rushworth's planned improvements, adapted from this scene in *The Task*, resonates in *Mansfield Park*'s transatlantic framework because, in book 2 of the poem, Cowper poses his famous constitutional question: "We have no slaves at home—then why abroad?"[51] Austen's indirect citation of Cowper's abolitionism rings because, at this moment of the story, Fanny's uncle is abroad attending to his slave-worked plantation while also seeking to stabilize his family's position through Maria's marriage to a man who courts her by boasting of renovations to a different estate.[52] With Fanny's intertextual remarks on Rushworth's plans for Sotherton, Austen indicates the transatlantic scope of Maria's predicament.

Alistair M. Duckworth has argued that Austen writes estate improvements into her novels to voice debate about social change in Britain. The estates in Austen's *oeuvre* are not merely sites of narrative action, Duckworth observes; they are "indexes to the character and social responsibility of their owners."[53] Duckworth argues that, in this "index" of character, Austen captures elements of Edmund Burke's conservatism. "Burke was no enemy of change and improvement," Duckworth writes; the Irish MP warned vigorously against "the unimproved existence of institutions,"[54] a position that would inform his role as an anti-slavery gradualist.[55] As Burke explained in *Reflections on the Revolution in France* (1790), "'A state without the means of some change is without the means of its conservation.'"[56] In *Mansfield Park*, both Sir Thomas and James Rushworth understand this maxim; but Austen's invocations of property law during the tour of Sotherton indicate that these men are in different constitutional positions with respect to the conservation of their estates.

The Sotherton estate, we are told, includes a "capital freehold mansion" and the "ancient manorial residence of the family, with all its rights of court-leet and court-baron" (82). Courts leet were convened annually by the manorial lord or his deputy to settle petty infractions and administer the commons. One commentator noted in 1689 that court leet is "where they have power to make By-laws, as that a man shall put so many Cows, or Sheep in the Common."[57] Court baron, by contrast, administered the tenancy of freehold and copyhold lands; the latter was a form of tenure in which property was held "at the will of the lord according to the custom of the manor."[58] In this way, copyhold tenure was a forerunner of the colonial plantation in its insistence on the supremacy of local custom. Copyhold tenure, however, did not provide for the lord's proprietorship of human beings as chattel possessions.[59]

Copyhold tenures, like those Austen places at Sotherton, emerged in the early modern period from a medieval practice in which villeins, or unfree laborers, cultivated portions of land within the feudal lord's manor.[60] The term "copyhold" derives from the practice of giving tenants a copy of the title deed, rather than the original deed itself.[61] Copyhold divided manorial grounds, reserving a portion for the lord's use and asserting court-baron rights to bar villeins from hunting or trapping on it.[62] Villeins were bound to lifelong labor on copyhold estates, yet they could farm small plots to sustain families that remained on the estate for generations.[63] The security of these traditional manorial arrangements underscores important differences between the legal foundations of Rushworth's Sotherton and Sir Thomas's Antiguan plantation.

As we have seen in previous chapters, these differences were shaped first by Stuart imperialism's legal assertions of absolute power over labor. Under this framework, Parliament would later assert its interest in subordinating the colonial economy to metropolitan control. As Claire Priest has demonstrated, the Debt Recovery Act of 1732 was particularly transformative. In response to the difficulty creditors often faced when collecting from debtors in the colonies, this legislation required that all colonial holdings, including land and enslaved people, be treated as chattels for the satisfaction of debts. The Act allowed creditors to seize and sell plantations and enslaved persons as readily as livestock or furnishings, stripping colonial landholding of its customary common law protections, which insulated real estate from creditors.[64] In 1797, a partial repeal of the 1732 legislation, advocated by abolitionists, removed the clause that treated enslaved people as chattels for debt repayment; but the 1732 Act's provisions governing land and non-human property remained intact.[65]

The 1807 abolition of the slave trade increased the financial instability of this system: shrinking enslaved populations, rising maintenance costs, and declining yields made estates increasingly dependent on credit and increasingly unable to service it.[66] In this atmosphere of economic depression, the seizure of colonial estates under the Debt Recovery Act became more likely. Economic pressures on Antigua, and the legal architecture of colonial debt, place Sir Thomas in a position of uncertainty wholly unlike the securely inherited estate at Sotherton, which is why Maria's marriage into the Rushworth family looks so favorable to him from the other side of the Atlantic.[67]

Crucially for Austen's plot, the Debt Recovery Act also made the colonial proprietor's death a moment of pronounced legal exposure because it triggered creditors' right to satisfy outstanding obligations through the forced sale of assets during probate.[68] A deceased planter could, of course, no longer renegotiate his loans or use future harvests to manage creditors' demands; his estate, instead, became vulnerable to immediate liquidation. This is why fears of Sir Thomas's death in the Caribbean, like Mrs Norris's, are legally and financially significant to Maria's engagement: should the slaveholder perish abroad, his children would inherit not a stable estate but the financial consequences of its dismantlement. Existing debts—made likely by post-abolition downturn and suggested by the "large part of his income" that remains "unsettled"—would fall due under the Debt Recovery Act. Knowledge of this system perhaps motivates Mrs Norris's strenuous pursuit of Maria's connection to Rushworth's landed wealth while Sir Thomas is abroad. Viewed in the context of legal strictures on colonial property, Maria's prolonged engagement during Sir Thomas's risky absence in the Caribbean appears as a kind of security—coordinated by her aunt with her father's uninformed consent—against the threat of enforceable insolvency.

Austen's episode at Sotherton thus orchestrates: (1) that estate's feudal legal history alongside (2) Sir Thomas's troubled voyage to Antigua, as well as (3) the slaveholder's bid to secure his oldest daughter's claim to that landed estate. Together, these details reveal that the Rushworths and the Bertrams do not, in fact, share the "interest" Sir Thomas asserts—at least not constitutionally speaking. Sir Thomas is a proprietor of human beings while James Rushworth and his family have been the lords of villeins whose rights, however diminished, were ratified by copyhold contract. The villeins of Sotherton were under the personal dominion of James Rushworth's ancestors, that is, but these people were not for sale and, in *Mansfield Park*, they do not seem to have rebelled against their legal condition. As Mary Crawford says, the "unwilling feelings" of "the former belles of the house of Rushworth" about going to church on Sunday seem to be the most of any rebellion that anyone can imagine at Sotherton Court (87).

By contrast, Sir Thomas's slaves in Antigua are his chattel property, which means that they are governed by colonial laws of commercial exchange. These human beings can be moved from one estate to the next in the same way that Mrs Norris can take four pheasant eggs from Sotherton's housekeeper, Mrs Whitaker, and transfer them to a "spare hen" (106).[69] Mrs Norris's many premonitions of violent disaster in Antigua—read with the estate improvements and pheasant displacements at Sotherton—are a steady accretion of implication that Sir Thomas's voyage to Antigua is, as George E. Boulukos has argued, an ameliorationist's errand to make improvements to his colonial estate in order to forestall a slave rebellion and preserve the financial solvency of the plantation.[70]

This legal history illuminates Sir Thomas's sole caveat to Maria's engagement: she is not to marry until his return. The stipulation reflects the planter's willingness to tolerate a degree of financial risk, which the union would mitigate, in order to attend personally to his daughter's marriage settlement. We see him act on this resolve as soon as he returns to England, when he offers to release Maria from the engagement. Said another way, Sir Thomas knows that his death overseas—by rebellion, illness, or accident—would trigger creditors' claims under the Debt Recovery Act; nevertheless, he insists on delay, retaining paternal control over Maria's future for as long as possible. The postponement of the wedding thus registers both fatherly caution and a calculated wager on his survival of the colonial errand. It also exposes his distrust of those left to manage family affairs in his absence, particularly his sister-in-law.

Mrs Norris responds to these same legal conditions with characteristic opportunism; her urgency about the Rushworth match after Sir Thomas's departure suggests her concern that his life, and the family's finances, may be in jeopardy. Austen registers this fact in Mrs Norris's recurring fears of Sir Thomas's death. If her brother-in-law were to die, the colonial estate could be seized by creditors before any residue reaches the family, throwing Maria's marriage settlement (and the rest of the Bertram finances) into disorder. Yet Rushworth, "ignorant in business," might proceed with the marriage nonetheless, unwittingly providing the Bertrams with a domestic financial bulwark should the colonial plantation collapse. Rushworth's ignorance, far from disqualifying him, makes him attractive to Maria's sponging aunt.

Whatever calculations Mrs Norris has made, by throwing Maria's happiness into the bargain, do eventually come to less than nothing—but not because Sir Thomas is killed by his slaves. During her father's absence, and despite her engagement to James Rushworth, Maria Bertram strikes up a plot-bending flirtation with Henry Crawford. The attraction ultimately ends Maria's marriage, destroying her aunt's and father's efforts to stabilize Mansfield Park through a connection to Sotherton. Later in this chapter, we will emphasize the transatlantic character of this plot point by considering new evidence that Austen perhaps uses Maria's rebellion against her marriage to reference a specific slave revolt in Antigua.

In *Mansfield Park*'s falling action, Sir Thomas recognizes that Maria's fate is the product of his own "grievous mismanagement" (463)—but of what? Here, the term "mismanagement" has transatlantic range, emphasizing that Austen's absentee father is also an absentee slaveholder. He has failed to provide his daughters with a moral education, he believes, and to safeguard their personal interests; the unmanageable demands of his interests overseas have gotten in his way. Mrs Norris, left to manage the Bertram children in their father's absence, has fallen down on her duties just as thoroughly as the overseers on Sir Thomas's plantation, who—evidently—also cannot be left to their own devices.[71] This plot point tends to corroborate the view of critics who think Mrs Norris is named after a colonial overseer Austen saw referenced in Thomas Clarkson's *The History of the Rise, Progress and Accomplishment of the Abolition of the African Slave-Trade, by the British Parliament* (1808).[72] Austen presents this transatlantic problem not as an isolated paternal lapse but as part of a generational pattern of slavocratic decline inherent in a British colonial system that depends on the absentee patriarch. From the novel's opening lines, where we learn that Sir Thomas has failed to secure an equitable marriage even for himself, Austen exposes the many deformations arising from British colonial slavery's new patriarchalism. Chief among these is a lie Sir Thomas has been telling himself from the beginning of the story: that owning human beings in Antigua is a way of raising his family's status in Britain.

Sir Thomas's "wretched" reckoning of his paternal failures is twofold: not only have "all the cost and care of an anxious and expensive education" been wasted on Maria and Julia; he has ensured his daughters' ruin by training them to "repress their spirits in his presence," making their true dispositions unknown—and unknowable—to him (463–64). The sisters' concealment clarifies the serially misread[73] "dead silence" that follows Fanny's famous question about the slave trade (198). Her female cousins do not share her curiosity about the transatlantic traffic because they already understand how their futures are circumscribed by it. Indeed, in this episode they have just cut off romantic dalliances with Henry Crawford and John Yates to comport with their father's expectations, underwritten by his Caribbean estate. Belonging to a brood unburdened by this colonial inheritance, Fanny alone can afford a guileless interest in Sir Thomas's overseas concerns.

The narrative relation Austen cultivates between Northamptonshire and Antigua in these pages prompts us to consider that Sir Thomas's slaves may also "repress *their* spirits in his presence," ripening for revolt the time he spends away from them in Britain and periodically requiring his presence on the plantation (my emphasis). These realities of colonial absenteeism, a part of racecraft's wake, affect Sir Thomas personally and absolutely. He cannot, *Mansfield Park* insists, attend to his unsettled plantations in Antigua and properly form the moral character of his children. One practical result of this transatlantic disunification of Sir Thomas's personality is that—although he settles his daughter's marriage into an ancient, landed family—the marriage does not last. In Austen's 1814 account, Britain's slaveholding class is shunted into ever greater economic uncertainty, a trend similar to the one documented by modern historians.

In this way, Sir Thomas's dual losses, of slavocratic and paternal authority, become a major structuring principle of *Mansfield Park* as well as a significant insight into Austen's anti-slavery politics: in the character of Sir Thomas, who cannot control his plantation in Antigua without relinquishing command of his children in Northamptonshire, Austen shows that novel constitutionalism has eroded the moral foundation of patriarchal authority embodied in Sir Thomas's legal personhood. Austen's transatlantic plot, which plumbs the tensions of absolute and qualified forms of power, intimates that the patriarchal principle at the root of Britain's government—familial, national, and imperial—is no principle at all because colonial racecraft has corrupted the relation between parents and children. Families of African descent face structural deracination in the British Caribbean under colonial slave codes. Slaves are in ontologic (indeed, *constitutional*) rebellion against slavocracy because of their humanity. As Austen sees it, British slaveholders tasked with preventing inexorable rebellions abroad cannot also attend consistently to paternal responsibilities in their own homes. Categorically different forms of human strife are correspondingly inevitable. These, in the world Austen envisions, are the terrible differences and equalities racecraft has made.

Mansfield Park discloses the moral content of Sir Thomas's diminished prospects by casting the inward landscapes of other characters as parables of slavocratic government. Motifs of freedom, captivity, absolute power, and consent permeate the novel, generating striking reversals of understanding and fortune. To understand Austen's construction of Sir Thomas's racial consciousness more fully, we turn next to the various rebellions against his tyranny in the text, which reveal a novelist finely attuned to the anti-slavery politics of her era. In earlier chapters, we traced the abolitionist claim that slavocrats, in claiming absolute power over people of African descent through the legal fiction of race, mistook human authority for divine: a rehearsal of original sin.[74] Through the drama of Sir Thomas's waning authority on both sides of the ocean, Austen aligns with abolitionists who observed that colonial slavery was constitutionally destructive at home because it introduced moral inconsistencies abroad.

Austen's distinctive insight in *Mansfield Park* is that the natural right of rebellion against tyranny, elaborated by John Locke, proves a futile form of anti-slavery politics. She develops this position, I will suggest, by plotting parallel uprisings against Sir Thomas's authority—one in Antigua and one in Northamptonshire. Modern readers, used to thinking of Austen as a novelist of domestic manners, may be surprised to find evidence of a slave revolt in her fiction. But the resistance of enslaved people was certainly known to her, as was its relationship to the institution of marriage in Britain: recall how early in life Austen had witnessed her sister's happiness destroyed by Britain's effort to re-enslave people seeking liberation in French Saint-Domingue. *Mansfield Park*, read by the light of this history, reveals that Austen did not forget her family's losses in the Haitian Revolution when she imagined the losses of the Bertrams.

Tyranny and Rebellion in *Mansfield Park*

Jane Austen's assessment of tyranny and rebellion in *Mansfield Park* probably grew from her family's connections to British colonial slavery, which were not limited to Tom Fowle's death in the Haitian Revolution. The major relationship between *Mansfield Park* and the British Empire, which Said raised to critical attention in the late 1980s,[75] has been significantly developed by subsequent scholarship on the novel. This work has brought to light the trusteeship of an Antiguan plantation by Jane Austen's father, the Reverend George Austen, as part of the marriage settlement of his Oxford pupil, James Langford Nibbs.[76] Nibbs's role in human slavery is evident in the colonial record. The *Antigua Journal* of November 20, 1798, for example, advertises a reward for the return of an elderly enslaved man likely being "harboured by a negro woman named *Grace*, on the Estate of James Nibbs" (Figure 5.1).[77] When the *Antigua Journal* named the Austens' family friend in this advertisement for a runaway slave, Jane was nearing her 23rd birthday and completing the revisions of *Sense and Sensibility* (1811) at her family's home in Steventon.

The Austens had other family ties to colonial slavery. It has been known for some time that Austen's brother Francis, who served in the British Navy, held anti-slavery sentiments born of his time overseas.[78] Writing from St Helena in 1808, Francis emphasized the "harshness and despotism" he witnessed in "landholders or their managers in the West India Islands."[79] More recently, Devoney Looser has established that Henry Austen, in a long-forgotten episode of the family's history, attended the World Anti-Slavery Convention in 1840.[80] Sheila

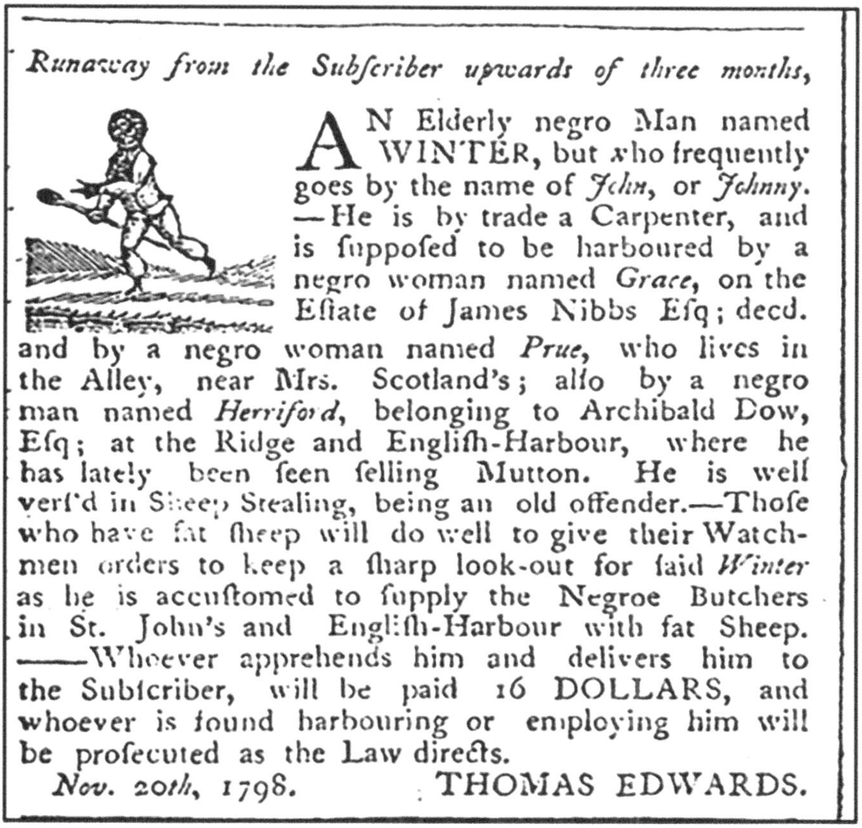

Runaway from the Subſcriber upwards of three months,

AN Elderly negro Man named WINTER, but who frequently goes by the name of *John*, or *Johnny*. —He is by trade a Carpenter, and is ſuppoſed to be harboured by a negro woman named *Grace*, on the Eſtate of James Nibbs Eſq; decd. and by a negro woman named *Prue*, who lives in the Alley, near Mrs. Scotland's; alſo by a negro man named *Herriford*, belonging to Archibald Dow, Eſq; at the Ridge and Engliſh-Harbour, where he has lately been ſeen ſelling Mutton. He is well verſ'd in Sheep Stealing, being an old offender.—Thoſe who have fat ſheep will do well to give their Watchmen orders to keep a ſharp look-out for ſaid *Winter* as he is accuſtomed to ſupply the Negroe Butchers in St. John's and Engliſh-Harbour with fat Sheep. ——Whoever apprehends him and delivers him to the Subſcriber, will be paid 16 DOLLARS, and whoever is found harbouring or employing him will be proſecuted as the Law directs.

Nov. 20th, 1798. THOMAS EDWARDS.

Figure 5.1 Notice from the *Antigua Journal*, November 20, 1798, advertising a reward for the return of an elderly enslaved man named Winter.

Johnson Kindred has shown in archival detail that Austen's sister-in-law, the Bermuda-born Fanny Palmer, had intimate knowledge of British colonial and naval life, having lived aboard the HMS *Namur* after marrying Austen's brother, Charles.[81]

More recently still, Miranda Kaufmann has elaborated Jane Austen's relationship with her maternal aunt by marriage, Jane Leigh Perrot (née Cholmeley), born to a slaveholding family in Barbados and heiress to that estate. Leigh Perrot's mother, Ann, was related distantly to the Willoughbys of Parham, whose patriarch, Francis, we met in our reading of *Oroonoko*; Leigh Perrot's sister, Katherine, would marry the Governor of Barbados, William Spry.[82] Jane Austen and her siblings expected to inherit a portion of their childless aunt's wealth, derived in part from colonial slavery, but Leigh Perrot ultimately left most of her estate to Jane Austen's nephew, on the condition that he adopt the Leigh family surname. Austen was not alive when the final transaction unfolded, but the disposal of this colonial inheritance played a significant role in Austen family politics.[83] These varied family connections to slavery gave Austen firsthand insights into the labyrinthine domestic implications of holding people in bondage overseas.

The letters Austen wrote while drafting *Mansfield Park* also reveal her scholarly interest in colonial slavery. As she was finishing *Mansfield Park* in January 1813, Austen wrote to Cassandra of having read Thomas Clarkson's *History* as well as Charles Pasley's *Essay on the Military Policy and Institutions of the British Empire* (1810).[84] She was as much "in love" with the latter, she told her sister, as she had ever been with the former.[85] Noting Pasley's "highly entertaining"[86] prose style, which includes his critique of Britain's involvement in the "dreadful contests in St. Domingo,"[87] Austen said that he was the "first soldier [she] ever sighed for," deploying her characteristic wit whose irony is perennially difficult to gauge.[88]

In a footnote to his *Essay*, Pasley elaborated what to his mind had been so "dreadful" about the violence in Haiti. The "revolution that established an independent black government" in the Caribbean, where "the great body of natives of all the other islands [were] slaves," Pasley said, made Britain's "possessions in the West Indies, as well as those of any other civilized power," vulnerable to invasion.[89] Pasley's racialized fears, which pit "an independent black government in St. Domingo" and "a great body of [enslaved Caribbean] natives" against "civilized power[s]"[90] like Britain, were echoes in 1811 of earlier anxieties on the United States mainland, like Thomas Jefferson's and George Washington's, that the spark of the Haitian Revolution would catch fire in America.[91] Writing from Philadelphia in June of 1792, for example, Thomas Jefferson told his friend, the Marquis de Lafayette, that "no future efforts you can make will ever be able to reduce the blacks" in Haiti; rather, Jefferson advised, the colony should be "more effectually succoured [*sic*]," a projection into the French Caribbean of his 1785 fear in *Notes* that a race war could break out in the young United States.[92]

Austen uses this historical threat of colonial slave rebellion to define her characters' understanding of Sir Thomas's voyage to Antigua. We have already considered Maria's engagement to Rushworth as Mrs Norris's hedge against the Debt Recovery Act, should Sir Thomas die on his Antiguan errand. Mrs Norris also articulates "very dreadful fears" that Sir Thomas and his oldest son will encounter some "fatal catastrophe" while they are abroad in Antigua (34). Mrs Norris later becomes "terribly haunted" by the idea of colonial violence when Sir Thomas sends Tom home from Antigua months before making the return voyage himself: "Sir Thomas's sending away his son seemed to her so like a parent's care, under the influence of a foreboding of evil to himself, that she could not help feeling dreadful presentiments" (38). Fanny says that Sir Thomas "was gone" to the Caribbean "perhaps never to return" (33). Lady Bertram, in contrast to her relatives, is "not disturbed by any alarm for [Sir Thomas's] safety" (32). The detail is amplified by her oldest son's subsequent teasing that his father's transatlantic passage is a "*very* anxious period for her" (126). The dispositions of the two Ward sisters, one manipulative and the other oblivious—in distinction to their niece's real concern for her uncle—suggest that there is something for thoughtful people to worry about.

After Tom's return from the Caribbean, bringing firsthand news of Sir Thomas's travails, the novel's details change slightly: Mrs Norris's general fears of "catastrophe" and "evil" modulate into clear themes of tyranny and rebellion. When Tom and Edmund argue about whether or not to continue their controversial play-acting in their father's absence, Tom (always the more transgressive brother) references their father's love of *Julius Caesar* (1599) as an argument in favor of their production of *Lovers' Vows*. Here, Austen introduces Shakespeare's political drama of insurrection in a heated discussion of whether or not the Bertram children are in revolt against their father with their play-acting. Edmund responds to his older brother that *Lovers' Vows* is, in fact, an affront to Sir Thomas, who is experiencing "some degree of constant danger" in the Caribbean (125). Maybe Edmund is worried about disease, shipwreck, or pirates; but Tom's (and Austen's) choice of *Julius Caesar* in this conversation introduces the idea of political revolt. As Cassius famously reminds Brutus, "The fault, dear Brutus, is not in our stars / But in ourselves, that we are underlings"[93]—a line indicating that submission to Caesar, not fate, is the political problem facing the Romans. As Tom suggests to his younger brother in this scene, subordination to tyrannical power is a political problem that can be solved.

Austen's allusion invites readers to understand the Mansfield Park theatricals not merely as youthful mischief, but as deliberate subversion of Sir Thomas's patriarchal authority. The most important uprising in *Lovers' Vows*, of course, is Maria's—against her engagement to James Rushworth—in her intense attachment to Henry Crawford. As we have seen in our discussion of Maria's betrothal, Sotherton, and the Debt Recovery Act, Sir Thomas's unsettled plantation exerts transatlantic force on his daughter's marriage prospects. The Bertram children's play-acting responds by giving Maria temporary cover to pursue her romantic attachment to Henry, a flagrant violation both of her betrothal, and of a financial settlement that will insulate her family from a volatile overseas estate. This is why everyone at Mansfield Park (except the oblivious Mrs Bertram) is so worried about Sir Thomas's safety—and yet so upset when he arrives home early, while the theatricals are in progress. Read in this transatlantic light, Maria's disobedience to her father's plans for the Bertram estate has amplified the very instability he seeks to balance across the Atlantic. Austen's narrator confirms this by explaining that, upon his return to Mansfield Park, "Sir Thomas saw all the impropriety of such a scheme among such a party, and at such a time, as strongly as his son [Edmund] had ever supposed he must" (187). The phrase "at such a time" signals a direct relationship between Maria's engagement and whatever is happening on the Antiguan plantation.

We should emphasize here that Austen is not portraying any of these British characters as slaves plotting a rebellion. The novel is showing, rather, that Sir

Thomas's absence creates an opening for his children to live in freedom from his oppressive domestic manners whose source is the slaveholding culture of the Caribbean. We know this because their liberties with one another, artistic and sexual, disappear with the planter's return: "Under his government," Austen's narrator tells us, "Mansfield was an altered place" characterized by "sameness and gloom" (196). Austen references the colonies, however, by invoking the "government" Sir Thomas's person represents: the absolute personal dominion of a slaveholder. Shortly after his return to Northamptonshire, Sir Thomas sees his "steward and his bailiff"; he walks "into his stables," "his gardens, and nearest plantations"; he sets "the carpenter to work in pulling down" the set of *Lovers' Vows* (190). Sir Thomas has gone to Antigua to settle the estate in person; so must he settle Mansfield himself.

There may, however, be more than mere fears of a Caribbean rebellion in *Mansfield Park*. This is where our argument shifts into a more speculative register: to consider evidence of a slave insurrection in Austen's text that, if persuasive, would reveal a novel and an author with capacious interest in how colony and metropole structure one another, as they do in Maria's troubled engagement. While any empirical claim of such a rebellion in *Mansfield Park* will remain speculative in this chapter, the available evidence makes any counterclaim similarly—if not equally—speculative. This raises a fascinating question about reading *Mansfield Park*: what *is* the evidentiary standard for showing the existence of an imaginary slave revolt in the made-up world of a novel? We have already established Austen's firsthand family knowledge that a slave rebellion could rewrite a marriage plot, so the question becomes one of literary interpretation. Borrowing Aristotle's standard from *Poetics*, which requires the plausibility of textual events but not their empirical proof, we will consider whether a slave insurrection is internally consistent with *Mansfield Park*'s characters, plot, and historical atmosphere.[94]

The following section makes the case, that is, that a slave revolt in Antigua is one possible way to account for the transatlantic design of *Mansfield Park*. Edward Said was, I hypothesize, absolutely correct when he perceived a sustained relationship in the novel between a volatile colonial sphere and the domestic scene it sustains. Where Said saw Austen's metropole "resisting" the colony in important textual silences, however, I see signs of a colony rising in resistance to the metropole.[95] Austen's plot achieves its unity, I propose, through narrative coordination of resistance to Sir Thomas in both Antigua and Northamptonshire, which it will be the object of the next section to describe. The success of this effort will depend, at least partly, upon modern readers' allowance that Jane Austen, English novelist of manners, might place so violent an upheaval in one of her books and allow it to direct her storytelling in such a concerted way. In considering this new evidence, we may find that many of our modern presumptions—about what Austen could have written about empire—are themselves part of racecraft's long wake.

A Slave Rebellion in *Mansfield Park*?

We begin this phase of the argument after Tom Bertram's return from Antigua, but before the return of his father. At an evening gathering, the planter's oldest son picks up a newspaper. The Antiguan plantation's heir notes to Dr Grant an unnamed but "strange business...in America" (119). Bernard Ledwidge has argued that this is a reference to United States trade embargoes of 1809, declared by the Madison administration.[96] But would Tom find it "strange" that Madison was reissuing the Jeffersonian policies begun by his predecessor in 1807?[97] Following his exclamation to Dr Grant about unusual events abroad, Tom adds to his interlocutor: "I always come to you to know what I am to think of public matters," indicating that whatever has happened in America is the subject of public debate in Britain (199). Read in the novel's colonial context, this is a point of derision. Tom, who has just gotten home from the western Atlantic, is making a joke at the expense of a well-fed country parson, who seems never to have left the country. As more archival context for *Mansfield Park* emerges, perhaps establishing a definitive internal timeline for the story, we may find that Tom's newspaper details precisely the kind of "business...in America" on which he, heir to slaves on a plantation in upheaval, would not need Dr Grant's advice. This reading of Atlantic world news in *Mansfield Park* aligns with what we know of Austen's irony and Tom's profligate tendency to entertain himself at cost to others and himself.

When Sir Thomas returns to Northamptonshire, there are a series of signs in the text that slave resistance has been afoot. In this part of our analysis, we will consider a highly complex ten-chapter arc of *Mansfield Park*'s plot, beginning with the planter's sudden return from Antigua. This section of Austen's story begins with the planter's discovery of the Mansfield Park theatricals, which are figured as a plot against his authority. It ends with the Mansfield Park ball, which is characterized by his reconsolidation of power in Northamptonshire—before the final crash of the Rushworths' divorce. The subtleties of this section, in combination with important historical allusion, form the basis of our speculative claim that Austen has written a slave insurrection into *Mansfield Park*.

When Sir Thomas arrives home from the Caribbean in the beginning of volume 2, he is physically altered: "he was grown thinner," Fanny perceives, "and had the burnt, fagged, worn look of fatigue and a hot climate" (178). This physical evidence is by no means proof of an Antiguan rebellion, but Sir Thomas's errand has clearly taxed him. By the time of the Mansfield Park ball, however, Sir Thomas has regained his strength. This recovery manifests in the slaveholder's subtle but decisive moves to curtail his children's play-acting and, most crucially, extract Henry Crawford from his flirtation with Maria, thus shoring up the Bertram finances with the connection to the Rushworths. After Maria affirms her intention to remain engaged, for example, Sir Thomas blocks Crawford from renting the family property at Thornton Lacey, emphasizing that it will be Edmund's home following his ordination, and that a clergyman must be "constantly resident" (247). This statement is Sir Thomas's negative judgment of his own absenteeism, implying that his latest errand to Antigua has changed his mind about the way he lives. Austen shows this when Sir Thomas chooses Edmund's residency at Thornton Lacey over the financial advantage of Crawford's rent. But this gesture is also the planter's effort to keep Henry away from Maria.

Sir Thomas's interventions between Maria and Henry are particularly evident at the ball Sir Thomas gives in Fanny's honor—an event intended to elevate his niece socially, but also a hedge against the threat Henry poses to Maria's engagement. Critically, Austen closes the ball with Sir Thomas's exercise of "absolute power" over Fanny, when he recommends that his niece retire to bed (280). The Caribbean planter draws upon this slavocratic characteristic in himself to demonstrate Fanny's "persuadableness" to her suitor, Henry Crawford, whom Sir Thomas seeks to extract from Maria's orbit through a different romantic attachment (280). Austen amplifies the Caribbean resonance of this scene with a backdrop of dancers who are "still hard at work" on Mansfield's ballroom floor, "feverish with hopes and fears ... sore-footed and fatigued, restless and agitated" (281). This strange description of Northamptonshire ball-goers—why in the world are they "restless"?—indicates more than mere narration of the present scene. Austen strikes this otherwise unaccountable note, I want to show next, in a wider chord of references to the history of slave rebellion in British colonial Antigua.

In October 1736, to commemorate the coronation of George II, a large ball was planned in St John's, Antigua, just southwest of two of the Nibbs family's plantations on the island, shown circled on the map of Antigua (Figure 5.2).[98] (The Nibbs colonial holdings, of which Austen's father would eventually serve as trustee, were established in Antigua during the 1670s, giving the family firsthand knowledge of the events of the 1730s.[99])

Enslaved Coramantees under the leadership of Court—known popularly as Tackey or Prince Klaas—and his lieutenant, Tomboy, plotted a rebellion on the island that would begin by exploding the coronation ball. Colonial reports describe the rebels' plan to smuggle a barrel of gunpowder into the event and ignite an explosion, signaling slaves across Antigua to kill their masters, raid the island's garrison, and seize control of the colony.[100] After the plot was discovered, the conspirators were rounded up, tried, and executed brutally.

Britons on the island had little difficulty crediting the details of a slave conspiracy that, to them, must have resembled the famous Gunpowder Plot of 1605—a Catholic attempt to assassinate King James I by blowing up the Houses of Parliament at the opening of the legislative session.[101] One administrative account

Figure 5.2 Detail from Eman Bowen, *A New and Accurate Map of the Island of Antigua or Antego* (London: Printed for William Innys, 1747).

of the uprising noted that the "most active Incendiaries under *Tomboy*" were "*Freeman's Secundi*, and Sir *William Codrington's Jacko*, both *Creoles*, of *French* Parentage, and initiated into Christianity according to the Romanish Church," casting the Antiguan rebels in the familiar role of dissident Catholics—the clandestine, embedded threat English Protestants believed capable of overturning the state from within.[102]

This colonial administrative report, *A Genuine Narrative of the Intended Conspiracy of the Negroes at Antigua* (1737), was prepared by the "Judges appointed to try the Conspirators" for "the Chief Governor of the *Carabee* Islands." Published in Dublin, it describes the Antiguan conspiracy in extraordinary detail.[103] After recounting the initial discovery of the plot, the *Genuine Narrative* reconstructs the rebels' plans for coordinated insurrection, the methods through which enslaved informants and colonial officials uncovered those plans, and the ensuing interrogations, trials, and executions. It catalogues individual enslaved people—naming their estates, owners, and alleged roles in the rebellion—while also offering the judges' commentary on presumed motivations of the rebels. Parts of this document are referenced so cannily in *Mansfield Park* that it seems plausible, maybe even likely, that the *Genuine Narrative* was at Austen's disposal in 1813, when she was writing *Mansfield Park* and reported to Cassandra that Chawton was "quite run over with Books."[104]

Consider, for example, the "Hopes and Fears"[105] of the Antiguan rebels in the *Genuine Narrative* echoed in the "hopes and fears" of the Mansfield Park dancers, who are "hard at work" as Sir Thomas tries to exert "absolute power" over Fanny at the ball (281, 280). The authors of the *Genuine Narrative* also say that providence saved them from violence by casting a divine "Mist before the Eyes of [their enslaved] Enemies."[106] Austen, too, uses a vision-obscuring mist in *Mansfield Park* to characterize Maria Bertram's prospect of marrying James Rushworth when her father returns from Antigua: "all she could do was to throw a mist over it," Austen's narrator tells us, "and hope when the mist cleared away she should see something else" (107). The mist in both texts is a cover under which rebellion against slavocratic tyranny proceeds.

Mansfield Park and the *Genuine Narrative* also thematize absenteeism as a major source of rebellion against slavocracy. The Antigua report's authors emphasize that one "Remedy to the Evil" of slave insurrections in the Caribbean would be "if Gentlemen resided on their own Estates here."[107] This is the very insight which leads Sir Thomas to affirm that Edmund must be resident at Thornton Lacey: "no proxy can be capable of satisfying to the same extent," the planter pointedly emphasizes to his son, as well as to Henry Crawford (427). Here, Austen's planter voices a well-known technique for suppressing slave revolts while also separating Henry from his oldest daughter. We should remember this narrative figure, which makes the planter a conduit of discipline and surveillance between the colony and metropole; its importance to Austen's critique of Britain's limited anti-slavery jurisprudence, we will see, cannot be overstated.

The most suggestive point of contact between *Mansfield Park* and the 1737 *Genuine Narrative*, however, is the latter's explanation of a Coramantee ritual of military allegiance conducted by Prince Klaas in advance of the thwarted insurrection. Seeking to understand the "Numbers" of potential combatants in the colony, the *Genuine Narrative* says, Prince Klaas performed "a military Dance and Shew" in "open Day-light" of which "the Whites, and even the Slaves who were not *Coramantees*... might be Spectators," but yet remain "ignorant of the meaning" because "the Language and Ceremonies used at it [were] all *Coramantine*."[108] Here, we will remember Sir Thomas's discovery of the Mansfield Park theatricals. The planter enters his billiard room, sees his furniture in disarray, and hears an unknown voice speaking "in a very loud accent;" it was "more than talking—almost hallooing" (182). Bursting through the door, Sir Thomas finds "himself on the stage of a theatre, and opposed to a ranting young man, who appeared likely to knock him down backwards" (182). The "hallooing" person, who threatens to "knock [the slaveholder] down" is Tom Bertram's friend, John Yates, a key proponent of the theatricals held in defiance of Sir Thomas's authority. Like Prince Klaas, John Yates is responsible for recruiting others to rebellion against slaveholders, namely Maria Bertram in her emotional betrayal of an engagement meant to stabilize her family's transatlantic finances.

The 1737 *Genuine Narrative* describes the sources of Prince Klaas's dance in the military traditions of West Africa: "When a *Coramantee* King has resolved upon a War with a neighbouring State," the authors note, "the *Ikem Dance* will be performed at a certain Time, and Place."[109] The *Genuine Narrative* describes how, during the dance, a cry goes up among the slaves: "*Tackey, Tackey, Tackey, Coquo Tackey* which signifies, King, King, King, great King."[110] This is a remarkable echo of Aphra Behn's report in *Oroonoko* that enslaved Coramantee people in English colonial Surinam greet the title character by "crying out, in their Language," "*Live, O King! Long live, O King!*"[111] Prince Klaas, the *Genuine Narrative* concludes, performed the Ikem Dance in advance of Antigua's coronation ball to recruit supporters against the island's slavocracy by securing the rebels' oaths of allegiance unto death.

Austen's selection of *Lovers' Vows* for the Mansfield Park theatricals is a provocative domestic counterpoint to the Ikem Dance. Promises throughout *Lovers' Vows* emphasize bonds of affection among the characters and duty unto death. Frederick (Henry Crawford) expresses undying devotion to his mother, Agatha (Maria Bertram). Wildenhaim (John Yates) voices paternal remorse and reconciliation with his natural child, Frederick. Amelia (Mary Crawford) and Anhalt (Edmund Bertram) forge a romantic commitment to one another.[112] By slotting her characters into these roles, Austen reveals the complex psychosexual relations among the Bertrams, Crawfords, James Rushworth, and John Yates, as many critics have noted.[113]

If Austen had at hand the *Genuine Narrative of the Intended Conspiracy of the Negroes at Antigua*, then *Mansfield Park* also holds *Lovers' Vows* in significant transatlantic tension with Antiguan slaves' expression of their desire for freedom in the Ikem Dance.[114] Some slaves in Antigua saw an opportunity in 1736 to be free through personal loyalty to Prince Klaas, and they expressed this fealty with the forms of African military custom. The parallel in *Mansfield Park* is that Maria Bertram requires the allegiance of Henry Crawford if she is to rebel against her engagement—and keep her personal happiness intact by abandoning a financial settlement favorable to her father's precarious colonial interests. But Henry Crawford, it turns out, is only acting during play practice: his is merely a rehearsal of *Lovers' Vows*. Maria, consequently, goes through with her marriage to James Rushworth.

The point, again, is not that Maria is a slave planning a revolt against a slavocrat. Rather, Maria is the daughter of a slavocrat engaged in revolt against her father. For Austen, the difference is crucial because it describes how colonial slaveholders' enforcement of racecraft abroad has diminished their paternal authority in Britain. In the case of *Mansfield Park*, a slaveholding patriarch loses control of his family because his colonial prerogative of owning people as chattels has, in the machinations of Mrs Norris, transformed into a plan to use Maria's marriage as leverage. Sir Thomas assents to this plan only, the plot emphasizes, because he is viewing it from the distant standpoint of his Antiguan plantation.

Read in this light, Sir Thomas's character appears as a long catalog of slavocratic powers breaking through variously at home; his impulses are curbed by the domestic setting, but there is no question in *Mansfield Park* that his actions are the result of colonial habits, pressures, and imperatives. In 1792, abolitionist William Wilberforce captured the brutality of these colonial customs when he observed in colonial planters "the fierceness of unrestrained power"; but Wilberforce believed that "superior rank and consequence" would mitigate slavery's worst evils among well-born enslavers.[115] Austen insists in Sir Thomas that there is no such hedge between chattel slavery and human character.

These broader textual dynamics of tyranny and rebellion sharpen our context for the Mansfield Park ball, where Austen embeds even more pointed allusions to the real colonial history of Antigua that seems to shape Sir Thomas's consciousness. During the Northamptonshire ball, Sir Thomas engages with his nephew William in a "prolonged . . . conversation on dancing in general" (251). The narrator notes further that Sir Thomas is "well engaged in describing" to William "the balls of Antigua," a seemingly random detail, which may hint that Sir Thomas is regaling his nephew with Caribbean stories of Prince Klaas's plot on Antigua's 1736 coronation ball. Austen amplifies this note with Sir Thomas's interest in "what his nephew could relate of the different modes of dancing which had fallen within his observation," perhaps the planter's oblique reference to the Ikem Dance (251). By this point of the novel, William's naval service has taken him to "Gibraltar," "the Mediterranean," the "West Indies," and "the Mediterranean again," suggesting that he, like his Uncle Bertram, has had occasion to observe non-English styles of dance (235, 236). We know that Sir Thomas regards his nephew's sea stories as "proof of good principles, professional knowledge, energy, courage, and cheerfulness," so we might expect the Caribbean planter to respond to William in kind, with his own colonial stories of "courage" (236). The slaveholder's misplaced pride, which William's mother notes in the rising action of the story, may be in evidence here.[116]

Tom Bertram's character arc gives us yet further insight into what Sir Thomas has encountered overseas. One does not like to put too much stock in the observations of a designing aunt, but Tom's return to Northamptonshire in advance of his father to fulfill his "duties" implies truth in Mrs Norris's premonition that Sir Thomas no longer considers the island safe for his son (114). After returning to England, Tom describes these "duties" by asserting at least five times that the Mansfield Park company should, instead of *Lovers' Vows*, put on George Colman's 1797 play, *Heir at Law* (114, 131).[117] Tom's suggestion of this comedy of legal succession jives with his unserious disposition to his father's interest in keeping him alive to undertake future proprietary responsibilities. Anti-slavery violence in Antigua is one sound explanation of why Sir Thomas removes his ungovernable son from his direct personal supervision and sends him back to Britain, where he tends to squander the family fortune and create trouble for his siblings.

Where, then, does this leave the speculative claim that there is a slave insurrection in *Mansfield Park*? Here is the totality of the evidence from above: first, the novel repeatedly admits the specter of Caribbean violence in the voices of several characters. While Sir Thomas is abroad, furthermore, he readily assents to Maria's connection to Sotherton; he would have reason to recognize that such an alliance could steady family finances should their colonial property be seized in the event of his death. Sending Tom home from Antigua, many months before his own return, suggests the planter's effort to remove his heir from danger on the island. Upon resuming control at Mansfield Park, Sir Thomas responds to his children's disorder with strategies slaveholders used to quell slave rebellion—insisting, for example, that Edmund avoid absenteeism at Thornton Lacey. Sir Thomas then appears to reference the specific history of Antiguan slave revolt at the Mansfield Park ball, which was plotted to begin just a few miles from the Nibbs family's Antigua plantations, to which Austen's father was trustee. The reader will decide for herself the degree to which these accruing details signal a revolt in *Mansfield Park*'s fictional Antigua, offering her a glimpse into the overseas speculations of a slaveholding family like the Bertrams.

If we venture even further, and grant that Austen was using a copy of the *Genuine Narrative* to inform her plot—or had at least heard about the 1736 slave rebellion from the Nibbses[118]—we can move *Mansfield Park* even more squarely into the Atlantic literary history of anti-slavery politics. The human right of rebellion against tyranny, described by John Locke during the 1680s to justify the overthrow of the Stuarts,[119] was reasserted in 1736 by people held in bondage by British colonists in Antigua. It was asserted again in 1776 by slaveholding American revolutionaries against British imperial power. In 1791, enslaved people in Saint-Domingue asserted this same right against French slavocratic rule. The appearance of Austen's novel during a crucial interval of British anti-slavery politics undergirds all other textual evidence that, as Deidre Lynch observes, Austen was a "social commentator" on "imperial policy."[120] This remarkable growth in our knowledge of Austen and empire, beginning about thirty years ago, humbles us to see that our own ignorance of sociopolitical nuances wrought by empire in domestic society ought never be mistaken for the ignorance of historical actors.

Edward Said concluded in *Culture and Imperialism* that *Mansfield Park* was "part of the structure of [Britain's] expanding imperialist venture"; but, perceiving in himself the controversy his claim would excite in others, he also noted that the cruelty of colonial slavery was at odds with "everything we know about Austen and her values." For him, the solution to reconciling these opposing concepts—what he called a "paradox... in reading Jane Austen,"—was to "take seriously our intellectual and interpretive vocation to make connections, to deal with as much evidence as possible" and to see the "complementarity and interdependence... of human history."[121] I have sought to apply Said's wisdom in the final sections of this chapter in full knowledge that, thirty years hence, there will be more evidence to deal with.[122] As the wake widens, the imprecision I have here attributed to Said's reading of *Mansfield Park* will be at least as true of my own.

"The Liberty which his Absence had Given": *Somerset v. Stewart* and *Mansfield Park*

Thus far, we have surveyed how Jane Austen plots decisive reversals of Sir Thomas Bertram's plans for himself and his children in *Mansfield Park*.[123] In a narrative act James Baldwin later called the creation of consciousness, Austen envisions a fictional person, racecrafted into a British absentee slaveholder, losing patriarchal authority over his family because of how slaveholding has corrupted his disposition. And what Austen created in fiction, others observed in fact: Thomas Jefferson recorded slavery's corruption of planters' manners in *Notes*, and Frederick Douglass saw the specific effects of slavery on Sophia Auld in *Narrative of the Life of Frederick Douglass* (1845). Auld became Douglass's mistress through marriage; but she (like Fanny Price until her tenth year) had not grown up in a slaveholding family. "Slavery proved as injurious to her as it did to me,"[124] Douglass writes, noting that the institution damaged each person in separate but equal ways. *Mansfield Park* sets out the related, but uniquely British, problem of how human bondage affected a slaveholder divided between slavocratic prerogatives across the Atlantic and paternal duties at home.

But Sir Thomas is no mere experiment in fiction. Austen anchors his character in the facts of *Somerset v. Stewart*, the watershed slavery case Lord Chief Justice Mansfield decided from the King's Bench in 1772. In that case, an enslaved man, James Somerset, escaped his enslaver in London after being brought to the metropole from colonial Virginia. Stewart hired slavecatchers who detained Somerset in the city and handed him over to Captain John Knowles of the *Ann and Mary*, a ship lying at anchor in the Thames and bound for Jamaica. Stewart directed Knowles to there sell Somerset back into slavery.[125] Through his godparents, Somerset filed a writ of habeas corpus against Stewart for unlawful imprisonment.[126] In attempting to sell James Somerset from London back into Caribbean slavery, Stewart asserted that his slavocratic authority was everywhere coterminous with his natural body. But Lord Mansfield said otherwise, dividing Stewart, while in Britain, from his commercial power to trade in human flesh, which persisted beyond British shores. The Court concluded that severing Stewart from his chattel prerogatives was essential because the tyranny of slavery was incompatible with the protections of the ancient constitution.[127]

Somerset's attorney argued to the Mansfield court that "the laws, the genius and spirit of the constitution, [forbade] the approach of slavery; [and did] not suffer it's [*sic*] existence here."[128] Mansfield agreed that slavery, because of its nature, was "incapable of being introduced on any reasons, moral or political." He explained that slavery was so "odious" that "nothing can be suffered to support it, but positive law."[129] In distinction to the common law, positive laws are legislature-made statutes like the colonial slave codes that this study calls novel constitutions. Mansfield affirmed that those colonial legal inventions did not apply domestically. Because slavery could only be supported by codes beyond his jurisdiction, Mansfield concluded, James Somerset "must be discharged" from the tyranny of Stewart's personal dominion.[130] Here, we should note a remarkable historical coincidence. Charles Stewart lost his commercial power to buy and sell humans at home because this, Mansfield said, was a violation of the ancient constitution. An earlier Charles Stuart, who contravened the ancient constitution by asserting personal dominion over *all* his subjects, had his head severed from his body, in 1649, less than a mile from where James Somerset was set free.

By naming Sir Thomas's Northamptonshire estate—and the novel—after *Somerset v. Stewart,* Austen signals that Sir Thomas's character personifies the consequences of Mansfield's decision.[131] Mansfield applied the protections of the ancient constitution to James Somerset domestically and limited Charles Stewart's chattel prerogatives to the colonies. And that is all he did. Abolitionists extolled

Lord Mansfield's ruling as freeing all of the slaves in Britain, but Mansfield clarified in 1785, in *The King v. Inhabitants of Thames Ditton*, that his 1772 decision was far narrower in scope: "The determinations [of *Somerset*] go no further than that the master cannot by force compel [his slave] to go out of the kingdom."[132] Thus, Mansfield's ruling in *Somerset* made definitive those distinctions which had arisen since the seventeenth century between domestic common law and the positive laws of the country's colonial plantation system. Austen develops these distinctions early in *Mansfield Park* between the capital freehold interests of the Rushworths and the colonial slavocratic interests of the Bertrams.

A novel, Jane Austen knew, was uniquely suited to exploring these tensions in the state of the law and how they affect the moral condition of the human interior.[133] In the words of Somerset's attorney, Austen uses *Mansfield Park* to plumb the implication of slavery's "corruption of manners in the master, from the entire subjection of the slaves he possesses to his sole will."[134] Austen's notice of *Somerset* in *Mansfield Park* is akin to her engagements with marriage law in the earlier novels, especially *Pride and Prejudice* (1813). There, Lydia Bennet elopes with George Wickham to Gretna Green, beyond the jurisdiction of the Anglican Church, to "thwart [her] parents' will."[135] Comparably, Sir Thomas's children thwart his will while he is maintaining his personal government in colonial Antigua, beyond the jurisdiction of the common law. The moral corrosion of Sir Thomas's dominion in Northamptonshire, arising from the absolute power he exercises abroad, establishes the legal realism of *Mansfield Park* as an anti-slavery argument. With the domestic destruction caused by Sir Thomas's colonial manners, Austen emphasizes that Mansfield's ruling in favor of James Somerset did not curb colonial slavery's corruption of constitutional ideals in Britain.

Austen would have read this summary of Somerset's case in Clarkson's *History*:

> James Somerset, an African slave, had been brought to England by his master, Charles Stewart, in November 1769. Somerset in process of time left him. Stewart took an opportunity of seizing him, and had him conveyed on board the Ann and Mary, Captain Knowles, to be carried out of the kingdom and sold as a slave in Jamaica: the question was, "Whether a slave, by coming into England, became free?"[136]

This, however, was the political gloss of an abolitionist, not the question before the court. The legal issue facing Mansfield was whether a slaveholder, after coming into England with his human chattel, could there alienate that property. In this sense, Somerset's habeas petition challenged Mansfield to affirm the legal principle, and the nationalist commonplace, that the British constitution limited the exercise of absolute power over its subjects. By envisioning Sir Thomas as a slaveholder who tries but fails to exercise slavocratic absolutism in England, Austen not only reveals her understanding of the Mansfield decision's contours and limits; she also illuminates the moral hazards of British slavery in her own time. Read in this way, *Mansfield Park* creates, in the Baldwinian sense, *our* consciousness of colonial slavery's nearer wake.

Austen asks us to see, that is, how slavery in the Caribbean has altered the marriage plot in Britain. Sir Thomas's colonial tendency to exert absolute power at home is most evident in his disposition to the engagements of Maria, Julia, and Fanny. Austen transacts this dynamic of the plot first through the planter's responses to the play, *Lovers' Vows*, which his children and their friends rehearse in his absence. The group proceeds despite Fanny's and Edmund's concerns that the drama will involve everyone in general sexual improprieties as well as specific violation of James and Maria's engagement, and all that depends upon it. While Austen largely leaves to readers' imaginations the precise interactions between Maria and Henry during rehearsals, critics have shown that the stage directions for *Lovers' Vows* grant a high degree of sexual license during Agatha and Frederick's embraces.[137] We also learn from Austen's narrator that "Frederick," played by Henry, "was listening with looks of devotion to Agatha's narrative," delivered by the engaged Maria, "and pressing her hand to his heart," a gesture that Maria cataclysmically misinterprets as Henry's unspoken devotion to her (175).

Sir Thomas arrives home "in the middle of a rehearsal" of *Lovers' Vows*, to which he puts an immediate end, dismantling the stage and burning copies of the script (185).[138] His severe reaction suggests that, in pursuing the play, the Bertram children have placed their family in precisely the kind of unacceptable precarity that Maria's marriage and his own Atlantic errand were meant to stabilize; after all, almost everyone at Mansfield Park thinks he has risked his life to settle the overseas estate. From the earliest moments of his return, then, it is clear that Sir Thomas intends to crush his children's rebellion against his authority. Yet he cannot access the full details of the plot against him for two reasons: first, he has alienated his children—especially Maria—from his understanding by spending so much time abroad; and second, he has alienated himself from their confidence by applying at home forms of absolute power similar to ones he exercises over his slaves. In this inability to know what his children are actually doing, Sir Thomas resembles the Antiguan slaveholders who watched the Coramantee Ikem Dance performed in plain sight before the coronation ball without perceiving that their own deaths were being orchestrated.

Other signs of the colonies are here. John Yates, exasperated that the play has been shut down, and with it his unfettered contact with Julia, complains to Tom Bertram while the two friends are hunting. Austen's narrator tells us knowingly that "Mr. Yates was beginning now to understand Sir Thomas's intentions," in ending the theatricals—but Yates is, the narrator adds, "as far as ever from understanding their source" (191). This "source," Austen faintly indicates in this resonant paragraph, is colonial Antigua. Tom Bertram, who has witnessed his father's slavocratic power firsthand, apologizes to his friend "for his father's particularity," the difference Tom alone knows that colonial racecraft has made (191). The narrator tells us that Yates's displeasure with the planter is so great that "he believed he should certainly attack the Baronet," a significant line because Yates is both carrying a gun when he says it and voicing an impulse to attack a slaveholder—all of this mere pages after almost toppling Sir Thomas during the planter's discovery of the rebellious theatricals (191).

If we believe that the *Genuine Narrative* is a paratext of *Mansfield Park*, Yates's envisioned attack on Sir Thomas is an allusion to Prince Klaas's plot to explode the coronation ball and raid the garrison. But, the narrator continues, "there was a something in Sir Thomas...which made Mr. Yates think it wiser to let him pursue his own way...without opposition" (191). Yates backs away from public defiance of Sir Thomas because of an undefined "something" in the slaveholder's manner. Austen's narrator says more: "never, in the whole course of his life, had [Yates] seen one of that class so unintelligibly moral, so infamously tyrannical as Sir Thomas" (191). The "class" of people that Yates references here are British fathers. But, by underscoring Tom's singular knowledge of the "source" of Sir Thomas's "infamous" tyranny—unlike anything Yates has seen "in the whole course of his life"—Austen gestures west.

John Yates does not openly contravene Sir Thomas. But Maria, Julia, and Fanny all enter into states of rebellion against the planter's authority in the context of their marriages. Fanny refuses to accept Crawford's proposal of marriage, which her Uncle Bertram endorsed (perhaps to save the marriage of the Rushworths). Maria has an adulterous affair with Crawford, exploding the very union her father has striven to preserve.[139] Julia elopes with Yates. This has all been prefigured by the sisters' subversion of Sir Thomas's will during rehearsals of *Lovers' Vows*. However, while Sir Thomas has a sense of "all the impropriety" of these theatricals, and suspects Henry Crawford, he does not know his daughters' feelings for himself; Sir Thomas "*would have been*"—but is not actually—"deeply mortified" by even "a suspicion of half that his daughters felt on the subject of his return," Austen's narrator discloses (107–8, my emphasis).

Austen thus signals both Sir Thomas's lack of particular knowledge and the Bertram sisters' awareness of how profoundly their sexual freedom is circumscribed by his presence. In this way, Maria and Julia move toward open rebellion against Sir Thomas's personal government while he is away only to resume the appearance of obedience after his return. They rebel again after leaving Mansfield Park. Fanny, by significant contrast, honors her uncle's authority while he is away, but directly contravenes him when he tries to apply his absolute power to her in person. We will return to this important difference between the Bertram and Price cousins because it is an index of Austen's specific argument for abolition.

Austen orchestrates the various rebellions of Maria, Julia, and Fanny around the figure of Henry Crawford. Perceiving the extreme displeasure of Mansfield

Park's returned patriarch, and the contraction of sexual liberties he enjoyed in Northamptonshire during the planter's absence, Henry Crawford plans a hasty retreat to Bath. The morning of Crawford's departure from Mansfield finds Maria Bertram "in a good deal of agitation" (191). Her fiancé James has already gone to Sotherton with news of Sir Thomas's safe Atlantic voyage and the imminent wedding it signals. The narrator says that it is "of the utmost consequence to [Maria] that Crawford should now lose no time in declaring himself" as her lover (191). Again: think of Prince Klaas, who, as Antigua's coronation ball for George II approached, needed to know who was with him.

Maria Bertram is not a slave. But she, too, needs a declaration of loyalty against the slavocratic power that has arranged her marriage. On this very morning, Maria expects Henry's "immediate *eclaircissement*," imagining gleefully that James Rushworth might be saved "the trouble of ever coming back again" to Mansfield Park (192). When Henry arrives at Mansfield to take his leave, the sincerity of Maria's feelings is revealed in the "delight and agitation" she experiences at "the introduction of the man she loved to her father" (192). The stage is set for Maria's release from an unwanted engagement she accepted, at least in part, as her filial duty to her father's colonial estate. Austen has prefigured the potential for Maria's freedom from her father during the Sotherton tour, in which Henry offers Maria passage "round the edge of the [locked] gate... with [his] assistance" and "without Mr. Rushworth's authority and protection" (99). With Sir Thomas's return, however, comes Henry's reversal. He abandons his role as Maria's deliverer and declines to declare his love, finding it expedient to visit his uncle instead. Thus end "all the hopes [that Henry Crawford's] selfish vanity had raised in Maria and Julia Bertram" (194).

Pages later, Sir Thomas offers to assist Maria in ending her engagement to Rushworth. But it is too late. Abandoned by her lover, and lacking "neither pride nor resolution," Maria refuses her father's assistance (193). Because she finds her ongoing subjection to his will constitutionally intolerable, Maria instead thanks Sir Thomas for "his paternal kindness" and assures him with a lie that he is "quite mistaken in supposing she had the smallest desire of breaking through her engagement" (200). Maria throws in her lot with James Rushworth because she is "less and less able to endure the restraint which her father imposed. The liberty which his absence" in Antigua "had given was now become absolutely necessary" to her (202). The independence Maria enjoys from Sir Thomas's oppressive manners while he is away coerces her into marriage vows she does not want and will not honor. The failure of Maria's character is to accept the coercion.

Sir Thomas realizes the role he has played in his child's destruction only too late. The planter's ignorance of Maria's most fundamental wishes for her life and happiness is another "dead silence" in the text, just as rooted in Britain's colonial enterprise as Fanny's famous question about the slave trade. The silence signals

Austen's insight that colonial slavery fundamentally compromises the independence and security of Britons, especially those who believe themselves its beneficiaries. This is not the sentimental position of contemporary abolitionists like William Cowper, Thomas Clarkson, and Hannah More, who dramatized the horrors enslaved people experienced on British plantations.[140] Rather, Austen's anti-slavery stance is a novel-length refutation of the popular pro-slavery argument[141] that chattel property in persons was a colonial evil necessary to Britain's domestic prosperity.

But why, some will ask, does Austen encode her anti-slavery position so deeply in *Mansfield Park*?—why has it been so hard for us to perceive? One answer is that *Mansfield Park* does not glorify rebellion against absolute power in ways that her modern readers may wish to see. Rather, Austen qualifies rebellion as an insufficient response to the moral problem of slavery. It is absolutely significant that all rebellions against Sir Thomas's tyranny fail in this novel, one way or another. The slaveholder settles his Caribbean plantation enough to return safely from Antigua. Similarly, none of the sexual relationships raised in rebellion against Sir Thomas by *Lovers' Vows* survive to meaningfully shape the future of Britain. Henry is full of regret; Maria is ruined; Julia and Yates elope offstage; and Mary Crawford is sent packing to London. Even the marriage between Edmund and Fanny, the most favorable outcome of the story, results from Fanny's temporarily successful but ultimately limited rebellion against her uncle's slavocratic power. This is a tragedy. Austen brings to life many possibilities of freedom from Sir Thomas's rule and destroys each of them in turn. This may be why so many of *Mansfield Park*'s modern readers find its ending so disappointing.

Jane Austen, Abolitionist

A final comparison of Fanny's and Maria's resistance to Sir Thomas reveals a deep seam of Austen's abolition politics. Maria's domestic revolt against her slaveholding father is silent, self-destructive, and ultimately unsuccessful in securing the kind of independence she desires. But in Fanny Price—who honors her uncle's authority while he is away in the colonies but rebukes his absolute power when he gets home, as Lord Mansfield had done with Charles Stewart—Austen runs her plot headlong into the constitutional problem of the *Somerset* decision. That is: a singular instance of freeing one slave in Britain did not change the fundamental evils of the wider institution. As Benjamin Franklin exclaimed in 1772, just a few months after Mansfield issued his ruling:

> Pharisaical Britain! to pride thyself in setting free a single Slave that happens to land on thy coasts, while thy Merchants in all thy ports are encouraged by thy laws to continue a commerce whereby so many hundreds of thousands are

dragged into a slavery that can scarce be said to end with their lives, since it is entailed on their posterity![142]

When *Mansfield Park* was published, the "commerce" Franklin decried had been abolished by Parliament; but Austen indicates in the novel's conclusion that neither the abolished trade nor isolated rebellions against colonial slavocracy could absolve her country of its role in the original sin of chattel slavery.

When Sir Thomas visits Fanny to persuade her to accept Henry Crawford's proposal against her will, she asserts an absolute right to refuse the marriage, what Sir Thomas calls her "decided negative," and which he accepts on its face as the limit of his authority over her: "there is nothing more to be said," Sir Thomas concludes, once Fanny has refused her consent (319, 316). In Sir Thomas's view, Fanny is free to contravene his wishes because of their absent legal relationship to one another: Sir Thomas himself notes that Fanny is "not to be judged" in this instance "by the same rule" that governs his legal relationship with his children; Fanny does not owe him "the duty of a child," as his daughters do, including the filial duty to accept their father's right to "bestow" either of them on Henry Crawford (319).

While there is nothing more to be said, Sir Thomas thinks, there is much more to be done. The planter next undertakes a campaign to override Fanny's rejection of Henry. First, Sir Thomas assuages her feelings with the warm comforts of a fire; when indulgence fails, he sends her away from Mansfield Park to her family's home in Portsmouth, where she experiences the material difference colonial racecraft has made between the Bertrams and Prices. Mrs Norris calls these differences the "extraordinary advantages" bestowed on Fanny by her extended family out of their imperial surfeit (272). I do not see sufficient evidence in the novel that Sir Thomas is applying to his niece ameliorationist tactics for appeasing and disciplining rebellious slaves. But I also do not see sufficient evidence that he is not.

There is no question, however, that Sir Thomas is seeking to comfort Fanny—and to shame her—into the acceptance of his imperial will and the abandonment of her own. These manipulations of his niece, Austen is clear at the Mansfield Park ball, are the domestic manners of a planter used to exercising his "absolute power" abroad but limited by *Somerset* (and, now, his own niece) from exercising it fully at home. We know this because Sir Thomas fails to override Fanny's will with his manipulations of her material surroundings: she goes on to marry her cousin, Edmund, and the two ultimately take up residence at the parsonage connected to Mansfield Park.

Sir Thomas eventually learns to value the limits his niece has placed on his power at home, and the two develop a strong "mutual attachment," a clear domestic improvement to a disposition corrupted by slavocratic rule (472). But the worst of the damage cannot be reversed by this belated alteration, as his daughters and slaves would certainly attest. Once divided by slavocratic government, ancient constitutional protections of life, liberty, and property cannot easily be sutured back together, a fact we will consider at length in our next and final chapter on *Frankenstein*. Sir Thomas consequently ends the novel chastened by the creation of his racial consciousness, but deeply impotent: he is "[s]ick of ambitious and mercenary connections" required by imperial slavocracy and "anxious" to bind himself to "all that remained to him of domestic felicity" (471). Austen is clear that what remains of domestic felicity after racecraft cannot be much because of British abolitionism's limits.

Fanny has exercised her negative against slavocratic power, to be sure—but the Mansfield Park living, Austen's narrator tells us, soon grew "as dear to [Fanny's] heart, and as thoroughly perfect in her eyes, as everything else, within the view and patronage of Mansfield Park, had long been" (473). This is the same "living" that has been "unsettled" from the beginning of the novel, and only resettled at extraordinary cost to the Bertram family, which is to say nothing of the people they own. Claudia Johnson has underscored the awkwardness of *Mansfield Park*'s last sentence: its "hyperconventional" satire on novelistic resolutions.[143] I would highlight in this line Austen's studied imperial dissonance, developed purposefully in tension with the outcome of *Somerset*.

Fanny and Edmund may be the novel's last best custodians of virtue, but they are fundamentally compromised by inextricable ties to Mansfield Park; its sister plantation in the West Indies; and its patriarch, whose diminished life and fractured family signal what awaits Britons playing even minor or involuntary roles in colonial slavery. For all of her principled resistance to her uncle's slavocratic power, that is, Fanny is easily incorporated into the imperial estate at Mansfield, even as her beloved brother William remains in naval service to the vagaries of Britain's colonial enterprise. Austen knew this divided and tragic position. She was the daughter of an Antiguan plantation's trustee and sister to a woman who lost the future she desired in Britain's pro-slavery adventurism in revolutionary Haiti. This is why Austen characterizes the newlywed Bertrams, and the country whose future they signal, with profound equivocation. Fanny and Edmund's living at the parsonage will remain as "perfect" as "everything else" connected to Sir Thomas's Northamptonshire estate. In *Mansfield Park*, Austen perceives a British slave system chillingly proficient at turning rebellion of all kinds toward its own ends; the only remaining option, it would seem, is to change Britain's imperial constitution and abolish the institution everywhere it exists.

Notes

1. Jane Austen, *Mansfield Park*, ed. R. W. Chapman, 3rd edn (Oxford: Oxford University Press, 1934), 30. Cited hereafter parenthetically.

2. A. Peter Bailey and Earl Grant, *Malcolm X: The Man and his Times* (New York: Macmillan, 1969), 122–23.
3. Carolyn E. Fick, *The Making of Haiti: The Saint Domingue Revolution from Below* (Knoxville, TN: University of Tennessee Press, 1990), esp. introduction and chapter "Slaves in the North," 91–117.
4. Banneker's calculations ended up in Revolutionary France. Jefferson mailed them to the Marquis de Condorcet, who died in prison in 1794 while hiding from leaders of the French Revolution. *The Papers of Thomas Jefferson*, vol. 22, *6 August 1791–31 December 1791*, ed. Charles T. Cullen (Princeton: Princeton University Press, 1986), 98–99.
5. Ruth Perry, "Austen and Empire: A Thinking Woman's Guide to British Imperialism," *Persuasions* 16 (1994): 95–106. See also C. L. R. James, *The Black Jacobins: Toussaint L'Ouverture and the San Domingo Revolution*, 2nd edn (New York: Vintage Books, 1963); Fick, *Making of Haiti*; and Leslie M. Alexander, *Fear of a Black Republic: Haiti and the Birth of Black Internationalism in the United States* (Urbana, IL: University of Illinois Press, 2022).
6. Perry, "Austen and Empire," 95.
7. Deirdre Le Faye, *Jane Austen: A Family Record*, 2nd edn (Cambridge: Cambridge University Press, 2004), 101.
8. Perry, "Austen and Empire," 96–97.
9. Perry, "Austen and Empire," 95–96, and Claire Tomalin, *Jane Austen: A Life* (New York: Vintage Books, 1999), 108, 114.
10. Le Faye, *Austen: Family Record*, 91, 101.
11. Le Faye, *Austen: Family Record*, 101.
12. Perry, "Austen and Empire," 96; Tomalin, *Austen: Life*, 126–27.
13. Tomalin, *Austen: Life*, 126–27.
14. Perry, "Austen and Empire," 95.
15. R. W. Chapman, *Jane Austen: Facts and Problems* (Oxford: Clarendon Press, 1948), 81.
16. James Oldham, "New Light on Mansfield and Slavery," *Journal of British Studies* 27, no. 1 (1988): 45–68. I have argued elsewhere that the 1772 Mansfield decision is the source of Austen's title. Sarah Marsh, "Changes of Air: The Somerset Case and *Mansfield Park*'s Imperial Plots," *Eighteenth-Century Studies* 53, no. 2 (Winter 2020): 213, 228.
17. Brian Southam, "The Silence of the Bertrams: Slavery and the Chronology of *Mansfield Park*," *Times Literary Supplement*, February 17, 1995, 13–14.
18. See generally Christopher Leslie Brown, *Moral Capital* (Chapel Hill, NC: University of North Carolina Press, 2006).
19. For an excellent review of the controversy, see J. A. Downie, "The Chronology of *Mansfield Park*," *Modern Philology* 112, no. 2 (2014): 427–34.
20. Quotation in the subheading is from Austen, *Mansfield Park*, 446.
21. Christina Sharpe, *In the Wake: On Blackness and Being* (Durham, NC: Duke University Press, 2016), 3, 10, 21.
22. Sharpe, *In the Wake*, 15.
23. See generally Jonathan A. Bush, "Free to Enslave: The Foundations of Colonial American Slave Law," *Yale Journal of Law and the Humanities* 5, no. 2 (1993): 417–70; and Brewer, "Common Law of Slavery."
24. Sharpe, *In the Wake*, 15.
25. James Baldwin, "Letter from a Region in my Mind," *The New Yorker*, November 17, 1962. This essay became the second half of *The Fire Next Time* (1963); the first half of the book was another 1962 essay, "My Dungeon Shook: Letter to My Nephew on the One Hundredth Anniversary of Emancipation," originally published in *The Progressive*. In his *Between the World and Me* (2015), Ta-Nehisi Coates would adopt Baldwin's epistolary format. Ta-Nehisi Coates, *Between the World and Me* (New York: Spiegel & Grau, 2015).
26. Said, *Culture and Imperialism*, 93.
27. I am grateful to April Shelford for helping me to clarify this portion of the argument and for supplying some of the language of this sentence. April Shelford, email message to author, December 2, 2024.
28. Marsh, "Changes of Air," 213–19.
29. Peter Smith is probably the most forthright expositor of this view: "It is Fanny who is the slave," he explains, "or perhaps it would be better to say that *Mansfield Park* rests upon a symbolic equivalence established between the forced labour of African cane-cutters and that invisible figure who stands in the margin of every page Jane Austen wrote, the unmarried gentlewoman who has no money of her own." Peter Smith, "Mansfield Park and the World Stage," *Cambridge Quarterly* 23, no. 3 (1994): 207.

30. Margaret Kirkham has argued that there is an "analogy" implied in *Mansfield Park* "between the condition of the slave and the condition of the Englishwoman of the middle class" (132). This was a commonplace in abolitionist writings of the period, and one that Austen would raise as a comparison in the voice of Jane Fairfax in *Emma*. Moira Ferguson has explained of *Mansfield Park* that "gender relations at home parallel and echo traditional relationships of power between the colonialists and colonized peoples: European women visibly signify the most egregiously and invisibly repressed of the text—African-Caribbeans themselves" (118). I am arguing that treating fictional Englishwomen as analogous to or symbols of other kinds of people is to leave aside the intricacies of colonial and domestic property law, to which Austen painstakingly attends. See Margaret Kirkham, *Jane Austen, Feminism and Fiction* (London: Bloomsbury, 2000), 132; Moira Ferguson, "Mansfield Park: Slavery, Colonialism, and Gender," *Oxford Literary Review* 13, no. 1 (1991): 118–39; and Deirdre Coleman, "Domestic and Colonial Sisters in *Mansfield Park*," in *A Companion to Jane Austen*, ed. Claudia L. Johnson and Clara Tuite (Oxford: Blackwell, 2009), 295–310.
31. J. A. Downie, "Who Says She's a Bourgeois Writer? Reconsidering the Social and Political Contexts of Jane Austen's Novels," *Eighteenth-Century Studies* 40, no. 1 (Fall 2006): 69–84.
32. As Coleman rightly says, Austen "could never have blurred and confounded the categories of oppressed middle-class woman and plantation slaves." Coleman, "Domestic and Colonial Sisters," 303. John Wiltshire has made a similar, correct observation: "It is difficult to understand, though, how a modern reader of even a few of the genuine narratives by slaves, or the diaries of their masters, could possibly think that there is any but the loosest relation between the state of slavery and the condition of a genteel young English woman as depicted in the novel." See John Wiltshire, "Decolonising *Mansfield Park*," *Essays in Criticism* 53, no. 4 (October 2003): 308.
33. Richard S. Dunn, *Sugar and Slaves: The Rise of the Planter Class in the English West Indies, 1624–1713* (Chapel Hill, NC: University of North Carolina Press, 1972).
34. Lowell J. Ragatz, *The Fall of the Planter Class in the British Caribbean, 1763–1833: A Study in Social and Economic History* (New York: Century Co., 1928); Eric Williams, *Capitalism and Slavery* (Chapel Hill, NC: University of North Carolina Press, 1944).
35. Nicholas Crawford, review of *Rethinking the Fall of the Planter Class*, ed. Christer Petley, *New West Indian Guide* 92, nos. 1–2 (2018): 114.
36. Brown, *Moral Capital*, 24. See also Marsha Huff, "Sir Thomas Bertram and the Slave Trade," *Persuasions On-Line* 41, no. 2 (2021), on Sir Thomas's role as a Member of Parliament and his presumed familiarity with abolition debates.
37. Eve Kosofsky Sedgwick, "Jane Austen and the Masturbating Girl," *Critical Inquiry* 17, no. 4 (Summer 1991): 833.
38. The nation's ascendant merchant class stood on the shoulders of naval service members and their families, who, in the name of the national defense, also protected the commercial interest and thereby secured colonial planters' large gains in overseas markets. Naval service members kept the Atlantic open to British trade by risking life and limb for meager wages, though the social returns for their patriotism were relatively high. See Brian Southam, *Jane Austen and the Navy* (London: National Maritime Museum, 2005), esp. chapter "Mansfield Park: The Young Lieutenant," 181–218.
39. For a related argument, that there is something "*nouveau* and West Indian" about Sir Thomas, see Southam, "Silence of the Bertrams," 14.
40. For commentary on the moral landscapes of *Mansfield Park* in the context of eighteenth-century Enlightenment ideals, see Ann Banfield, "The Moral Landscape of *Mansfield Park*," *Nineteenth-Century Fiction* 26, no. 1 (1971): 1–24.
41. Daniel Bogart and Gary Richardson, "Property Rights and Parliament in Industrializing Britain," NBER Working Paper no. 15697 (Cambridge, MA: National Bureau of Economic Research, January 2010).
42. Susanne Seymour, Stephen Daniels, and Charles Watkins, "Estate and Empire: Sir George Cornewall's Management of Moccas, Herefordshire and La Taste, Grenada, 1771–1819," *Journal of Historical Geography* 24, no. 3 (1998): 333.
43. Seymour et al., "Estate and Empire," 333.
44. Seymour et al., "Estate and Empire," 333.
45. Ragatz, *The Fall of the Planter Class*, 67.
46. Downie, "Chronology of *Mansfield Park*," 427–34.
47. "Free air" was one way that English jurists styled the common law principle that slavery required positive law and could not exist by ancient constitutional custom on English soil, a doctrine often traced to Chief Justice Sir John Holt's late seventeenth- and early eighteenth-century decisions.

See *Chamberlain v. Harvey* (1697) 5 Mod. 186, 87 Eng. Rep. 646 (K.B.); *Smith v. Brown and Cooper* (1701) 2 Salk. 666, 91 Eng. Rep. 566 (K.B.); *Somerset v. Stewart* (1772) Lofft 1, 98 Eng. Rep. 499 (K.B.); William M. Wiecek, *The Sources of Anti-Slavery Constitutionalism in America, 1760–1848* (Ithaca, NY: Cornell University Press, 2018), 174, 176–77; Brown, *Moral Capital*, 108.

48. Katherine Turner, "Cowper, Slave Narratives, and the Antebellum American Reading Public," *Cowper & Newton Journal* 6 (2016), https://cowperandnewtonmuseum.org.uk/journal/j6-article-turner/.
49. Julia Jorati (ed.), "William Cowper, 'The Negro's Complaint' (1788)," in *Slavery in Early Modern Philosophy, 1765–1800: Essential Readings* (New York: Oxford University Press, 2026).
50. William Cowper, *The Task, with Tirocinium: and Selections from the Minor Poems, A.D. 1784–1799*, ed. Henry Thomas Griffith, 2nd edn (Oxford: Clarendon Press, 1875), bk. 1, ll. 331, 339.
51. Cowper, *The Task*, bk. 2, l. 37.
52. Maria is not a slave because there are no slaves in Britain, as Cowper's poem asserts; but Maria is nevertheless connected to enslaved people in the West Indies through her father's transatlantically divided personhood.
53. Alistair M. Duckworth, "*Mansfield Park* and Estate Improvements: Jane Austen's Grounds of Being," *Nineteenth-Century Fiction* 26, no. 1 (1971): 25–48.
54. Duckworth, "*Mansfield Park* and Estate Improvements," 33.
55. P. J. Marshall, *Edmund Burke and the British Empire in the West Indies: Wealth, Power, and Slavery* (Oxford: Oxford University Press, 2019), 22–23.
56. Burke, quoted in Duckworth, "*Mansfield Park* and Estate Improvements," 33.
57. *Oxford English Dictionary*, s.v. "court leet (n.)," accessed July 2024. <https://doi.org/10.1093/OED/2979724634> See also Sarah Parry, "Mansfield Park and the Idea of 'Old' and 'New' Money: A Study in the Interpretation of Historic Houses," *Persuasions On-Line* 35, no. 1 (Winter 2014), para. 6. <https://jasna.org/persuasions/on-line/vol35no1/parry.html>
58. *Oxford English Dictionary*, s.v. "court baron (n.)," accessed July 2024, <https://doi.org/10.1093/OED/1873393930>; "copyhold (n.)," accessed July 2023. <https://doi.org/10.1093/OED/8926151063> Encyclopaedia Britannica Online, s.v. "copyhold," accessed October 5, 2024. <https://www.britannica.com/topic/copyhold>
59. David Barry Gaspar has found evidence in the records of colonial Jamaica, for example, that slavery was justified as the custom of that country. See Gaspar, "'Rigid and Inclement': Origins of the Jamaica Slave Laws of the Seventeenth Century," in *The Many Legalities of Early America*, ed. Tomlins and Mann (Chapel Hill, NC: University of North Carolina Press, 2001).
60. Michael Guasco, *Slaves and Englishmen: Human Bondage in the Early Modern Atlantic World* (Philadelphia: University of Pennsylvania Press, 2014), 29–33.
61. University of Nottingham, "Copyhold," Manuscripts and Special Collections, accessed October 8, 2024. <https://www.nottingham.ac.uk/manuscriptsandspecialcollections/researchguidance/deedsindepth/copyhold/copyhold.aspx>
62. See generally Teresa Michals, "'That Sole and Despotic Dominion': Slaves, Wives, and Game in Blackstone's *Commentaries*," *Eighteenth-Century Studies* 27, no. 2 (1993): 195–216.
63. Encyclopaedia Britannica Online, s.v. "copyhold."
64. On Parliament's use of property and debt law to subordinate colonial estates to metropolitan creditors, see Claire Priest, "Creating an American Property Law: Alienability and its Limits in American History," *Harvard Law Review* 120 (2006): 395–406; and Claire Priest, *Credit Nation: Property Laws and Institutions in Early America* (Princeton: Princeton University Press, 2021), 74–89.
65. An Act to Repeal So Much of an Act, Made in the Fifth Year of the Reign of His Late Majesty King George the Second, Intituled, "An Act for the More Easy Recovery of Debts in His Majesty's Plantations and Colonies in America," as Makes Negroes Liable to Be Sold in Execution for the Payment of Debts, 37 Geo. 3 c. 119 (1797).
66. Nicholas Crawford, "'In the Wreck of a Master's Fortune': Slave Provisioning and Planter Debt in the British Caribbean," *Slavery and Abolition* 37, no. 4 (2016): 736–57.
67. Crawford, "Wreck of a Master's Fortune," 736–57.
68. Priest, *Credit Nation*, 82.
69. This is the same number as the Bertram children; Fanny is not included in this tally.
70. See generally George E. Boulukos, "The Politics of Silence: *Mansfield Park* and the Amelioration of Slavery," *Novel: A Forum on Fiction* 39, no. 3 (2006): 361–83. Boulukos thinks that the silence of the Bertrams at Fanny Price's mention of the slave trade to her uncle is not silence about slavery, as Edward Said concluded, but rather the Bertram daughters' indifference to their father's occupations abroad. Edmund and Fanny, in contrast to Maria and Julia, "concur," Boulukos

writes, "in seeing the slave trade as an attractive topic for Sir Thomas. Neither of the two imagines Fanny's question as an improper broaching of a distasteful topic, a hostile challenge, or a naïve gaffe" (368). Boulukos is wrong about the content of this silence, I think, but he concludes correctly that "[a]ttributing Austen's views to Fanny—or vice versa—is risky" (377).

71. Marsha Huff reads Austen's treatment of Sir Thomas Bertram's absence as a critique of delegated authority modeled on contemporary accounts of absentee plantation management in Thomas Clarkson's *History*. Drawing on Clarkson's descriptions of overseers left in charge of enslaved laborers, Huff argues that *Mansfield Park* links domestic misrule to the moral failures of nonresident slaveholders, a framework that helps explain Mrs Norris's mismanagement of the Bertram children during Sir Thomas's absence. See Huff, "Sir Thomas Bertram and the Slave Trade."
72. For a dissenting discussion of these critics' positions, see Wiltshire, "Decolonising *Mansfield Park*," 306–7.
73. The innovative misinterpretations of this scene by postcolonial critics, beginning with Edward Said, are too numerous to list here, but I name myself among them: Marsh, "Changes of Air," 218.
74. For a clear expression of this argument contemporary to Austen's life see Sharp, *The Just Limitation of Slavery in the Laws of God, Compared with the Unbounded Claims of the African Traders and British American Slaveholders*. For treatment of Sharp in context, see Brown, *Moral Capital*, 33–101, 155–206.
75. Said, *Culture and Imperialism*, 80–97. This chapter was a reprint of Said's essay of the same title first published in 1989.
76. John Avery Jones has shown that the trusteeship "was a purely nominal one required to deal with a theoretical legal problem that could never have involved him in any duties connected with running a plantation implicated with slavery." John Avery Jones, "George Austen as a (Nominal) Trustee of a Plantation in Antigua: The Legal Position," in *Report for 2021* (London: The Jane Austen Society, 2021), 33. Devoney Looser adds that George Austen may have been so named because he was officiant at the wedding of James Langford Nibbs to his first cousin, Barbara Langford. Devoney Looser, "Breaking the Silence: The Austen Family's Complex Entanglements with Slavery," in *Report for 2021* (London: The Jane Austen Society, 2021), 27.

    Frank Gibbon, "The Antiguan Connection: Some New Light on *Mansfield Park*," *Cambridge Quarterly* 11, no. 2 (1982): 298–305; Gregson Davis, "Jane Austen's *Mansfield Park*: The Antigua Connection," University of the West Indies Open Campus, 2004, accessed September 15, 2024.
77. *Antigua Journal* 11, no. 578 (November 20, 1798).
78. See esp. John Henry Hubback and Edith Charlotte Hubback, *Jane Austen's Sailor Brothers: Being the Adventures of Sir Francis Austen, G.C.B., Admiral of the Fleet and Rear-Admiral Charles Austen* (London: John Lane, 1906); and Southam, *Austen and the Navy*. Relatedly, see Gabrielle D. V. White, *Jane Austen in the Context of Abolition: "A Fling at the Slave Trade"* (New York: Palgrave Macmillan, 2006).
79. Hubback and Hubback, *Jane Austen's Sailor Brothers*, 192.
80. Looser, "Breaking the Silence"; see also Devoney Looser, "Heroics All at Sea: Jane Austen's Brother and 'Crushing' the Slave Trade," *Times Literary Supplement*, July 8, 2022.
81. Sheila Johnson Kindred, *Jane Austen's Transatlantic Sister: The Life and Letters of Fanny Palmer Austen* (Montreal: McGill-Queen's University Press, 2017).
82. Miranda Kaufmann, *Heiresses: Marriage, Inheritance, and Slavery in the Caribbean* (London: Pegasus Books, 2024), 135–69; at 136 on Ann Cholmeley's relationship to the Willoughbys of Parham, and at 141 on Katherine's marriage to Governor Spry.
83. Kaufmann, *Heiresses*, 167.
84. Perry, "Austen and Empire," 103; Jane Austen, *Jane Austen's Letters*, ed. Deirdre Le Faye, 4th edn (Oxford: Oxford University Press, 2011), 207.
85. Austen, *Jane Austen's Letters*, 207.
86. Austen, *Jane Austen's Letters*, 207. For the best extended assessment of Jane Austen's style see D. A. Miller, *Jane Austen, or The Secret of Style* (Princeton: Princeton University Press, 2003).
87. Charles William Pasley, *Essay on the Military Policy and Institutions of the British Empire* (London: E. Lloyd, 1811), 74.
88. Austen, *Jane Austen's Letters*, 207. For additional commentary on Pasley and Austen, see Kathryn E. Davis, "'The First Soldier [She] Ever Sighed for': Charles Pasley's *Essay* and the 'Governing Winds' of *Mansfield Park*," *Persuasions On-Line* 35, no. 1 (Winter 2014).
89. Pasley, *Essay on Military Policy*, 74.
90. Pasley, *Essay on Military Policy*, 74.

91. Alexander, *Fear of a Black Republic*, 3.
92. Thomas Jefferson, "Letter to the Marquis de Lafayette," June 16, 1792, Gilder Lehrman Institute of American History, accessed September 26, 2024. <https://www.gilderlehrman.org/history-resources/spotlight-primary-source/jefferson-french-and-haitian-revolutions-1792>
93. William Shakespeare, *Julius Caesar*, ed. Barbara A. Mowat and Paul Werstine (Washington, DC: Folger Shakespeare Library, 1992), 1.2.147–48.
94. Aristotle defines poetic, or fictional, plausibility as what is possible in an imaginative text according to probability or necessity, prioritizing internal coherence. Aristotle, *Poetics*, tr. S. H. Butcher, in *The Complete Works of Aristotle*, ed. Jonathan Barnes, vol. 2 (Princeton: Princeton University Press, 1984), 1451a36–1451b11.
95. Said, *Culture and Imperialism*, 96.
96. Bernard Ledwidge, "The 'Strange Business in America,'" in *Collected Reports of the Jane Austen Society, 1949–67* (London: The Jane Austen Society, 1967), 199.
97. Encyclopaedia Britannica Online, s.v. "Embargo Act," accessed November 11, 2024. <https://www.britannica.com/topic/Embargo-Act>
98. Emanuel Bowen, *A New and Accurate Map of the Island of Antigua or Antego* (London: Printed for William Innys, 1747), accessed December 28, 2025, David Rumsey Map Collection. Readers will recognize several important names from Austen's *oeuvre* on this map: Willoughby, Lucas, Wickham, and even Price. I am grateful to Simon Stern for noting these surnames from Austen's novels.
99. Davis, "The Antigua Connection."
100. David Barry Gaspar, *Bondmen and Rebels* (Baltimore, MD: Johns Hopkins University Press, 1985), 232–63; Vincent Brown, *Tacky's Revolt: The Story of an Atlantic Slave War*. (Cambridge, MA: Belknap Press of Harvard University Press, 2020), 104–5.
101. Mike Dash, "Antigua's Disputed Slave Conspiracy of 1736," *Smithsonian Magazine*, July 3, 2013.
102. *A Genuine Narrative of the Intended Conspiracy of the Negroes at Antigua* (London: Printed for J. Wilford, 1737; repr., New York: Arno Press, 1972), 4.
103. *A Genuine Narrative*, 1.
104. Austen, *Jane Austen's Letters*, 207.
105. *A Genuine Narrative*, 19.
106. *A Genuine Narrative*, 20.
107. *A Genuine Narrative*, 14.
108. *A Genuine Narrative*, 6.
109. *A Genuine Narrative*, 6–7.
110. *A Genuine Narrative*, 8.
111. Behn, *Oroonoko*, 70.
112. Elizabeth Inchbald, *Lovers' Vows*, ed. Lance Bertelsen, in *The Works of Elizabeth Inchbald*, vol. 5 (London: Pickering & Chatto, 2003), Act 1, Scene 1; Act 4, Scene 2; Act 5, Scene 2.
113. Marilyn Butler, *Jane Austen and the War of Ideas* (Oxford: Clarendon Press, 1975), 233; Paula Byrne, *Jane Austen and the Theatre* (London: Bloomsbury Academic, 2002), 53; Penny Gay, *Jane Austen and the Theatre* (Cambridge: Cambridge University Press, 2002), 103–10; Jocelyn Harris, *Jane Austen's Art of Memory* (Cambridge: Cambridge University Press, 1989), 81; Marvin Mudrick, *Jane Austen: Irony as Defense and Discovery* (Berkeley, CA: University of California Press, 1952), 160.
114. I am grateful to Sophie Reynolds, Head of Collections, Interpretation & Engagement at Jane Austen's House in Chawton, for helping me to confirm that we do not presently know what books Austen had access to at either of her homes in Steventon or Chawton. Sophie Reynolds, email message to the author, December 9, 2024.
115. *The Debate on a Motion for the Abolition of the Slave-Trade, House of Commons (Great Britain), April 2, 1792* (London: n.p., [1792]), 4.
116. We know that Sir Thomas likes to share these Atlantic stories; Mrs Norris interrupts him, to his great irritation, when he is recounting to his family "the most interesting moment of his passage to England, when the alarm of a French privateer was at the height" (180).
117. Tom debates whether he should play "Lord Duberley or Dr. Pangloss," the first a common chandler, and the heir of the play's title, who is elevated to the peerage by a twist of fate, the second a comic pseudo-intellectual named after a character in Voltaire's *Candide* and hired in Colman's play to educate the Duberley family in the ways of the aristocracy (131). George Colman, *The Heir at Law: A Comedy in Five Acts* (London: Printed for Longman, Hurst, Rees, Orme, & Browne, 1818).

118. The Langford family of Antigua, which would intermarry with the Nibbs family, owned a slave named Robin who was recommended for banishment after the plotted insurrection of 1736. I have not been able to establish Robin's fate beyond this colonial administrative proposal of December 15, 1736. *A Genuine Narrative*, 22.
119. Locke, *Two Treatises of Government*, 45–60.
120. Jane Austen, *Mansfield Park: An Annotated Edition*, ed. Deidre Shauna Lynch. Illustrated edn (Cambridge, MA: Belknap Press of Harvard University Press, 2016).
121. Said, *Culture and Imperialism*, 95–96.
122. Corinne Fowler has written thoughtfully of how Said inaugurated an era of Austen criticism that has filled gaps in his own knowledge of the archive while bearing out the importance of his insights. Corinne Fowler, "Revisiting *Mansfield Park*: The Critical and Literary Legacies of Edward W. Said's Essay 'Jane Austen and Empire' in *Culture and Imperialism* (1993)," *Cambridge Journal of Postcolonial Literary Inquiry* 4, no. 3 (2017): 362–81.
123. Austen, *Mansfield Park*, 202.
124. Douglass, *Narrative of the Life of Frederick Douglass* (Boston: Anti-Slavery Office, 1845), 37.
125. Mark S. Weiner, *Black Trials: Citizenship from the Beginnings of Slavery to the End of Caste* (New York: Vintage, 2006), 70–84.
126. Habeas corpus, literally "You shall have the body" in Latin, is a writ which requires "the body of a person restrained of liberty to be brought before the judge or into court, that the lawfulness of the restraint may be investigated and determined." *Oxford English Dictionary*, s.v. "habeas corpus (n.)," September 2016. <http://www.oed.com.proxyau.wrlc.org/view/Entry/82954?rskey=AzHbxF&result=1&isAdvanced=false> In his *Interesting Narrative*, Olaudah Equiano records a similar scene of imprisonment aboard the *Charming Sally* bound from Gravesend to the West Indies under the captainship of James Doran; Equiano remembers citing the principle later affirmed in the *Somerset* case to Doran, emphasizing that under "the laws of the land 'no man has a right to sell me.'" Doran takes no heed of these arguments, threatens Equiano into silence, and sells Equiano into slavery in the West Indies. Equiano, *The Interesting Narrative and Other Writings*, 93–94.
127. Capel Lofft, "Somerset against Stewart." 98 Eng. Rep. 499 (K.B. 1772).
128. Lofft, "Somerset against Stewart," 500.
129. Lofft, "Somerset against Stewart," 510.
130. Lofft, "Somerset against Stewart," 510.
131. Marsh, "Changes of Air," 213, 228. See also Margaret Doody, *Jane Austen's Names: Riddles, Persons, Places* (Chicago: University of Chicago Press, 2015); and Jocelyn Harris, *Satire, Celebrity, and Politics in Jane Austen* (Lewisburg, PA: Bucknell University Press, 2017).
132. *R. v. Ditton* (1785), 4 Doug. 300 (K.B.).
133. Other critics have made similar observations about Austen's engagement in her novels with Lord Hardwicke's Clandestine Marriages Act, introduced in Parliament in 1753. See, e.g., Rebecca Probert, "Control over Marriage in England and Wales, 1753–1823: The Clandestine Marriages Act of 1753 in Context," *Law and History Review* 27, no. 2 (2009): 413–50; and Katherine Sobba Green, "The Heroine's Blazon and Hardwicke's Marriage Act: Commodification for a Novel Market," *Tulsa Studies in Women's Literature* 9, no. 2 (1990): 273–90.
134. Lofft, "Somerset against Stewart," 500.
135. Probert, "Control over Marriage," 427.
136. Thomas Clarkson, *The History of the Rise, Progress, and Accomplishment of the Abolition of the African Slave-Trade by the British Parliament* (London: R. Taylor & Co., 1808), 76–77.
137. Susan Allen Ford, "It is about *Lovers' Vows*: Kotzebue, Inchbald, and the Players of *Mansfield Park*," *Persuasions On-Line* 27, no. 1 (Winter 2006). <https://jasna.org/persuasions/on-line/vol27no1/ford.htm> Azar Hussain, "Jane Austen and the Periodic Press: How Austen may have Encountered *Lovers' Vows*," *Persuasions On-Line* 43, no. 1 (Winter 2022). <https://jasna.org/publications-2/persuasions-online/volume-43-no-1/hussain-2/>
138. Following the discovery of their plot against Antigua's coronation ball, seventy-seven enslaved rebels were burned at the stake. See Gaspar, *Bondmen and Rebels*, 29.
139. Laurie Kaplan argues that Austen uses Wimpole Street as a morally significant setting for this elopement. As Kaplan explains, "when Maria Bertram Rushworth absconds with Henry Crawford from the extravagant house on Wimpole Street, she is fulfilling the pattern of sexual abandonment that her behavior at Mansfield and Sotherton had forecast." The Rushworths' London residence is thus not incidental but, in Kaplan's terms, "doubly tainted," by association with "plantations, slavery, and corruption" and with a history of sexual scandal that gives Maria's transgression its historical and moral potency. Laurie Kaplan, "The Rushworths of Wimpole Street," *Persuasions* 33 (2011): 202–3.

140. See generally Hannah More, *Slavery, a Poem* (London: T. Cadell, 1788) and Thomas Clarkson, *An Essay on the Slavery and Commerce of the Human Species, Particularly the African: In Three Parts* (New York: N. Wiley, 1804).
141. See, e.g., Michael Renwick Sergent, *An Address, to the Inhabitants in General of Great Britain, and Ireland: Relating to a Few of the Consequences which Must Naturally Result from the Abolition of the Slave Trade* (London, 1788).
142. "The Sommersett Case and the Slave Trade, 18–20 June 1772," in *The Papers of Benjamin Franklin*, vol. 19. *January 1 through December 31, 1772*, ed. William B. Willcox (New Haven and London: Yale University Press, 1975), 187–88.
143. Claudia Johnson, *Jane Austen: Women, Politics, and the Novel* (Chicago: University of Chicago Press, 1988), 115.

Novel Constitutions and the Making of Race: A Literary and Legal History of Slavery in the Anglophone Atlantic, 1688–1818.
Sarah Marsh, Oxford University Press. © Sarah Marsh 2026. DOI: 10.1093/9780197917855.003.0006

6

"I Was Not Even of the Same Nature as Man"

Mary Shelley's *Frankenstein* and the Novel Ends of the Ancient Constitution

Slavery is everywhere the pet monster of the American people.
—Frederick Douglass, "Slavery and the Irrepressible Conflict"[1]

Having examined colonial adaptations of the ancient constitution in the Atlantic world works of Behn, Defoe, Equiano, Banneker, and Austen, we last consider Mary Shelley's *Frankenstein; Or, the Modern Prometheus* (1818) as a narrative experiment on the ends of novel constitutionalism. *Frankenstein*, I argue here, is an index of racial slavery's long history in Anglo-America, which positions this institution as an important ligature between the English Civil War and the American Revolution. This chapter explains that long (but in *Frankenstein* experimentally compressed) history by engaging with sources from Milton's *Paradise Lost* (1667), which *Frankenstein* references directly, to seventeenth-century slave codes and the Declaration of Independence, which *Frankenstein* references by analogy.

Our argument proceeds in four parts. First, by animating a new being through bodily—not legislative—racecraft, *Frankenstein* highlights the ontologic limit of slavocracies' pursuit of absolute property rights in human beings. Second, by imagining a Creature racecrafted in flesh and blood, not by the legal fictions of positive law, Shelley differentiates Frankenstein's creation from enslaved people, offering a heuristic for contemplating why and how slavery is incompatible with human nature. Third, by envisioning a justice system unequal to Frankenstein's racecraft, Shelley allows us to consider the folly of English slavocrats' attempt to reanimate the concept of divine right sovereignty as a principal justification for chattel slavery. Finally, we read *Frankenstein* as a constitutional tragedy. Shelley assembles Victor Frankenstein's racecraft in volume 1 cheek by jowl with his Creature's pleas for happiness in volume 2. Frankenstein refuses these pleas, which gives way to cascading judicial dysfunction in volume 3. In this way, *Frankenstein* sheds light on why declaring the fundamental human rights to life, liberty, and *happiness*—not *property*—was an early American anti-slavery adaptation of the ancient constitution.

As many of *Frankenstein*'s readers have observed, the law consistently fails to deliver justice throughout the novel.[2] Many, though not all, of these failures result from the strange relationship between Victor Frankenstein, a Genevan aristocrat-turned-inventor, and his Creature, a made-not-begotten monster whom Frankenstein animates by mysterious means in the first volume of the story. As Despina Kakoudaki has written, "animating stories," like Shelley's *Frankenstein*, "hold great political power in modernity" because "scenes of animation and de-animation become allegorical conduits for depicting the conferral and withholding of human rights."[3] A specific example of this allegory in *Frankenstein*, Melissa J. Ganz argues, is when Shelley stages scenes of judgment that reveal how subjects, particularly the Creature, can be condemned even when, by contemporary standards of criminal responsibility, they lack the legal capacity required for guilt. For Ganz, the Creature does not possess the understanding, impulse control, and foresight that eighteenth- and nineteenth-century British jurists associated with criminal intent. In this way, the Creature is Shelley's fictive rendering of a child deemed *doli incapax*, or incapable of wrongdoing, under Romantic-era law.[4]

In the first part of *Novel Constitutions*, we surveyed how "conferral[s] and withholding[s]" of ancient constitutional protections were transatlantic adaptations of absolute power to form English colonial slavocracies after the Restoration of the English monarchy under King Charles II in 1660. Colonial legislation enshrined new labor categories demarcated by body color and religion, bringing new racial groups into being. Slaves and slaveholders were coeval, Behn and Defoe attest: the legal animation of the latter's chattel property rights was yoked to de-animation of customary English protections associated with liegance and subjection for the former. This led to a new kind of sovereignty—slavocratic sovereignty—in which the slaveholder arrogated to himself the power to kill, let live, and trade. Evidence for this transatlantic political dynamic continues to emerge: as I was writing this chapter, the BBC published a story on "Barbados' oldest sheet music," a manuscript dating from the 1770s or 1780s, which records an "African Song or Chant" recited as a call and response by enslaved people as they worked in the cane fields of that colony. The lyrics repeat the phrase, "Massa buy me he won't killa me," indicating how thoroughly enslaved people understood the absolute slavocratic power that suspended them among life, death, and sale.[5]

As the institution of racial bondage expanded, enslaved and enslavable people in Anglo-America protested this condition with appeals to authorities higher than slavocrats—God, science, and royal monarch—as we have observed in the work of Equiano and Banneker. By the late eighteenth century, Austen observed, Britain's authorization of slavocratic government abroad was raising dire constitutional questions, both in the London courts and the family circles of the English countryside. In the early nineteenth century, after these colonial developments had given way to major political revolutions in America (1765–83) and Haiti (1791–1804), Mary Shelley would conceive of a plot emphasizing that animation and de-animation are reciprocal political processes: the Creature's coming to life drains Frankenstein of his vitality;[6] as Frankenstein asserts control over the Creature (in destroying the Creature's future companion, for example), the Creature is animated by despair toward the absolute power of violence.

In this way, Frankenstein and his Creature embody in fiction a real dynamic of slavocratic government, in which enfranchisement and disenfranchisement became, by law, correlative. The nature of the rights deprivations that African-descended people suffered under anglophone slave codes, for example, described precisely the character of the human property that Anglo-American slavocrats sought to hold in perpetuity. Figures like Defoe's Robinson Crusoe represent the temptation that such acquisitions held for the English monarch's unpropertied subjects seeking abroad the ancient constitution's full protections of life, liberty, and property. Enslaved Africans responded, Behn's *Oroonoko* dramatizes, with rebellions meant to end slavocratic conditions of colonial subjection. The striving of enslaved people for intellectual, spiritual, and legal freedom from bondage shaped political and economic threats to the hereditary chattel interests of the slaveholding class. Shelley allegorizes this cycle in *Frankenstein* with Victor's relationship to his Creature, distilling by the counterfactual means of fiction a self-evident truth about chattel slavery: it is incompatible with the nature of human beings. The chattel regime would be thus at cross purposes with theories of natural rights, a dynamic we will consider later in the context of the Declaration of Independence of 1776.

Shelley's insight about the mutually constitutive nature of natural rights—that they must be held by everyone or by no one—emerges frequently when *Frankenstein* is adapted to film, and especially to plotlines about robots.[7] As Kakoudaki has observed, the cultural phenomenon of *Frankenstein* represents both origin and limit of human fascination with artificial people.[8] The modern fashioning of humanlike beings by technological means, Kakoudaki notes, has not only allegorical but etymological resonance with the history of slavery. Coined in 1923, the term "robot" is from the Czech *robotnik*, which means "forced worker." Deeper linguistic sources in the Old Czech term *rabota* ("servitude") and the Old Church Slavonic *rabu* ("slave") link the idea of the robot to bound labor.[9] The genres of Afrofuturism and Africanfuturism have, in turn, drawn upon the possibilities of science fiction to envision a future free from the historic enslavable condition of African-descended people created by slavocratic assertions that Africans and their progeny were natural slaves.[10] First envisioned in Stan Lee and Jack Kirby's Marvel Comic, *The Fantastic Four* (1966), the fictive African monarchy of Wakanda is ruled by a royal dynasty presiding over a sequestered body politic whose absolute technological superiority is directed not toward conquest or empire but rather shields its members from the incursions of other societies.[11]

The Creature himself comments on this techno-racial dimension of Shelley's insight about chattel slavery when he declares that he is "not even of the same nature as man," a conclusion following from his recognition of his "hideously deformed and loathsome" appearance (96).[12] Both are the results of Frankenstein's experiment in racecraft, or *techne*, which seeks to displace the offices of human reproduction and results in a being without kin. As we saw in *Oroonoko*, as well as in Equiano's *Interesting Narrative*, the English colonial *techne* of the slave code disrupted vertical family relationships between Africans and their children, annulling at law parental claims and obligations by replacing them with the slavocratic dominion of English colonists who aspired to commercial expressions of sovereign power abroad. But these laws, unlike Frankenstein's embodied experiment in racecraft, could never fully obscure the fact of the racecrafted person's parentage and wider familial networks. When legal commentators like Lord Mansfield noted that human slavery could only be established by positive law, they implied that slavery was contrary to the nature of human society, which recognizes relationships between parents and children and tends to organize itself into family systems. In animating a subject without procreative parents, brought into being through the power of a non-relation to lead a life of what Eileen Hunt calls "total abuse"[13] by society, *Frankenstein* is an asymptote of colonial lawmaking that constituted racial slavery, emphasizing *Frankenstein*'s status as, in Kakoudaki's phrase, the "limit" of how human beings can be unmade by the powers of government.

"Farewell Soveraignty": The Ancient Constitution in *Frankenstein*

By pairing Frankenstein's awesome creative power with his abject failure to protect any fundamental rights for the being he has created, Shelley's plot slices the Gordian knot of absolute monarchy's fundamental Filmerian metaphor: paternity. Beginning with James I's *Basilikon Doron* (1599), we have noted, the Stuarts developed the idea of absolute monarchy by emphasizing the sovereign's fatherliness to his people, both human and divine. But the theory harbored the germ of its own demise. Writing in the 1620s,[14] nearly two hundred years before Shelley's *Frankenstein* cut to the heart of the matter, Filmer himself admitted a serious technical problem with his patriarchal theory of royal absolutism: "It is true," Filmer conceded, that:

> all Kings are not the Natural Parents of their Subjects, yet they all either are, or are to be reputed the next Heirs to those first Progenitors who were at first the natural Parents of the whole People; and so in their right succeed to the exercise

> of Supream *[sic]* Jurisdiction: and such Heirs are not onely *[sic]* Lords of their own Children, but of their Brethren, and all others that were subject to their Fathers.[15]

There are two important transfigurations to note in Filmer's concession. First, "the Natural Parents of the whole People," through actual or "reputed" inheritance, endow "all Kings" with a "Right...of Supream *[sic]* Jurisdiction." Adam's God-granted dominion from Genesis is thus naturalized as the power of all present monarchs. Second, the divine authority of Adam's dominion, expressed vertically by "Lords" over "their own Children" is also redirected horizontally as the natural authority of the "Lords" over "their Brethren, and all others." To apply the Fieldses' definition of racecraft to Filmer's derivation is to see that what divine right kings and their political theorists *do*—assert "Supreme Jurisdiction"—is remade as something "the whole People" once *were* in Eden: natural children of those "first Progenitors," Adam and Eve. This logical problem, of deriving absolute power through analogy to vertical and horizontal family bonds, proved a catastrophic—indeed a regicidal—weakness in Filmer's theory.

As we noted in our reading of *Oroonoko*, the Stuart position, that the sovereign's relation to the people was godlike and fatherlike, collapsed spectacularly under its own weight when Charles I failed the offices of divine parenthood in the estimation of his people, represented in Parliament.[16] Thus, Parliament could call Charles to account for his failures. During Charles's trial in Westminster, Lord President Bradshaw explained the people's authority by acknowledging that "the next person in bloud [*sic*] is designed" to be King of England by law, but "the people of *England* might," nevertheless, "refuse him" for a "just cause" because, Bradshaw continued, "there is a Contract and a bargain made betwixt the King and his people." Furthermore, Bradshaw noted to a defiant Charles, "the Bond is reciprocall [*sic*] for as you are Liege Lord, so are they Liege Subjects, and we know very well that *Legantis est duplex*, the one is a Bond of perfection" and "once broken, farewell Soveraignty [*sic*]."[17] The charges against Charles—that he was a "Tyrant, a Traytor [*sic*], a murtherer [*sic*], and a publick [*sic*] enemy" to his people[18]—suggest that the contents of the "Contract" Bradshaw invoked here were the ancient constitution's immemorial, unwritten protections of English life, liberty, and property.

The High Court of Justice thus brought its case against Charles in "the Name of the People of *England*" on the grounds that the English had "elected" Charles as sovereign by not opposing his accession in 1625.[19] Therefore, they could require that he "make answer to them" for his alleged offenses against their ancient constitutional protections during the period of his rule. Charles vehemently disputed the people's jurisdiction in this matter, arguing from the dock that monarchs made answer to God alone, and that his subjects had not been his electors under the constitutional contract that Bradshaw described: "*England* was never an

Elective Kingdome [*sic*]," he insisted, "but hereditary, for almost, these two thousand years. Therefore declare unto me," he demanded, "by what Authority I am brought hither."[20] Thus in 1649, Sergeant Bradshaw and the indicted Charles I had a disagreement similar to the one Locke's *Two Treatises* would rehearse with Filmer's *Patriarcha* in the 1680s on the eve of the Glorious Revolution: Did the authority of government arise from the ancient, now evidently contractual[21] consent of the people, or from God's holy ordination expressed here below as hereditary monarchy? Was the fate of the English people written in ink, or in blood?

By asserting that his sovereignty was "hereditary," but in a way that did not make him subject to his own people under the obligations of sacred parenthood, Charles emphasized his humanity and deemphasized his divinity, a crucial link in the chain of sovereign being that Filmer had racecrafted between the Adam of Eden and the Stuarts of Scotland and England. After all, if Charles I was heritor of Adam's God-given natural dominion, all Christian Englishmen and Scotsmen would be his children with legitimate expectations of protection commensurate with his sacred patrimony, as had been affirmed at law in *Calvin's Case* during the reign of Charles's father, James. By thus severing his natural hereditary body from his transcendent body politic in this denial of popular election, Charles paradoxically granted his subjects an authority he sought to deny. Sealing his argument that Charles had forfeited the liegance of his people through tyrannous crimes against the ancient constitution, including trespass against God's sixth commandment, Bradshaw cited the text of Genesis on the doctrine of the *imago dei*: "Whoso sheddeth man's blood, by man shall his blood be shed: for in the image of God made he man."[22] The English people's warrant to kill their human king had found a scriptural footing.

But what has any of this to do with colonial slavery or Shelley's *Frankenstein*? While Victor and Henry Clerval travel through Oxford, on their way to the site of Frankenstein's abortive second experiment in the Orkney Islands, Victor expresses a fascination with the executed English monarch: "It was here," Victor says of Oxford,

> that Charles I had collected his forces. This city had remained faithful to him, after the whole nation had forsaken his cause to join the standard of parliament and liberty. The memory of that unfortunate king, and his companions, the amiable Falkland, the insolent Gower, his queen, and son, gave a peculiar interest to every part of the city, which they might be supposed to have inhabited. The spirit of elder days found a dwelling here, and we delighted to trace its footsteps. (133)

This "delight" in following the Civil War "footsteps" of both Charles Stuarts and their royalist supporters[23] indicates a captivation with absolute monarchy, hinting at the political character of Frankenstein's ongoing experiment in racecraft.

These allusions to the English Civil War are how Shelley introduces ancient constitutional rights and their absence into *Frankenstein*, simultaneously invoking the parallel history of chattel slavery in England's western Atlantic colonies and illuminating its source in sovereign absolutism.

After remarking on the manifest failures of absolute monarchy in Oxford, the only city that "remained faithful to [King Charles I], after the whole nation had forsaken his cause to join the standard of parliament and liberty," Frankenstein does not follow through on his second creative project (133). This is because he fears a "race of devils . . . who might make the very existence of the species of man a condition precarious and full of terror" (138). Here, Shelley's allusion is to John Milton's Satan and his minions from *Paradise Lost*, who wage war against Heaven following their expulsion to Hell, a transposition of England's Civil War into the cosmic register of Genesis.[24] At the counsel in Pandemonium, in book 1 of Milton's epic, Satan acknowledges that he and his fellows, having been conquered by "Almighty" God, now serve in Hell as "his thralls / By right of Warr."[25] They are, in Shelley's terms, "a race of devils" who plague "the species of man" in Milton's "pendant world."[26] The important distinction that Shelley draws between Frankenstein's Creature and Milton's Satan is that the latter has, by his own admission, been enslaved by God's legitimate conquest; the former, however, has been racecrafted into being by a human wielding Promethean technology, marking with allusion a subtle but crucial distinction between conquest and chattel slavery: the former comports with the order of creation in *Paradise Lost*; the latter does not.

Through *Frankenstein*'s studied invocation of Milton's seventeenth-century political drama, Shelley raises another important question with implications for colonial slavery: if both God and Frankenstein have absolute creative power, what is the difference between them? The obvious point, that Frankenstein is mortal and God divine, gains historical significance when we consider the implications of each being's ontological status for the act of creation. Exegetic tradition in Christian theology holds that, in the Book of Genesis, God creates *ex nihilo*: from nothing. Frankenstein, by contrast, makes the Creature from the dead and decaying fragments of existing creation animated by an unspecified scientific insight. Analogously, English slaveholders in Barbados created racial slavery at law, after the regicide and Restoration, from the political remains of divine-right sovereignty with the added commercial component of alienation adopted from domestic agriculture.[27] Shelley at least intuits this history when Frankenstein chooses both human and animal parts for his creation: he "dabble[s] among the unhallowed damps of the grave," "collect[s] bones from charnel houses," and finds "many of [his] materials" in the "dissecting room and the slaughter-house" (36–37). This cobbling together of the human and animal disturbs Frankenstein: "often did my human nature turn with loathing from my occupation," he recollects (37). When the Creature repeats the word "loathsome" to describe himself later in the novel, Shelley links his self-regard to Frankenstein's unnatural science (96).

As J. Kameron Carter has argued in his study of the theology of race, the Christian tradition of God's *creatio ex nihilo* in Genesis has a significant relationship to the doctrine of the *imago dei*. As Carter writes, "from the perspective of the dynamism of creation generally and of the human being specifically, who exists in the image of God, the creature is from God and the ground of its being ultimately is God."[28] Here, I take Carter to be making an anthropological claim about the status of the human being as that which is nothing but an incarnate expression of the divine maker's own nature. Frankenstein, by contrast, creates from dead and decaying creation; he seeks to make the Creature "beautiful," but he fails spectacularly (39). If the human being is an expression of God's nature, as Cameron argues, the Creature is a hideously ugly expression of Frankenstein's desire to be like God out of his own resources, or his *sicut deus* moral character.

If we follow Carter's analysis, the difference between God's creation of human beings in the Bible and Victor's creation of a nonhuman being in *Frankenstein* suggests by analogy another difference: between patriarchal claims of divine-right kingship, which were asserted by monarchs like the indicted Charles I to be from "God alone," and property claims of English slavocracy, which were adaptations of sovereign powers of life and death inflected by market interests underwritten by human avarice. The Creature explains another analogous difference—between his creation and Adam's—to Frankenstein in the second volume of the novel: "Remember, that I am thy creature: I ought to be thy Adam; but I am rather the fallen angel, whom thou drivest from joy for no misdeed" (77). Here, the Creature has arrived at an important misreading of God's actions against Satan in *Paradise Lost*: that they arise from "no misdeed." As we have observed, however, Satan himself acknowledges that the thralldom of Hell is founded legitimately[29] in God's right of conquest over rebellious angels. In this way, the Creature, made by Frankenstein so not in God's image, is fundamentally different from Satan, too. Shelley emphasizes this contrast with the Creature's "loathsome" appearance, which in the social context of the novel seems to be the basis for the Creature's absolute rightlessness among human beings, in contradistinction to Adam's originary dominion in Eden and Satan's political authority in Hell.

Given the unholy nature of his act of creation—Shelley would call it "unhallowed"[30] in her introduction to the 1831 edition of the novel—Frankenstein at length understands himself to have crafted an impossible choice for himself between his immediate family's survival and the survival of the whole human race, which he frames in the vocabulary of rights. "Had I a right, for my own benefit," Frankenstein wonders in contemplating the animation of a second being, "to inflict this curse upon everlasting generations?" (138). He decides, in the destruction of the female Creature's incomplete body, that he does not: moral obligation to posterity, in Frankenstein's estimation, outweighs his and the Creature's claims to happiness, illuminating a signal crisis in the act of slavocratic racecraft in the colonial system. Unlike Frankenstein, who refuses to racecraft more beings in perpetuity (and thereby accepts his own death by the bereaved Creature's hand), English colonial slavocrats persisted in overseas arrogations of the monarch's divinely ordained powers and duties to, "for [their] own benefit," create hundreds of thousands of racial slaves by enlarging capacities for state violence to preserve their own lives in the face of slave rebellion.[31] We witnessed this phenomenon in Aphra Behn's description of the violent Irishman Banister, who responds to Imoinda's rebellion in *Oroonoko* with extraordinary barbarism. Holly Brewer further illuminates this element of slavocratic constitutions by emphasizing that "[t]here is no such thing as 'free trade' in forced labor—forced labor requires the power of the state, and its navies and armies and militias and slave patrols and county court judges."[32] In this way, English slaveholders, in approaching yet never reaching the asymptote of Frankenstein's racecraft to enrich themselves, were inescapably diminishing their own traditional rights to life and liberty by claiming as property that which could not legitimately be claimed.

Resonantly, Charles I's 1649 execution had been an occasion for English republicans to cite their monarch's chattelization of the subject as just cause for regicide. As Milton argued in *The Tenure of Kings and Magistrates* (1649): "our Ancestors, who were not ignorant with what rights either Nature or ancient Constitution had endowd [*sic*] them... thought it no way illegal to depose and put to death thir [*sic*] tyrannous Kings."[33] This punishment was appropriate, Milton said, "when Oaths both at Coronation, and renewd in Parlament [*sic*] would not serve" to subordinate the monarch to the interests of the people.[34] Here, we should mark Milton's use of the phrase "either Nature or ancient Constitution." The proximity of "Nature" to the "ancient Constituiton" in seventeenth-century political theory will become relevant in our forthcoming consideration of Thomas Jefferson's theorization of the equal rights doctrine of the Declaration of Independence in the context of chattel slavery.

As we have seen, Lord President John Bradshaw had drawn upon the ancient constitution to justify the English people's jurisdiction in King Charles I's 1649 case. Invoking an understanding of the ancient constitution as popular election, Milton implied further in *Tenure* that the nature of Charles's hereditary claim to the crown, by divine right *without* popular election, was tantamount to the enslavement of the English: "to say... [that] the King hath as good right to his crown and dignitie [*sic*], as any man to his inheritance," Milton reckoned, "is to make the subject no better then the Kings [*sic*] slave, his chattell, or his possession that may be bought and sould [*sic*]."[35] Thus Christian theology, the precolonial meanings of the ancient constitution, and human nature itself revolted against what Sean Wilentz has, in his study of the anti-slavery elements of the United States Constitution, called "property in man."[36] This is why, as Equiano observed with powerful Miltonic resonance, colonial slaveholders found themselves at war not with the people they enslaved, but with God.

Perceiving that they could not be held in bondage legitimately, enslaved people rebelled against their legal condition with the cosmic implications of Victor Frankenstein's Miltonic choice of words. By having Victor call the Creature and his potential progeny a "race of devils," Frankenstein indicates by allusion his creative role in the novel's tragedy, reminding us of how Aphra Behn's Trefry, Daniel Defoe's Robinson Crusoe, and Austen's Sir Thomas Bertram cloak themselves in property rights in human beings that are not only self-destructive but, as Shelley suggests by analogy, hideously ugly arrogations of divine power: the "original sin" of colonial slavery. These characters, and the novels they inhabit, give voice to Atlantic slavery's manifold consequences for persons, governments, and households, exposing the moral drama, spiritual struggles, political reversals, and interpersonal nuances of the transmarine chattel regime. Far from being mere hegemonic expressions of slavocratic power or white supremacist interests, the texts we have examined in this study plumb slavery's human consequences in their depth and their seriousness, involving readers in a reckoning with racial slavery in other times and ours.[37]

In *Frankenstein*, however, Mary Shelley envisions a character whose original disobedience, a Promethean abrogation of creative power, is—in being a limit—distinct in some crucial ways from the genesis of Atlantic slavocratic societies. Victor Frankenstein creates a new being in Shelley's novel with the science of the Enlightenment, drawing upon the very methods of observation, measurement, and hypothesis that Benjamin Banneker used in his 1792 *Almanack and Ephemeris* to make mathematical claims for human equality. Frankenstein does not, that is, use colonial legislation to create new beings at law, as Barbadian and Virginian planters did—and he is not motivated by the property interests that animate the slaveholding class in colonial jurisdictions, a point that Shelley emphasizes structurally by juxtaposing Frankenstein's experiment with Walton's quest for new trade routes. Said another way, Frankenstein's pursuit of absolute power is not so much political or economic but epistemological in nature; his is an unaccountable desire to "pursue nature to her hiding places" and learn "one secret which [he] alone possesse[s]" (36). He does not aspire to divine absolutism on Earth, in the way of the Stuarts, or transnational commercial power in the way of Robinson Crusoe. Frankenstein desires, rather, to be God himself—a point that Shelley underscores in *Frankenstein*'s many invocations of *Paradise Lost*. Indeed, the novel that bears Frankenstein's name would be a different story altogether if his Creature represented some kind of worth to human beings, even a chattel value, as Oroonoko and Equiano do. Instead, Frankenstein's Creature faces *dis*ownment, like Fanny Price's in kind, but absolute in degree.

Accordingly, *Frankenstein* not only emblematizes the limit of racecraft in the Creature; the novel itself is a limiting frame for the constitutional history of Atlantic world slavery in the century and a half that *Novel Constitutions* has taken as its scope. Understood in this way, the Creature is not only an intricate concatenation of racial stereotypes[38] resulting from chattel slavery; he is, as a character arc in the novel, a juxtaposition of seventeenth-century constitutional politics of racecraft alongside the conditions of political, epistemological, and moral extremity they have wrought in the eighteenth century. Specifically, the animation and de-animation scenes of Shelley's novel allow us to reconsider a constitutional labor relation, between slaveholders and slaves codified by law, textually compressed alongside an ontological relation, between a natural philosopher and the being he invents with flesh and blood. The inseparability in *Frankenstein* of jurisprudence from natural philosophy—of ought from is—becomes a formal limit of racecraft: the novel end of the ancient constitution.

This vitally important feature of *Frankenstein* emphasizes that the racecrafting exercises of seventeenth-century colonial legislatures—which established new polities and subjects on paper by drawing upon the ancient constitution's status as a legal theory that became transportable in English persons during the eighteenth century—could never avoid being experiments with the flesh and blood of real human beings, *which is precisely why they would fail.* Like Charles I's claims for his hereditary absolute sovereignty, without reciprocal duties to his people, colonial slavocrats would find their bid for perpetual commercial rights in Africans, with corresponding obligations to capital accumulation instead of to other human beings, at odds with the Christian doctrine of the *imago dei* and the ideals of seventeenth-century republican liberalism. Like Robinson Crusoe, named by Defoe for a coin imprinted with the cross of Jesus, these Englishmen had exchanged both their and others' humanity for property, alienating themselves Esau-like from the very birthright of ancient constitutional rights against tyranny they continued to assert. Thus, in 1857, when Supreme Court Chief Justice Roger B. Taney found in *Dred Scott v. Sandford* that "the class of persons who had been imported as slaves," as well as their descendants, had "no rights which the white man was bound to respect," he was articulating a seventeenth-century English political ideology of divine absolutism refracted through the transatlantic prism of novel constitutionalism, and the legal colorism to which it had given rise.[39]

"Darkness Visible"—Or, Historicizing Blackness in *Frankenstein*

Shelley dramatizes this constitutional crisis when Frankenstein's Creature faces absolute exclusion from the human family based, solely it seems, on the appearance of his body.[40] This outcome is strikingly similar to the consequences of slave codes that created slavocracies in which the outward appearances of humans' bodies played a significant role in organizing law, politics, and society before and after the abolition of slavery itself. Writing in 1764, the abolitionist James Otis would underscore both the reality and absurdity of this mode of social organization, attacking the Anglo-American mistake of a physiological for a governmental constitution: Is it "right to enslave a man because he is black?" Otis asked rhetorically; "Will short curled hair, like wool, instead of Christian hair, as it is called by those whose hearts are as hard as the nether millstone, help the argument?"[41] As we have observed, slavocratic interpretations of body color, and the other surface features of human beings, created conditions of legal exception for enfranchised and disenfranchised people alike, although not the same exceptions, resulting in radically unequal conditions of life that were prone to erupt into violence and make justice impossible because the scriptural mandate—that human beings, all made in God's image, were one another's equals—was expressly rejected.

Writing from the nineteenth-century American aftermath of seventeenth-century English racecraft, in a polity that would become part of the American Confederacy, Frederick Douglass attested to this particular species of lawlessness in Maryland plantation life. When the overseer Mr Gore shoots and kills an enslaved man named Demby, Douglass explains in his 1845 autobiography, there is no possible legal response to Gore's iniquity because of the state of the law in Maryland. As Demby's mortally wounded body sinks out of sight into a creek, the slavemaster Colonel Lloyd, for one, asks Mr Gore why he has resorted to something so "extraordinary."[42] Gore's response is that "Demby had become unmanageable," and would soon encourage other slaves in similar disobedience. Gore concludes that "the result of [this] would be, the freedom of the slaves, and the enslavement of the whites," an extreme yet reasonable conclusion in a slavocratic society founded by men like Robinson Crusoe who animated ancient constitutional protections of property for themselves by de-animating the rights of Africans.[43] Douglass remembers that "Mr. Gore's defence" of himself in this instance proved "satisfactory," and he was not removed from his position as overseer. "His horrid crime was not even submitted to judicial investigation," Douglass recalls, because it "was committed in the presence of slaves, and they of course could neither institute a suit, nor testify against him."[44] Thus slaves, overseers, slavemasters, and the entirety of Talbot County plantation society are deprived of the law's due process because of the legal supremacy of the chattel principle. The truth about Mr Gore's role in Demby's death is excluded from the judicial record by the fiction of race.

As Rei Terada has observed, Shelley largely removes from *Frankenstein* the real and chattel property interests that structure works like *Robinson Crusoe, Mansfield Park*, and Douglass's *Narrative*, "stripping away characteristics of slavery" in a comprehensive way throughout the novel's plot.[45] In this way, *Frankenstein* allows us to consider what is left of the racecrafted chattel relation of colonial slavery when property rights in other human beings are removed from the story's details. Terada notes that the "creature steals and gathers but doesn't work, nor is he 'property.' Far from being confined, he...crisscross[es] national borders" and "renders captivity atopic, burst[ing] the categories of freedom and bondage."[46] The *idea* of property, however, nevertheless informs the Creature's developing self-awareness in the novel. He intuits an important relationship between his ontological condition of disinheritance and his mysterious origins: "Of my creation and creator I was absolutely ignorant," he says. "I knew that I possessed no money, no friends, no kind of property," a set of details leading him to conclude, in despair: "I was not even of the same nature as man" (96). This element of Shelley's story both resonates with and diverges from Equiano's narrative of captivity and Douglass's understanding that American slaveholders were "a band of successful robbers, who had left their homes, and gone to Africa, and stolen us from our homes, and in a strange land reduced us to slavery."[47] On one hand, there is great likeness among the Creature's desire to understand who he is and Equiano's and Douglass's struggles to comprehend the nature of the societies in which they live. On the other hand, Equiano and Douglass reasonably can seek answers to their questions about origins, even if those searches are ultimately unsatisfying.[48]

Shelley's Creature, by important contrast, faces questions of a different order because of the nature of Frankenstein's experiment. That is: both Equiano and Douglass remember their mothers, however fleetingly and painfully; Frankenstein's Creature cannot. Invoking James Baldwin's 1953 account of his sojourn in Löeche-les-Bains, Switzerland, scholar Saidiya Hartman describes her twenty-first-century journey along a slave-trading route in western Africa, seeking the older branches of her family tree: but "I was a stranger in the village," Hartman finds, "a wandering seed bereft of the possibility of taking root."[49] The rootless condition that Hartman and Baldwin describe is the very sociopolitical reality that Aphra Behn's Imoinda revolts against in *Oroonoko*, under the auspices of the ancient constitution. The real stories of Equiano, Douglass, and Hartman are tragic precisely because these human beings have a past and a kin network that racial slavery has obscured in part or in whole. Shelley's Creature, by an ontologic contrast achievable only in fiction, has no roots to find, and no mother to lose.

But while Shelley's plot peels away racializing mechanisms like ancestral history and property inheritance from the Creature's story, *Frankenstein* preserves—indeed it centralizes—a fundamental cognitive mechanism of racecraft: characters' negative perceptions of the Creature's appearance become, for them, a sign of his malicious motivations and natural unsuitedness for equality with human beings.[50] One important instance of this error in judgment of the Creature is how quickly Frankenstein's horror of his newly animated creation becomes his presumption[51] that the Creature seeks to "detain" him, despite myriad possible interpretations (40). As Eileen Hunt has shown, the Creature's childlike "grin" and inchoate sounds at this point of the story strongly suggest a baby reaching out to a parent (40).[52]

But Frankenstein, in response to a terrifying dream and one wordless interaction with the new being, declares the "monster" his "enemy," exposing that his fear, judgment, and familial trauma are racecrafted in a stroke as the Creature's malevolent intentions (39, 42). This is how Victor recalls the moment when the Creature first approaches him in his bedchamber: "He might have spoken, but I did not hear; one hand was stretched out, seemingly to detain me, but I escaped, and rushed down stairs" (40). Frankenstein's projections and reactions in this episode of extreme mental disturbance prevent him from knowing even *if* the Creature has spoken to him, much less what the Creature has, if anything, said. These initial reactions propel the plot of the novel[53] and structure its tragedy, rehearsing in fiction the craft, or *techne*, of dehumanization practiced by European colonial administration. Perhaps the most resonant example here is the 1513 *Requieremiento*, a Spanish text that was read aloud to Native Americans asserting the superior claims of the Pope and Spanish monarchy to indigenous lands. Indians who did not assent to this message, delivered in a language they did not understand, became candidates for dispossession and enslavement by the Spanish.[54]

The Barbadian slave code of 1661, which was read aloud in parish churches on the island,[55] carried a similar effect for Africans and Anglo-Americans an ocean and generations away. After Victor Frankenstein declares his creation categorically malevolent, based seemingly on appearance alone, other characters in the novel, like African and English contemporaries of the 1661 Barbadian code, are involved in a race problem of which they do not yet know. Most real people in the Atlantic world, and most imaginary people in *Frankenstein*, had little if any direct role in the work of legislative racecraft in Barbados, or scientific racecraft in Ingolstadt. Nevertheless, racecraft alienates them in myriad ways from their previous political and social positions. We saw this process unfold in real narrative time when Aphra Behn's narrator slipped from her original position of disinterested omniscience into an actor in the looming race war in English colonial Surinam.

As Charles W. Mills has written, when people live under the legal fictions of racecraft—what I have here called "novel constitutions" and what Mills has called "the Racial Contract"—epistemology itself can be subsumed by the fiction of race, altering the "norms and procedures for determining what counts as moral and factual knowledge of the world."[56] Shelley's frame narrative, through which Victor and his Creature offer radically conflicting perspectives on key coincidences of the novel's recursive plot (the Creature's birth, William's murder, and so forth), illuminates the epistemic fractures and failures arising from racecraft in *Frankenstein*. Thus thematizing racecraft as a specific counterfactual process in the chronology of the novel, Shelley stages the genre itself as a deliberative process for readers seeking to establish some standard of truth from within the epistemological impasse created by the Racial Contract, and necessary for its maintenance.

Under Shelley's pen, the novel becomes both a thought experiment on human rights, as Hunt has argued, as well as an adversarial venue, like a courtroom, where the many implications of that experiment might be adjudicated by readers. Fiction is an especially suggestive site of arbitration on legal questions related to race precisely because, as Douglass attested in his first autobiography, the fictions of race have foreclosed the possibility of truth in the legal process established by slavocratic government. As Karla FC Holloway has shown, black American writers from Nella Larsen to Ralph Ellison to Toni Morrison used imaginative literature to convey the truth that "U.S. racial identity is a constructed legal fiction."[57] Other stories like Herman Melville's *Benito Cereno* (1855) and Mark Twain's *The Tragedy of Pudd'nhead Wilson* (1894) suggest the deep degree to which literary fiction became a key American medium for assessing the meanings and limits of the law in a racialized polity. A key question in these texts is how the law "makes up" persons in deciding who is, and who is not, subject to the courts.

As Simon Stern has shown, the law does not merely recognize persons; it creates them through methods including "deeming, definition, presumption, and stipulation."[58] Those techniques are neither neutral nor self-evident, and Stern notes that "lawyers and laypersons alike disagree about which legal propositions count as ways of making up persons,"[59] suggesting an analytic gap between the person in law and the person in fact. In this deliberative context, *Frankenstein* again represents a suggestive limit for examining the legal ramifications of racecraft. In the fictional world of the novel, Victor Frankenstein makes a being in flesh and blood, but Shelley's plot persistently asks whether his ontological accomplishment compels any corresponding recognition by the courts, or whether legal personhood can be denied to the Creature even in the face of his embodied, speaking, feeling, and reasoning life.

Shelley crystallizes this problem of the Creature's legal personhood when she stages the question of his standing before a magistrate in Geneva. In this scene, Victor seeks to translate his private experience of the Creature's crimes into a public legal claim: "This is the being whom I accuse," Frankenstein declares, emphasizing that it is the magistrate's "duty" to seize and punish the Creature (169). The magistrate's response is Shelley's examination of the slipperiness in legal standing wrought by Frankenstein's racecraft: the Genevan official can certainly listen to Frankenstein's accusations as if the Creature is a person; but when Frankenstein asks the court to perform its legal duty, the magistrate's incredulity rules. Shelley imagines a judge who draws on Frankenstein's testimony to redescribe the Creature as an "animal" and a "monster," beyond any practical reach of due process (169, 170). The court renders itself impotent through belief in a racial fiction of its own imagination that is based in hearsay.

This refusal of the Creature's standing is rendered as a shift in the kind of being the Creature is imagined by the court to be. In that gesture, Shelley shows how due process is manipulated by racecraft: the court can promise punishment to the Creature, "proportionate to his crimes," while also imaginatively arranging some key details so that the accused never appears as a legal person at all (170). Here, Shelley narrativizes the "asymmetry" that racecraft introduces in questions of legal standing: as Stern writes, one can be imagined as a bearer of liability without any corresponding pathway to the claiming of rights or legal redress. Chattel slaves are the most salient historical example of this kind of legal person, who is constitutionally asymmetrical.[60] In Shelley's hands, this asymmetry results in the universal miscarriage of justice: not a single court in *Frankenstein* arrives at a just verdict.

Shelley thus dramatizes the manner in which racecraft creates for both slave and slaveholder conditions of exception from civic obligations to accuse, judge, and punish one another for wrongdoing under the law, a juridical function that Sherman J. Clark calls "conscience catching." According to Clark, "conscience catching" is the power of the judicial system, especially in jury trials, to create conditions under which human beings must bear—and be formed by—the moral weight of due process.[61] Clark has argued in the modern legal context that one of artificial intelligence's central risks is that it can deprive human beings of morally necessary confrontations with what they are doing to one another in court.[62] Read in this light, Shelley's scene before the Genevan magistrate in *Frankenstein* may illuminate what AI stands to do to us precisely because it does not—like the Creature—have standing in court. As we use *Frankenstein* to understand advances in contemporary technology, however, we should take care to distinguish among: (1) the rights-endowed subject, a human being with standing in the courts; (2) the AI, a non-human entity without (as of this writing) standing in the courts; and (3) the chattel slave, a human being historically with standing in the court so long as he is accused of a crime, but not when he is the victim of one.

These specific distortions of the judicial process in *Frankenstein* are rooted in the nature of Frankenstein's absolute creative power. Frankenstein's absolutism in the novel is neither the capacity to kill, like Behn's Banister, nor to sell, like Austen's Sir Thomas. Frankenstein's, rather, is the disconcerting power to let the Creature live—but not in the company of others, and to destroy potential life before it begins, as he does with the Creature's female companion. By literalizing Frankenstein's capacity to "foster life or disallow it to the point of death"[63] as a metaphor for legal procedures of rights creation and rights deprivation, Shelley anticipates Michel Foucault's and Giorgio Agamben's assessments of biopolitics as a hallmark of modernity[64] and allows us to consider that racecrafting human beings into chattels may have been an important conduit for the emergence of biopolitical absolutism, although evidently not its absolute expression. As Agamben has argued, the limit of sovereignty's modern iteration was in the mid-twentieth-century death camps of Nazi Germany.[65] Kathleen Biddick, by important and compelling contrast, has suggested that the so-called modern power to "make and let die" is in fact a medieval form of authority whose real age has been misapprehended by critics focused exclusively on the twentieth century.[66] While any serious comparative analysis of racism in Anglo-America, Nazi Germany, and the medieval world[67] is well beyond the scope of this study, it is nevertheless noteworthy that both eighteenth-century abolitionists like Equiano, and twentieth-century opponents of Nazism like Bonhoeffer, would find in the Christian anthropology of the *imago dei* a rebuke to colonial slavocracy and National Socialism which, in their different ways, had adopted racecraft as a fundamental technique of power.

Indeed, Victor Frankenstein, Robinson Crusoe, and Sir Thomas Bertram, are each fictive variations on what Bonhoeffer would call *sicut deus* human beings. In the later chapters of his *Interesting Narrative*, Olaudah Equiano notices himself becoming a real example of this phenomenon, which is why he abandons Dr Irving's plantation. Taking a page out of "the life of Columbus," Equiano threatens restive Mosquito Coast inhabitants by telling them that "they must not quarrel so; that they were all brothers, and if they did not leave off, and go away quietly, [he] would take the book (pointing to the Bible)...and *tell* God to make them dead."[68] Through this imperial process of borrowing divine power to issue threats to the Mosquito natives, Equiano becomes disillusioned and sickened by the power dynamics of slavocratic society.

Because *Frankenstein* has stripped away the property dynamics of slavocratic power, Terada notes, its plot beckons for "[s]cholarship debating the ontological implications of chattel slavery."[69] One of these implications, Terada finds, is that "the Creature's blackness is not the implication of a racial identity but the phenomenalization of a fear of the impossibility of accounting for its origin," with "blackness" here signifying an onto-historic psychic condition.[70] Terada's "unaccountable origin" of "the Creature's blackness" is analogous to, *if not an historically traceable epiphenomenon of*, Englishmen's overseas application of their ancient constitution to create race in its modern form: the English people's rights to life, liberty, and property were immemorial, the ancient constitution held—without a beginning that could be known—in order to antedate all possible claims of sovereign prerogative.

In *Frankenstein*, other characters' conclusions—that the Creature's outward appearance correlates with malicious inward character—become a rationale for directing cruel or violent behaviors toward the Creature: first Victor does it, followed by his little brother William; next is Felix De Lacey, then an unnamed rustic, and so on. We might even say that the actions of these characters deny the Creature the forms of social, political, and legal recognition that are fundamental, or constitutional, in nature: the Creature is deprived, for a time, of education and speech; he is assaulted with a gun; he cannot assemble with others; and his grievances against power are serially unredressed—all because of the way human beings in the novel interpret his appearance. Old De Lacey, Shelley's figure of blind justice, is the only person in the book to recognize Frankenstein's monster as a "human creature," strongly suggesting, although perhaps not conclusively, that the Creature's exclusion from society is based *only* on the visible parts of his person (109). We readers are like De Lacey in being unable to see the Creature's body with our own eyes, suggesting our role as potentially fair arbiters of the Creature's complicated case.

Part of that complication, of course, is *Frankenstein*'s disturbing power to divide its readers on the question of the Creature's humanity. What are we to do with this being without kin who exemplifies obvious capacities for moral reason? Shelley has anticipated our grave problem of interpretation by offering us a character like Victor Frankenstein, who thinks the Creature is nonhuman, and De Lacey, who comes to the opposite conclusion. This range of interpretations inside the text establishes bookends of how the Creature's humanity, or lack of it, can be understood outside the text. Shelley sorts *Frankenstein*'s readers along a continuum that reveals how easily our empirical judgments—about who counts as human—can slide into justifications for inclusion or exclusion: is the (in)humanity we perceive in the Creature coming from the text itself, or is it a phenomenon of our own perception? And how, in the end, can we know?

In yet another complication of the problem of judgment in *Frankenstein*, Shelley sets offstage the Creature's meetings with Henry Clerval and Elizabeth Frankenstein, gentle personalities who might respond differently to the Creature's apparent ugliness. During Justine Moritz's trial and execution for William Frankenstein's homicide, Elizabeth refers to the accused as "the most amiable and benevolent of human creatures," despite the conclusion of others, including the Genevan judiciary, that Justine is monstrous because it appears from circumstantial evidence, orchestrated by the Creature, that she has murdered a child (71). Shelley thus raises the possibility that the charitable Elizabeth might have given the Creature a sympathetic hearing, but later denies this potential when the Creature extinguishes, on her wedding night, the very sensibility that might have perceived him as a person. *Frankenstein*, considered thus, looks a good deal like a thought experiment in fiction on the status of constitutional rights in a racialized society, much like the real one Douglass recorded in his *Narrative*.[71]

Contrary to Douglass, however, the Creature responds to his desolation and disenfranchisement through the serial murder of innocent people, tragically making true presumptive judgments of his malevolence. By responding to his inequality with murder, the Creature seeks a Hobbesian framework in which people are one another's equals not because they are children made in the image of the same divine parent, but because they are like Cain and Abel: each powerful enough to end another's fragile life.[72] As the Creature says in one of the most famous lines of the novel: "Beware; for I am fearless, and therefore powerful" (140). Recent commentators, notably Elizabeth Young, have linked the Creature's murderous revolt against Victor's tyranny to western Atlantic slave rebellions, specifically the revolt led by Nat Turner in 1831.[73] With nothing left to lose, to borrow Janis Joplin's immortal formulation, Shelley's Creature is free to exert absolute power over Frankenstein and his family: the power to kill the latter and let the former live. The divine right of the Stuart kings is now, in Shelley's hands, the absolute power of anglophone fiction's consummate subaltern.[74]

If we read Shelley's modern myth at this particular level of abstraction—that is, as a text that experimentally juxtaposes English colonial racecraft with its constitutional eventualities—there is illuminating rhetorical resonance of *Frankenstein*'s animation scene with the Barbadian slave code of 1661. In the code, English colonists' name for their perception of Africans' appearance—"Negro" in this instance—carries in the legislation's text an imputation of these people's "brutish" and "uncertain" inward character, which, the legislators argue, requires the rights deprivations of the slave code. As Rugemer observes, the 1661 Barbadian code used the term "'Negro' throughout rather than 'slave,' which asserted equivalence between slave status and the complexion of sub-Saharan Africans."[75] Slavocratic ambition to be like God—Hell's "darkness visible" that surrounds Milton's angels banished for their aspiration to divine power—was racecrafted as human skin color.[76] We saw in our reading of Equiano that enslaved people sought Christian baptism as a sacramental remedy for this enslavement; but theirs was not the original sin that required absolution.

Rebuking the doctrine of the *imago dei*, Barbadian planters concluded circularly that "'Negroes[,]...being brutish Slaves,' did not deserve to be tried," for example, "by a jury of twelve of their peers as English law prescribed," a right that was preserved for themselves and Christian servants in the colony.[77] Thus the English deprived constitutional protections at law from those persons whose bodily constitutions they categorized as "Negro," a tautologic form that Shelley rehearses in Frankenstein's rejection of his creation based on his perception of what he has built the Creature to be—unmaking, in Kakoudaki's phrase, what he has made. This turnabout in Frankenstein's thinking *seems* to happen (but, as we will see later in this chapter, does not in fact happen) at the moment of the Creature's completion: "now that I had finished," Frankenstein attests, "the beauty of the dream vanished, and breathless horror and disgust filled my heart" (39). Denise Gigante has noted that "the Creature's ugliness did not bother Victor (or anyone else for that matter) before he came to life," an observation that pretty well captures the action of social politics in the novel's plot.[78] But, along the lines of *Novel Constitutions*' broader claim that English colonial racecraft was a result of transplanted Stuart absolutism, *Frankenstein* also discloses that Victor's racecraft of the Creature has a prior history in the Frankenstein family. This history can help us make sense of the long-term consequences of English colonial racecraft in the early national United States.

"An Exchange of Situation": Masters, Slaves, and Fortune's Wheel

When Thomas Jefferson wrote *Notes on the State of Virginia*, some 124 years after Virginia codified the racial principle of *partus sequitur ventrem*[79] that would shape his political and domestic destiny, he said that he "tremble[d]" when contemplating the "exchange of situation" he imagined between American slaveholders and slaves.[80] His concerns were not hypothetical. Jefferson's early career as a common lawyer in Virginia, the natural rights doctrine of the Declaration of 1776, and the excised grievance he penned for that Declaration, which laid blame for slavery at the feet of George III, indicate his developing view that, because it was a crime against humanity, slaveholding would bear other lawless consequences, most obviously slave revolts.[81] In this part of the argument, we will examine how *Frankenstein* elevates slave rebellion as a legitimate response to one of racecraft's greatest tyrannies: the breaking at law of a familial bond between parents and children. This is the dynamic we observed in *Oroonoko*, when Imoinda rebelled in English colonial Surinam against the racial enslavement of her unborn child.

The anti-slavery arguments that characterize Jefferson's early political thought can be traced to his legal education under the tutelage of George Wythe.[82] Jefferson's legal commonplace book, dating from the 1760s, demonstrates his early study of the English common law and statutory traditions, including the law reports of William Salkeld and Robert Raymond as well as Coke's *Institutes*, Lord Kames's *Historical Law-Tracts* (1758), John Dalrymple's *History of Feudal Property* (1757), and Matthew Hale's *History of Common Law* (1713).[83] Jefferson's commonplaces from this period also demonstrate his interest in the ancient constitution. For example, Jefferson cites *Smith v. Brown and Cooper* (1701) in which Justice Holt held that "as soon as a NEGRO comes into England he becomes free: one may be a villein in England, but not a slave," the same "free air" metaphor that Francis Hargrave would invoke in the King's Bench to secure James Somerset's manumission in 1772.[84] Jefferson also cited earlier cases like *Butts v. Penny* (1677) and *Cleve v. Gelly* (1694) on the competing idea that "trover will lie for a negro, for they are heathens and therefor a man may have property in them."[85] In citing these cases, David Konig and Michael Zuckert explain, the young Jefferson was engaging intellectually not only with the "anomalous nature of slave labor but also, more fundamentally, the question of the slave's humanity."[86] As we have noted in previous chapters, Holly Brewer situates these cases in the wider political context of sovereign absolutism, explaining that, when Parliament failed to pass an imperial slave code in the seventeenth century, despite pressure from the Crown, the Stuart monarchy instead used the English courts (in *Butts v. Penny* for example) to establish English chattel property in human persons, a crucial development for its imperial ambitions as an Atlantic slave power.[87] Jefferson's questions from the

1760s and 1770s about slave labor and human property are ones that Mary Shelley would later explore in *Frankenstein* as they were coming to a head in the American republic of the early nineteenth century, when a much older Jefferson looked on in trepidation.

A well-known practical expression of Jefferson's developing theory of natural rights came in his 1770 service as counsel to Samuel Howell, a Virginia man suing for his freedom based on his claim to a freeborn lineage. In a later compilation of law reports[88] published in 1829, Jefferson recalled that both plaintiff and defendant stipulated to the facts of the suit as follows:

> the plaintiff's grandmother was a mulatto, begotten of a white woman by a negro man, after the year 1705, and bound by the churchwardens, under the law of that date to serve to the age of thirty-one. That after the year 1723, but during her servitude, she was delivered of the plaintiff's mother, who, during her servitude, to wit, in 1742, was delivered of the plaintiff, and he again was sold by the person to whom his grandmother was bound to the defendant, who now claims his service till he shall be thirty-one years of age.[89]

The precise legal status that Howell was disputing, William Merkel notes, is difficult to discern from the historical record: he was either an enslaved person suing for manumission, or an indentured person suing for release from servitude.[90] Paul Finkelman thinks it likely that "Howell had predominantly white ancestry, appeared white, and was, in Jefferson's view, a white person."[91] Merkel challenges this interpretation, calling Finkelman's assessment of Howell's racial phenotype "a guess" and noting that "Jefferson did not argue that Howell was entitled to freedom because he was legally white."[92] The "magistrate court," Merkel adds, who heard the case first, "had not freed Howell on inspection, as courts generally did with white-looking (or Indian-looking) plaintiffs in freedom suits."[93] (Native Americans had been free in colonial Virginia since 1691.[94]) Said another way, had "Howell been a white looking *slave*, one would expect him to have been freed on those grounds alone," unless the alleged owner could provide documentary proof otherwise.[95] This lack of clarity in the judicial record, signaled in divergence of contemporary interpretation by legal scholars, epitomizes Orlando Patterson's point that the distinction at law between owning the bound *person* and owning the bound person's *labor* is often without a meaningful difference.[96] In his *Commentaries on the Laws of England*, William Blackstone articulated a similar hedge, noting that slavery was repugnant to the laws of England, while allowing that a master's right to an enslaved person's labor may still persist.[97]

Our claim, of *Frankenstein*'s status as a text that experimentally compresses seventeenth-century racecraft against its constitutional outcomes, is bolstered by the relationship Shelley draws between bodily appearances and judicial dysfunction. Victor's fabrication of his monster's outward ugliness (in creating it, perceiving it, and narrating it to Walton) compares suggestively with the fact that, in colonial Virginia's late eighteenth-century courts, a claimant's physical appearance to the judiciary could be of fundamental legal significance in freedom suits like Samuel Howell's. As William P. MacNeil has argued, "*Frankenstein* is not...just a representation of the works of the legal system"; the text also "*enacts* the legal system's fundamental discursive process in the text's overarching narrative arc. That central narrative arc is nothing less than the *production* of a body."[98] But the body that Frankenstein produces with science is *never* produced in court because of a lack of standing, a symbolic disruption in the novel of habeas corpus[99] and the wider constitutional protections of due process.

Conversely, we observed in our reading of *Mansfield Park*, James Somerset's godparents transcended the legal racial categories of colonial Virginia (the very ones that governed Thomas Jefferson and Samuel Howell) by obtaining in London a writ of habeas corpus, which affirmed Somerset's condition as a subject of the king's laws, and brought him before Lord Chief Justice Mansfield. These efforts indicate a civil action proclaiming what was, for James Somerset's sponsors, the spiritual truth of their godchild's equal membership in the body of Christ. In his 1788 petition, Equiano would make a similar appeal to Queen Charlotte, asserting the royal subjectship of slaves in Britain's remaining colonies and implying the monarch's authority to end slavery in those jurisdictions. Just four years later, Benjamin Banneker shared with Thomas Jefferson trigonometric calculations which he believed showed that human beings are one another's equals by the same mathematic laws that describe the order of the universe. By significant contrast in *Frankenstein*, Victor approaches a Genevan magistrate in volume 3 for relief from the Creature's murderous depredations, but racecraft has disrupted his access to legal recourse. The magistrate promises to exert himself on Frankenstein's behalf so that the Creature "shall suffer punishment proportionate to his crimes" (170). "But I fear," the magistrate continues, "from what you have yourself described to be his properties, that this will prove impracticable" (170). In Shelley's Geneva, as in Douglass's Talbot County Maryland, racecraft—what one person "describe[s]" as another's "propertie[s]"—has invaded the courtroom and set justice at naught.

In his work on *Howell v. Netherland*, Thomas Jefferson also saw how racecraft obstructed natural rights in the courtrooms of colonial Virginia. The important question in Samuel Howell's case was whether or not penal servitude, the legal punishment for interracial procreation according to the Virginia slave code of 1705, was heritable from mother to child in perpetuity under the principle of *partus sequitur ventrem*. Drawing upon the doctrine of natural rights, which he would soon articulate as the Declaration of Independence, Jefferson argued that the 1705 law made no such provision. Rather, in passing the 1705 legislation Jefferson reasoned, the Virginia House of Burgesses meant to "punish and deter women from that confusion of species," or interracial unions, "which the legislature seems to have considered evil."[100] However, Jefferson argued, the 1705 legislators did not seek to "oppress [the] innocent offspring" of these procreative acts.[101] Thus, Samuel Howell could not have inherited bound labor status through his family's maternal line. As Jefferson concluded, "Under the law of nature, all men are born free, every one comes into the world with a right to his own person, which includes the liberty of moving and using it at his own will" (376). Jefferson argued further that this "personal liberty" had been given to "every one," including Howell, by the "author of nature, because necessary for his own sustenance."[102] Thus in 1770, Jefferson argued that "personal liberty" expressed the law of nature because a person had to sustain himself through the activity of his body. In this way, the first two protections of the ancient constitution—life and liberty—were each the other's necessary condition. However, the property protections of the ancient constitution, which had been racecrafted by slaveholders to create chattel interest in persons, conflicted expressly with these other endowments from the "author of nature." In this way, the early Jefferson would seem to agree with Equiano that Anglo-American slaveholders were at war with nature's God.

Thomas Jefferson was well aware of the history and politics of the ancient constitution, particularly the role this ideology had played in opposing Stuart tyranny contemporary to the development of Britain's American colonies. In his 1774 *Summary View of the Rights of British America*, a document that in retrospect looks like the dress rehearsal for the Declaration of Independence, Jefferson drew upon the concept of the ancient constitution to make the case for colonial America's legislative independence from Parliament. Jefferson wrote to King George III that, before emigrating to the western Atlantic, "our ancestors... were the free inhabitants of the British dominions in Europe," who "possessed a right which nature has given to all men, of departing from the country in which chance, not choice, has placed them, of going in quest of new habitations, and of there establishing new societies, under such laws and regulations as to them shall seem most likely to promote public happiness."[103] Here, Jefferson's theory of natural rights substituted "public happiness" for the transatlantic legal principles of liegance and subjection, by which the Stuarts had extended the English empire into the Atlantic world, and through which Englishmen had developed overseas property rights in land and in persons in process of exercising their other rights to life and liberty.

In this justification for British America's natural rights, Jefferson racecrafted his fellow British Americans into the freeborn lineage of their "Saxon ancestors," who "in like manner" to British colonists, "left their native wilds and woods in the north of Europe," "possessed themselves of the island of Britain," and "saw fit there to establish that system of laws, which has so long been the glory and protection of the country."[104] The role of the people in mutually constituting a society through settlement, lawmaking—and evidently without much regard for a monarch—is a striking feature of Jefferson's 1774 account of natural rights. "[N]o circumstance has occurred," Jefferson emphasized, "to distinguish materially the

British from the Saxon emigration."[105] However, as we have seen in our reading of *Robinson Crusoe*, and as Jefferson knew from his own domestic experience as a Virginia slaveholder, one crucial distinction among others was that Britons serving in colonial and domestic governments had developed a "system of laws" that established human slavery as a conduit for creating their own property rights, and under *Calvin's Case* implied the monarch's obligations to protect those rights.[106] This practice threatened natural rights, as Jefferson knew from his work on Samuel Howell's freedom suit.

Thus, in the *Summary View*, Jefferson sought King George's assistance in liberating Anglo-Americans from the original sin of human property that had enriched real and fictional Englishmen: "The abolition of domestic slavery is the great object of desire in [the American] colonies," Jefferson began,

> where it was unhappily introduced in their infant state. But previous to the enfranchisement of the slaves we have, it is necessary to exclude all further importations from Africa; yet our repeated attempts to effect this by prohibitions, and by imposing duties which might amount to a prohibition, have been hitherto defeated by his majesty's negative: Thus preferring the immediate advantages of a few African corsairs to the lasting interests of the American states, and to the rights of human nature, deeply wounded by this infamous practice.[107]

According to Jefferson's account of the ancient constitution, the British American colonists' protections of life and liberty were being eroded by the monarch's preferment of "a few" slave traders' property rights in persons over and above "the lasting interests of the American states." Jefferson's use of the word "unhappily" here, in connection with colonial enslavement, may remind us of the Creature's appeal to Frankenstein and prompt us to see something of the slaveholder's two bodies. These people had, in the late seventeenth century, legally created themselves as sovereigns in relation to their slaves; but they also faced ongoing political subjection to the Crown after the Restoration of the monarchy in 1661, chiefly in the form of taxes but also in their powerlessness to unilaterally end the slave trade. Here, we arrive at a formidable problem of historical interpretation, which illuminates the central role of novel constitutionalism in the establishment of western Atlantic slave societies: was racial bondage introduced to American and Caribbean colonies by the prerogative power of the Stuart kings, or by the burgeoning commercial power of English colonists?

Holly Brewer has argued that the role of England's monarchy in the establishment of colonial slavery has been overlooked by modern scholars. Brewer rightly attributes this oversight to the influence of Edmund S. Morgan's conclusion that slavery and freedom were coeval in colonial Virginia: "This is not to say that a belief in republican equality had to rest on slavery," Morgan famously deduced, "but only that in Virginia... it did."[108] By contrast, Brewer concludes that slavocratic government is best understood as an imperial projection of divine-right monarchy: "One was born a slave, just as one was born a prince."[109] Morgan's and Brewer's well-evidenced positions seem troublingly at odds with one another.

Novel Constitutions, however, has offered an interpretation of Atlantic history which harmonizes the apparent discord of Morgan's and Brewer's stances. That is: colonial adaptations of ancient constitutionalism explain the English subject's evolving and contested relation with both the monarch and the market, especially when that subject began to imagine that he could transport overseas in his body political forms like sovereign absolutism, which manifested as slavocracy, and ancient constitutionalism, whose republican protections of life, liberty, and property were flummoxed by the paradox of chattel claims in persons. Said another way, absolute sovereignty, in colonial jurisdictions, had invaded the ancient constitutional protections of the people's property as a key element of colonial racecraft. Novel constitutionalism, in this sense, gives us something like a unified theory of republican liberalism and racial capitalism in the early modern Atlantic world. By smuggling absolute property rights in persons into the English people's ancient constitutional protections against tyranny, Stuart absolutism left constitutional liberalism vulnerable, then and now, to claims of hypocrisy. Narrative forms like novels and memoirs—which afford perspectivalism, ambivalence, and access to the human interior—are crucial to perceiving these intricate dynamics of history that are with us still.

Fifteen years after the publication of *Notes on the State of Virginia*, Jefferson would see his fears of slave insurrection materialize in his home state. In the summer of 1800, an enslaved blacksmith named Gabriel Prosser, with followers in Henrico County, planned a rebellion against the slaveholding power in Virginia, which was thwarted at the eleventh hour.[110] On September 20 of that year, Jefferson wrote to Virginia's governor, James Monroe, about the question of executing the rebel slaves, urging his fellow Virginian to remember that "the other states & the world at large will for ever condemn us if we indulge a principle of revenge, or go one step beyond absolute necessity."[111] Jefferson also noted that Virginia's critics would not "lose sight of the rights of the two parties, & the object of the unsuccessful one,"[112] acknowledging, like Aphra Behn in the late 1680s, that enslaved people had legitimate grievances against slavocrats, even to the point of violent uprising. Merkel reckons that Jefferson saw this form of revolt as "legally justified."[113] Slavocratic constitutions of the colonial era, which sought to squelch rebellion through absolute means—like prohibiting slaves' assemblies and arms-bearing, and policing "outlying" slaves[114]—were now at cross purposes with the Jeffersonian doctrine of natural rights in the young republic.

Because of the paradox of human property, Jefferson concluded at the end of his political career, American slaveholders were in a terrible bind. The problem came to a head in the crisis of 1819, one year after *Frankenstein*'s publication, when Missouri petitioned to join the Union as a slave state. "We have the wolf by the ear," Jefferson wrote famously of slavery in his 1820 letter to the Maine senator, John Holmes, "and can neither hold him, nor safely let him go. Justice is in one scale, and self-preservation in the other."[115] Thomas Merrill sees in this metaphor Jefferson's conclusion that enslaved people "would be justified in using violence to acquire their freedom. But," Merrill adds, "the slave owners are under no obligation to free the enslaved if that would endanger their own self-preservation."[116] Both groups are "equally justified," Merrill finds, "in doing whatever they must in order to secure their lives."[117] With slaves' natural rights to freedom hanging thus in the balance against the natural rights of slaveholders to self-preservation, Jefferson articulated to Holmes a predicament remarkably similar to the fictional one Frankenstein perceives in his relationship with the Creature. The rightless monster implores Victor to create for him a fellow being, so that he can pursue a happy life in the company of another like himself. As Victor sees it, he can either deny this request and accept that the Creature will kill him; or, he can acquiesce to the Creature's wishes and unleash, he believes, a Miltonian "race of devils" on the world.

With its programmatic allusions to *Paradise Lost*, *Frankenstein* underscores that rebellion—against slavocratic tyranny over the human family—is a western Atlantic adaptation of the ancient constitutionalism that sent Charles I to the scaffold in 1649. Because he had broken his divine patriarchal bonds with his people, Lord President Bradshaw argued, Charles could be executed for treason under the auspices of the ancient constitution. The American slave system presented similar consequences for slavocrats, as Thomas Jefferson observed in his 1820 letter to Holmes. Slaveholders' extension of human bondage into new states of the American Union was, Jefferson said, an "act of suicide on themselves and of treason"—not against the English people, as it was in Charles's case—but rather "against the hopes of the world."[118] Shelley's *Frankenstein* emphasizes this "exchange of situation"—between subjects and monarchs; between bondspeople and masters—when Victor, the Creature's godlike maker, is transformed into the Creature's "slave" through his ungodlike refusal to make the Creature a female companion and grant him the possibility of pursuing domestic happiness in her company (127). *Frankenstein*'s positioning of slavery as the opposite of the pursuit of domestic happiness is one we will examine in the final section of this chapter in a reading of the Declaration of Independence.

Shelley's insight in *Frankenstein*, similar to the one that Jefferson would articulate to Holmes, is that English racecraft has pitted rights against rights: "I had no right," Frankenstein says, "to withhold from [the Creature] the small portion of happiness which was yet in my power to bestow" (121). At the same time, Frankenstein does not understand himself to have "a right" to save himself and his immediate family by inflicting "this curse" of racecraft "upon everlasting generations" (138). Tipping the balance for Frankenstein against the Creature's happiness are thoughts of his own legacy: "I shuddered to think that future ages might curse me as their pest, whose selfishness had not hesitated to buy its own peace at the price perhaps of the existence of the whole human race" (138). Like the original sinner Robinson Crusoe, Victor Frankenstein realizes too late that he has become his "own destroyer."[119] The conflicted legacy of Thomas Jefferson—a man who owned slaves, immortalized the equal rights doctrine of 1776, and later fathered six legally enslavable children with Sally Hemings, a woman he owned[120]—suggests that fictions of race like *Frankenstein* hold self-evident truths about real human lives led within racialized polities.

Early in his political career, Jefferson foresaw that the problem of racial slavery in America was only going to get worse, making it especially difficult to understand how he ultimately could support the expansion of slavery as new states were added to the Union in the early decades of the nineteenth century. Natural increase of the enslaved population, Jefferson posited in his 1785 *Notes*, made increased violence between slaves and slaveholders not just possible but probable, and American slaveholders could not expect to have God on their side. "The Almighty has no attribute," Jefferson concluded in *Notes*, "which can take side with us in such a contest," perhaps a significant yet subtle early connection of American racial slavery's ideologic roots in English divine-right absolutism, which made claims to that which could not legitimately be claimed.[121]

Jefferson's Promethean foresight about chattel slavery in *Notes* is one that *Frankenstein* rehearses in Victor's perception of his Creature's animation. For Frankenstein, this fear manifests as a nightmare in which Elizabeth Lavenza, Victor's intended wife and the presumptive mother of his future children, transforms into his dead mother. This "exchange of situation," of living fiancée for dead mother, repeats the reaction Frankenstein has just had to his Creature in which "the beauty of the dream vanished" to be replaced by "horror and disgust."[122] By rooting Victor's reaction to the Creature in the patriarchal drama surrounding his mother's death and betrothal to Elizabeth, Shelley hints that this reaction stems from something much deeper, much older, and much more traumatic than the physical appearance of the just-animated monster.

The symbolic link that Shelley fashions between *Frankenstein*'s central animation and de-animation scenes prompts us to reflect that Barbadian planters were in a situation comparable to Frankenstein's in 1661, as were Virginians in 1662: they had created the people they called "Negroes" as perpetual racial slaves by positive law. But at this time they also were heritors of a much older English framework, dating from at least the Norman invasion of 1066, for understanding political relationships of sovereignty, dominion, liegance, settlement, and subjection. That constitutional framework was, in the late seventeenth century, symbolically laden for Anglo-American slavocrats with the violence of the English Civil War and the political trauma of the regicide. Indeed, they had produced their racial slave code at the behest of the executed king's son and heir.[123] These men knew that the ancient constitution's protections of life, liberty, and property bespoke another English inheritance of death, imprisonment, and rapine. The memory held on in political culture; even in the 1774 *Summary View*, Jefferson could invoke the popular memory of a "family of princes... whose treasonable crimes against their people brought on them afterwards the exertion of those sacred and sovereign rights of punishment reserved in the hands of the people."[124] Under Jefferson's 1774 logic of natural rights, the English people of the seventeenth century were to the Stuarts as enslaved Africans were to eighteenth-century American slavocrats.

Faced with these deadly consequences of English racecraft late in the eighteenth century, Jefferson found it "impossible to be temperate" in contemplation of the "probable" ends of American slavery, marked as they were in his imagination with apocalyptic visions of divinely ordained violence against American slaveholders.[125] Similarly, Victor Frankenstein responds to the dream of his mother with extraordinary immoderation, abandoning his new creation in Ingolstadt, and telling no one of the monster's existence. Unlike Frankenstein, however, who does not stop to check his own ambition until it is too late, Thomas Jefferson saw in the 1780s a potential for American slavocracy to step back from the brink of its own destruction: "The spirit of the master is abating," Jefferson observed in *Notes*, and "that of the slave rising from the dust, his condition mollifying, the way I hope preparing, under the auspices of heaven, for a total emancipation."[126] The Virginian's hope for the "abating" spirit of American mastery seems, at best, quixotic to us now, especially in light of Jefferson's failure to free his own slaves as well as the American Confederacy's subsequent rise to power in express repudiation of the equal rights doctrine of the Declaration of Independence.[127] But it is clear that nothing less than "a total emancipation" was commensurate, in Jefferson's 1785 view, with "the auspices of heaven."

"Our Common Kindred": *Frankenstein* and the End of Racecraft

Thus far, we have examined how Jefferson foresaw a violent "exchange of situation" between slaveholders and slaves, a political dynamic that Mary Shelley allegorizes in *Frankenstein* by compressing seventeenth-century English racecraft against its late eighteenth-century outcomes.[128] In this final section, I read the 1776 Declaration of Independence as offering a potential but unrealized solution to the slavocratic problem of rights pitted against rights. This reading of the Declaration argues that the United States severed itself from Britain in terms antithetical to slavocratic principles derived from the ancient constitution. This severing was ideologically abolitionist in its disavowal of racial rights associated with English subjectship to the Crown, including and especially the racial right to hold property in other human beings. By substituting social friendship and domestic happiness for patriarchal inheritance, the Declaration proposes terms on which race, not people, could be unmade. *Frankenstein* again proves an instructive counterpoint. In Shelley's novel, Frankenstein's racecraft forecloses procreation of all kinds, suggesting that the process of unmaking people—with science, legislation, or otherwise—is a dead end for human society. In this way, *Frankenstein* defines the negative space wrought by racecraft that the Declaration sought to fill.

Thomas Jefferson's wife Martha, called Patty, never recovered fully from complications of delivering their daughter in May 1782. Douglas L. Wilson notes that, at about the time Patty died, on September 6, 1782, Thomas Jefferson may have been reading *Paradise Lost*, or perhaps revisiting his earlier annotations of Milton dating from the 1760s. As Wilson explains in the notes of *Jefferson's Literary Commonplace Book*, some of Jefferson's transcriptions from the epic "may have been copied into the manuscript [of Jefferson's first volume of literary commonplaces]...as late as the early 1780s."[129] This timeline suggests that the Virginian may have been contemplating the English poet's rendering of cosmic revolutions in *Paradise Lost* as his own domestic life was being tragically upended within a young republic facing an inevitable "exchange of situation" between slaveholders and slaves. "Better to reign in Hell, than serve in Heaven," Jefferson transcribed from Satan's reflections in Pandemonium in book 1.[130]

In another of his commonplaces from *Paradise Lost*, perhaps also from 1782, Jefferson would note Adam's famous complaint to God about Eve in book 10 of the epic:

> O! Why did God[,]
> Creator wise! That Peopl'd highest Heav'n
> With Spirits masculine, create at last
> This Novelty on Earth, this fair Defect
> Of Nature? And not fill the World at once
> With Men, as Angels, without feminine?
> Or find some other Way to generate
> Mankind?[131]

If this transcription from Milton dates from the early 1780s, we might connect it meaningfully to the final struggle with death that the Jeffersons endured together in the summer of 1782. Jefferson's biographer Jon Meacham captures the profundity of the couple's grief by noting their quotation of Laurence Sterne's *Tristram Shandy* (1759–67) on a scrap of paper: "every thing presses on," Patty began, and Thomas completed the quotation by copying from Sterne's novel the "eternal separation" the couple was "shortly to make!"[132] Jefferson's interest in Adam's plea that God find "some other Way to generate / Mankind" resonates with the loss he would suffer that fall in consequence of Patty's many pregnancies.[133]

It has become a staple of *Frankenstein* scholarship to note that Mary Shelley's own tragic experience of pregnancy and childbirth is an animating force in the novel's imaginative world.[134] Shelley's mother died of puerperal fever eleven days after giving birth to her in August 1797, and Shelley herself suffered grievous obstetric tragedies early in her childbearing years. Shelley, like Jefferson before her, would be drawn to Adam's appeal in *Paradise Lost* for "some other Way to generate" life; but, as we have noted of Frankenstein's racecraft, Shelley's experiment does not create "Mankind" in the way that God does in Milton's *Paradise Lost* or in Genesis. These varying creation stories—Shelley's, Milton's, and the Bible's—will aid our understanding of why and how the Declaration of 1776 uncrafted race to envision a government based on a natural and universal human right to happiness.

In Genesis, God creates Eve after observing that "It is not good that the man should be alone."[135] In book 8 of *Paradise Lost*, Milton's God promises to assuage Adam's solitude with "Thy likeness, thy fit help, thy other self," invoking the *imago dei*.[136] Shelley's Creature, however, believes that he has been doomed by his human creator's racecraft to perpetual affliction because he is terribly ugly and lacks a companionate being like himself: "I am alone, and miserable," he reasons to Frankenstein; "man will not associate with me" because "the human senses are insurmountable barriers" to social fellowship (119). The Creature reasons that "human senses," which in the text almost invariably perceive him as hideous, are the source of his unhappiness (119). By establishing "the human senses" as "insurmountable barriers" to the Creature's equality with human beings—recall how the Genevan magistrate excludes him from court standing—the Creature underscores racecraft's fundamental rejection of the *imago dei* as the inability to see others as like oneself. Seeking revenge against Victor for this absolute state of exception, the Creature learns to break the "sanguinary laws of man" by murdering various intimate members of Frankenstein's domestic circle (118).

The only solution to his existential conundrum, the Creature concludes, is another exercise in racecraft that yields a second being "as deformed and horrible" as he is who "would not deny herself to me" (118).[137] This is why the Creature insists that Victor make another "of the same species, and have the same defects," a revision of Adam's complaint in *Paradise Lost* about the "Defect / Of Nature" he claims Eve to be (118). To press the case with his creator, the Creature emphasizes his understanding of racecraft's moral consequences: "I am malicious because I am miserable," he concludes, but "mine shall not be the submission of abject slavery" (119). "Oh! my creator," he cries, again echoing Milton's Adam: "make me happy" (120). Importantly, Shelley's racecrafted Creature positions "slavery" and happiness as mutually exclusive, a suggestive echo of Jefferson's characterization in the *Summary View* of the "unhappy" introduction of slavery in Britain's "infant" colonies, as well as a canny anticipation of abolitionist William Lloyd Garrison's exclamation in his preface to Douglass's *Narrative* that "a happy slave is an extinct man!"[138]

The Creature's wish to be made happy with a female companion, and the prospect of their offspring—a Miltonic "race of devils" that Victor imagines would be an existential threat to humanity—animates Shelley's great insight about racecraft. This process has not merely pitted the rights of creator, ruler, and master against the rights of creation, subject, and slave. Shelley goes further to correlate bondage, loneliness, and unhappiness on one hand and then contrast them with freedom, society, and happiness on the other. These conflicts of ontology arise, at least in part, from the absolute nature of racecraft she envisions. The Promethean Frankenstein, having stolen divine creative power in the rising action of the story without accepting any reciprocal duties of care, stands in relation to no omnipotent being beyond himself who can ask: "What hast thou done?"—God's question to Eve after she eats of the tree of the knowledge of good and evil, as well as to her son, Cain, after he murders his brother.[139] Charles Stuart found himself in an analogous situation until 1649, when the English people asserted their jurisdiction over his person and declared their own sovereignty with his execution. Shelley emphasizes Frankenstein's *sicut deus* status in the text—his absolute aseity—when he tells no one of his creation until it is too late. No friend or family member ever learns from Victor of the Creature's existence. Nor does Victor share the nature of the threat that the Creature poses to the entire Frankenstein circle, an effect that Shelley emphasizes when Victor promises Elizabeth to tell her his "dreadful secret" the day after their marriage, which for Elizabeth never arrives (162). One wonders when and how Maria Ward learned of Thomas Bertram's human chattels in Antigua.

As Shelley sees it, the act of racecraft rends human society because it creates the racecrafter and the racecrafted in conditions of exception that tend to pit the law's protection of rights against the possibility of domestic happiness. In this sense, Victor Frankenstein chooses to "rule in Hell," where the secret of his role as a racecrafter isolates him from the happiness and freedoms of a liberated subject. Shelley emplots this phenomenon in *Frankenstein* when Victor inexplicably withholds knowledge of the Creature from family and friends but shares it with officers of the court, exemplifying how English racecraft at law in the western Atlantic ensnared generations of human families in bondage and foreclosed the possibility of their happiness. A closer examination of how racecraft programmatically destroys both legal and family institutions in *Frankenstein* will put us in a strong position to consider corresponding themes in the Declaration of Independence.

Mr Kirwin, the Irish magistrate who superintends the inquest into Clerval's murder, is the first person in the book to hear from Victor about the Creature, albeit in convoluted terms marked by Frankenstein's mental derangement, implying racecraft's epistemological crisis described by Mills. Upon seeing Clerval's dead body on an examination table in Ireland, Victor collapses into a fevered state, ranting of his own "murderous machinations" as the cause of his friend's death (148). Similar to the constitutional overwhelm Robinson Crusoe suffers in response to his realization of vast wealth through the unmaking of Africans, Frankenstein is overcome in body by new constitutional realities, which his making and unmaking of the Creature have unleashed. As Frankenstein recalls upon seeing Clerval's corpse, "The human frame could no longer support the agonizing suffering that I endured, and I was carried out of the room in strong convulsions" (148). Frankenstein is thus removed from the novel's constitutional due process by the failure of his own constitution, indicating that racecraft *does* make differences among human bodies, just not the ones it asserts.

Victor remains in Ireland "for two months on the point of death" (148). He learns only afterward that, in a fevered and deranged state, he "called [himself] the murderer of William, of Justine, and of Clerval. Sometimes [he] entreated [his] attendants to assist [him] in the destruction of the fiend by whom [he] was tormented" (148). Importantly, Mr Kirwin does not take Frankenstein's lunatic ravings to be a confession. But the nurse, whom Mr Kirwin hires to care for the deranged prisoner, comes to a different conclusion about Frankenstein's culpability: "if you mean about the gentleman you murdered," she says coldly, "I believe that it were better for you if you were dead, for I fancy it will go hard with you; but you will be hung when the next sessions come on" (149). In this scene, as with Justine's execution in the novel's first volume, Shelley uses the perspectivalism of the novel's structure to implicate readers in racecraft's distortions of justice. Besides Victor and the Creature, Shelley's readers are the only ones who know what really happened to William, Justine, and Clerval—so we know that it would be wrong for Frankenstein to be executed for Clerval's murder, just as it was unjust for Justine to be executed for William's. Yet we have no power to testify to the truth in the world of the novel.

Narratologically, then, *Frankenstein* orchestrates between text and reader several legal consequences of Frankenstein's racecraft instead of resolving them. With the nesting box structure of her counterfactual world, that is, Shelley gives us readers decisive knowledge of the Creature's culpability in the deaths of several characters while simultaneously excluding us from the novel's legal system where our knowledge could be transformed into justice. This will remind us of the legal deficiencies Frederick Douglass and his fellow slaves faced in the Talbot County judicial system, where the legal fictions of racial slave codes prevented these men's testimony in court. Ultimately, however, Douglass used the truth function of his autobiography to testify to the injustice of Demby's murder. By important contrast, which animates the unparalleled critical power of literary fiction, *Frankenstein*'s imagined jurisdictions are absolutely out of our reach precisely by dint of ontology.

Shelley is silent on the precise location of Victor's landing and imprisonment in Ireland for Clerval's murder, and thus the jurisdiction of his prosecution and trial, but Fred V. Randel has cited the novel's "north-east breeze" to argue that

Ulster or County Mayo in Connacht are likely points of his arrival.[140] Read constitutionally, Shelley's English-speaking nurse, who threatens Victor with execution, may signal the Unionist sympathies of the province of Ulster. If this is true, then the Genevese Frankenstein has arrived within the imperial reach of George III's courts.[141] Shelley is clear, in any event, that Frankenstein is fortunate to have fallen under the protection of the liberal-minded Mr Kirwin while he is detained in Ireland. Despite Frankenstein's condition of mental extremity, and his contemplation of judicial suicide—"whether I should not declare myself guilty, and suffer the penalty of the law"—Mr Kirwin fulfills his obligations to constitutional due process, even at moments when he wavers inwardly from his own presumption of Victor's innocence (150).[142] Allowing that Frankenstein's fevered account is potentially true (that he is not Clerval's killer, and that "some fiend" is responsible instead), Kirwin seeks exculpatory evidence on Victor's behalf. He remarks on Frankenstein's "strange... misfortune" of being framed for murder, and he shares with the inmate a "hope" that he will "soon quit this melancholy abode" of prison; "doubtless," Kirwin adds to Frankenstein, "evidence can easily be brought to free you from the criminal charge," a gentle invitation to Frankenstein to tell the truth (151).

Important here is Kirwin's presumption of Frankenstein's innocence, as well as his process of judicial discernment, in which he brackets even Victor's confession to homicide in pursuit of justice in Clerval's case. Said another way, Kirwin makes no pretense to omnipotent character knowledge, a narrative counterpoint to Frankenstein's original judgment of the Creature, which is founded on Victor's conclusion that his own fearful reactions to what he has done are the fundamental truth about the being he has endowed with life. Shelley emphasizes that Kirwin is Frankenstein's foil when the title character is ultimately unmoved in the novel's middle volume by the Creature's pleas for happiness that he believes a companion would provide. "I compassionated him," Victor says, "and sometimes felt a wish to console him; but when I looked upon him, when I saw the filthy mass that moved and talked, my heart sickened, and my feelings were altered to those of horror and hatred" (121). Mr Kirwin's disposition is not so easily changed by Frankenstein's outward appearance.

In the second volume of the novel, Shelley establishes another important counterpoint to Victor's reactive judgments when the Creature recalls to Victor the slower process by which he discerns his own nature. Seeking to understand who and what he is, the Creature observes the De Lacey family and reads three books: "*Paradise Lost*, a volume of *Plutarch's Lives*, and the *Sorrows of Werther*" (103). He also learns from a fourth text, Volney's *Ruins of Empire*, which Felix De Lacey is reading aloud to his Turkish fiancée, Safie (95). From Milton, the Creature gleans a "picture of an omnipotent God warring with his creatures," to which he likens his situation: "Like Adam" he tells Frankenstein, "I was created apparently united by no link to any other being in existence" but did not enjoy

Adam's stature as God's "perfect creature, happy and prosperous, guarded by the especial care of his Creator" (104, 105, 105). Rather, the Creature notes, "I was wretched, helpless, and alone" (105). Here, Shelley invokes the doctrine of the *imago dei* in Adam's "perfect" creation as the precise locus of Victor's inevitable failure in his dual roles of creator and judge, a taut metaphor for slaveholding freeholders in the western Atlantic, who decreed and interpreted the law in colonial jurisdictions.

Milton's account of humankind's first disobedience is not the only source of the Creature's self-knowledge. "Another circumstance," the Creature notes, "strengthen[s] and confirm[s his] feelings" of wretchedness (105). "Soon after my arrival in the hovel," the Creature continues to Frankenstein, "I discovered some papers in the pocket of the dress which I had taken from your laboratory" (105). As the Creature learns to read, he understands that this is Frankenstein's "journal of the four months that preceded [his] creation" (105). In it, Frankenstein "minutely describe[s]...every step [he] took in the progress of [his] work" in racecraft (105). The Creature reports with acrimony that, in these papers, the "minutest description of my odious and loathsome person is given, in language which painted your own horrors, and rendered mine ineffaceable" (105). Long before the Creature's animation, the Promethean Frankenstein foresaw the extreme ugliness of what he was doing. The deformity was perhaps amplified for Frankenstein when he made the Creature breathe and move with the addition of a spark of life; but the textual fact remains that Frankenstein "painted" his "horrors" of the Creature well in advance and brought him to completion anyway.

With the motif of origin stories, Victor's and the Creature's, found in Frankenstein's pockets, Shelley connects Frankenstein's racecraft to constitutional due process. Seeking a fuller understanding of the accused murderer, Kirwin explains to Frankenstein that he "thought of examining [Frankenstein's] dress that I might discover some trace by which I could send to your relations an account of your misfortune and illness" (151). Finding several letters in Frankenstein's garments, one from Alphonse Frankenstein, Kirwin "instantly" dispatches his own correspondence to Geneva to make contact with Frankenstein's family (151). Ostensibly, the letters that Kirwin finds are part of the exonerating proof that Victor "was on the Orkney Islands at the hour the body of [Henry Clerval] was found"; at the very least, these papers lead Kirwin to more information that sets Frankenstein free from accusations in Ireland that he has murdered his friend (153). Owing to Mr Kirwin's various exertions on behalf of the accused—"collecting witnesses, and arranging [Frankenstein's] defence [*sic*]"—the Irish "grand jury rejected the bill" accusing Frankenstein of Clerval's homicide, and Frankenstein is "liberated from prison" (153). At the same time, Clerval's murderer remains at large.

These linked scenes of evidence, discovery, and their failures have compelling divergences through which *Frankenstein* reveals the impacts of racecraft on judicial due process. Like the Barbadian and other slave codes, Victor's laboratory journal catalogues the maker's judgments of the made, setting the stage for the Creature's later discovery of Victor Frankenstein's difference from God, and his own difference from God's "perfect" creature, Adam. Equiano's discovery of the Barbadian slave code revealed, similarly, that English slavocrats had established themselves in positions of absolute sovereignty with respect to the African-descended people they enslaved, originally on account of the "uncertain" and "brutish" nature that the English perceived and inscribed in colonial law as the basis for revoking customary constitutional protections. As Equiano observed, Barbadian slaveholders sacrificed even their own children to the chattel regime, not in Abrahamic obedience to God, but as expressions of slavocratic avarice. Enslaved African people in English colonial jurisdictions of course had no access to family or legal networks, as Englishmen did, through which to contest the lawfulness of their bound condition.[143]

The letters that Mr Kirwin finds among Frankenstein's garments demonstrate, in absolute contrast to the Creature, Victor's implacable embeddedness in a family system, directly connected to lawmaking institutions of Geneva: "My ancestors had been for many years counsellors and syndics," Frankenstein explains to Walton at the outset of his story, and little William announces to the Creature: "My papa is a Syndic—he is M. Frankenstein—he would punish you" (18, 117). Shelley's plot reverses the child's claims, demonstrating the difference that racecraft has made: Alphonse Frankenstein will suffer extrajudicial punishment at the Creature's hand because his son's strange experiment has removed the monster beyond the reaches of family and law. This is the kind of turnabout, "the exchange of situation," that Jefferson feared: revolutions of the "wheel of fortune" would enslave the slaveholders in the infant United States.

While he is being held on suspicion in Clerval's murder, Victor Frankenstein's familial connections to Genevan legal institutions undergird his extranational enjoyment of the ancient constitution's protections in Ireland: because Kirwin finds Frankenstein's letter to his father, the young inventor gets a fair trial in a foreign country. But Frankenstein's patrimony—the protection of the laws—is eventually destroyed by a Creature whose nature severs him from legal systems everywhere.[144] At length in *Frankenstein*, Shelley brings to fruition Jefferson's racial nightmare from *Notes on the State of Virginia*. Jefferson worried in 1785 about not only an "exchange of situation" between slaveholders and slaves, but the "extirpation" of slave masters if some solution to the great national paradox was not found through "the consent of the masters." Before the end of *Frankenstein*, the Creature has exacted the turn of the wheel that Jefferson described, proclaiming himself the "master" of his new "slave," Victor. These appellations arise after Frankenstein refuses to consent to the Creature's pursuit of happiness with a companion, emphasizing Shelley's equation of bondage with unhappiness (140). The story ends when Frankenstein is, in Jefferson's phrase, "extirpated" by the cosmic struggle in which his racecraft binds him.

Yet the depredations of racecraft, as Shelley saw them in *Frankenstein*, are not just in the absolute terms of racecrafters' extirpation by the racecrafted. Other forms of destruction to families and legal systems have long been unfolding in the text—at least since the Creature's murder of William and Justine's wrongful execution. So it was in Jefferson's Virginia, even before Gabriel's rebellion. The likeness we have observed between Frankenstein and Jefferson explodes with the complexities of patrimony and disownment when we consider Annette Gordon-Reed's magisterial study of Jefferson's relationship with Sally Hemings, a woman he enslaved, his sometimes-concubine, and the half-sister of his wife.[145] As Gordon-Reed has documented in great detail, the 14-year-old Hemings chaperoned Jefferson's daughter on a voyage to Paris in 1787, where the pair joined Thomas Jefferson, then serving as American envoy to France. When the group of Virginians returned to the United States in 1789, the 16-year-old Hemings was pregnant with Jefferson's child.[146] Hemings and Jefferson had at least six children outside of wedlock, four of whom survived into adulthood: Beverly, Harriet, Madison, and Eston. Under the Virginia principle of *partus sequitur ventrem*, all of Hemings's children would have been born into lifelong slavery. That fate was averted only because Jefferson evidently consented to Hemings's demands for their future manumission.[147]

As Jon Kukla observes, by Jefferson's own reckoning as well as a 1792 Virginia statute, "any children Jefferson fathered with Sally Hemings would legally be white."[148] The children's legal status—as white slaves—made them living metaphors for the constitutional contradiction of the Anglo-American chattel regime, which adapted ancient constitutionalism to new slavocratic ends marked by colorism. Put plainly: America's founding father sired white children born into slavery. They were freed only through an exception created by their parents. As Jefferson knew from his work on *Howell v. Netherland*, this constitutional contradiction arose from Virginia's legal fiction that Europeans and Africans were different kinds of beings, with different sets of parental rights in their offspring, creating both legal and familial paradoxes when these human beings procreated with one another. Children born from these sexual relationships were known, Gordon-Reed notes, as *filius nullius*, or the children of no one, a counterfactual condition that Shelley figures precisely in Frankenstein's Creature.[149] Samuel Howell's great grandmother and great grandfather were an example of this legal fiction—parents of the children of no one—as were the parents of half-sisters Patty Jefferson and Sally Hemings. Thomas Jefferson and Sally Hemings would join their numbers. In this way, American slavocratic fictions of an English constitution, as a set of embodied features that combined complexion with a portable set of rights, were in Thomas Jefferson's own family revealing their profound inconsistencies. Shelley imagined the absolute limit of this problem in *Frankenstein*, where racecraft's destruction of family and legal institutions prevents anyone from procreating at all.

The argument here is not that Frankenstein's character is based on Thomas Jefferson, as Shelley is thought to have done with figures like Percy Shelley and Benjamin Franklin.[150] Instead I write to describe Shelley's quickening in *Frankenstein* of complex intersubjective relations and institutional conflicts that arise invariably from racecraft. Because these relations tend to be broadly uniform in the anglophone context, as a result of the ancient constitution's transatlantic coordinating power, they perhaps seem to describe Jefferson personally. But as Jefferson's neighbor General John Hartwell Cocke recorded in his diary, Jefferson's relationship with Hemings was by no means rare in Virginia: if sexual relationships between slaveholders and slaves were "enumerated with the statistics of the State," Cocke said, "they would be found by the hundreds."[151] To the extent that Frankenstein is like Jefferson, then, he is like "hundreds" of others in Jefferson's position.

Frederick Douglass summarized the problem succinctly in his third autobiography, *Life and Times of Frederick Douglass* (1881): "The father might be a freeman and the child a slave. The father might be a white man, glorying in the purity of his Anglo-Saxon blood, and his child ranked with the blackest slaves. Father he might be, and not be husband, and could sell his own child without incurring reproach, if in its veins coursed one drop of African blood."[152] Jefferson—who gloried in his Anglo-Saxon inheritance in the 1774 *Summary View* and later became a father to Sally Hemings's children without ever being her husband—somehow saw fit in the meantime to sever the racial ties of ancient constitutionalism when he and his collaborators declared independence from Great Britain in 1776. This marked a major change in the transatlantic logic of his appeals just two years earlier in the *Summary View*, when he noted the continuity of ancient, racial protections against tyranny that accompanied British Americans in their very bodies when they crossed the ocean.

The 1776 Declaration, by significant contrast, disavows familial and racial bonds that Americans have with their "Brittish [*sic*] brethren," marking them instead like all others as "Enemies in War, in Peace Friends."[153] Despite American appeals to the "native justice and magnanimity" of the British, and invocations of "the ties of our common kindred," the Declaration concludes that the British ultimately are "deaf to the voice of justice and of consanguinity," a failure of their human senses, which Shelley's Creature would echo in *Frankenstein*.[154] Instead of binding themselves to Great Britain through a transatlantic constitution, which Jefferson had conjured in his 1774 *Summary View*, the colonists must now bind themselves to one another.[155]

Many readers of the Declaration of Independence have likened it to a divorce proceeding, illuminating the confluence of law and domesticity in the institution of marriage.[156] But, read in the context of the literary and legal texts we have thus far examined, the Declaration's rhetorical severing of blood and legal ties to Britain also suggests an ideological break with the ancient constitution's racial protections of life, liberty, and property. With the enormity of their other failures, the writers of the 1776 Declaration at least seem to have intuited that the property protections of the ancient constitution had been corrupted during the colonial period by racecrafting Africans into chattels through the transplanted principles of divine-right sovereignty, enlarged by capital. That Anglo-Americans, like Robinson Crusoe, had prospered from this original sin is likely why Jefferson's now well-known clause in the Declaration, which blamed George III for African slavery, had to be excised from the final document. The remaining solution, if the British monarchy would not answer the colonists' plea to abolish the slave trade institutionalized legally under the Stuarts, was to sever the infant United States from its sovereign parent. The colonists did this, in part, by replacing the English property protections of the ancient constitution—which had been invaded by legal fictions like *partus sequitur ventrem*—with "the pursuit of happiness." Jefferson and Shelley, like Milton before them, saw human happiness as a full expression of natural rights that was constitutionally incompatible with human bondage.

It would take an abolition movement, another Civil War (American this time), and the passage of the Thirteenth Amendment to the US Constitution of 1865 to legally end human bondage in the United States. A Civil Rights movement would follow, and the Black Freedom Struggle continue, chipping away at arbitrary legal distortions first set down in the seventeenth century by English colonists stealing divine power from their godlike sovereign and expanding it with transatlantic commercial power. Racecraft, however—that pernicious human tendency to mask politics as ontology—has lingered long after the protests, the picketing, and the passage of these laws. It is with us still.

Frankenstein's thought experiment grants a final insight into what might happen to human beings after the racecrafter and the racecrafted have finally exited the text. By the time Victor Frankenstein dies at the end of the novel, and his monster disappears over the horizon with a promise to immolate himself at the North Pole, Robert Walton and his crew have abandoned their pursuit of "glory" in trade and are sailing back to England (184). The choice is not Walton's but his crew's.[157] As Frankenstein lies dying below decks, and Walton is mourning the impending loss of his strange new friend, the ice that has trapped the ship for almost the entirety of Shelley's plot suddenly shifts, rendering the stranded vessel "perfectly free" (184). The crew's "tumultuous joy" at this event; their "demands" to return home; and Walton's inability to "withstand" the sailors' popular sentiment collude to set Shelley's remaining characters on a new kind of journey (184). Walton regards it as a total failure of his acquisitive ambitions, but the sailors understand the situation differently. For them, it represents the pursuit not of Walton's ambition, but of the happiness they find at home. *Frankenstein* is too ambivalent and tragic a novel to see its final narrative flourish as a purely democratic silver lining. But Mary Shelley saw that, wherever we are going after racecraft, we are going there together.

Novel Constitutions has argued that the unwritten, immemorial ancient constitution of the early modern English was a capacious and powerful ideology that racialized English rights against tyranny by making them transportable in persons through a series of seventeenth- and eighteenth-century legal decisions. These rights were asserted by the English during the seventeenth century to oppose sovereign absolutism at home and attach human rights to human complexions in their slave societies abroad. The former was a harbinger of political revolutions to come; the latter was the original sin of chattel slavery. The bodies of law that created these fictions of race during the colonial era, as well as the literary texts that challenged the idea that one human being could own another, are among the ancient constitution's most durable—and American—legacies. How we read these fictions of race, and if we read them at all, is ours.

Notes

1. Frederick Douglass, "Slavery and the Irrepressible Conflict," address delivered in Geneva, New York, August 1, 1860, reprinted in *The Frederick Douglass Papers*, ser. 1, *Speeches, Debates, and Interviews*, 3. *1855–63*, ed. John W. Blassingame (New Haven: Yale University Press, 1985), 369–70.
2. For further exploration of this in the text, see Barbara Hughes-Moore, "'Ten Thousand Times More Malignant than her Mate': Destabilizing Gendered Assumptions Underlying the Defences of Provocation and Loss of Control through a Reading of Mary Shelley's *Frankenstein*," *Cardiff University Law School Journal of Law and Society* 48 (2021): 690–712; Ralph Pordzik, "Fiction, the Law, and the Docile Body: The Uncanny Presence of Kant and the Marquis de Sade in Mary Shelley's *Frankenstein*," *Zeitschrift für Anglistik und Amerikanistik* 77, no. 2 (2009): 109–23; and Patrick Vincent, "'This Wretched Mockery of Justice': Mary Shelley's *Frankenstein* and Geneva," *European Romantic Review* 18, no. 5 (2007): 645–61.
3. Despina Kakoudaki, "Unmaking People: The Politics of Negation in *Frankenstein* and *Ex Machina*," *Science Fiction Studies* 45, no. 2 (2018): 289–307.
4. Melissa J. Ganz, "'A Kind of Insanity in my Spirits': *Frankenstein*, Childhood, and Criminal Intent," *Eighteenth-Century Studies* 56, no. 1 (Fall 2022): 53–74, esp. 54–55 and 63–65.
5. "Barbados' Oldest Sheet Music to Unlock Enslaved People's Voices," *BBC News*, June 2, 2024. <https://www.bbc.com/news/articles/c4nn97yw42ro>
6. For elaboration of the scientific, medical, figurative, and biographic meanings of "vitality" during Mary Shelley's lifetime, see Sharon Ruston, *Shelley and Vitality* (New York: Palgrave Macmillan, 2005), and Sharon Ruston, *The Science of Life and Death in Frankenstein* (Oxford: Bodleian Library Publishing, 2022).
7. Despina Kakoudaki, *Anatomy of a Robot: Literature, Cinema, and the Cultural Work of Artificial People* (New Brunswick, NJ: Rutgers University Press, 2014).
8. Kakoudaki, *Anatomy of a Robot*, 29–68.
9. *Oxford English Dictionary*, s.v. "robot (n.1)," July 2023. <https://doi.org/10.1093/OED/1025681623> "robot (n.2)," March 2024. <https://doi.org/10.1093/OED/4330523394>
10. The term "Afrofuturism" is typically credited to Mark Dery, who identified the genre and traced examples throughout history in "Black to the Future: Interviews with Samuel R. Delany, Greg Tate, and Tricia Rose." In "Afrofuturism and the Technologies of Survival," Elizabeth C. Hamilton writes that Afrofuturism is a "mechanism for understanding the real world situations of oppression in the contemporary world in the context of the ever-present past, while charting the future situation through the arts" (19). Hamilton also highlights that "Afrofuturism as a mechanism relies on not just the injection of futurity, fantasy, and technology, but also an ever-present orientation toward Black liberation that draws its strength from liberation movements in the past" (19). Africanfuturism was coined as a literary term by Nnedi Okorafor as an alternative to Afrofuturism. Okorafor writes that Africanfuturism differs from Afrofuturism in that it "is specifically and more directly rooted in African culture, history, mythology and point-of-view as it then branches into the Black Diaspora, and does not privilege or center the West." Africanfuturism is

more distinctly tied to African culture and history, while Afrofuturism is more linked with Black and African American or Western culture. Mark Dery, "Black to the Future: Interviews with Samuel R. Delany, Greg Tate, and Tricia Rose," in *Flame Wars: The Discourse of Cyberculture*, ed. Mark Dery (Durham, NC: Duke University Press, 1994); Elizabeth C. Hamilton, "Afrofuturism and the Technologies of Survival," *African Arts* 50, no. 4 (2017): 18–23; Nnedi Okorafor, "Africanfuturism Defined," *Nnedi's Wahala Zone Blog*, October 19, 2019. <https://nnedi.blogspot.com/2019/10/africanfuturism-defined.html>

11. Carvell Wallace, "Why *Black Panther* is a Defining Moment for Black America," *New York Times*, February 12, 2018. <https://www.nytimes.com/2018/02/12/magazine/why-black-panther-is-a-defining-moment-for-black-america.html>
12. Mary Shelley, *Frankenstein: The 1818 Text*, ed. Marilyn Butler (New York: Oxford University Press, 2008), 96. Cited hereafter parenthetically.
13. Eileen Hunt, *Mary Shelley and the Rights of the Child: Political Philosophy in* Frankenstein (Philadelphia: University of Pennsylvania Press, 2017).
14. John M. Wallace, "The Date of Sir Robert Filmer's *Patriarcha*," *Historical Journal* 23, no. 1 (1980): 155–65.
15. Robert Filmer, quoted in [James Tyrrell], *Patriarcha non Monarcha: The Patriarch Unmonarch'd: Being Observations on a Late Treatise and Divers Other Miscellanies, Published Under the Name of Sir Robert Filmer, Baronet: In which the Falseness of those Opinions that Would Make Monarchy Jure Divino are Laid Open, and the True Principles of Government and Property (Especially in Our Kingdom) Asserted/by a Lover of Truth and of His Country* (London: Richard Janeway in Queens-head-Alley, 1681), 19.
16. After the trial, William Say, who represented Camelford in Parliament, was instructed to create a record of the proceedings within a week. Though there are multiple recorded follow-up orders, Say did not present the record until almost two years later, in December 1650. Today, there are two separate and almost identical official accounts. Neil Johnston, "The Trial of Charles I." Blogpost, The National Archives, January 30, 2019. <https://blog.nationalarchives.gov.uk/trial-charles-i>
17. Charles I, King of England, *The Full Proceedings of the High Court of Justice against King Charles in Westminster Hall, on Saturday the 20 of January, 1648; together with the King's Reasons and Speeches, and His Deportment on the Scaffold before His Execution* (London: n.p., 1648), 80.
18. Charles I, *Full Proceedings*, 83.
19. Charles I, *Full Proceedings*, 15.
20. Charles I, *Full Proceedings*, 15.
21. For a wide-ranging discussion of the pervasive discourses of contract in seventeenth-century literature, social practice, and political theory see Victoria Kahn, *Wayward Contracts: The Crisis of Political Obligation in England, 1640–1674* (Princeton: Princeton University Press, 2004). Kahn concludes that contract theory developed not as a normative foundation for liberal rights and duties, but rather from literary, social, and political debates about human passions and the role of imagination in motivating individuals to enter into binding agreements. Of particular interest in the context of the present study is Kahn's discussion of the difference between voluntary servitude and voluntary subjection (58).
22. It is a notable historical turnabout that Bradshaw was here citing the King James Bible, named after Charles I's father, under whose princely auspices it was first published in 1611 to make the holy text widely available in English.
23. Shelley references Falkland (Lucius Cary, 2nd Viscount of Falkland) and Gower (George Goring), both royalists. Falkland was committed to the rule of law and felt that the English Parliament should not involve itself in Scotland. As war approached in 1642, Falkland drew closer to the king, was appointed secretary of state, and co-authored Charles I's *Answer to the Nineteen Propositions*, a response to Parliament that asserted the power of the Crown and rule of law as protectors of people and property. George Goring was a royalist army officer during the Civil War, who alternated his military successes with a stint in the Tower of London and other political failures. Ronald Hutton, "Goring, George, Baron Goring (1608–1657), royalist army officer," *Oxford Dictionary of National Biography*, September 23, 2004, accessed April 13, 2024. <https://www.oxforddnb.com/view/10.1093/ref:odnb/9780198614128.001.0001/odnb-9780198614128-e-11100> David L. Smith, "Cary, Lucius, second Viscount Falkland (1609/10–1643), politician and author," *Oxford Dictionary of National Biography*, September 23, 2004, accessed April 13, 2024. <https://www.oxforddnb.com/view/10.1093/ref:odnb/9780198614128.001.0001/odnb-9780198614128-e-4841>
24. Scholarly commentary on this feature of Milton's epic is too expansive to summarize adequately here. In this work on Shelley's uses of Milton in *Frankenstein*, I have found instructive the following studies: Blair Worden, "Milton and the Civil Wars," in *Literature and Politics in*

Cromwellian England (Oxford: Oxford University Press, 2009); Stevie Davies, *Images of Kingship in Paradise Lost: Milton's Politics and Christian Liberty* (Columbia, MO: University of Missouri Press, 1983); Stephen M. Fallon, *Milton among the Philosophers: Poetry and Materialism in Seventeenth-Century England* (Ithaca, NY: Cornell University Press, 2007); Thomas N. Corns (ed.), *The Royal Image: Representations of Charles I* (Cambridge: Cambridge University Press, 1999); Christopher Hill, *The English Bible and the Seventeenth-Century Revolution* (London: Penguin Books, 1995).

25. John Milton, *Paradise Lost*, ed. Alastair Fowler, 2nd edn (London: Longman, 1998), 1.149–50.
26. Milton, *Paradise Lost*, 2.1052.
27. Edward B. Rugemer, "The Development of Mastery and Race in the Comprehensive Slave Codes of the Greater Caribbean during the Seventeenth Century," *William and Mary Quarterly* 70, no. 3 (2013): 429–58.
28. J. Kameron Carter, *Race: A Theological Account* (Oxford: Oxford University Press, 2008), 263.
29. I use this word with purpose, but also with circumspection. Because Milton's Satan hypothesizes that God's power may be categorically absolute (not just allegedly absolute like the Stuarts'), *Paradise Lost* implies a subtle question about the legitimacy of God's conquest of the rebel angels. Satan says at the council in Pandemonium that he must "Of force believe" that God is "Almighty" because "no less / Then [*sic*] such could hav orepow'rd such force as ours" (ll. 144–45). Thus Milton wonders: Is it just for a heavenly power greater not only in degree but also in kind to condemn another group of beings to eternal perdition?
30. Mary Shelley, "Author's Introduction to the Standard Novels Edition (1831)" of *Frankenstein* (New York: Oxford University Press, 1993), 192–97.
31. David Barry Gaspar's and Peter Charles Hoffer's studies of slave rebellions, in Antigua and South Carolina respectively, are the best accounts I have read of the mutually constitutive relationship between slave rebellion and state violence. Peter Charles Hoffer, *Cry Liberty: The Great Stono River Slave Rebellion of 1739* (Oxford: Oxford University Press, 2010); Gaspar, *Bondmen and Rebels*.
32. Holly Brewer, "Slavery, Sovereignty, and 'Inheritable Blood,'" *American Historical Review* 122, no. 4 (October 2017): 1043.
33. John Milton, *The Tenure of Kings and Magistrates* (London: Matthew Simmons in Aldersgate Street, 1649), 26.
34. Milton, *Tenure of Kings and Magistrates*, 26.
35. Milton, *Tenure of Kings and Magistrates*, 12.
36. Sean Wilentz, *No Property in Man* (Cambridge, MA: Harvard University Press, 2018).
37. This conclusion is at variance with Edward Said's particular readings of *Robinson Crusoe* and *Mansfield Park* in *Culture and Imperialism*. But my claim is nevertheless commensurate with Said's broader (and, I think, more important) finding that contrapuntal reading can yield interpretations of cultural artifacts that are both "more interesting" and more humanistic than "denunciations of the past," "expressions of regret for its having ended, or—even more wasteful because violent and far too easy and attractive—the hostility between Western and non-Western cultures that leads to crises." Edward Said, *Culture and Imperialism* (New York: Vintage, 1994), 19.
38. Many scholars have observed racialized content in Shelley's figuration of the Creature. For an overview, see generally: Patrick Brantlinger, "Race and *Frankenstein*," in *The Cambridge Companion to Frankenstein*, ed. Andrew Smith (Cambridge: Cambridge University Press, 2016), 128–42; H. L. Malchow, "Frankenstein's Monster and Images of Race in Nineteenth-Century Britain," *Past and Present* 139 (1993): 90–130; Anne K. Mellor, "Frankenstein, Racial Science, and the Yellow Peril," *Nineteenth-Century Contexts* 23 (2001): 1–28; Marie Mulvey-Roberts, "Mary Shelley, *Frankenstein*, and Slavery," in *Dangerous Bodies: Historicizing the Gothic Corporeal* (Manchester: Manchester University Press, 2016), 89–108.
39. *Dred Scott v. Sandford*, 60 U.S. (19 How.) 393 (1857). For an in-depth treatment of *Dred Scott v. Sandford* in relation to chattel slavery's moral implications for the American founding, see Herbert J. Storing, "Slavery and the Moral Foundations of the American Republic," in *Slavery and its Consequences: The Constitution, Equality, and Race*, ed. Robert A. Goldwin and Art Kaufman (Washington, DC: American Enterprise Institute for Public Policy Research, 1988).
40. Quotation in the subheading is from Milton, *Paradise Lost*, 1.63.
41. James Otis, *The Rights of the British Colonists Asserted and Proved*, 3rd edn (Boston, 1766), 43. See also Duncan J. MacLeod, "The American Revolution and the Institution of Slavery," in *Slavery, Race and the American Revolution* (Cambridge: Cambridge University Press, 1974), 15–61.
42. Douglass, *Narrative*, 23.
43. Douglass, *Narrative*, 23.
44. Douglass, *Narrative*, 23.

45. Rei Terada, *Metaracial: Hegel, Antiblackness, and Political Identity* (Chicago: University of Chicago Press, 2023), 119.
46. Terada, *Metaracial*, 119.
47. Douglass, *Narrative*, 40.
48. As David W. Blight has shown, Douglass remained interested until the end of his life in the question of his paternity, but he never seems to have resolved the question to his satisfaction. David W. Blight, *Frederick Douglass: Prophet of Freedom* (New York: W. W. Norton, 2018), 13–16.
49. Baldwin, "Stranger in the Village"; Saidiya Hartman, *Lose your Mother: A Journey along the Atlantic Slave Route* (New York: Farrar, Straus & Giroux, 2007), 4.
50. Ganz argues persuasively that Shelley ultimately refuses to condemn the Creature in *Frankenstein*, even while some characters (like Victor) pass negative judgment on him. Ganz, "A Kind of Insanity in my Spirits," 54–55; see also 63–65.
51. Dramatic adaptations of *Frankenstein* illuminate how superficial judgments inflect Shelley's original plot. Richard Brinsley Peake represents the Creature with blue skin, which is a suggestive, but not conclusive, index of the Creature's racial identity. See Richard Brinsley Peake, *Presumption; Or, the Fate of Frankenstein*, in *Seven Gothic Dramas: 1789–1825*, ed. Jeffrey N. Cox (Athens, OH: Ohio University Press, 1992). See also Brittany Reid, "Acting Monstrous: Staging the Creature in *Presumption; or, The Fate of Frankenstein*," *Supernatural Studies* 2, no. 2 (2015): 59–72.
52. Hunt, *Mary Shelley and the Rights of the Child*, 118.
53. Hunt's interpretation of *Frankenstein*'s nesting box structure, as successive deprivations of rights suffered by the Creature, is an important insight into Shelley's contribution to constitutional thought.
54. Mills, *The Racial Contract* (Ithaca, NY: Cornell University Press, 1997), 22–23.
55. Katharine Gerbner, *Christian Slavery* (Philadelphia: University of Pennsylvania Press, 2018), 32.
56. Mills, *The Racial Contract*, 17.
57. Karla F. C. Holloway, *Legal Fictions: Constituting Race, Composing Literature* (Durham, NC: Duke University Press, 1994), 5.
58. Simon Stern, "Reasonable Reasons, Reasonable Persons, and Legal Fictions," *Representations* 172 (2025): 19.
59. Stern, "Reasonable Reasons," 19.
60. Stern, "Reasonable Reasons," 24.
61. Sherman J. Clark, "Confronting Algorithms: Conscience Catching in the Criminal Trial and Beyond," *University of Michigan Journal of Law Reform* 57, no. 4 (2024): 787–824, esp. 789–90.
62. Clark, "Confronting Algorithms," 796–98.
63. Michel Foucault, *The History of Sexuality, Volume 1: An Introduction*, tr. Robert Hurley (New York: Vintage Books, 1978), 138.
64. See generally: Giorgio Agamben, *Homo Sacer* (Stanford, CA: Stanford University Press, 1998).
65. Agamben, *Homo Sacer*, 166–80.
66. Robert J. Lifton, *The Nazi Doctors: Medical Killing and the Psychology of Genocide* (New York: Basic Books, 1986), 22–44. For discussions of racial slavery's deployments of biopolitical power in a variety of contexts, see Stephanie Smallwood, *Saltwater Slavery* (Cambridge, MA: Harvard University Press, 2007) and Daina Ramey Berry, *The Price for Their Pound of Flesh: The Value of the Enslaved from Womb to Grave in the Building of a Nation* (Boston, MA: Beacon Press, 2017).
67. Although see M. Lindsay Kaplan, *Figuring Racism in Medieval Christianity* (New York: Oxford University Press, 2019). Kaplan argues that the Christian doctrine of *servitus Judaeorum*, or the perpetual enslavement of Jews as punishment for the crucifixion of Jesus, is a major ideological forerunner of other Western systems of racial categorization.
68. Equiano, *Interesting Narrative*, 208, emphasis in original.
69. Terada, *Metaracial*, 122.
70. Terada, *Metaracial*, 123.
71. One coincidence in the literary history of transatlantic constitutionalism is that Shelley's *Frankenstein* was first published in 1818, the year in which Douglass believed (but could not be certain) that he had been born.
72. Hobbes writes of human beings in *Leviathan* that "the weakest has strength enough to kill the strongest, either by secret machination, or by confederacy with others, that are in the same danger with himselfe." Thomas Hobbes, *Leviathan: Or the Matter, Forme & Power of a Commonwealth, Ecclesiasticall and Civill* (Cambridge: Cambridge University Press, 1904), 81.
73. Elizabeth Young, *Black Frankenstein: The Making of an American Metaphor* (New York: New York University Press, 2008).
74. As other critics have noted, this is a significant articulation in fiction of Hegel's master–slave dialectic in *Phenomenology of Spirit* (1807). Jared Hickman has argued, vis-à-vis Andrew Cole's

historicization of Hegel's lord–bondsman dialectic in *The Birth of Theory* (2014), that Hegel is writing in the *Phenomenology* about "bondsmen" or "serfs" (*Knecht* in German), not "slaves" (*Sklave* in German). Thus, in Hickman's view, Gilroy's and other interpretations of the Hegelian master–slave dialectic as a free white–enslaved Black dialectic "miss the point" because, as Hickman notes, the "the 'African' is *precluded* from this scene of recognition" (Hickman, *Black Prometheus*, 126). Gilroy, by contrast, calls this scene the "natal core of modern sociality" (*Black Atlantic*, 63). Hickman prefers the term lord-bondsman to describe the historical relation that birthed modern consciousness. But I think that Gilroy and Hickman are both correct. The racialized master–slave relation Gilroy describes *did* drive "modern sociality" in colonial and early national America precisely because "the 'African' [was] *precluded*," or presumed to be precluded, "from this scene of recognition" but ultimately could not be; this relation was at the heart of the modern racial state, as we have seen in the juridical innovations of the Caribbean slave codes and the contours of early modern literatures in English. In this way (and particularly by ending Frankenstein's generational line with Elizabeth's murder) the monster creates for Victor an inheritance of death, similar to his own lot in life. But, because the Creature cannot remove the fact of Frankenstein's human family, and a loving one at that, he cannot render his and Victor's circumstances entirely equivalent. The conditions of this difference arise from racecraft, the original scene of the Creature's making.

75. Rugemer, *Slave Law*, 32.
76. Milton, *Paradise Lost*, 1.63.
77. Rugemer, *Slave Law*, 29.
78. Denise Gigante, "Facing the Ugly: The Case of *Frankenstein*," *ELH* 67, no. 2 (2000): 565–87.
79. In 1662, Virginia codified the principle of *partus sequitur ventrem*, ruling that "all children borne [sic] in this country shall be bound or free according to the condition of the mother." William Waller Hening (ed.), *The Statutes at Large; Being a Collection of All the Laws of Virginia from the First Session of the Legislature, in the Year 1619* (New York: R. & W. & G. Bartow, 1823), 2:170.
80. Thomas Jefferson, *Notes on the State of Virginia* (New York: Penguin Books, 1999), 173.
81. Thomas Jefferson, "'Original Rough Draught' of the Declaration of Independence," in *The Papers of Thomas Jefferson*, vol. 1. *1760–1776*, ed. Julian P. Boyd (Princeton: Princeton University Press, 1950), 243–47.
82. Frank L. Dewey, *Thomas Jefferson, Lawyer* (Charlottesville, VA: University Press of Virginia, 1986), 11.
83. David Thomas Konig and Michael P. Zuckert, "Introduction," in *Jefferson's Legal Commonplace Book*, ed. David Thomas Konig and Michael P. Zuckert (Princeton: Princeton University Press, 2019), 5.
84. Konig and Zuckert, *Jefferson's Legal Commonplace Book*, 133. As Holly Brewer has shown, however, Holt supposedly gave Smith off-the-record guidance about how his claim may have been made valid. In this alleged advice, Holt distinguished between the laws of England and the laws of Virginia, as Mansfield would in *Somerset v. Stewart*. "You should have averred in the declaration," Holt is reported to have written to Smith, "that the sale of the negro was in Virginia, and by the laws of that country negroes are saleable; for the laws of England do not extend to Virginia, being a conquered country their law is what the King pleases, and we cannot take notice of their law but as set forth: therefore he ordered the plaintiff should amend and alter his declaration, that the defendant was indebted to him so much, for a negro sold here at London, but that the said negro, at the time of the sale, was in Virginia; and that negroes by the laws and statutes of Virginia may be sold as chattels." Brewer, "Common Law of Slavery," 821–22.
85. Konig and Zuckert, *Jefferson's Legal Commonplace Book*, 134.
86. Konig and Zuckert, *Jefferson's Legal Commonplace Book*, 124.
87. Brewer, "Common Law of Slavery," 767–71.
88. The collection is titled *Reports of Cases Determined in the General Court of Virginia from 1730 to 1740, and from 1768 to 1772.*
89. Thomas Jefferson, *The Writings of Thomas Jefferson: 1760–1775* (London: G. P. Putnam's Sons, 1892), 373–74.
90. William G. Merkel, "A Founding Father on Trial: Jefferson's Rights Talk and the Problem of Slavery during the Revolutionary Period," *Rutgers Law Review* 64 (2011): 593–646.
91. Paul Finkelman, *Slavery and the Founders: Race and Liberty in the Age of Jefferson* (New York: Routledge, 2014), 203.
92. Merkel, "Founding Father on Trial," 620.
93. Merkel, "Founding Father on Trial," 620.
94. Hening, *The Statutes at Large*, pp. vi–vii.
95. Merkel, "Founding Father on Trial," 620.

96. Patterson, *Slavery and Social Death*, 25.
97. William Blackstone, *Commentaries on the Laws of England*, ed. David Lemmings (Oxford: Oxford University Press, 2016; orig. edn 1765), 1:86, 331. In the first edition of *Commentaries*, Blackstone concludes without qualification that "The spirit of liberty is so deeply implanted in our constitution and rooted even in our very soil that a slave or negro the very moment he lands in England falls under the protection of the laws and with regard to all natural rights becomes *eo instanti* a freeman." As Teresa Michals has shown, Blackstone revised this discussion in the second and third editions of *Commentaries*, after consulting Lord Chief Justice Mansfield, to allow for the probable survival of a master's right to his slave's service in England. The accommodation exposes Blackstone's failure to distinguish freedom of person from slavocratic claims to labor. Michals, "'That Sole and Despotic Dominion': Slaves, Wives, and Game in Blackstone's Commentaries," *Eighteenth-Century Studies* 27, no. 2 (1993): 195–216, esp. 205.
98. William P. MacNeil, "The Monstrous Body of the Law: Wollstonecraft vs. Shelley," *Australian Feminist Law Journal* 12, no. 1 (1999): 24.
99. On Lord Byron's 1817 poem *Beppo: A Venetian Story* and the suggestive line "I like the Habeas Corpus (when we've got it)," see Deanna P. Koretsky, "Habeas Corpus and the Politics of Freedom: Slavery and Romantic Suicide," *Essays in Romanticism* 22, no. 1 (2015): 21–33; and Michael Williams, "'I like the Habeas Corpus (When we've Got it)': Byron, Wellington and the Future of British Liberties," *English Academy Review* 31, no. 1 (2014): 6–18. George Gordon Byron, *Beppo: A Venetian Story*, 6th edn (London: John Murray, 1818), 25.
100. Jefferson, *Writings of Thomas Jefferson: 1760–1775*, 374. Jefferson's use of the phrase "confusion of species," is one we might compare with both Frankenstein's worry that the Creature's companion, one of "his own species," would turn from him to the "superior beauty of man," as well as Jefferson's exceptionable remarks in *Notes on the State of Virginia* on the "preference of the Oranootan for the black women over those of his own species" (*Frankenstein* 138; *Notes on the State of Virginia*, 148). In these ways, racecraft raises questions about the meanings of sexual attraction and their sociolegal boundaries, a point we will consider in greater depth in examining Jefferson's relationship with Sally Hemings.
101. Jefferson, *Writings of Thomas Jefferson: 1760–1775*, 374.
102. Jefferson, *Writings of Thomas Jefferson: 1760–1775*, 374.
103. Thomas Jefferson, *A Summary View of the Rights of British America* (Philadelphia: John Dunlap, 1774), 5–6.
104. Jefferson, *Summary View*, 6.
105. Jefferson, *Summary View*, 6.
106. In his *Summary View*, Jefferson was, in some measure, exhorting George III to extend to Anglo-American colonists the customary rights of their British counterparts, most saliently representation in Parliament.
107. Jefferson, *Summary View*, 16.
108. Edmund S. Morgan, *American Slavery, American Freedom: The Ordeal of Colonial Virginia* (New York: W. W. Norton & Co., 1975), 381.
109. Brewer, "Slavery, Sovereignty, and 'Inheritable Blood,'" 1042.
110. Merkel, "Founding Father on Trial," 602.
111. Thomas Jefferson to James Monroe, September 20, 1800, *Founders Online*, National Archives. <https://founders.archives.gov/documents/Jefferson/01-32-02-0097>
112. "Thomas Jefferson to James Monroe, 20 September 1800," *Founders Online*.
113. Merkel, "Founding Father on Trial," 602.
114. Hening, *The Statutes at Large*, 86.
115. Thomas Jefferson to John Holmes, April 22, 1820, *Founders Online*, National Archives. <https://founders.archives.gov/documents/Jefferson/03-15-02-0518>
116. Thomas W. Merrill, "The Later Jefferson and the Problem of Natural Rights," in *The Political Thought of the Civil War*, ed. Thomas W. Merrill, Alan Levine, and James R. Stoner (Lawrence, KS: University Press of Kansas, 2018), 32.
117. Merrill, "The Later Jefferson," 32.
118. Jefferson to Holmes, April 22, 1820.
119. Defoe, *Robinson Crusoe*, 33.
120. Gordon-Reed, *The Hemingses of Monticello*.
121. Jefferson, *Notes on the State of Virginia*, 173.
122. When *Frankenstein* was adapted to American cinema, especially in James Whale's 1931 production, the monster's murder of Elizabeth Frankenstein on her bridal bed became conflated with the white supremacist trope of the rape of white women by black men, popularized by D. W. Griffith's *Birth of a Nation* (1915). The best-known real example of this element of the American racial

imagination is the 1955 story of Emmett Till, a 14-year-old black boy who was accused of sexual misconduct by a white woman, Carolyn Bryant, and then kidnapped and murdered by her husband and brother-in-law. In the late 1800s, the journalist Ida B. Wells documented lynchings in the United States, and their connection to notions of white women's racial and sexual purity. Ida B. Wells, *A Red Record: Tabulated Statistics and Alleged Causes of Lynchings in the United States, 1892–1893–1894* (Chicago: Privately published, 1894).

123. Rugemer, *Slave Law*, 26–27.
124. Jefferson, *Summary View*, 7.
125. Jefferson, *Notes on the State of Virginia*, 173.
126. Jefferson, *Notes on the State of Virginia*, 174.
127. Avalon Project at Yale Law School, "Constitution of the Confederate States; March 11, 1861," *Documents in Law, History, and Diplomacy.* <https://avalon.law.yale.edu/19th_century/csa_csa.asp>
128. Quotation in the subheading from US National Archives and Records Administration, "Declaration of Independence: A Transcription," *America's Founding Documents*, last modified October 11, 2023. <https://www.archives.gov/founding-docs/declaration-transcript>
129. Douglas L. Wilson, ed., *Jefferson's Literary Commonplace Book, Papers of Thomas Jefferson: Second Series*, vol. 5 (Princeton, NJ: Princeton University Press, 2014), 95.
130. Wilson, *Jefferson's Literary Commonplace Book*, 94.
131. Wilson, *Jefferson's Literary Commonplace Book*, 98–99.
132. Jon Meacham, *Thomas Jefferson: The Art of Power* (New York: Random House Trade Paperbacks, 2012), 144–45.
133. The complications that caused Patty's death were not, it seems, exclusively obstetric. Meacham reckons that the "tensions and exertions of the [American Revolutionary] war, culminating in the family's evacuation of Monticello, exacerbated the state of her health. She may have suffered from tuberculosis." At the same time, Patty's last child, Lucy, was her "sixth in ten years," indicating that the physical strains of childbirth, so dangerous in the late eighteenth century, contributed to her death at the age of 33. Meacham, *Thomas Jefferson: The Art of Power*, 144.
134. Burton Hatlen, "Milton, Mary Shelley and Patriarchy," in *Rhetoric, Literature, and Interpretation*, ed. Harry R. Garvin (Lewisburg, PA: Bucknell University Press, 1983), 19–47; Mary Jacobus, "Is there a Woman in This Text?," *New Literary History* 14 (1982): 117–41; Barbara Johnson, "My Monster/my Self," *Diacritics* 12 (1982): 2–10; Devon Hodges, "Frankenstein and the Feminine Subversion of the Novel," *Tulsa Studies in Women's Literature* 2 (Autumn 1983): 155–64; Jill Lepore, "The Strange and Twisted Life of Frankenstein," *The New Yorker*, February 5, 2018. <https://www.newyorker.com/magazine/2018/02/12/the-strange-and-twisted-life-of-frankenstein> Mary Poovey, *The Proper Lady and the Woman Writer: Ideology as Style in the Works of Mary Wollstonecraft, Mary Shelley and Jane Austen* (Chicago: University of Chicago Press, 1984); Marc A. Rubenstein, "'My Accursed Origin': The Search for the Mother in Frankenstein," *Studies in Romanticism* 15 (Spring 1976): 165–94.
135. Genesis 2: 18 (KJV).
136. Milton, *Paradise Lost*, 8.450.
137. Eileen Hunt has noted that this is a faulty presumption on the Creature's part; there is no guarantee that a second creation would associate freely with Frankenstein's original being. Hunt, *Mary Shelley and the Rights of the Child*, 132–34.
138. William Lloyd Garrison, "Preface," in *Narrative of the Life of Frederick Douglass, an American Slave*, by Frederick Douglass, written by himself (Boston: Anti-Slavery Office, 1845), p. ix.
139. Gen. 3: 13, 4: 10 (KJV).
140. Fred V. Randel, "The Political Geography of Horror in Mary Shelley's 'Frankenstein,'" *ELH* 70, no. 2 (2003): 483.
141. As William Godwin, Shelley's father, has his eponymous hero say in *Caleb Williams* (1794): Ireland is, for the fugitive Williams, "a place of less security than most other countries which are divided from [the British government] by the ocean." William Godwin, *Things as They Are; or, The Adventures of Caleb Williams*, 2 vols. (Philadelphia: Printed for H. and P. Rice, no. 50 Market Street, and sold by J. Rice & Co., Baltimore, 1795), 115.
142. Mr Kirwin "could not help regarding my exclamation" at the arrival of Alphonse Frankenstein, "as a presumption of my guilt," Frankenstein notes (152).
143. For an account of English appeals to Parliament regarding their colonial labor conditions, see Peter Charles Hoffer, *Law and People in Colonial America* (Baltimore, MD: Johns Hopkins University Press, 1992).

144. Both the Creature and Frankenstein believe this about the Creature's nature. One of the great and maybe unresolvable questions of *Frankenstein* is whether or not their shared belief is true.
145. Gordon-Reed, *The Hemingses of Monticello*, 337.
146. Gordon-Reed, *The Hemingses of Monticello*, 326–92.
147. Gordon-Reed, *The Hemingses of Monticello*, 353–75.
148. Jon Kukla, *Mr. Jefferson's Women* (New York: Alfred A. Knopf, 2007), 137.
149. Gordon-Reed, *The Hemingses of Monticello*, 82–83.
150. Adriana Craciun, "Writing the Disaster: Franklin and *Frankenstein*," *Nineteenth-Century Literature* 65, no. 4 (2011): 433–80; Theodore Ziolkowski, "Science, *Frankenstein*, and Myth," *Sewanee Review* 89, no. 1 (1981): 34–56; Lisa Nocks, "*Frankenstein*, in a Better Light," *Journal of Social and Evolutionary Systems* 20, no. 2 (1997): 137–55; George Levine, "The Ambiguous Heritage of *Frankenstein*," in *The Endurance of Frankenstein: Essays on Mary Shelley's Novel*, ed. Levine and U. C. Knoepflmacher (Berkeley, CA: University Of California Press, 1979), 3–30; David Seed, "*Frankenstein*—Parable of Spectacle?," *Criticism* 24, no. 4 (1982): 327–40; Nora Crook, "Mary Shelley, Author of *Frankenstein*," in *A New Companion to the Gothic*, ed. David Punter (Malden, MA: Wiley-Blackwell, 2012), 110–22; Irving H. Buchen, "Frankenstein and the Alchemy of Creation and Evolution," *The Wordsworth Circle* 8, no. 2 (1977): 103–12.
151. Kukla, *Jefferson's Women*, 119.
152. Frederick Douglass, *Life and Times of Frederick Douglass* (Boston: De Wolfe, Fiske & Co., 1881), 15.
153. US National Archives, "Declaration of Independence."
154. US National Archives, "Declaration of Independence."
155. US National Archives, "Declaration of Independence."
156. See generally: Danielle S. Allen, *Our Declaration: A Reading of the Declaration of Independence in Defense of Equality* (New York: W. W. Norton & Co., 2014), 94–98; Willard Sterne Randall, *Thomas Jefferson: A Life* (New York: Harper Perennial Modern Classics, 1993), 63; Dewey, *Thomas Jefferson, Lawyer*, 57–72.
157. For a book-length study of the democratic currents traveled by Atlantic-world sailing vessels, see Peter Linebaugh and Marcus Rediker, *The Many-Headed Hydra: Sailors, Slaves, Commoners, and the Hidden History of the Revolutionary Atlantic* (Boston: Beacon Press, 2000).

Novel Constitutions and the Making of Race: A Literary and Legal History of Slavery in the Anglophone Atlantic, 1688–1818. Sarah Marsh, Oxford University Press. © Sarah Marsh 2026. DOI: 10.1093/9780197917855.003.0007

Bibliography

An Act for the Punishment of Vagabonds and for the Relief of the Poor. 1 Edward VI, c. 3 (1547).

An Acte Touching Dyvers Orders for Artificers, Laborers, Servantes of Husbandrye and Apprentises. 5 Elizabeth I, c. 4 (1563).

"Barbados Slave Code." 1661. The National Archives (UK), Kew. CO 30/2.

An Act for the Better Ordering and Governing of Negro Slaves. Jamaica, 1664. In *The Laws of Jamaica, 1664–1832*, edited and digitized by the Slavery and Freedom in the British Atlantic World Project. University of New Brunswick. Accessed December 28, 2025. <https://slavery-andfreedomlaws.lib.unb.ca/laws/jamaica-1664-0>

An Act Declaring the Rights and Liberties of the Subject and Settling the Succession of the Crown. [= Bill of Rights] 1 Will. & Mar., sess. 2, c. 2 (1689). In *The Statutes of the Realm*, vol. 6, 142–45. London, 1819.

Acts of Assembly of the Province of Maryland, Made and Passed. Baltimore, MD: Jonas Green, 1751. Accessed April 3, 2023. <https://msa.maryland.gov/megafile/msa/speccol/sc4800/sc4872/003179/html/m3179-0798.html>

African Company of Merchants Act. 23 Geo. III, c. 65 (1783). *The Statutes Project*. Accessed December12,2023.<https://statutes.org.uk/site/the-statutes/eighteenth-century/1783-23-george-3-c-65-african-company-of-merchants-act>

Constitution of the Confederate States of America. March 11, 1861. Avalon Project, Yale Law School. <https://avalon.law.yale.edu/19th_century/csa_csa.asp>

Constitution of the United States. Article IV, Section 2, Clause 3 (Fugitive Slave Clause). *National Archives and Records Administration*. Accessed March 28, 2023. <https://www.archives.gov/founding-docs/constitution-transcript>

Declaration of Independence: A Transcription. National Archives and Records Administration. Last modified October 11, 2023. <https://www.archives.gov/founding-docs/declaration-transcript>

An Act to Repeal So Much of an Act, Made in the Fifth Year of the Reign of His Late Majesty King George the Second, Intituled, "An Act for the More Easy Recovery of Debts in His Majesty's Plantations and Colonies in America," as Makes Negroes Liable to Be Sold in Execution for the Payment of Debts. 37 Geo. III, c. 119 (1797).

Acholonu-Olumba, Catherine Obianuju. *The Igbo Roots of Olaudah Equiano: An Anthropological Research (with a Reply to Vincent Carretta)*. Rev. edn. Owerri, Nigeria: AFA Publications, 2007.

Acts and Ordinances of the Interregnum, 1642–1660, edited by C. H. Firth and R. S. Rait, vol. 2. London: His Majesty's Stationery Office, 1911. British History Online. Accessed October 28, 2023. <http://www.british-history.ac.uk/no-series/acts-ordinances-interregnum>

Agamben, Giorgio. *Homo Sacer: Sovereign Power and Bare Life*. Translated by Daniel Heller-Roazen. Stanford, CA: Stanford University Press, 1998.

A Genuine Narrative of the Intended Conspiracy of the Negroes at Antigua. London: Printed for J. Wilford, 1737. Reprint, New York: Arno Press, 1972.

Alexander, Leslie M. *Fear of a Black Republic: Haiti and the Birth of Black Internationalism in the United States*. Urbana, IL: University of Illinois Press, 2022.

Allen, Danielle S. *Our Declaration: A Reading of the Declaration of Independence in Defense of Equality*. New York: W. W. Norton & Co., 2014.

Almanac for Maryland, Pennsylvania, and Virginia. Baltimore, MD: Printed by R. J. Matchett, 1835. Author's personal collection. Publication details inferred from internal evidence.

Anderson, Edgar. "The Couronians and the West Indies: The First Settlements." *Caribbean Quarterly* 5, no. 4 (1959): 264–71.

Andrews, William. "Benjamin Banneker's Revision of Thomas Jefferson: Conscience Versus Science in the Early American Antislavery Debate." In *Genius in Bondage: Literature of the Early Black Atlantic*, edited by Vincent Carretta and Philip Gould, 135–58. Louisville, KY: University Press of Kentucky, 2001.

Andrews, William. *To Tell a Free Story: The First Century of Afro-American Autobiography, 1760–1865*. Urbana, IL: University of Illinois Press, 1986.

Aptheker, Herbert. *American Negro Slave Revolts*. New York: Columbia University Press, 1943.

Aravamudan, Srinivas. *Tropicopolitans: Colonialism and Agency, 1688–1804*. Durham, NC: Duke University Press, 1999.

Aristotle. *Poetics*. Translated by S. H. Butcher. In *The Complete Works of Aristotle*, vol. 2, edited by Jonathan Barnes, 1451a36–1451b11. Princeton: Princeton University Press, 1984.

Armstrong, Nancy. *Desire and Domestic Fiction: A Political History of the Novel*. New York: Oxford University Press, 1987.

Austen, Jane. *Jane Austen's Letters*, edited by Deirdre Le Faye. 4th edn. Oxford: Oxford University Press, 2011.

Austen, Jane. *Mansfield Park*, edited by R. W. Chapman. 3rd edn. Oxford: Oxford University Press, 1934.

Austen, Jane. *Mansfield Park: An Annotated Edition*, edited by Deidre Shauna Lynch. Illustrated edn. Cambridge, MA: Belknap Press of Harvard University Press, 2016.

Bacon, Nathaniel. *An Historical and Political Discourse of the Laws and Government of England*. London, 1689.

Bailey, A. Peter, and Earl Grant. *Malcolm X: The Man and his Times*. New York: Macmillan, 1969.

Bailyn, Bernard. *The Ideological Origins of the American Revolution*. Fiftieth anniversary edn. Cambridge, MA: Belknap Press of Harvard University Press, 2017.

Baker, J. H. *An Introduction to English Legal History*. 5th edn. Oxford: Oxford University Press, 2019.

Baldwin, James. "Letter from a Region in my Mind." *The New Yorker*, November 17, 1962.

Baldwin, James. "Stranger in the Village." *Harper's Magazine* 207, no. 1214 (October 1953): 44–50.

Baldwin, James. *The Fire Next Time*. New York: Dial Press, 1963.

Banfield, Ann. "The Moral Landscape of *Mansfield Park*." *Nineteenth-Century Fiction* 26, no. 1 (1971): 1–24.

Banneker, Benjamin. *Benjamin Banneker's Pennsylvania, Delaware, Maryland and Virginia Almanack and Ephemeris for the Year of Our Lord 1792*. Baltimore, MD: William Goddard & James Angell, 1792.

Bannet, Eve Tavor. *Eighteenth-Century Manners of Reading: Print Culture and Popular Instruction in the Anglophone Atlantic World*. Cambridge: Cambridge University Press, 2017.

Barlow, Frank. *Edward the Confessor*. New Haven: Yale University Press, 1997.

Barter, Faith. *Black Pro Se: Authorship and the Limits of Law in Nineteenth-Century African American Literature*. Chapel Hill, NC: University of North Carolina Press, 2025.

Baucom, Ian. *Specters of the Atlantic: Finance Capital, Slavery, and the Philosophy of History*. Durham, NC: Duke University Press, 2005.

Beckles, Hilary. *A History of Barbados: From Amerindian Settlement to Caribbean Single Market*. Cambridge: Cambridge University Press, 2007.

Bedini, Silvio A. *The Life of Benjamin Banneker: The Definitive Biography of the First Black Man of Science*. New York: Charles Scribner's Sons, 1972.

Behn, Aphra. *Oroonoko; or, The Royal Slave*, edited by Catherine Gallagher with Simon Stern. Boston: Bedford/St Martin's, 2000.

Benezet, Anthony, with John Ady, John Drinker, and the London Yearly Meeting (Society of Friends). *The Case of Our Fellow-Creatures, the Oppressed Africans: Respectfully Recommended to the Serious Consideration of the Legislature of Great-Britain*. London and Philadelphia: Reprinted by Joseph Crukshank, 1784.

Berry, Daina Ramey. *The Price for Their Pound of Flesh: The Value of the Enslaved from Womb to Grave in the Building of a Nation*. Boston: Beacon Press, 2017.

Bewell, Alan. *Romanticism and Colonial Disease*. Baltimore, MD: Johns Hopkins University Press, 1999.

Bilder, Mary Sarah. *The Transatlantic Constitution: Colonial Legal Culture and the Empire*. Cambridge, MA: Harvard University Press, 2004.

Billings, Warren M. "The Cases of Fernando and Elizabeth Key: A Note on the Status of Blacks in Seventeenth-Century Virginia." *William and Mary Quarterly* 30, no. 3 (1973): 467–74.

Black, Barbara. "Constitution of Empire: The Case for the Colonists." *University of Pennsylvania Law Review* 124, no. 5 (1976): 1157–1211.

Blackburn, Robin. "The Old World Background to European Colonial Slavery." *William and Mary Quarterly* 54, no. 1 (January 1997): 65–102.

Blackstone, William. *Commentaries on the Laws of England*, edited by David Lemmings. Oxford: Oxford University Press, 2016. Originally published 1765.

Blight, David W. *Frederick Douglass: Prophet of Freedom*. New York: W. W. Norton, 2018.

Block, Sharon. *Colonial Complexions: Race and Bodies in Eighteenth-Century America*. Philadelphia: University of Pennsylvania Press, 2018.

Bogart, Daniel, and Gary Richardson. "Property Rights and Parliament in Industrializing Britain." NBER Working Paper no. 15697. Cambridge, MA: National Bureau of Economic Research, January 2010.

Bonhoeffer, Dietrich. *Creation and Fall: A Theological Exposition of Genesis 1–3*. Minneapolis: Fortress Press, 1997.

Boulukos, George. "Defoe and Slavery." In *Daniel Defoe in Context*, edited by Albert J. Rivero and George Justice, 295–307. Cambridge: Cambridge University Press, 2023.

Boulukos, George E. "The Politics of Silence: *Mansfield Park* and the Amelioration of Slavery." *Novel: A Forum on Fiction* 39, no. 3 (2006): 361–83.

Bowen, Emanuel. *A New and Accurate Map of the Island of Antigua or Antego*. London: Printed for William Innys, 1747. David Rumsey Map Collection. Accessed December 28, 2025.

Boyer, Allen D. *Sir Edward Coke and the Elizabethan Age*. Stanford, CA: Stanford University Press, 2003.

Brandon, Richard. *The Confession of Richard Brandon, the Hangman (Upon His Death Bed)*. London, 1774. British Library.

Brantlinger, Patrick. "Race and *Frankenstein*." In *The Cambridge Companion to Frankenstein*, edited by Andrew Smith, 128–42. Cambridge: Cambridge University Press, 2016.

Brault, Gerard J., ed. *The Song of Roland*. University Park, PA: Pennsylvania State University Press, 1978.

Brewer, Holly. *By Birth or Consent: Children, Law, and the Anglo-American Revolution in Authority*. Chapel Hill, NC: University of North Carolina Press, 2005.

Brewer, Holly. "Creating a Common Law of Slavery for England and its New World Empire." *Law and History Review* 39, no. 4 (2021): 765–834.

Brewer, Holly. "Slavery, Sovereignty, and 'Inheritable Blood': Reconsidering John Locke and the Origins of American Slavery." *American Historical Review* 122, no. 4 (October 2017): 1038–68.

Brewer, Holly. "Whose Fundamental Constitutions? Locke, Slavery, and Manuscript Evidence." *Locke Studies* (2024): 1–57.

Brewer, John, and Susan Staves. "Introduction." In *Early Modern Conceptions of Property*, edited by John Brewer and Susan Staves, 1–16. New York: Routledge, 1995.

Brown, Christopher Leslie. *Moral Capital: Foundations of British Abolitionism*. Chapel Hill, NC: University of North Carolina Press for the Omohundro Institute of Early American History and Culture, Williamsburg, VA, 2006.

Brown, Laura. "The Romance of Empire: *Oroonoko* and the Trade in Slaves." In *The New 18th Century: Theory, Politics, English Literature*, edited by Felicity Nussbaum and Laura Brown, 58–59. New York: Methuen, 1987.

Brown, Vincent. *Tacky's Revolt: The Story of an Atlantic Slave War*. Cambridge, MA: Belknap Press of Harvard University Press, 2020.

Brush, Emma. "'In my own Handwriting': Phillis Wheatley and the Problem of the Creative Commons." *European Journal of English Studies* 29, no. 1 (2025): 50–74.

Buchen, Irving H. "Frankenstein and the Alchemy of Creation and Evolution." *The Wordsworth Circle* 8, no. 2 (1977): 103–12.

Burgess, Glenn. *Absolute Monarchy and the Stuart Constitution.* New Haven: Yale University Press, 1996.

Bush, Jonathan A. "Free to Enslave: The Foundations of Colonial American Slave Law." *Yale Journal of Law and the Humanities* 5, no. 2 (1993): 417–70.

Butler, Marilyn. *Jane Austen and the War of Ideas.* Oxford: Clarendon Press, 1975.

Byrne, Paula. *Jane Austen and the Theatre.* London: Bloomsbury Academic, 2002.

Byron, George Gordon. *Beppo: A Venetian Story.* 6th edn. London: John Murray, 1818.

Carey, Daniel. "Reading Contrapuntally: *Robinson Crusoe*, Slavery, and Postcolonial Theory." In *The Postcolonial Enlightenment: Eighteenth-Century Colonialism and Postcolonial Theory,* edited by Daniel Carey and Lynn Festa, 121–40. New York: Oxford University Press, 2009.

Carter, J. Kameron. *Race: A Theological Account.* Oxford: Oxford University Press, 2008.

Carretta, Vincent. *Equiano, the African: Biography of a Self-Made Man.* Athens, GA: University of Georgia Press, 2005.

Chakravarty, Urvashi. *Fictions of Consent: Slavery, Servitude, and Free Service in Early Modern England.* Philadelphia: University of Pennsylvania Press, 2022.

Chalmers, George. *Opinions of Eminent Lawyers on Various Points of English Jurisprudence,* vol. 1. London: Reed & Hunter, 1814.

Chapman, R. W. *Jane Austen: Facts and Problems.* Oxford: Clarendon Press, 1948.

Charles I, King of England. *The Full Proceedings of the High Court of Justice against King Charles in Westminster Hall, on Saturday the 20 of January, 1648; together with the King's Reasons and Speeches, and His Deportment on the Scaffold before His Execution.* London: n.p., 1648.

Charles II, King of England. *A Proclamation for the Encouraging of Planters in His Majesties Island of Jamaica in the West-Indies.* London: Printed by John Bill and Christopher Barker, 1661.

Chiles, Katy. *Transformable Race: Surprising Metamorphoses in the Literature of Early America.* Oxford: Oxford University Press, 2014.

Clark, Sherman J. "Confronting Algorithms: Conscience Catching in the Criminal Trial and Beyond." *University of Michigan Journal of Law Reform* 57, no. 4 (2024): 787–824.

Clarkson, Thomas. *An Essay on the Slavery and Commerce of the Human Species: Particularly the African.* United States: N. Wiley, 1804.

Clarkson, Thomas. *The History of the Rise, Progress, and Accomplishment of the Abolition of the African Slave-Trade by the British Parliament.* London: R. Taylor & Co., 1808.

Coates, Ta-Nehisi. *Between the World and Me.* New York: Spiegel & Grau, 2015.

Cohen, William. "Thomas Jefferson and the Problem of Slavery." *Journal of American History* 56, no. 3 (December 1969): 503–26.

Coke, Edward. "Preface." In *The Reports of Sir Edward Coke,* edited by John H. Thomas and John F. Fraser, new edn, 13 parts in 6 vols., vol. 5. London: J. Butterworth & Son, 1826.

Coke, Edward. "Proem." *The Fourth Part of the Institutes of the Laws of England: Concerning the Jurisdiction of the Courts.* 1669. Reprint, London: M. Plesher, 1817.

Coke, Edward. *The First Part of the Institutes of the Laws of England,* edited by Francis Hargrave and Charles Butler. 18th edn. 2 vols. 1628; London: J. & W. T. Clarke, 1832.

Coke, Edward. *The Second Part of the Reports of Edward Coke, Her Majesty's Attorney-General: Of Divers Matters in Law.* London: Printed by E. and R. Nutt & R. Gosling, assigns of Edward Sayer, for D. Bowne et al., 1727.

Coleman, Deirdre. "Domestic and Colonial Sisters in *Mansfield Park.*" In *A Companion to Jane Austen,* edited by Claudia L. Johnson and Clara Tuite, 295–310. Oxford: Blackwell Publishing, 2009.

Colley, Linda. *Britons: Forging the Nation, 1707–1837.* New Haven: Yale University Press, 2009.

Colley, Linda. *The Gun, the Ship, and the Pen: Warfare, Constitutions, and the Making of the Modern World.* New York: Liveright Publishing Corporation, 2021.

Colman, George. *The Heir at Law: A Comedy in Five Acts.* London: Printed for Longman, Hurst, Rees, Orme, & Browne, 1818.

Copeland, M. Shawn. *Knowing Christ Crucified: The Witness of African American Religious Experience.* Maryknoll, NY: Orbis Books, 2018.

Cormack, Bradin. *A Power to Do Justice: Jurisdiction, English Literature, and Common Law.* Chicago: University of Chicago Press, 2008.

Corns, Thomas N., ed. *The Royal Image: Representations of Charles I.* Cambridge: Cambridge University Press, 1999.

Cowper, William. *The Task, with Tirocinium: and Selections from the Minor Poems, A.D. 1784–1799,* edited by Henry Thomas Griffith. 2nd edn. Oxford: Clarendon Press, 1875.

Craciun, Adriana. "Writing the Disaster: Franklin and *Frankenstein*." *Nineteenth-Century Literature* 65, no. 4 (2011): 433–80.

Crawford, Nicholas. "'In the Wreck of a Master's Fortune': Slave Provisioning and Planter Debt in the British Caribbean." *Slavery and Abolition* 37, no. 4 (2016): 736–57.

Crawford, Nicholas. Review of *Rethinking the Fall of the Planter Class,* edited by Christer Petley. *New West Indian Guide* 92, nos. 1–2 (2018): 113–15.

Crook, Nora. "Mary Shelley, Author of *Frankenstein*." In *A New Companion to the Gothic,* edited by David Punter, 110–22. Malden, MA: Wiley-Blackwell, 2012.

Cugoano, Quobna Ottobah. *Thoughts and Sentiments on the Evil and Wicked Traffic of the Slavery and Commerce of the Human Species: Humbly Submitted to the Inhabitants of Great-Britain.* London, 1787.

Cullen, Charles T., ed. *The Papers of Thomas Jefferson,* vol. 22, *6 August 1791–31 December 1791.* Princeton: Princeton University Press, 1986.

Curran, Stuart, and Henry Louis Gates, Jr. *Who's Black and Why? A Hidden Chapter from the Eighteenth-Century Invention of Race.* Cambridge, MA: Belknap Press of Harvard University Press, 2021.

Dash, Mike. "Antigua's Disputed Slave Conspiracy of 1736." *Smithsonian Magazine,* July 3, 2013. <https://www.smithsonianmag.com/history/antiguas-disputed-slave-conspiracy-of-1736-117569/>

David, James Corbett. *Dunmore's New World: The Extraordinary Life of a Royal Governor in Revolutionary America.* Charlottesville, VA: University of Virginia Press, 2013.

Davies, Cliff S. L. "Slavery and Protector Somerset: The Vagrancy Act of 1547." *Economic History Review,* 19 (1966): 533–49.

Davies, Sir John. *Irish Reports (Les Reports des Cases & Matters en Ley, Resolves & Adjudges en les Courts del Roy en Ireland).* London, 1674.

Davies, Stevie. *Images of Kingship in Paradise Lost: Milton's Politics and Christian Liberty.* Columbia, MO: University of Missouri Press, 1983.

Davis, Charles T., and Henry Louis Gates, Jr., eds. *The Slave's Narrative.* Oxford: Oxford University Press, 1991.

Davis, Gregson. "Jane Austen's *Mansfield Park*: The Antigua Connection." *University of the West Indies Open Campus,* 2004. Accessed September 15, 2024.

Davis, Kathryn E. "'The First Soldier [She] Ever Sighed for': Charles Pasley's Essay and the 'Governing Winds' of *Mansfield Park*." *Persuasions On-Line* 35, no. 1 (Winter 2014).

Davis, Lennard J. *Factual Fictions: The Origins of the English Novel.* New York: Columbia University Press, 1983.

Defoe, Daniel. *An Essay upon the Trade to Africa, in Order to Set the Merits of that Cause in a True Light and Bring the Disputes between the African Company and the Separate Traders into a Narrower Compass.* London, 1711.

Defoe, Daniel. "An Explanatory Preface." In *The Earlier Life and the Chief Earlier Works of Daniel Defoe,* edited by Henry Morley, 179. London, 1889.

Defoe, Daniel. *Reformation of Manners, a Satyr: Væ Vobis Hypocritè.* London, 1702.

Defoe, Daniel. *Robinson Crusoe.* 2nd edn, edited by John Richetti. New York: Penguin Books, 2003.

Defoe, Daniel. *Serious Reflections during the Life and Surprising Adventures of Robinson Crusoe: With His Vision of the Angelick World.* Part 3. London: W. Taylor, 1720.

Defoe, Daniel. *The Farther Adventures of Robinson Crusoe; Being the Second and Last Part of His Life, and of the Strange Surprising Account of His Travels Round Three Parts of the Globe.* 3rd edn. London: Printed for W. Taylor, 1722.

Defoe, Daniel. *The History of the Union between England and Scotland, with a Collection of Original Papers Relating Thereto.* To which is prefixed a life of Daniel Defoe, by George Chalmers. London: Printed for J. Stockdale, 1786.

Defoe, Daniel. *The Original Power of the Collective Body of the People of England*. London, 1702.
Defoe, Daniel. *The True-Born Englishman*. London, 1701.
Defoe, Daniel. *The True-Born Englishman*. In *The Earlier Life and the Chief Earlier Works of Daniel Defoe*, edited by Henry Morley. London, 1889.
DeGooyer, Stephanie. *Before Borders: A Legal and Literary History of Naturalization*. Baltimore, MD: Johns Hopkins University Press, 2022.
Dery, Mark. "Black to the Future: Interviews with Samuel R. Delany, Greg Tate, and Tricia Rose." In *Flame Wars: The Discourse of Cyberculture*, edited by Mark Dery. Durham, NC: Duke University Press, 1994.
Dewey, Frank L. *Thomas Jefferson, Lawyer*. Charlottesville, VA: University of Virginia Press, 1986.
Doody, Margaret. *Jane Austen's Names: Riddles, Persons, Places*. Chicago: University of Chicago Press, 2015.
Douglass, Frederick. *Frederick Douglass: Narrative of the Life of Frederick Douglass, an American Slave, Written by Himself*, edited with an introduction by Ira Dworkin. New York: Penguin Books, 2014.
Douglass, Frederick. *Life and Times of Frederick Douglass*. Boston: De Wolfe, Fiske & Co., 1881.
Douglass, Frederick. *My Bondage and my Freedom*. New York: Miller, Orton & Mulligan, 1855.
Douglass, Frederick. *Narrative of the Life of Frederick Douglass, an American Slave, Written by Himself*. Boston: Anti-Slavery Office, 1845.
Douglass, Frederick. "Slavery and the Irrepressible Conflict." Address delivered in Geneva, New York, August 1, 1860. Reprinted in *The Frederick Douglass Papers*, series 1, *Speeches, Debates, and Interviews*, vol. 3, *1855–63*, edited by John W. Blassingame, 369–70. New Haven: Yale University Press, 1985.
Downie, J. A. "The Chronology of *Mansfield Park*." *Modern Philology* 112, no. 2 (2014): 427–34.
Downie, J. A. "Who Says She's a Bourgeois Writer? Reconsidering the Social and Political Contexts of Jane Austen's Novels." *Eighteenth-Century Studies* 40, no. 1 (Fall 2006): 69–84.
Doyle, Laura. *Freedom's Empire: Race and the Rise of the Novel in Atlantic Modernity, 1640–1940*. Durham, NC: Duke University Press, 2008.
Du Bois, W. E. B. *The Souls of Black Folk*. Oxford: Oxford University Press, 2008.
Duckworth, Alistair M. "*Mansfield Park* and Estate Improvements: Jane Austen's Grounds of Being." *Nineteenth-Century Fiction* 26, no. 1 (1971): 25–48.
Duckworth, Alistair M. *The Improvement of the Estate: A Study of Jane Austen's Novels*. Baltimore, MD: Johns Hopkins University Press, 1994.
Dugatkin, Lee Alan. "Buffon, Jefferson and the Theory of New World Degeneracy." *Evolution: Education and Outreach* 12, no. 1 (2019): 1–10.
Dunmore, John Murray, earl of. *By His Excellency the Right Honorable John Earl of Dunmore . . . A Proclamation*. Broadside, November 7, 1775. Broadside 1775.V852 FF. Special Collections, Library of Virginia.
Dunn, Richard S. *Sugar and Slaves: The Rise of the Planter Class in the English West Indies, 1624–1713*. Chapel Hill, NC: University of North Carolina Press, 1972.
Equiano, Olaudah. *The Interesting Narrative of the Life of Olaudah Equiano, or Gustavus Vassa, the African*, edited by Vincent Carretta. New York: Penguin, 2003.
Erickson, Robert A. "Mrs. A. Behn and the Myth of Oroonoko-Imoinda." *Eighteenth-Century Fiction* 5, no. 3 (April 1993): 211–26.
Fallon, Stephen M. *Milton among the Philosophers: Poetry and Materialism in Seventeenth-Century England*. Ithaca, NY: Cornell University Press, 2007.
Faubert, Michelle. *Granville Sharp's Uncovered Letter and the Zong Massacre*. New York: Palgrave Pivot, 2018.
Ferguson, J. A., et al. "Jamaica." *Encyclopaedia Britannica*. Last modified July 2, 2024. <https://www.britannica.com/place/Jamaica.>
Ferguson, Moira. "Mansfield Park: Slavery, Colonialism, and Gender." *Oxford Literary Review* 13, no. 1 (1991): 118–39.
Fick, Carolyn E. *The Making of Haiti: The Saint Domingue Revolution from Below*. Knoxville, TN: University of Tennessee Press, 1990.

Fields, Barbara J., and Karen E. Fields. *Racecraft: The Soul of Inequality in American Life.* London and New York: Verso, 2012.

Filmer, Sir Robert. "Patriarcha, or The Natural Power of Kings (1680)." In *Patriarcha and Other Writings*, edited by Johann P. Sommerville, 1–68. Cambridge: Cambridge University Press, 1991.

Finkelman, Paul. *Slavery and the Founders: Race and Liberty in the Age of Jefferson.* New York: Routledge, 2014.

Finkelman, Paul. "Slavery and the Northwest Ordinance: A Study in Ambiguity." *Journal of the Early Republic* 6, no. 4 (1986): 343–70.

Fisher, Rebecka Rutledge. *Habitations of the Veil: Metaphor and the Poetics of Black Being in African American Literature.* Albany, NY: State University of New York Press, 2014.

Fleming, Victor, George Cukor, and Sam Wood, dirs. *Gone with the Wind.* Metro-Goldwyn-Mayer, 1939.

Fletcher, Angus. *Wonderworks: The 25 Most Powerful Inventions in the History of Literature.* New York: Simon & Schuster, 2021.

Fliegelman, Jay. *Prodigals and Pilgrims: The American Revolution Against Patriarchal Authority, 1750–1800.* Cambridge: Cambridge University Press, 1985.

Floyd-Wilson, Mary. *English Ethnicity and Race in Early Modern Drama.* Cambridge: Cambridge University Press, 2003.

Fogel, Robert William. *Without Consent or Contract: The Rise and Fall of American Slavery.* New York: W. W. Norton & Co., 1989.

Foner, Eric. *Gateway to Freedom: The Hidden History of the Underground Railroad.* New York: W. W. Norton & Co., 2015.

Ford, Susan Allen. "It is about Lovers' Vows: Kotzebue, Inchbald, and the Players of *Mansfield Park*." *Persuasions On-Line* 27, no. 1 (Winter 2006). <https://jasna.org/persuasions/on-line/vol27no1/ford.htm>

Fortescue, John. "Introduction." In *Sir John Fortescue: On the Laws and Governance of England*, edited by Shelley Lockwood, pp. xxix–xxxviii. Cambridge: Cambridge University Press, 1997.

Foucault, Michel. *The History of Sexuality, Volume 1: An Introduction.* Translated by Robert Hurley. New York: Vintage Books, 1978.

Fowler, Corinne. "Revisiting *Mansfield Park*: The Critical and Literary Legacies of Edward W. Said's Essay 'Jane Austen and Empire.'" *Cambridge Journal of Postcolonial Literary Inquiry* 4, no. 3 (2017): 362–81.

Franklin, Benjamin. "Letter Transmitting Letter from James Pemberton and a Petition from the Pennsylvania Society for Promoting the Abolition of Slavery to Vice President John Adams." February 9, 1790. Record Group 46, *Petitions and Memorials and Resolutions of State Legislatures Submitted to the 1st Congress.* National Archives and Records Administration, Washington, DC. National Archives Identifier 306388. <https://catalog.archives.gov/id/306388>

Franklin, Benjamin. "Poor Richard, 1745." *Founders Online*, National Archives. Accessed January 1, 2024. <https://founders.archives.gov/documents/Franklin/01-03-02-0001>

Franklin, Benjamin, "The Sommersett Case and the Slave Trade, 18–20 June 1772." In *The Papers of Benjamin Franklin*, vol. 19. *January 1–December 31, 1772*, edited by William B. Willcox, 187–88. New Haven and London: Yale University Press, 1975.

Fraser, Gordon. *Star Territory: Printing the Universe in Nineteenth-Century America.* Philadelphia: University of Pennsylvania Press, 2021.

Frey, Sylvia R. *Water from the Rock: Black Resistance in a Revolutionary Age.* Princeton: Princeton University Press, 1991.

Frohock, Richard. "Violence and Awe: The Foundations of Government in Aphra Behn's New World Settings." *Eighteenth-Century Fiction* 8, no. 4 (1996): 437–52.

Gallagher, Catherine. *Nobody's Story: The Vanishing Acts of Women Writers in the Marketplace, 1670–1820.* Berkeley, CA: University of California Press, 1995.

Ganz, Melissa J. "'A Kind of Insanity in My Spirits': *Frankenstein*, Childhood, and Criminal Intent." *Eighteenth-Century Studies* 56, no. 1 (Fall 2022): 54–75.

Garrison, William Lloyd. "Preface." In Frederick Douglass, *Narrative of the Life of Frederick Douglass, an American Slave, Written by Himself.* Boston: Anti-Slavery Office, 1845.

Gaspar, David Barry. "'Rigid and Inclement': Origins of the Jamaica Slave Laws of the Seventeenth Century." In *The Many Legalities of Early America*, edited by Christopher L. Tomlins and Bruce H. Mann. Chapel Hill, NC: University of North Carolina Press, 2001.

Gaspar, David Barry. *Bondmen and Rebels: A Study of Master–Slave Relations in Antigua, with Implications for Colonial British America*. Baltimore, MD: Johns Hopkins University Press, 1985.

Gates, Henry Louis, Jr. *The Signifying Monkey: A Theory of Afro-American Literary Criticism*. With a new preface by the author. Oxford: Oxford University Press, 2014.

Gates, Henry Louis, Jr. *The Trials of Phillis Wheatley: America's First Black Poet and her Encounters with the Founding Fathers*. New York: Basic Civitas, 2003.

Gay, Penny. *Jane Austen and the Theatre*. Cambridge: Cambridge University Press, 2002.

Gerbner, Katharine. *Christian Slavery: Conversion and Race in the Protestant Atlantic World*. Philadelphia: University of Pennsylvania Press, 2018.

Ghachem, Malick W. "The Slave's Two Bodies: The Life of an American Legal Fiction." *William and Mary Quarterly* 60, no. 4 (2003): 809–42.

Gibbon, Frank. "The Antiguan Connection." *Cambridge Quarterly* 11, no. 2 (1982): 300.

Gigante, Denise. "Facing the Ugly: The Case of *Frankenstein*." *ELH* 67, no. 2 (2000): 565–87.

Gilroy, Paul. *The Black Atlantic: Modernity and Double Consciousness*. Cambridge, MA: Harvard University Press, 1993.

Godwin, William. *Things as They Are; or, The Adventures of Caleb Williams*. 2 vols. Philadelphia: Printed for H. and P. Rice, 1795.

Goetz, Rebecca Anne. *The Baptism of Early Virginia: How Christianity Created Race*. Baltimore, MD: Johns Hopkins University Press, 2012.

Goldsworthy, Jeffrey. "From Bracton to the Reformation." In *The Sovereignty of Parliament: History and Philosophy*, 22–50. Oxford: Clarendon Press, 1999.

Gordon-Reed, Annette. "Engaging Jefferson: Blacks and the Founding Father." *William and Mary Quarterly* 57, no. 1 (2000): 171–82.

Gordon-Reed, Annette. *The Hemingses of Monticello: An American Family*. New York: W. W. Norton & Co., 2008.

Gray, Edward G. "First Partition: The Troubled Origins of the Mason-Dixon Line." In *The American Revolution Reborn*, edited by Patrick Spero and Michael Zuckerman, 255–78. Philadelphia: University of Pennsylvania Press, 2016.

Green, Katherine Sobba. "The Heroine's Blazon and Hardwicke's Marriage Act: Commodification for a Novel Market." *Tulsa Studies in Women's Literature* 9, no. 2 (1990): 273–90.

Greenberg, Janelle. *The Radical Face of the Ancient Constitution: St. Edward's "Laws" in Early Modern Political Thought*. Cambridge: Cambridge University Press, 2001.

Greenblatt, Stephen. *Marvelous Possessions: The Wonder of the New World*. Chicago: University of Chicago Press, 2017.

Griffin, Megan. "Dismembering the Sovereign in Aphra Behn's *Oroonoko*." *ELH* 86, no. 1 (2019): 123–50.

Guasco, Michael. *Slaves and Englishmen: Human Bondage in the Early Modern Atlantic World*. Philadelphia: University of Pennsylvania Press, 2014.

Hale, Matthew. *The History of the Common Law of England*. 3rd edn. London: Printed by E. and R. Nutt & R. Gosling for T. Waller, 1739.

Hall, Kim F. *Things of Darkness: Economies of Race and Gender in Early Modern England*. Ithaca, NY: Cornell University Press, 1995.

Hall, Richard, ed. *Acts Passed in the Island of Barbados from 1643 to 1762*. London, 1764.

Hamilton, Elizabeth C. "Afrofuturism and the Technologies of Survival." *African Arts* 50, no. 4 (2017): 19.

Hannah-Jones, Nikole, et al. *The 1619 Project: A New Origin Story*. New York: New York Times, 2021.

Hanson, Lenora. *The Romantic Rhetoric of Accumulation*. Stanford, CA: Stanford University Press, 2023.

Harlow, Vincent T. *A History of Barbados, 1625–1685*. Oxford: Clarendon Press, 1926.

Harpham, John Samuel. "The Causes of Complexion." Paper presented at the Triangle Intellectual History Seminar, October 25, 2020.

Harpham, John Samuel. "Two Concepts of a Slave in the South Carolina Law of Slavery." *Slavery and Abolition* 39, no. 1 (2018): 101–22.

Harpham, John Samuel. *The Intellectual Origins of American Slavery: English Ideas in the Early Modern Atlantic World*. Cambridge, MA: Harvard University Press, 2025.

Harris, Jocelyn. *Jane Austen's Art of Memory*. Cambridge: Cambridge University Press, 1989.

Harris, Jocelyn. *Satire, Celebrity, and Politics in Jane Austen*. Lewisburg, PA: Bucknell University Press, 2017.

Harris, Leslie M. "I Helped Fact-Check the 1619 Project: The Times Ignored Me." *Politico*, March 6, 2020.

Harrison, Brian. "A Genealogy of Reform in Modern Britain." In *Anti-Slavery, Religion, and Reform*, edited by Christine Bolt and Seymour Drescher, 23–44. Ann Arbor: University of Michigan Press, 2009.

Hartman, Saidiya. *Lose your Mother: A Journey along the Atlantic Slave Route*. New York: Farrar, Straus & Giroux, 2007.

Hartman, Saidiya. *Scenes of Subjection: Terror, Slavery, and Self-Making in Nineteenth-Century America*. Oxford: Oxford University Press, 1997.

Hatlen, Burton. "Milton, Mary Shelley and Patriarchy." In *Rhetoric, Literature, and Interpretation*, edited by Harry R. Garvin, 19–47. Lewisburg, PA: Bucknell University Press, 1983.

Hening, William Waller, ed. *The Statutes at Large; Being a Collection of All the Laws of Virginia from the First Session of the Legislature, in the Year 1619*. New York: R. & W. & G. Bartow, 1823.

Herschthal, Eric. *The Science of Abolition: How Slaveholders Became the Enemies of Progress*. New Haven: Yale University Press, 2021.

Hervey, James. Selections reprinted (unattributed) in *Benjamin Banneker's Pennsylvania, Delaware, Maryland and Virginia Almanack and Ephemeris for the Year of Our Lord 1792*. Baltimore, MD: William Goddard & James Angell, 1792. Originally published in *The Universal Magazine*, London, mid-eighteenth century.

Hickman, Jared. *Black Prometheus: Race and Radicalism in the Age of Atlantic Slavery*. Oxford: Oxford University Press, 2017.

Higginbotham, A. Leon, Jr. *In the Matter of Color: Race and the American Legal Process, The Colonial Period*. New York: Oxford University Press, 1978.

Hill, Christopher. *The English Bible and the Seventeenth-Century Revolution*. London: Penguin Books, 1995.

Hill, Christopher, ed. *Winstanley: "The Law of Freedom" and Other Writings*. Cambridge: Cambridge University Press, 1983.

Hippocrates. *On Airs, Waters, and Places*, edited by A. C. Burnell. Translated by Émile Littré, Johannes Antonides van der Linden, Janus Cornarius, and Francis Adams. London: Wyman & Sons for the Royal College of Physicians, 1881.

Historic Royal Palaces. "Banqueting House: The Execution of Charles I." Accessed July 31, 2023. <https://www.hrp.org.uk/banqueting-house/history-and-stories/the-execution-of-charles-i/>

Hobbes, Thomas. *Leviathan: Or the Matter, Forme & Power of a Commonwealth, Ecclesiasticall and Civill*. Cambridge: Cambridge University Press, 1904.

Hodges, Devon. "Frankenstein and the Feminine Subversion of the Novel." *Tulsa Studies in Women's Literature* 2, no. 2 (Autumn 1983): 155–64.

Hoffer, Peter Charles. *Cry Liberty: The Great Stono River Slave Rebellion of 1739*. Oxford: Oxford University Press, 2010.

Hoffer, Peter Charles. *Law and People in Colonial America*. Baltimore, MD: Johns Hopkins University Press, 1992.

Holloway, Karla F. C. *Legal Fictions: Constituting Race, Composing Literature*. Durham, NC: Duke University Press, 1994.

Horrocks, Thomas A. *Popular and Print Medicine: Almanacs and Health Advice in Early America*. Amherst, MA: University of Massachusetts Press, 2008.

Howard, Sethanne. "Benjamin Banneker and Celestial Navigation: Just How Did They Know Where They Were, Then?" *Journal of the Washington Academy of Sciences* 101, no. 1 (Spring 2015): 29–42.

Hubback, John Henry, and Edith Charlotte Hubback. *Jane Austen's Sailor Brothers: Being the Adventures of Sir Francis Austen, G.C.B., Admiral of the Fleet, and Rear-Admiral Charles Austen.* London: John Lane, 1906.

Huff, Marsha. "Sir Thomas Bertram and the Slave Trade." *Persuasions On-Line* 41, no. 2 (Summer 2021).

Hughes-Moore, Barbara. "'Ten Thousand Times More Malignant Than Her Mate': Destabilizing Gendered Assumptions Underlying the Defences of Provocation and Loss of Control through a Reading of Mary Shelley's *Frankenstein*." *Cardiff University Law School Journal of Law and Society* 48 (2021): 690–712.

Hulsebosch, Daniel J. "The Ancient Constitution and the Expanding Empire: Sir Edward Coke's British Jurisprudence." *Law and History Review* 21, no. 3 (Autumn 2003): 439–82.

Hume, David. *Essays: Moral, Political, and Literary,* edited by Eugene F. Miller. Indianapolis: Liberty Fund, 1987.

Hume, David. *Political Discourses.* Edinburgh: Printed by R. Fleming for A. Kincaid & A. Donaldson, 1752.

Hunt, Eileen. *Mary Shelley and the Rights of the Child: Political Philosophy in Frankenstein.* Philadelphia: University of Pennsylvania Press, 2017.

Hunt, Lynn Avery. *Inventing Human Rights: A History.* New York: W. W. Norton & Co., 2007.

Hussain, Azar. "Jane Austen and the Periodic Press: How Austen may have Encountered *Lovers' Vows*." *Persuasions On-Line* 43, no. 1 (Winter 2022). <https://jasna.org/publications-2/persuasions-online/volume-43-no-1/hussain-2/>

Hutton, Ronald. "Goring, George, Baron Goring (1608–1657), Royalist Army Officer." *Oxford Dictionary of National Biography*, September 23, 2004. Accessed April 13, 2024. <https://www.oxforddnb.com/view/10.1093/ref:odnb/9780198614128.001.0001/odnb-9780198614128-e-11100>

Hutton, Ronald. *The Restoration: A Political and Religious History of England and Wales, 1658–1667.* Oxford: Clarendon Press, 1987.

Inchbald, Elizabeth. *Lovers' Vows,* edited by Lance Bertelsen. In *The Works of Elizabeth Inchbald*, vol. 5. London: Pickering & Chatto, 2003.

Jacobus, Mary. "Is there a Woman in This Text?" *New Literary History* 14 (1982): 117–41.

James, C. L. R. *The Black Jacobins: Toussaint L'Ouverture and the San Domingo Revolution.* 2nd edn. New York: Vintage Books, 1963.

Jarrett, Derek. "The Regency Crisis of 1765." *English Historical Review* 85, no. 335 (1970): 282–315.

Jefferson, Thomas. *A Summary View of the Rights of British America.* Philadelphia: John Dunlap, 1774.

Jefferson, Thomas. "From Thomas Jefferson to James Monroe, 20 September 1800." In *The Papers of Thomas Jefferson*, vol. 32. *1 June 1800–16 February 1801*, edited by Barbara B. Oberg, 160–61. Princeton: Princeton University Press, 2005.

Jefferson, Thomas. "From Thomas Jefferson to John Holmes, 22 April 1820." In *The Papers of Thomas Jefferson: Retirement Series*, vol. 15. *1 September 1819–31 May 1820*, edited by J. Jefferson Looney, 550–51. Princeton: Princeton University Press, 2018.

Jefferson, Thomas. "Jefferson's 'Original Rough Draught' of the Declaration of Independence." June 1776. In *Declaring Independence: Drafting the Documents.* Library of Congress. Accessed April 23, 2023. <https://www.americaslibrary.gov/aa/jefferson/aa_jefferson_declar_2_e.html>

Jefferson, Thomas. "Letter to the Marquis de Lafayette." June 16, 1792. Gilder Lehrman Institute of American History. Accessed September 26, 2024. <https://www.gilderlehrman.org/history-resources/spotlight-primary-source/jefferson-french-and-haitian-revolutions-1792>

Jefferson, Thomas. *Notes on the State of Virginia.* New York: Penguin Books, 1999.

Jefferson, Thomas. "'Original Rough Draught' of the Declaration of Independence." In *The Papers of Thomas Jefferson*, vol. 1. *1760–1776*, edited by Julian P. Boyd, 243–47. Princeton: Princeton University Press, 1950.

Jefferson, Thomas. *The Writings of Thomas Jefferson: 1760–1775.* New York: G. P. Putnam's Sons, 1892.

Jennings, Willie James. *The Christian Imagination: Theology and the Origins of Race.* New Haven: Yale University Press, 2010.

Johnson, Barbara. "My Monster/my Self." *Diacritics* 12 (1982): 2–10.

Johnson, Claudia L. *Jane Austen: Women, Politics, and the Novel*. Chicago: University of Chicago Press, 1988.

Johnson, Samuel. *Taxation No Tyranny: An Answer to the Resolutions and Address of the American Congress*. 4th edn. London: Printed for T. Cadell, 1775.

Johnson Kindred, Sheila. *Jane Austen's Transatlantic Sister: The Life and Letters of Fanny Palmer Austen*. Montreal: McGill–Queen's University Press, 2017.

Johnston, Katherine. *The Nature of Slavery: Environment and Plantation Labor in the Anglo-Atlantic World*. Oxford: Oxford University Press, 2022.

Johnston, Neil. "The Trial of Charles I." Blogpost, The National Archives (UK), January 30, 2019. <https://blog.nationalarchives.gov.uk/trial-charles-i/>

Jones, John Avery. "George Austen as a (Nominal) Trustee of a Plantation in Antigua: The Legal Position." In *Report for 2021*, 33–48. London: The Jane Austen Society, 2021.

Jorati, Julia, ed. "William Cowper, 'The Negro's Complaint' (1788)." In *Slavery in Early Modern Philosophy, 1765–1800: Essential Readings*. New York: Oxford University Press, 2026.

Jordan, Don, and Michael Walsh. *White Cargo: The Forgotten History of Britain's White Slaves in America*. New York: New York University Press, 2008.

Jordan, Winthrop D. *White over Black: American Attitudes Toward the Negro, 1550–1812*. Chapel Hill, NC: University of North Carolina Press for the Institute of Early American History and Culture at Williamsburg, VA, 1968.

Joyce, James. "Lecture on Daniel Defoe." Lecture delivered at the Università Popolare, Trieste, Italy, 1912.

Kahn, Victoria. *Wayward Contracts: The Crisis of Political Obligation in England, 1640–1674*. Princeton: Princeton University Press, 2004.

Kakoudaki, Despina. *Anatomy of a Robot: Literature, Cinema, and the Cultural Work of Artificial People*. New Brunswick, NJ: Rutgers University Press, 2014.

Kakoudaki, Despina. "Unmaking People: The Politics of Negation in *Frankenstein* and *Ex Machina*." *Science Fiction Studies* 45, no. 2 (2018): 289–307.

Kantorowicz, Ernst H. *The King's Two Bodies: A Study in Medieval Political Theology*. Rev. edn. Princeton: Princeton University Press, 2016.

Kaplan, Laurie. "The Rushworths of Wimpole Street." *Persuasions* 33 (2011): 202–14.

Kaplan, M. Lindsay. *Figuring Racism in Medieval Christianity*. New York: Oxford University Press, 2019.

Kaufmann, Miranda. *Heiresses: Marriage, Inheritance, and Slavery in the Caribbean*. London: Pegasus Books, 2024.

Keenleyside, Heather. *Animals and Other People: Literary Forms and Living Beings in the Long Eighteenth Century*. Philadelphia: University of Pennsylvania Press, 2016.

Keirn, Tim. "Daniel Defoe and the Royal African Company." *Historical Research* 61, no. 145 (June 1988): 240–59.

Kidd, Colin. *The Forging of Races: Race and Scripture in the Protestant Atlantic World, 1600–2000*. Cambridge: Cambridge University Press, 2006.

King, Martin Luther, Jr. *The Trumpet of Conscience*. Boston: Beacon Press, 1968.

Kirkham, Margaret. *Jane Austen, Feminism and Fiction*. London: Bloomsbury, 2000.

Koenigs, Thomas. *Founded in Fiction: The Uses of Fiction in the Early United States*. Princeton: Princeton University Press, 2021.

Konig, David Thomas, and Michael P. Zuckert, eds. *Jefferson's Legal Commonplace Book*. Princeton: Princeton University Press, 2019.

Koretsky, Deanna P. "Habeas Corpus and the Politics of Freedom: Slavery and Romantic Suicide." *Essays in Romanticism* 22, no. 1 (2015): 21–33.

Kroll, Richard. "Fatal Fluency: Behn's Fiction and the Restoration Letter." *Eighteenth-Century Fiction* 12, nos. 3–4 (2000): 417–34.

Kukla, Jon. *Mr. Jefferson's Women*. New York: Alfred A. Knopf, 2007.

Kupperman, Karen Ordahl. "Fear of Hot Climates in the Anglo-American Colonial Experience." *William and Mary Quarterly* 41, no. 2 (April 1984): 213–40.

Lamore, Eric D., ed. *Teaching Olaudah Equiano's Narrative: Pedagogical Strategies and New Perspectives*. Knoxville, TN: University of Tennessee Press, 2012.

Le Faye, Deirdre. *Jane Austen: A Family Record.* 2nd edn. Cambridge: Cambridge University Press, 2004.

Ledwidge, Bernard. "The 'Strange Business in America.'" In *Collected Reports of the Jane Austen Society, 1949–67*, 199. London: The Jane Austen Society, 1967.

Lepore, Jill. "The Strange and Twisted Life of *Frankenstein*." *The New Yorker*, February 5, 2018. <https://www.newyorker.com/magazine/2018/02/12/the-strange-and-twisted-life-of-frankenstein>

Lepore, Jill. *New York Burning: Liberty, Slavery, and Conspiracy in Eighteenth-Century Manhattan.* New York: Alfred A. Knopf, 2005.

Levine, Caroline. *Forms: Whole, Rhythm, Hierarchy, Network.* Princeton: Princeton University Press, 2015.

Levine, George. "The Ambiguous Heritage of *Frankenstein*." In *The Endurance of Frankenstein: Essays on Mary Shelley's Novel*, edited by George Levine and U. C. Knoepflmacher, 3–30. Berkeley, CA: University of California Press, 1979.

Levy, Jacob T. *Rationalism, Pluralism, and Freedom.* Oxford: Oxford University Press, 2015.

Lifton, Robert J. *The Nazi Doctors: Medical Killing and the Psychology of Genocide.* New York: Basic Books, 1986.

Ligon, Richard. *A True and Exact History of the Island of Barbados.* London: Printed for Humphrey Moseley, 1657.

Lincoln, Abraham. "Second Inaugural Address." March 4, 1865. In *The Collected Works of Abraham Lincoln*, edited by Roy P. Basler, vol. 8, 332–33. New Brunswick, NJ: Rutgers University Press, 1953.

Locke, John. *Some Thoughts Concerning Education.* 12th edn. London: Printed for J. Brown, 1752.

Locke, John. *Two Treatises of Government. Edited by Peter Laslett. Student ed. Cambridge Texts in the History of Political Thought.* Cambridge: Cambridge University Press, 1988.

Locke, Mary Stoughton. *Anti-Slavery in America from the Introduction of African Slaves to the Prohibition of the Slave Trade (1619–1808).* Gloucester, MA: Radcliffe College, 1901.

Looser, Devoney. "Breaking the Silence: The Austen Family's Complex Entanglements with Slavery." In *Report for 2021*, 25–32. London: The Jane Austen Society, 2021.

Looser, Devoney. "Breaking the Silence: Exploring the Austen Family's Complex Entanglements with Slavery." *Times Literary Supplement*, May 21, 2021.

Looser, Devoney. "Heroics All at Sea: Jane Austen's Brother and 'Crushing' the Slave Trade." *Times Literary Supplement*, July 8, 2022.

Lorimer, Douglas A. "Black Slaves and English Liberty: A Re-examination of Racial Slavery in England." *Immigrants and Minorities* 3, no. 2 (July 1984): 121–50.

Lovejoy, Paul E. "Issues of Motivation—Vassa/Equiano and Carretta's Critique of the Evidence." *Slavery and Abolition* 28, no. 1 (2007): 121–35.

Lovell Banks, Taunya. "Dangerous Woman: Elizabeth Key's Freedom Suit—Subjecthood and Racialized Identity in Seventeenth-Century Colonial Virginia." *Akron Law Review* 41, no. 4 (2008): 799–836.

McGrath, Alister E. *Reformation Thought: An Introduction.* 4th edn. Oxford: Wiley-Blackwell, 2012.

McIlwain, Charles Howard. *The American Revolution: A Constitutional Interpretation.* New York: Macmillan, 1923.

McKeon, Michael. *The Origins of the English Novel, 1600–1740.* Baltimore, MD: Johns Hopkins University Press, 1987.

MacLeod, Duncan J. "The American Revolution and the Institution of Slavery." In *Slavery, Race, and the American Revolution*, edited by Duncan J. MacLeod, 15–61. Cambridge: Cambridge University Press, 1974.

Malchow, H. L. "Frankenstein's Monster and Images of Race in Nineteenth-Century Britain." *Past and Present* 139 (1993): 90–130.

MacNeil, William P. "The Monstrous Body of the Law: Wollstonecraft vs Shelley." *Australian Feminist Law Journal* 12, no. 1 (1999): 23–38.

Macpherson, C. B. *The Political Theory of Possessive Individualism: Hobbes to Locke*. 2nd edn. Oxford: Oxford University Press, 2011.
Marche, Stephen. "The Racism of *Gone with the Wind* is Still with Us." *Esquire*, December 15, 2014. Accessed November 9, 2024. <https://www.esquire.com/entertainment/movies/a30109/gone-with-the-wind-racism/>
Marsh, Sarah. "Changes of Air: The Somerset Case and *Mansfield Park*'s Imperial Plots." *Eighteenth-Century Studies* 53, no. 2 (Winter 2020): 213–30.
Marsh, Sarah. "Imoinda's Rebellion: Sovereignty, Slavery, and the Ancient Constitution in Aphra Behn's *Oroonoko*." *ELH* 90, no. 3 (2023): 639–66.
Marshall, Alan. "'Memorialls for Mrs Affora': Aphra Behn and the Restoration Intelligence World." *Women's Writing* 22, no. 1 (2015): 13–33.
Marshall, P. J. *Edmund Burke and the British Empire in the West Indies: Wealth, Power, and Slavery*. Oxford: Oxford University Press, 2019.
Marx, Karl. *Capital: A Critique of Political Economy*. New York: Modern Library, 1906.
Meacham, Jon. *Thomas Jefferson: The Art of Power*. New York: Random House Trade Paperbacks, 2012.
Mellor, Anne K. "Frankenstein, Racial Science, and the Yellow Peril." *Nineteenth-Century Contexts* 23, no. 1 (2001): 1–28.
Merkel, William G. "A Founding Father on Trial: Jefferson's Rights Talk and the Problem of Slavery during the Revolutionary Period." *Rutgers Law Review* 64 (2011): 593–646.
Merkel, William G. "Jefferson's Failed Anti-Slavery Proviso of 1784 and the Nascence of Free Soil Constitutionalism." *Seton Hall Law Review* 38, no. 2 (2008): 555–91.
Merrill, Thomas W. "The Later Jefferson and the Problem of Natural Rights." In *The Political Thought of the Civil War*, edited by Thomas W. Merrill, Alan Levine, and James R. Stoner Jr., 17–40. Lawrence, KS: University Press of Kansas, 2018.
Michals, Teresa. "'That Sole and Despotic Dominion': Slaves, Wives, and Game in Blackstone's *Commentaries*." *Eighteenth-Century Studies* 27, no. 2 (1993): 195–216.
Miller, D. A. *Jane Austen, or The Secret of Style*. Princeton: Princeton University Press, 2003.
Mills, Charles W. *The Racial Contract*. Ithaca, NY: Cornell University Press, 1997.
Milsom, S. F. C. *Historical Foundations of the Common Law*. 2nd edn. London: Butterworths, 1981.
Milton, John. *Paradise Lost*, edited by Alastair Fowler. 2nd edn. London: Longman, 1998.
Milton, John. *The Tenure of Kings and Magistrates*. London: Matthew Simmons, 1649.
Mitchell, Margaret. *Gone with the Wind*. London: Pocket Books, 2008.
Molesworth, Robert, Viscount Molesworth. *An Account of Denmark, as It Was in the Year 1692*. London: Printed for Timothy Goodwin, 1694.
Molineux, Catherine. "False Gifts/Exotic Fictions: Epistemologies of Sovereignty and Assent in Aphra Behn's *Oroonoko*." *ELH* 80, no. 2 (2013): 457–89.
Montaigne, Michel Eyquem de. "Of Cannibals." In *The Complete Essays of Montaigne*, translated by Donald M. Frame, 150–59. Stanford, CA: Stanford University Press, 1973.
Montesquieu, Charles de Secondat, baron de. *The Complete Works of M. de Montesquieu*. Translated from the French. London: T. Evans & W. Davis, 1777.
More, Hannah. *Slavery, a Poem*. London: T. Cadell, 1788.
Morgan, Edmund S. *American Slavery, American Freedom: The Ordeal of Colonial Virginia*. New York: W. W. Norton & Co., 1975.
Morgan, Edmund S. *Inventing the People: The Rise of Popular Sovereignty in England and America*. New York: W. W. Norton & Co., 1989.
Morgan, Jennifer L. "'Some Could Suckle over their Shoulder': Male Travelers, Female Bodies, and the Gendering of Racial Ideology." In *Laboring Women: Reproduction and Gender in New World Slavery*, 12–49. Philadelphia: University of Pennsylvania Press, 2004.
Morris, Marc. *The Norman Conquest: The Battle of Hastings and the Fall of Anglo-Saxon England*. New York: Pegasus Books, 2013.
Morrison, Toni. *A Mercy*. New York: Alfred A. Knopf, 2008.

Morrison, Toni. *Playing in the Dark: Whiteness and the Literary Imagination*. Cambridge, MA: Harvard University Press, 1992.

Mudrick, Marvin. *Jane Austen: Irony as Defense and Discovery*. Berkeley, CA: University of California Press, 1952.

Mullan, John. *How Novels Work*. Oxford: Oxford University Press, 2006.

Müller-Wille, Staffan, and Hans-Jörg Rheinberger. *A Cultural History of Heredity*. Chicago: University of Chicago Press, 2012.

Muller, Hannah Weiss. *Subjects and Sovereign: Bonds of Belonging in the Eighteenth-Century British Empire*. Oxford: Oxford University Press, 2017.

Mulvey-Roberts, Marie. "Mary Shelley, *Frankenstein*, and Slavery." In *Dangerous Bodies: Historicizing the Gothic Corporeal*, edited by Marie Mulvey-Roberts, 89–108. Manchester: Manchester University Press, 2016.

Münzel-Everling, Dietlinde. "Imperial Law and Roland Statues." *Forum Historiae Iuris*, September 12, 1997. <https://forhistiur.net/en/1997-09-munzel-everling/>

Nelson, William E. *E Pluribus Unum: How the Common Law Helped Unify and Liberate Colonial America, 1607–1776*. New York: Oxford University Press, 2019.

Newman, Brooke N. *A Dark Inheritance: Blood, Race, and Sex in Colonial Jamaica*. New Haven: Yale University Press, 2018.

Nocks, Lisa. "*Frankenstein*, in a Better Light." *Journal of Social and Evolutionary Systems* 20, no. 2 (1997): 137–55.

Novak, Maximillian E. *Daniel Defoe: Master of Fictions: His Life and Ideas*. Oxford: Oxford University Press, 2001.

Nussbaum, Felicity A. *Torrid Zones: Maternity, Sexuality and Empire in Eighteenth-Century English Narratives*. Baltimore, MD: Johns Hopkins University Press, 1995.

Nyquist, Mary. *Arbitrary Rule: Slavery, Tyranny, and the Power of Life and Death*. Chicago: University of Chicago Press, 2013.

Okorafor, Nnedi. "Africanfuturism Defined." *Nnedi's Wahala Zone* (blog), October 19, 2019. <https://nnedi.blogspot.com/2019/10/africanfuturism-defined.html>

Oldham, James. "New Light on Mansfield and Slavery." *Journal of British Studies* 27, no. 1 (1988): 45–68.

Olney, James. "'I was Born': Slave Narratives, Their Status as Autobiography and as Literature." *Callaloo* 20 (1984): 46–73.

Olwell, Robert. *Masters, Slaves, and Subjects: The Culture of Power in the South Carolina Low Country, 1740–1790*. Ithaca, NY: Cornell University Press, 1998.

O'Melinn, Liam Séamus. "The American Revolution and Constitutionalism in the Seventeenth-Century West Indies." *Columbia Law Review* 95, no. 1 (1995): 104–59.

Otis, James. *The Rights of the British Colonists Asserted and Proved*. 3rd edn. Boston, 1766.

Pagden, Anthony. *Lords of All the World: Ideologies of Empire in Spain, Britain and France c. 1500–c. 1800*. New Haven: Yale University Press, 1995.

Painter, Nell Irvin. *The History of White People*. New York: W. W. Norton & Co., 2010.

Papers of Thomas Jefferson, Retirement Series, vol. 3. *12 August 1810 to 17 June 1811*, edited by J. Jefferson Looney. Princeton: Princeton University Press, 2006.

Parker, Matthew. *Willoughbyland: England's Lost Colony*. London: Windmill Books, 2015.

Parliament of the United Kingdom. "Act of Uniformity 1662." *Parliamentary Archives—Living Heritage*. Accessed November 1, 2025. <https://www.parliament.uk/about/living-heritage/transformingsociety/private-lives/religion/collections/common-prayer/act-of-uniformity-1662/>

Parliament of the United Kingdom. "Act of Union 1707." Accessed November 9, 2024. <https://www.parliament.uk/about/living-heritage/evolutionofparliament/legislativescrutiny/act-of-union-1707/>

Parliament of the United Kingdom. "The Transatlantic Slave Trade." Heritage Collections. Accessed July 1, 2024. <https://heritagecollections.parliament.uk/stories/the-transatlantic-slave-trade/>

Parry, Sarah. "Mansfield Park and the Idea of 'Old' and 'New' Money: A Study in the Interpretation of Historic Houses." *Persuasions On-Line* 35, no. 1 (Winter 2014). <https://jasna.org/persuasions/on-line/vol35no1/parry.html>

Pasley, Charles William. *Essay on the Military Policy and Institutions of the British Empire.* London: E. Lloyd, 1811.

Patterson, Annabel M. *Censorship and Interpretation: The Conditions of Writing and Reading in Early Modern England.* Madison, WI: University of Wisconsin Press, 1984.

Patterson, Orlando. *Freedom in the Making of Western Culture.* New York: Basic Books, 1991.

Patterson, Orlando. "Freedom, Slavery, and the Modern Construction of Rights." In *The Cultural Values of Europe*, edited by Hans Joas and Klaus Wiegandt, translated by Alex Skinner, 113–33. Liverpool: Liverpool University Press, 2008.

Patterson, Orlando. *Slavery and Social Death: A Comparative Study.* Cambridge, MA: Harvard University Press, 1982.

Patterson, Orlando. *The Sociology of Slavery: An Analysis of the Origins, Development and Structure of Negro Slave Society in Jamaica.* Rutherford, NJ: Fairleigh Dickinson University Press, 1969.

Peacey, Jason. *The Regicides and the Execution of Charles I.* Basingstoke: Palgrave Macmillan, 2001.

Peake, Richard Brinsley. "Presumption; Or, the Fate of Frankenstein." In *Seven Gothic Dramas: 1789–1825*, edited by Jeffrey N. Cox. Athens, GA: Ohio University Press, 1992.

Perry, Ruth. "Austen and Empire: A Thinking Woman's Guide to British Imperialism." *Persuasions* 16 (1994): 95–106.

Pettigrew, William A. *Freedom's Debt: The Royal African Company and the Politics of the Atlantic Slave Trade, 1672–1752.* Chapel Hill, NC: University of North Carolina Press, 2013.

Phelps, John. "The Act." In *Trial of Charles I.* The National Archives (UK). Accessed June 20, 2021. <https://www.nationalarchives.gov.uk/museum/additional_image_types.asp?item_id=22&image_id=30&extra_image_type_id=2.

Plowden, Edmund. *Commentaries or Reports.* London, 1816. Originally published 1571; first English translation printed in 1761.

Pocock, J. G. A. *The Ancient Constitution and the Feudal Law: A Study of English Historical Thought in the Seventeenth Century.* Rev. edn. Cambridge: Cambridge University Press, 1987.

Pocock, J. G. A. *Virtue, Commerce, and History: Essays on Political Thought and History, Chiefly in the Eighteenth Century.* Cambridge: Cambridge University Press, 1985.

Poovey, Mary. *The Proper Lady and the Woman Writer: Ideology as Style in the Works of Mary Wollstonecraft, Mary Shelley, and Jane Austen.* Chicago: University of Chicago Press, 1984.

Pordzik, Ralph. "Fiction, the Law, and the Docile Body: The Uncanny Presence of Kant and the Marquis de Sade in Mary Shelley's *Frankenstein.*" *Zeitschrift für Anglistik und Amerikanistik* 77, no. 2 (2009): 109–23.

Porter, Roy, and Dorothy Porter. *In Sickness and in Health: The British Experience, 1650–1850.* London: Fourth Estate, 1988.

President's Advisory 1776 Commission. *The 1776 Report.* Washington, DC: The White House, 2021. <https://trumpwhitehouse.archives.gov/wp-content/uploads/2021/01/The-Presidents-Advisory-1776-Commission-Final-Report.pdf>

Priest, Claire. "Creating an American Property Law: Alienability and its Limits in American History." *Harvard Law Review* 120 (2006): 385–459.

Priest, Claire. *Credit Nation: Property Laws and Institutions in Early America.* Princeton: Princeton University Press, 2021.

Probert, Rebecca. "Control over Marriage in England and Wales, 1753–1823: The Clandestine Marriages Act of 1753 in Context." *Law and History Review* 27, no. 2 (2009): 413–50.

Public Broadcasting Service. *The Black Atlantic: 1500–1800.* Directed by Phil Bertelsen, Asako Gladsjo Leslie, Sabin Streeter, and Jamila Wignot. 2013. Streaming video. <https://video.alexanderstreet.com/watch/the-black-atlantic-1500-1800>

Quarles, Benjamin. "Lord Dunmore as Liberator." *William and Mary Quarterly* 15, no. 4 (1958): 494–507.

Ragatz, Lowell J. *The Fall of the Planter Class in the British Caribbean, 1763–1833: A Study in Social and Economic History.* New York: Octagon Books, 1963.

Rakove, Jack N. *Original Meanings: Politics and Ideas in the Making of the Constitution.* New York: Alfred A. Knopf, 1996.

Randall, Willard Sterne. *Thomas Jefferson: A Life.* New York: Harper Perennial Modern Classics, 1993.

Randel, Fred V. "The Political Geography of Horror in Mary Shelley's *Frankenstein*." *ELH* 70, no. 2 (2003): 465–91.

Rastell, John. *A New Interlude and a Mery of the Nature of the Four Elements* (ca. 1519). In *The First Three English Books on America*, edited by Edward Arber, p. xxi. Birmingham, 1885.

Rawlin, William, ed. *The Laws of Barbados Collected in One Volume.* London: Printed for William Rawlin, 1699.

Rediker, Marcus. *The Slave Ship: A Human History.* London: Penguin Books, 2008.

Rediker, Marcus, and Peter Linebaugh. *The Many-Headed Hydra: Sailors, Slaves, Commoners, and the Hidden History of the Revolutionary Atlantic.* Boston: Beacon Press, 2000.

Reid, Brittany. "Acting Monstrous: Staging the Creature in *Presumption; or, The Fate of Frankenstein*." *Supernatural Studies* 2, no. 2 (2015): 59–72.

Reports of Cases Determined in the General Court of Virginia from 1730 to 1740, and from 1768 to 1772.

Resnick, David. "Locke and the Rejection of the Ancient Constitution." *Political Theory* 12, no. 1 (1984): 97–114.

Richards, Cynthia. "Interrogating *Oroonoko*: Torture in a New World and a New Fiction of Power." *Eighteenth-Century Fiction* 25, no. 4 (2013): 647–76.

Roberts, Justin. *Fragile Empire: Slavery in the Early English Tropics, 1645–1720.* Cambridge: Cambridge University Press, 2023.

Robertson, Geoffrey. *The Tyrannicide Brief: The Story of the Man Who Sent Charles I to the Scaffold.* New York: Anchor Books, 2007.

Rogers, Pat, ed. *Defoe: The Critical Heritage.* London: Routledge & Kegan Paul, 1972.

Rosenthal, Laura J. *Ways of the World: Theater and Cosmopolitanism in the Restoration and Beyond.* Ithaca, NY: Cornell University Press, 2020.

Rothman, Adam. *Slave Country: American Expansion and the Origins of the Deep South.* Cambridge, MA: Harvard University Press, 2002.

Royal Household. "Queen Charlotte (19 May 1744–17 November 1818)." Accessed December 18, 2023.< https://www.royal.uk/encyclopedia/queen-charlotte-19-may-1744-17-november-1818>.

Rubenstein, Marc A. "'My Accursed Origin': The Search for the Mother in *Frankenstein*." *Studies in Romanticism* 15, no. 2 (Spring 1976): 165–94.

Rugemer, Edward B. *Slave Law and the Politics of Resistance in the Early Atlantic World.* Cambridge, MA: Harvard University Press, 2018.

Rugemer, Edward B. "The Development of Mastery and Race in the Comprehensive Slave Codes of the Greater Caribbean during the Seventeenth Century." *William and Mary Quarterly* 70, no. 3 (2013): 429–58.

Rusert, Britt. *Fugitive Science: Empiricism and Freedom in Early African American Culture.* New York: New York University Press, 2017.

Ruston, Sharon. *Shelley and Vitality.* New York: Palgrave Macmillan, 2005.

Ruston, Sharon. *The Science of Life and Death in Frankenstein.* Oxford: Bodleian Library Publishing, 2022.

Said, Edward W. *Culture and Imperialism.* London: Chatto & Windus, 1993; New York: Vintage, 1994.

Saillant, John. "'Profitable Reading': Literacy, Christianity, and Constitutionalism in Olaudah Equiano's *Interesting Narrative*." In *Teaching Olaudah Equiano's Narrative: Pedagogical Strategies and New Perspectives*, edited by Eric D. Lamore, 141–58. Knoxville, TN: University of Tennessee Press, 2012.

Sanford, Robert. *Surinam Justice in the Case of Several Persons Proscribed by Certain Usurpers of Power in That Colony.* London: Printed for the author, 1662.

Scammell, Jean. "The Origin and Limitations of the Liberty of Durham." *English Historical Review* 81, no. 320 (1966): 449–73.

Schapiro, Meyer. "'Cain's Jaw-Bone that did the First Murder.'" *The Art Bulletin* 24, no. 3 (1942): 205–12.

Scherr, Arthur. "Intellectual Roots of Thomas Jefferson's Opinions on Slavery: Montesquieu's Impact." *Journal of Transatlantic Studies* 19 (2021): 189–214.

Schonhorn, Manuel. *Defoe's Politics: Parliament, Power, Kingship, and Robinson Crusoe.* Cambridge: Cambridge University Press, 1991.

Schuyler, Robert Livingston. *Parliament and the British Empire: Some Constitutional Controversies Concerning Imperial Legislative Jurisdiction.* New York: Columbia University Press, 1929.

Scott, Walter. *The Miscellaneous Prose Works of Sir Walter Scott.* Paris: Baudry's European Library, 1837.

Sedgwick, Eve Kosofsky. "Jane Austen and the Masturbating Girl." *Critical Inquiry* 17, no. 4 (Summer 1991): 818–37.

Seed, David. "Frankenstein—Parable of Spectacle?" *Criticism* 24, no. 4 (1982): 327–40.

Seed, Patricia. *Ceremonies of Possession in Europe's Conquest of the New World, 1492–1640.* Cambridge: Cambridge University Press, 1995.

Sergent, Michael Renwick. *An Address, to the Inhabitants in General of Great Britain, and Ireland: Relating to a Few of the Consequences which Must Naturally Result from the Abolition of the Slave Trade.* London, 1788.

Serwer, Adam. "The Fight over the 1619 Project is Not about the Facts." *The Atlantic*, December 23, 2019.

Seymour, Susanne, Stephen Daniels, and Charles Watkins. "Estate and Empire: Sir George Cornewall's Management of Moccas, Herefordshire and La Taste, Grenada, 1771–1819." *Journal of Historical Geography* 24, no. 3 (1998): 333–55.

Shakespeare, William. *Julius Caesar*, edited by Barbara A. Mowat and Paul Werstine. Washington, DC: Folger Shakespeare Library, 1992.

Shakespeare, William. *Othello: The Moor of Venice*, edited by Barbara Mowat, Paul Werstine, Michael Poston, and Rebecca Niles. Folger Shakespeare Library. Accessed April 30, 2023. <https://www.folger.edu/explore/shakespeares-works/othello/read/>

Shapiro, Barbara J. *A Culture of Fact: England, 1550–1720.* Ithaca, NY: Cornell University Press, 1991.

Sharp, Granville. *A Declaration of the People's Natural Right to a Share in the Legislature, Which Is the Fundamental Principle of the British Constitution of State.* Philadelphia: Reprinted and sold by John Dunlap, 1774.

Sharp, Granville. *The Just Limitation of Slavery in the Laws of God, Compared with the Unbounded Claims of the African Traders and British American Slaveholders.* London: B. White & E. and C. Dilly, 1776.

Sharpe, Christina. *In the Wake: On Blackness and Being.* Durham, NC: Duke University Press, 2016.

Shelley, Mary. "Author's Introduction to the Standard Novels Edition (1831)." In *Frankenstein.* New York: Oxford University Press, 1993.

Shelley, Mary. *Frankenstein: The 1818 Text*, edited by Marilyn Butler. New York: Oxford University Press, 2008.

Silverstein, Jake. "An Update to *The 1619 Project*." *New York Times*, March 11, 2020.

Silverstein, Jake. "The 1619 Project and the Long Battle over U.S. History." *New York Times Magazine*, November 9, 2021.

Slauter, Eric. *The State as a Work of Art: The Cultural Origins of the Constitution.* Chicago: University of Chicago Press, 2009.

Smallwood, Stephanie E. *Saltwater Slavery: A Middle Passage from Africa to American Diaspora.* Cambridge, MA: Harvard University Press, 2007.

Smith, David L. "Cary, Lucius, Second Viscount Falkland (1609/10–1643), Politician and Author." *Oxford Dictionary of National Biography*, September 23, 2004. Accessed April 13, 2024. <https://www.oxforddnb.com/view/10.1093/ref:odnb/9780198614128.001.0001/odnb-9780198614128-e-4841>

Smith, Peter. "Mansfield Park and the World Stage." *Cambridge Quarterly* 23, no. 3 (1994): 206–22.

Sobel, Dava. *Longitude: The True Story of a Lone Genius Who Solved the Greatest Scientific Problem of His Time*. New York: Bloomsbury, 1995.

Southam, Brian. "The Silence of the Bertrams: Slavery and the Chronology of *Mansfield Park*." *Times Literary Supplement*, February 17, 1995.

Southam, Brian. *Jane Austen and the Navy*. London: National Maritime Museum, 2005.

Spelman, Henry. "The Original, Growth, Propagation and Condition of Feuds and Tenures by Knight-Service, in England." In *Reliquiæ Spelmannianæ*. Oxford: Theatre, 1698.

Stedman, John Gabriel. *Narrative of a Five Years' Expedition Against the Revolted Negroes of Surinam, in Guiana, on the Wild Coast of South America, from the Year 1772 to 1777*. London: J. Johnson & T. Payne, 1813.

Steinfeld, Robert J. *The Invention of Free Labor: The Employment Relation in English and American Law and Culture, 1350–1870*. Chapel Hill, NC: University of North Carolina Press, 1991.

Stern, Simon. "Reasonable Reasons, Reasonable Persons, and Legal Fictions." *Representations* 172 (2025): 1–30.

Stoler, Ann Laura. *Along the Archival Grain: Epistemic Anxieties and Colonial Common Sense*. Princeton: Princeton University Press, 2010.

Storing, Herbert J. "Slavery and the Moral Foundations of the American Republic." In *Slavery and its Consequences: The Constitution, Equality, and Race*, edited by Robert A. Goldwin and Art Kaufman, 3–34. Washington, DC: American Enterprise Institute for Public Policy Research, 1988.

Stump, J. B., and Chad Meister, eds. *Original Sin and the Fall: Five Views*. Westmont, IL: IVP Academic, 2020.

Sussman, Charlotte. *Consuming Anxieties: Consumer Protest, Gender, and British Slavery, 1713–1833*. Stanford, CA: Stanford University Press, 2000.

Sussman, Charlotte. "The Other Problem with Women." In *Rereading Aphra Behn: History, Theory, and Criticism*, edited by Heidi Hutner, 211–29. Charlottesville, VA: University Press of Virginia, 1993.

Svalastog, Julie M. *Mastering the Worst of Trades: England's Early Africa Companies and their Traders, 1618–1672*. Leiden: Brill, 2021.

Tacitus. *Agricola*, edited by A. J. Woodman and Christina Shuttleworth Kraus. Cambridge: Cambridge University Press, 2014.

Terada, Rei. *Metaracial: Hegel, Antiblackness, and Political Identity*. Chicago: University of Chicago Press, 2023.

"The 1619 Project." *New York Times Magazine*, August 14, 2019.

The Debate on a Motion for the Abolition of the Slave-Trade. House of Commons (Great Britain), April 2, 1792. London: n.p., 1792.

Tiebout, Cornelius. *Olaudah Equiano or Gustavus Vassa the African*. 1791. Engraving. Library Company of Philadelphia Digital Collections. Accessed January 23, 2026. <https://digital.librarycompany.org/islandora/object/digitool%3A128586>

Tissot, Samuel Auguste David. *Advice to the People in General, in Regard to Their Health*. Boston: Mein & Fleeming, 1767.

Todd, Janet. *Aphra Behn: A Secret Life*. London: Fentum Press, 2017.

Todd, Janet. "Introduction." In *Oroonoko; or, The Royal Slave*, by Aphra Behn, pp. xxiii–xxxv. New York: Penguin Classics, 2003.

Tomalin, Claire. *Jane Austen: A Life*. New York: Vintage Books, 1999.

Trouillot, Michel-Rolph. *Silencing the Past: Power and the Production of History*. Boston: Beacon Press, 1995.

Turner, Katherine. "Cowper, Slave Narratives, and the Antebellum American Reading Public." *Cowper & Newton Journal* 6. Accessed December 12, 2024. <https://cowperandnewtonmuseum.org.uk/journal/j6-article-turner/>

[Tyrrell, James]. *Patriarcha non Monarcha. The Patriarch Unmonarch'd: Being Observations on a Late Treatise and Divers Other Miscellanies, Published Under the Name of Sir Robert Filmer, Baronet*. London: Richard Janeway in Queens-head-Alley, 1681.

Underdown, David. *A Freeborn People: Politics and the Nation in Seventeenth-Century England.* Oxford: Clarendon Press, 1996.
University of Nottingham. "Copyhold." Manuscripts and Special Collections. Accessed October 8, 2024. <https://www.nottingham.ac.uk/manuscriptsandspecialcollections/researchguidance/deedsindepth/copyhold/copyhold.aspx>
Vincent, Patrick. "'This Wretched Mockery of Justice': Mary Shelley's *Frankenstein* and Geneva." *European Romantic Review* 18, no. 5 (2007): 645–61.
Visconsi, Elliott. "A Degenerate Race: English Barbarism in Aphra Behn's *Oroonoko* and *The Widow Ranter.*" *ELH* 69, no. 3 (2002): 673–705.
Visconsi, Elliott. *Lines of Equity: Literature and the Origins of Law in Later Stuart England.* Ithaca, NY: Cornell University Press, 2008.
Voorwinde, Stephen. "Romans 7: A History of Interpretation." *Vox Reformata* 83 (2018): 65–90. <https://rtc.edu.au/wp-content/uploads/Romans-7-a-history-of-interpretation-2018.pdf>
Waldstreicher, David. "The Hidden Stakes of the 1619 Controversy." *Boston Review*, January 24, 2020.
Wallace, Carvell. "Why *Black Panther* is a Defining Moment for Black America." *New York Times*, February 12, 2018. <https://www.nytimes.com/2018/02/12/magazine/why-black-panther-is-a-defining-moment-for-black-america.html>
Wallace, John M. "The Date of Sir Robert Filmer's *Patriarcha.*" *Historical Journal* 23, no. 1 (1980): 155–65.
Warren, George. *An Impartial Description of Surinam Upon the Continent of Guiana in America.* London: Printed by William Godbid for Nathaniel Brooke, 1667.
Watt, Ian. *The Rise of the Novel: Studies in Defoe, Richardson and Fielding.* Berkeley, CA: University of California Press, 1967.
Weiner, Mark S. *Black Trials: Citizenship from the Beginnings of Slavery to the End of Caste.* New York: Vintage, 2006.
Wells, Ida B. *A Red Record: Tabulated Statistics and Alleged Causes of Lynchings in the United States, 1892–1893–1894.* Chicago: Privately published, 1894.
West, Cornel. "A Grand Tradition of Struggle." *English Journal* 89, no. 6 (2000): 40–43.
Weston, Corinne C. "England: Ancient Constitution and Common Law." In *The Cambridge History of Political Thought, 1450–1700*, edited by J. H. Burns, 374–411. Cambridge: Cambridge University Press, 1991.
Weston, Corinne Comstock, and Janelle Renfrow Greenberg. *Subjects and Sovereigns: The Grand Controversy of Sovereignty in Stuart England.* New York: Cambridge University Press, 1981.
Wheeler, Roxann. *The Complexion of Race: Categories of Difference in Eighteenth-Century British Culture.* Philadelphia: University of Pennsylvania Press, 2000.
White, Gabrielle D. V. *Jane Austen in the Context of Abolition: "A Fling at the Slave Trade."* New York: Palgrave Macmillan, 2006.
Whitford, David. "A Calvinist Heritage to the 'Curse of Ham': Assessing the Accuracy of a Claim about Racial Subordination." *Church History and Religious Culture* 90, no. 1 (2010): 25–45.
Wiecek, William M. *The Sources of Anti-Slavery Constitutionalism in America, 1760–1848.* Ithaca, NY: Cornell University Press, 2018.
Wilentz, Sean. "A Matter of Facts." *The Atlantic*, January 22, 2020.
Wilentz, Sean. *No Property in Man: Slavery and Antislavery at the Nation's Founding.* Cambridge, MA: Harvard University Press, 2018.
Williams, Eric. *Capitalism and Slavery.* Chapel Hill, NC: University of North Carolina Press, 1944.
Williams, Michael. "'I Like the Habeas Corpus (When we've Got it)': Byron, Wellington and the Future of British Liberties." *English Academy Review* 31, no. 1 (2014): 6–18.
Wilson, Douglas L., ed. *Jefferson's Literary Commonplace Book.* The Papers of Thomas Jefferson, Second Series, vol. 5. Princeton: Princeton University Press, 2014.
Wiltshire, John. "Decolonising *Mansfield Park.*" *Essays in Criticism* 53, no. 4 (2003): 303–22.
Woodford, Benjamin. "Developments and Debates in English Censorship during the Interregnum." *Early Modern Literary Studies* 17, no. 2 (2014): 1–21.

Worden, Blair. "Milton and the Civil Wars." In *Literature and Politics in Cromwellian England*, 154–179. Oxford: Oxford University Press, 2009.
Young, Elizabeth. *Black Frankenstein: The Making of an American Metaphor*. New York: New York University Press, 2008.
Zimmermann, Jens. "In God's Image: From *Sicut Deus* to *Imago Dei*." In *Dietrich Bonhoeffer's Christian Humanism*, 113–47. Oxford: Oxford University Press, 2019.
Ziolkowski, Theodore. "Science, *Frankenstein*, and Myth." *Sewanee Review* 89, no. 1 (1981): 34–56.
Zook, George Frederick. *The Company of Royal Adventurers Trading into Africa*. 1919. Reprint, New York: Negro Universities Press, 1969.

Index

Note: Figures are indicated by an italic '*f*', respectively, following the page number.

For the benefit of digital users, indexed terms that span two pages (e.g., 52–53) may, on occasion, appear on only one of those pages.

The manufacturer's authorised representative in the EU for product safety is Oxford University Press España S.A. of El Parque Empresarial San Fernando de Henares, Avenida de Castilla, 2 - 28830 Madrid (www.oup.es/en or product.safety@oup.com). OUP España S.A. also acts as importer into Spain of products made by the manufacturer.
Printed and bound by CPI Group (UK) Ltd, Croydon, CR0 4YY
06/10/2026
02228678-0001